Governance, Risk, and Compliance Handbook for Oracle Applications

Written by industry experts with more than 30 years combined experience, this handbook covers all the major aspects of Governance, Risk, and Compliance management in your organization

Nigel King

Adil R Khan

[PACKT] enterprise 🎴
PUBLISHING
professional expertise distilled

BIRMINGHAM - MUMBAI

Governance, Risk, and Compliance Handbook for Oracle Applications

First published: August 2012

Production Reference: 1170812

Published by Packt Publishing Ltd.
Livery Place
35 Livery Street
Birmingham B3 2PB, UK.

ISBN 978-1-84968-170-4

www.packtpub.com

Cover Image by Artie Ng (artherng@yahoo.com.au)

Credits

Foreword

Governance is nothing less than running a company well, and Oracle has proved itself a well-run company for over 30 years. It has found the need to provide the management team and directors many tools and facilities to plot course and help guide this huge enterprise. Though we steer through many storms, the risks are known, the course is plotted, the equipment is lashed to the decks, or properly stowed. The crew is prepared to sheet or drop sail.

These are the same tools that we make available to our customers, and while I have jokingly drawn the parallels to a sport with some connections to Oracle, the governance of an enterprise is a very broad and serious topic. What Nigel and Adil have shown in this book is just how broad it is and how many facets of Governance, Risk, and Compliance are handled through those tools. We have great tools that specialize in GRC and we have many other tools that intersect with it.

Just like the winds and the seas, the commercial, legal, and technological environment and the tools that we provide to help you manage them are varied and changing. This book gives you a great map on which you can chart your GRC journey, both present and near future. It is a journey that we are honored to share with you, as one of the many customers that has entrusted Oracle to provide the vessel and seamanship.

Chris Leone
Senior Vice President, HCM and GRC Products,
Oracle Corporation

About the Authors

Nigel King is the Vice President for Functional Architecture at Fusion Applications. As such he leads a band of architects whose job is to steward the designs and underpinnings for those things that span product families. He has been working with Oracle for the past 17 years. In that time he has worked mostly in Applications Development. He has worked in many areas of Applications, starting off in Distribution Management and then leading Oracle Applications' first venture into Business Intelligence, and Product Lifecycle Management Applications. A restless observer and inventor, his real passion has always been to see a problem defined, and in being defined well; resolved. By first profession he is a Chartered Management Accountant. He is also a Certified Internal Auditor (CIA), Certified Information Systems Auditor (CISA), Certified Information Security Manager (CISM), and Certified Information Security Professional (CISSP). He swears that as soon as he gets the book finished, he will catch up with his continuing professional education credits (CPE). His patents include, *Methods and systems for portfolio planning*, *Audit management workbench*, *Internal audit operations for Sarbanes Oxley compliance*, and *Audit planning*. He was fortunate to be hanging around at Oracle when the whole Enron issue happened. A decade later, GRC Apps was born, was new, then grew old, and is now suffused into many of the applications that surround it.

He is also Chairman of the Open Applications Group. The Open Applications Group is a 501(c)(6) not-for-profit standards development organization (SDO). This community is focused on building process-based business standards for e-commerce, Cloud Computing, Service Oriented Architecture (SOA), Web Services, and Enterprise Integration.

The OAGI Specification includes ICXML, an XML specification for the exchange, or risk and control libraries.

Before joining Oracle, he worked in what he now considers the "real world", first as an Accountant and then selling and implementing business systems. He gained insights in the high technology sector working for Philips, the consumer packaged goods sector working for Homepride Foods and Jeyes Group, and was introduced to the software world through Business Technology Consultants.

He is also a licensed boxer, keen soccer player and coach, and a qualified Boston marathon runner.

He lives with his beautiful wife Anita and their soccer fanatic son Ansel in San Mateo, California.

He also co-authored the *E-Business Suite, Manufacturing and Supply Chain, Oracle Press* handbook. You can also trace his thinking on GRC at ISACA's international conferences over the years: An Overview of Emerging Tools and Technologies for Auditors in 2005, Compliant Access Provisioning in 2006, and Security Provisioning for Outsourced Services in 2008.

Prior to getting interested in the GRC space, you can trace his articles on subjects as diverse as *The Convergence of Financial and Supply Chain Planning* in *Control*, the journal of the British Production and Inventory Control Society and *Knowledge Management, The Application of Manufacturing Theory in Knowledge Based industries* in *Management Accounting*, the journal of the Chartered Institute of Management Accountants.

Acknowledgement

Firstly I would like to thank Steve Miranda, the head of Oracle's Fusion applications development for granting us the permission to write this book. He also made the grave mistake of recruiting me onto his team and paying attention to me when I was bleating that this Enron issue was going to mean that audit was going to have to be automated. Steve really is a great leader and it has been a great learning experience to watch him guide the ship of impossible dreams that is Fusion, and quell the storms, not only of outrageous fortune, but the tempestuous spirits that are the management team at Oracle.

I need to thank my great friend and co-conspirator Adil, without whom the mountain would have been twice as high and the load twice as heavy.

There have been many people at Oracle who have given assistance: Georginna Manning and the Demo Solution Services team—their support for my constant requests for demo environments was invaluable; Swanarli Bag and the GRC team for making screenshots from the edge of possibility.

I would like to thank Bastin Gerald, Mumu Pande, Saye Arumugam, and the team that helped take Internal Controls Manager to market. Their minds are onto other great ventures now, but it was great to ride those rapids in the early days with them. We really did shape an industry.

I need to thank Mr. Kurt Robson, who brought me into Oracle and taught me the science and discipline of design. It is not possible to work at Oracle among so many shining intellects without having that brilliance reflect off the surface of your own mind, however dully.

I need to thank my friends and trainers Pat Regan and Mike Marshall, who through all this kept me fit and asked me to keep my hands up and my head moving.

There is no thanks that is enough for my beautiful wife Anita without whose support my life would be pretty unmanageable. My thanks as well to my son Ansel, who has to tolerate weekends spent in libraries and coffee shops watching me write and research.

About the Authors

Adil R Khan is the Managing Director at FulcrumWay, a firm that has delivered governance, risk, and compliance solutions to more than 200 Fortune-500 and middle-market Oracle customers in America, EMEA, and Asia Pacific since 2003. He also serves on the board of the Oracle Applications Users Group (OAUG) and GRC Special Interest Group. He has given over 50 presentations on GRC trends, best practices, and case studies at many industry conferences including Gartner GRC Summit, IIA, ISACA, Collaborate, and Oracle OpenWorld.

Prior to joining FulcrumWay, he served as the Chief Executive Officer and board member at Alternate Marketing Networks, Inc., a NASDAQ listed company where he was responsible for growth strategy, financial restructuring, and corporate governance. He also co-founded Hencie, Inc. in 1996, which was ranked 157th on Inc-500 list of the fastest growing companies and he was nominated as the Entrepreneur of the Year in 2001 by Ernst and Young Company.

He has also worked for Oracle Corporation, a Big-4 audit firm, and several startups to gain 20 years of combined experience in enterprise software and audit services. He graduated from Virginia Tech University in 1987 and attended an executive MBA program at the University of Texas in Dallas in 1993-1994.

Acknowledgement

I have dedicated this book to my father, Rasheed H Khan, who sparked my interest in learning, critical thinking, and innovation through books, tutoring, and travel at an early age.

I thank my close friend and co-author, Nigel for encouraging me to write this book on a subject that both of us have followed with a deep passion for the past ten years.

I also want to thank all my clients and colleagues at FulcrumWay who have given me the opportunity to develop the knowledge and experience to write this book. I specially want to recognize the following individuals and clients who have given me their personal time and shared their governance, risk, and compliance lessons at industry conferences: Heather Brown, US Restaurant Properties; Stephen Bateman, Allied Healthcare; Guy Mayberry, Alliance Resource; Shazia Hussainishah, Beckman Coulter; Karan Kapoor, GE; Gloria Chandler, ITT; Danny Dodds, PCL Contractors; Deirdre Centrillo, Readers Digest; Alison MacMillan, GFI Group; Bridget Kravchenko, Arvin Meritor; Bob Heinz, Oxy Petroleum; Becky Jackson, Boardwalk; Patrick Palmer, Oxbow; Jennifer Troiani, Genesis; and Rose Campbell, Hitachi.

About the Reviewers

Sam Bicheno is a Manager in PricewaterhouseCoopers (PwC) Risk Assurance practice focused on bringing specialist Oracle security and controls experience to a range of clients in the service, retail, and manufacturing sectors in both commercial and public sector environments.

He has over five years experience in Oracle consulting and is a subject matter expert in Oracle Governance, Risk, and Compliance (GRC) having helped numerous clients understand, evaluate, and implement improved control frameworks and business processes as well as implementing the core Oracle GRC products.

Sam Monarch is a Sr. Principal Oracle GRC Consultant. He has more than eight years of Oracle Database and Oracle GRC Implementation experience. He has worked with clients in both the Commercial and Public Sector markets. Most recently, he has been working for a variety of clients providing governance, risk, and compliance related services including SOD Remediation, Oracle GRC Training, Implementation Services, Project Management, and GRC Interface expertise. He also has direct experience in serving companies during 404, SOX, and FDA compliance reviews.

He holds a BS degree from Wayland Baptist University in MIS. He is a combat veteran, and has served our country in the United States Air Force.

www.PacktPub.com

Support files, eBooks, discount offers and more

You might want to visit www.PacktPub.com for support files and downloads related to your book.

Did you know that Packt offers eBook versions of every book published, with PDF and ePub files available? You can upgrade to the eBook version at www.PacktPub.com and as a print book customer, you are entitled to a discount on the eBook copy. Get in touch with us at service@packtpub.com for more details.

At www.PacktPub.com, you can also read a collection of free technical articles, sign up for a range of free newsletters and receive exclusive discounts and offers on Packt books and eBooks.

http://PacktLib.PacktPub.com

Do you need instant solutions to your IT questions? PacktLib is Packt's online digital book library. Here, you can access, read and search across Packt's entire library of books.

Why Subscribe?

- Fully searchable across every book published by Packt
- Copy and paste, print and bookmark content
- On demand and accessible via web browser

Free Access for Packt account holders

If you have an account with Packt at www.PacktPub.com, you can use this to access PacktLib today and view nine entirely free books. Simply use your login credentials for immediate access.

Instant Updates on New Packt Books

Get notified! Find out when new books are published by following @PacktEnterprise on Twitter, or the *Packt Enterprise* Facebook page.

Table of Contents

Preface

This book covers the topic of Governance Risk and Compliance management. It seems that every year since the Enron collapse, there has been a fresh debacle that refuses to lower the spotlight from this area. Before Sarbanes-Oxley forced the management of companies to become risk conscious, if you asked a Chief Executive whether he thought he had adequate internal controls, I think the most likely the answer would have been "What is an internal control?" This is clearly no longer the case. Every week some story of lack of good governance, failure to plan for a foreseeable catastrophe, or failure to comply with an important law or regulation, brings the GRC themes into public view and scrutiny and this makes management and directors keen to show they have put their best efforts forward to govern their companies well, manage risks to the enterprise, and to comply with all applicable laws.

Perhaps only Oracle and SAP are in a position to really address all three aspects of Governance, Risk, and Compliance. The mission of the GRC applications is to ensure that the managers and directors of the enterprises that run our applications have a strong defensible position. The mission is to provide:

- Controls that provide the highest degree of mitigation to the risks to the enterprise
- Efficiency in testing and consistency in enforcement of Controls
- Highest degree of certainty in the risk assessment
- Lowering the costs of collating the Management Assertions of the effectiveness of the controls for investors

What this book covers

Chapter 1, Introduction, introduces the GRC Concepts and shows you the breadth of tools that Oracle has to address the GRC problems. We introduce the fictional company with whom we will be taking the governance risk and compliance journey.

We introduce the key roles that have a stake in the Governance Risk and Compliance process and explain what that stake is. We show the overall risk management and compliance process at a very high level to see how the information comes together for the signing officers to certify to the investors in the enterprise that the risks are managed and the controls effective.

Chapter 2, Corporate Governance, covers the governance problem from the perspective of the board of directors and very senior management. We have taken a cursory glance at the array of corporate governance problems and reviewed some candidate applications from Oracle that address those problems.

Chapter 3, Information Technology Governance, covers governance of enterprise IT. We develop an IT strategy and document that strategy in Oracle's Balanced Scorecard. We review the alignment between the projects and that scorecard. We help the CIO see the ranking of those projects with respect to financial and non-financial goals. We sit with the IT Director to ensure that the configuration of the systems is baselined at an agreed state and that configuration is under an effective change management. Lastly, we work with the IT Director to ensure that Infission has good processes for support of end users.

Chapter 4, Security Governance, constructs a Security Balanced Scorecard with objectives for security management that are in concert with the overall corporate objectives. We then demonstrate how principles of least privilege are implemented through the role. We look at how the principle of accountability is implemented. We explain how employee on-boarding, off-boarding, transfers, and promotions are reflected in the security system. We show the CSO how the policies of what duties must be segregated are articulated, enforced, and violations reported. We explain how to harden the system to address security threats. Lastly, we take the CSO through security incident tracking and response.

Chapter 5, Risk Assessment and Control Verification, examines the process of evaluating the risks to the enterprise and its mission that is generally executed as part of a Sarbanes-Oxley Program Management Office established by the Chief Financial Officer. We review the Enterprise Risk Management (ERM) framework, established by COSO for risk assessment and controls verification.

Chapter 6, Documenting Your Controls, provides details to help you create and maintain control documentation such as process, procedures, risk controls, and business units.

Chapter 7, Managing Your Testing Phase: Management Testing and Certifying Controls, describes the Management Testing process, approach, and automation to help identify risks and provide reasonable assurance that an entity is able to meet its business and financial reporting objectives under an Enterprise Risk Management (ERM) framework.

Chapter 8, Managing Your Audit Function, explains the management of Internal Audit function to provide independent assessment of internal controls that provide the independent assurance to the Board of Directors and stockholders that financial and operational information is reliable, operations are performed efficiently, objectives are achieved, assets are safeguarded, and actions and decisions of the organization are in compliance with laws, regulations, and contracts.

Chapter 9, IT Audit, covers the IT Audit management function that mitigates information technology risks. The scope of an IT Audit plan includes testing general computer controls as well as application controls. The domains of IT Audit include access controls to reduce the segregation of duties risk, transaction controls to indentify if the user with access to the ERP system has created a transaction that violates a business policy, and configuration controls to track configuration changes in the ERP system.

Chapter 10, Cross Industry Cross Compliance, covers compliance issues that will be faced by companies in almost any industry. We start off by looking at Sarbanes-Oxley and then move on through ISO 27000 that defines the Security Management System Requirements and on to COBIT that defines control objectives for Information Technology. We look at the California Breach Law, Health Information Portability, and Payment Card Industry regulations. These have the common theme of privacy and we showed Oracle capabilities for hiding, encrypting, and masking values. We also looked at federal sentencing guidelines and showed how a learning management solution provides a defensible position and demonstrates due diligence.

Chapter 11, Industry-focused Compliance, covers regulations that apply to particular industries. We show the major compliance issues in high-tech manufacturing, pharmaceutical and life sciences, and banking. These compliance issues will generally still involve audit staff, but require specialized tools for each of the compliance issues.

Chapter 12, Regional-focused Compliance, covers Canada's Bill 198, the United Kingdom's Corporate Governance Code, the European Union's 8th Directive, Japan's Financial Instruments and Exchange Law, and Australia's Corporate Law Economic Reform Program (CLERP).

We neither stay in the narrow definition of the GRC applications, nor limit ourselves to the Business Applications but take you to the most appropriate places in the full Oracle footprint. For example, some of the configuration management and change control problems are addressed within the GRC Applications and some of them are addressed within enterprise manager.

This means that the book is not organized by product, but is organized by the governance and risk assurance processes. A given product may be represented in multiple places within the book and a given process may contain multiple product references.

In the governance chapters we take you through Oracle Balanced Scorecard, Oracle ilearning, Oracle Human Resources, Oracle Universal Content Management - Records Management, Project Portfolio Analysis, Oracle Enterprise Manager, and Oracle Service.

In the risk management chapters we take you through Oracle GRC Manager, Oracle Fusion GRC Intelligence, Oracle Enterprise GRC Manager, Application Access Controls Governor, Transaction Controls Governor, Oracle Preventive Control Governor, and Oracle Configuration Controls Governor.

In the compliance chapters we take you through Enterprise Manager, Oracle Payments, Oracle Database Vault, Oracle Data Masking Packs, Oracle E-records Management, Agile's Product Governance and Compliance, Oracle Reveleus, and Oracle Mantas.

We have baselined the book at the 11GR2 Database, 11GR2 Middleware, and release 12.1 of E-Business Suite.

What you need for this book

You will need to download the following software for this book:
- Oracle GRC Manager 7.8

- Oracle Fusion GRC Intelligence 2.01

- Oracle Enterprise GRC Manager 8.6.4

- Oracle GRC Controls Suite (AACG and TCG) 8.6.3

- Oracle Preventive Control Governor 7.3.2

- Oracle Configuration Controls Governor 5.5

Who this book is for

The audience for this book are the people who advise the board, the Internal Audit department, and CIO office on controls, security, and risk assurance. Consultants that are implementing Financials or GRC Applications who wish to gain an understanding of the Governance Risk and Compliance processes, and how they are represented in Oracle, should find it a useful primer. Risk Assurance professionals should find it a reliable companion and constant friend.

Conventions

In this book, you will find a number of styles of text that distinguish between different kinds of information. Here are some examples of these styles, and an explanation of their meaning.

Code words in text are shown as follows: "Use the configuration files `httpd.conf` and `httpd_pls.conf` to limit web page access to a list of trusted hosts."

A block of code is set as follows:

```
<Location ~ "/(dms0|DMS|Spy|AggreSpy)">
</Location>
<Location ~ "/dev60html/run(form|rep).htm">
</Location>
```

Any command-line input or output is written as follows:

```
*.dispatchers='(PROTOCOL=TCP) (SERVICE=sidXDB)'
```

New terms and **important words** are shown in bold. Words that you see on the screen, in menus or dialog boxes for example, appear in the text like this: "When you are in the Hyperion® System 9 Workspace, from the **Applications** tab select **Performance Scorecard** in order to access the scorecard."

> Warnings or important notes appear in a box like this.

> Tips and tricks appear like this.

Reader feedback

Feedback from our readers is always welcome. Let us know what you think about this book—what you liked or may have disliked. Reader feedback is important for us to develop titles that you really get the most out of.

To send us general feedback, simply send an e-mail to feedback@packtpub.com, and mention the book title through the subject of your message.

If there is a topic that you have expertise in and you are interested in either writing or contributing to a book, see our author guide on www.packtpub.com/authors.

Customer support

Now that you are the proud owner of a Packt book, we have a number of things to help you to get the most from your purchase.

Errata

Although we have taken every care to ensure the accuracy of our content, mistakes do happen. If you find a mistake in one of our books—maybe a mistake in the text or the code—we would be grateful if you would report this to us. By doing so, you can save other readers from frustration and help us improve subsequent versions of this book. If you find any errata, please report them by visiting http://www.packtpub.com/support, selecting your book, clicking on the **errata submission form** link, and entering the details of your errata. Once your errata are verified, your submission will be accepted and the errata will be uploaded to our website, or added to any list of existing errata, under the Errata section of that title.

Piracy

Piracy of copyright material on the Internet is an ongoing problem across all media. At Packt, we take the protection of our copyright and licenses very seriously. If you come across any illegal copies of our works, in any form, on the Internet, please provide us with the location address or website name immediately so that we can pursue a remedy.

Please contact us at copyright@packtpub.com with a link to the suspected pirated material.

We appreciate your help in protecting our authors, and our ability to bring you valuable content.

Questions

You can contact us at questions@packtpub.com if you are having a problem with any aspect of the book, and we will do our best to address it.

1
Introduction

This is a book about **governance**, **risk management**, and **compliance management** of a large modern enterprise and how the IT infrastructure, in particular the Oracle IT Infrastructure, can assist in that governance. The IT infrastructure both presents a risk and also provides the infrastructure to mitigate and manage that risk. The IT infrastructure must be shown to be in compliance with policies, laws, and regulations, and assists in establishing and confirming that compliance. We have written this book from the perspective of big GRC. There have been many solutions springing up around fashionable pieces of the compliance problem. At the start of the Sarbanes gold rush, it was document management. For a while that was the management of the close process. Then for a very long time it was segregation of duties. These are all important components. We have tried our best to take the perspective of those who are responsible for the stewardship of the company, and see the GRC problem from their perspective. We have written at length about governance To this end, our book is aimed at risk assurance professionals, executives, directors, and those who advise them. It is not an implementation manual for the GRC products, although we hope you can get the best out of the GRC products after reading this book. In this book, we have discussed many applications and technology products that are not in the GRC product family. Again, we are not attempting to write an implementation guide for those products. We can hopefully show you how those products participate and assist in the governance process, how they introduce or mitigate risk, and how they can be brought into compliance with best practice as well as applicable laws and regulations.

How this book is organized

We have written this book with a section dedicated to each of the following three blocks:

- **Governance**: Here we discuss the strategic management of the enterprise, setting the plans for the managers, making disclosures to investors, and ensuring that the board knows that the enterprise is meeting its goals and staying within its policies.

- **Risk management**: Here we discuss the audit disciplines. This is where we work out what can go wrong, document what we have to do to prevent it from going wrong, and check that what we think prevents it from going wrong actually works. We move through the various sub disciplines within the audit profession and show what tools are best suited from within the Oracle family to assist.

- **Compliance management**: Here we map the tools and facilities that we have discovered in the first two sections for frameworks and legislations. We will give this from an industry and geography agnostic viewpoint and then drill in to some specific industries and countries.

We neither stay in the narrow definition of the GRC applications, nor limit ourselves to the business applications but take you to the most appropriate places in the full Oracle footprint. For example, some of the configuration management and change control problems are addressed within the GRC applications and some of them are addressed within Enterprise Manager.

This means that the book is not organized by product. It is organized by the governance and risk assurance processes. A given product may be represented in multiple places in the book and a given process may contain multiple product references.

Definitions

Before we go much further, we should lay down some basic definitions of these three key terms.

Governance

The www.businessdictionary.com has a great definition of governance:

Traditionally defined as the ways in which a firm safeguards the interests of its financiers (investors, lenders, and creditors). The modern definition calls it the framework of rules and practices by which the board of directors ensure accountability, fairness, and transparency in the firm's relationship with all the stakeholders (financiers, customers, management, employees, government, and the community). This framework consists of (1) explicit and implicit contracts between the firm and the stakeholders for distribution of responsibilities, rights, and rewards; (2) procedures for reconciling the sometimes conflicting interests of stakeholders in accordance with their duties, privileges, and roles; and (3) procedures for proper supervision, control, and information-flows to serve as a system of checks-and-balances. It is also called corporation governance.

I really like this definition, partly because it lets you know where the real accountability for Governance lies in the enterprise, but mostly because it is pretty much undefined in most of the frameworks that have had influence on the GRC market.

Risk

Probability of loss inherent in a firm's operations and environment (such as competition and adverse economic conditions) that may impair its ability to provide returns on investment. The leading framework in risk management was published by the **Committee of Sponsoring Organizations (COSO)** of the Treadway Commission. COSO ERM extends the definition from not meeting a financial objective to not meeting any of the enterprise's objectives. It makes it pretty clear that the body that is responsible for signing off on the corporate strategy should also ensure that there is a process to identify the risks of not meeting the goals.

Compliance

Certification or confirmation that the doer of an action such as the writer of an audit report, or the manufacturer or supplier of a product, meets the requirements of accepted practices, legislation, prescribed rules and regulations, specified standards, or the terms of a contract.

Oracle's Governance Risk and Compliance Footprint

The following figure gives an overview of the major functional areas of the governance, risk, and compliance problems and the Oracle Component that best addresses that problem:

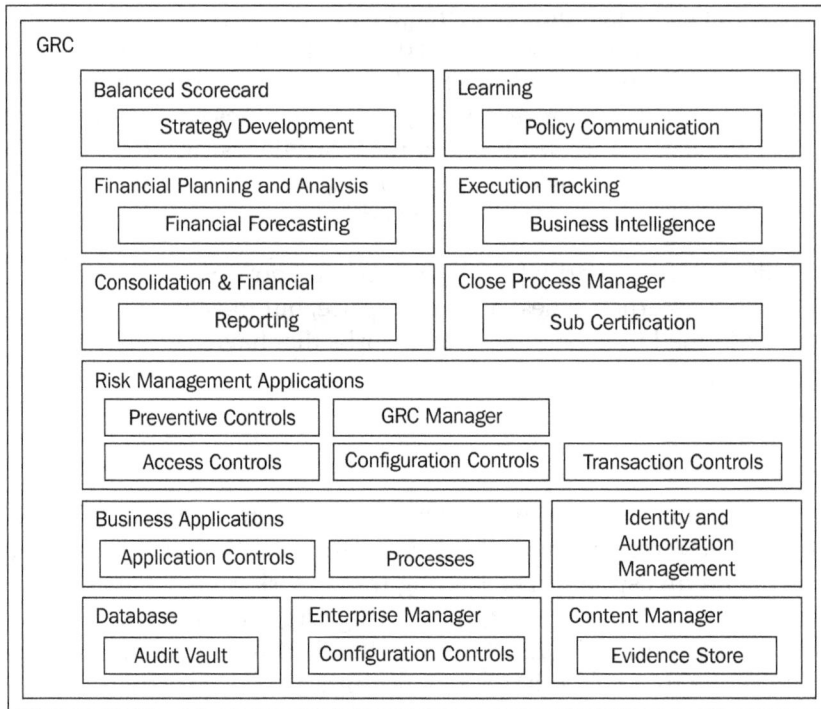

```
GRC
  ┌──────────────────────────────┐  ┌──────────────────────────────┐
  │ Balanced Scorecard           │  │ Learning                     │
  │   ┌──────────────────────┐   │  │   ┌──────────────────────┐   │
  │   │ Strategy Development │   │  │   │ Policy Communication │   │
  │   └──────────────────────┘   │  │   └──────────────────────┘   │
  └──────────────────────────────┘  └──────────────────────────────┘

  ┌──────────────────────────────┐  ┌──────────────────────────────┐
  │ Financial Planning and       │  │ Execution Tracking           │
  │ Analysis                     │  │   ┌──────────────────────┐   │
  │   ┌──────────────────────┐   │  │   │ Business Intelligence│   │
  │   │ Financial Forecasting│   │  │   └──────────────────────┘   │
  │   └──────────────────────┘   │  │                              │
  └──────────────────────────────┘  └──────────────────────────────┘

  ┌──────────────────────────────┐  ┌──────────────────────────────┐
  │ Consolidation & Financial    │  │ Close Process Manager        │
  │   ┌──────────────────────┐   │  │   ┌──────────────────────┐   │
  │   │ Reporting            │   │  │   │ Sub Certification    │   │
  │   └──────────────────────┘   │  │   └──────────────────────┘   │
  └──────────────────────────────┘  └──────────────────────────────┘

  Risk Management Applications
    ┌───────────────────┐  ┌───────────────────┐
    │ Preventive Controls│  │ GRC Manager       │
    └───────────────────┘  └───────────────────┘
    ┌───────────────────┐  ┌───────────────────┐  ┌───────────────────┐
    │ Access Controls   │  │ Configuration     │  │ Transaction       │
    └───────────────────┘  │ Controls          │  │ Controls          │
                           └───────────────────┘  └───────────────────┘

  Business Applications                    Identity and
    ┌───────────────────┐ ┌────────────┐   Authorization
    │ Application Controls│ │ Processes │   Management
    └───────────────────┘ └────────────┘

  Database           Enterprise Manager    Content Manager
    ┌───────────┐      ┌───────────────┐     ┌───────────────┐
    │ Audit Vault│     │ Configuration │     │ Evidence Store│
    └───────────┘      │ Controls      │     └───────────────┘
                       └───────────────┘
```

When you consider who is involved in the governance, risk, and compliance process, you start to appreciate the tools that you need to complete the footprint.

Balanced Scorecard

This tool is used to express and communicate the mission of the enterprise.

Business Intelligence

This tool is used to measure the degree to which the strategy that has been communicated is actually executing.

Financial Planning and Analysis

This tool is used to convert the mission of the enterprise into financial goals, forecasts that can be discussed with investors through the management)discussion, and analysis.

Consolidations and Financial Reporting

This set of tools is used to report to investors the progress toward the goals expressed in the financial plan.

Learning

This tool is used to ensure delivery of ethics and policy education and confirm their understanding.

Risk Management Applications

This tool is used to discover and document risks to the mission of the enterprise, and to ensure that management has well-designed and effective operating controls to mitigate those risks. Such tools cover the following:

- **Access Controls Governor**: To ensure that appropriate access is granted to systems.

- **Transaction Controls Governor**: To ensure that transaction policies are followed and fraudulent transactions found.

- **Configuration Controls Governor**: To ensure that recommended settings of the applications that themselves constitute great automated controls are appropriately configured and that changes are authorized and recorded.

- **Preventive Controls Governor**: To extend the controls footprint of the delivered application.

- **Oracle Enterprise Manager**: Enterprise Manager also has great capabilities to extract configuration settings and measure them against baseline. The settings that are tracked within EM by default tend to be deeper technical settings.

- **GRC Manager**: To provide self assessment, testing operations, and to aggregate the results of the documentation and testing phases of the governance program for managers of the risk assurance activity.

- **GRC Intelligence**: To provide the most potent and important information to the executive suite and directors on the residual risk to the enterprise.

Sub Certification

Sub Certification applications are used to allow management to confirm the controls within processes that they are responsible for. Such tools include Hyperion Close Process Manager.

Process Management Applications

These applications are used to provide the pivot point for the risk analysis and management accountability. Largely, these are the processes within the applications themselves. The process may be orchestrated through Oracle Workflow as in the case of purchase order approval or journal approval.

Content Management Applications

These applications are used to provide evidence store for unstructured information. They also provide a store for standard working papers and completed working papers that have been part of the testing activity.

Identity and Authorization Management Applications

These applications are used to provide authentication of users, accountability for their actions in the system, and authorization to information assets required to do their jobs.

Our case study

In order to ensure that we keep ourselves grounded in real problems, we have written the book as a journal of a fictional company establishing its governance processes. We will introduce managers and directors responsible for various aspects of the governance, risk, and compliance problem and where that problem is exposed and how it is addressed in the technology and business applications.

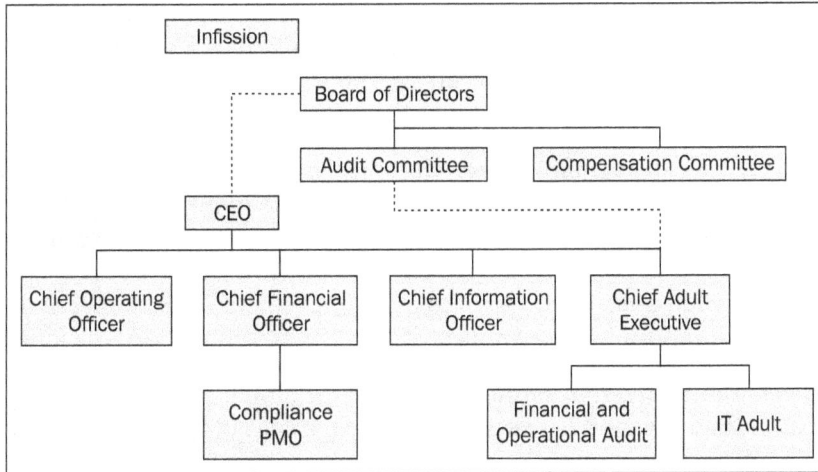

In the previous figure, we have seen the key roles that are directly engaged in the governance, risk management, and compliance activities in a typical organizational chart.

Their IT infrastructure is comprised of Sun Hardware and are running Oracle database, middleware, and business applications. We do have one of the subsidiaries of InFission running JD Edwards just to allow us to illustrate GRC working in a heterogeneous applications environment.

Roles involved in GRC activities

It is worth examining what function is responsible for what activity and what part of the Oracle footprint each is most interested in.

Audit Committee member

The audit committee of the board of directors must have at least three members. One member must have accounting or financial management expertise and all other members must be financially literate. All members must be independent.

The Audit Committee is charged with the oversight of the **Financial Reporting** process, including review of quarterly and annual financial statements on behalf of the investors and to discuss annual financial statement with management and auditors.

They need to review **Management Discussion and Analysis (MD&A)** with management and auditors. This is where management gives guidance on where the business is going. Such guidance is also given in Earnings Announcements, press releases, and guidance provided to rating agencies.

They need to monitor the system of internal control and compliance with legal and regulatory requirements. In order to do this, they need to monitor the system of risk assessment and risk management. This may be synonymous with overseeing the internal audit function, but in recent years many enterprises have set up a separate risk management program office reporting it to the management. This oversight means that the audit plan and the scope of the audits are signed off by the audit committee.

In order to ensure that the tone at the top is appropriate, received, and understood the audit committee is generally responsible for an ethics program, and responsible to manage whistle-blower complaints.

Signing Officers

The CEO and CFO of the company are responsible for signing the Sarbanes-Oxley Section 302 Certifications.

These certifications, referred to by the Securities and Exchange Commission as "Rule 13a-14(a)/15d-14a Certifications", must be signed separately by the CEO and the CFO, and filed as an exhibit to quarterly reports on Form 10-Q or 10-Q(SB) and to annual reports on Form 10-K or Form 10-KSB, as Exhibit 31, or, for foreign private issuers, as an exhibit to Form 20-F. The SEC has specified the form and wording of these certifications, which cannot be changed.

Briefly, the Signing Officer certifies that he has reviewed the report, that he believes that it does not contain any misleading misstatement or omission, and that it fairly presents the company's financial position and results of operations. The officer also certifies his responsibility for the company's disclosure controls and procedures and internal controls over financial reporting and as to their effectiveness.

Chief Audit Executive

The Chief Audit Executive is a part of the company but generally has reporting relationships to the Audit Committee of the board of directors.

The duties of the Chief Audit Executive include:

- Status, strategy, and organization of the Internal Audit Department
- Management/supervision of the internal audit activity

- Ensuring the timely completion of internal auditing engagements
- Ensuring that reports on internal auditing engagements are provided to the audit committee with minimum delay
- Providing an annual holistic opinion on the effectiveness and adequacy of risk management, control, and governance processes

Chief Financial Officer

As well as being one of the signing officers, the CFO obviously heads the departments that are involved in processing of transactions that most directly affect the subledgers and general ledger, the preparation of financial statements, and financial planning and analysis.

Chief Information Officer

In addition to Sarbanes-Oxley (SOX), CIOs and CSOs must understand and achieve compliance with the **Health Insurance Portability and Accountability Act (HIPAA)** the **Payment Card Industry Data Security Standard (PCI DSS)** for organizations processing credit card transactions, and the **Federal Information Security Management Act (FISMA)** for federal agencies as well as many other global, national, and industry-wide regulations and mandates.

IT governance includes writing IT policies that define who within an organization is responsible for key decisions with regards to IT adoption and usage, who is held accountable for such decisions, and how results are monitored and measured. Implementing IT governance strategies includes assigning committees to steer technology adoption, architectural reviews, and project analysis. Governance is about processes, which should support consistent and transparent methods for managing your information technology acquisitions and usage.

The CIO is also responsible for IT risk management. Risk management requires adapting to constantly changing business requirements and monitoring what technologies are deployed within the organization Risk management encompasses surviving a constantly changing threat landscape by tightening and optimizing an organization's information security, both perimeter and internal, while improving business agility and efficiency.

The CIO is also responsible for IT compliance approaches, governance by designing, assessing, and implementing controls. These controls must map back to the various industry requirements and *best practices* that ultimately determine success or failure during an IT audit.

Chief Operating Officer

Many of the controls in the business are part of the processes and procedures operating in the Business Units themselves. For example, your revenue line might be unreliable due to side contracts that are made by your salespeople. Management in the business is responsible for the design of the controls and certifying their effectiveness.

The Audit and Compliance process

The following figure explains the Audit and Compliance process starting with the establishment of the program office and ending with certified financial statements:

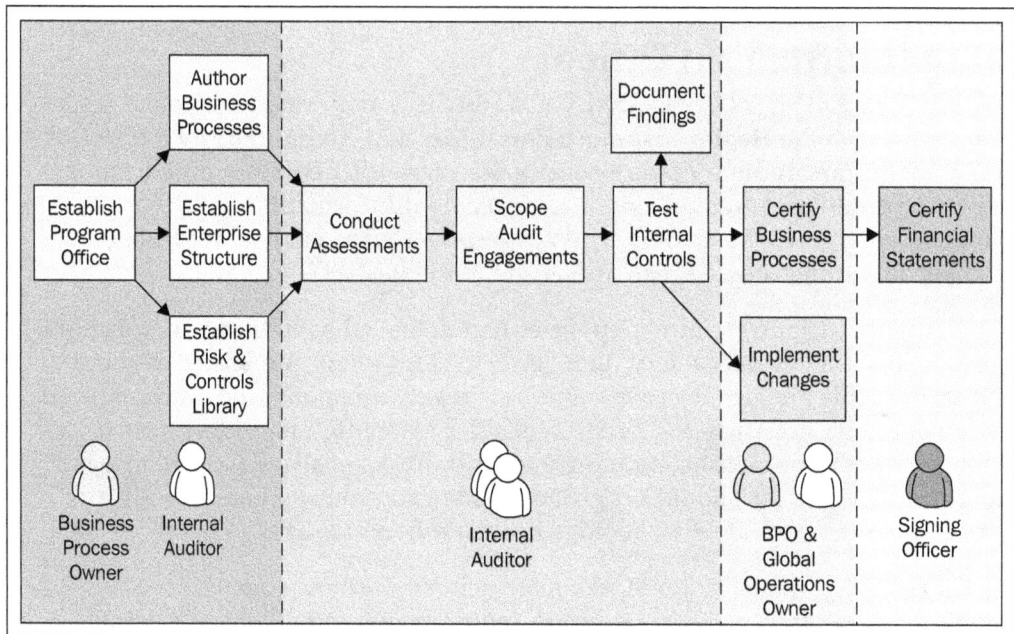

While there are many processes that support and feed into the audit processes process, it is important to realize who the players are at the end of top level process. The process has to make evident to investors and regulators that risks are managed. Once an Audit and Compliance process is established, it goes through a risk assessment, audit planning, documentation phase, a testing phase, and a reporting phase, before the results are combined with the financial disclosures and signed by the management.

Risk Assessment phase

In the Risk Assessment phase, you will be cataloging the risks to the objectives of the business and asking questions such as "What can go wrong?". There are many methodologies, tools, and focuses for this. One methodology is to review the financial statements by subsidiary and highlight the lines that are material and then start to investigate the risks to which that line is exposed. For example, if a subsidiary constitutes less than five percent of the revenue of the enterprise, its revenue line may not be material. For one of the subsidiaries, the revenue line may be subject to risks of mistatement. For example, if revenue is claimed when customers have vouchers outstanding. Other methodologies include facilitated workshop methods and survey methods.

Audit Planning phase

In the Audit Planning phase, you will create a set of audit engagements, each with a defined scope and projected timeframe. Scope may be defined in terms of process, business units, and subsidiaries. The scope sets a boundary around the set of risks and controls that will be tested. An engagement itself is a project that has an engagement manager and a set of auditors assigned. The audit and its scope is generally authorized through an engagement letter addressed to the management and authorized from the Chief Audit Executive or audit committee. It may well include a records request for access to records that are within the scope of the audit.

Documentation phase

As you kick off the program, you will probably establish a program office. The controls will need to be cataloged, but they are generally organized by processes, and the processes and procedures themselves may be controls in and of themselves. The testing phase will be performed within the legal entities and business units of the enterprise, so the enterprise structure needs to be documented.

Testing phase

The testing phase will include a risk assessment to prompt the management to think about the risks to the mission of the enterprise. When the risks have been cataloged, the scope of the audit and the audit plan can be set. The scope may be set in terms of the processes, business units, or individual controls. The audit plan is broken down into individual engagement projects that have their own scope, where controls are tested and the results reported back to the Chief Audit Executive. Management may also be testing controls themselves and providing self assessments of the effectiveness of those controls.

Reporting phase

The reporting phase brings together management testing and the results of audit operations to be able to arm management and the directors with the information they need to certify the financial statements.

The Chief Audit Executive will need to keep the audit committee apprised of the findings in the audit engagements.

Relationships between entities, accounts, process, risk controls, and tests

We should always remember that the end goal is that we can prove to the investors that management and directors have worked with due diligence to govern the company, assess risks to the enterprise and its mission, and comply with applicable laws and regulations.

We should look at an example of a process, a risk, a control, and a test:

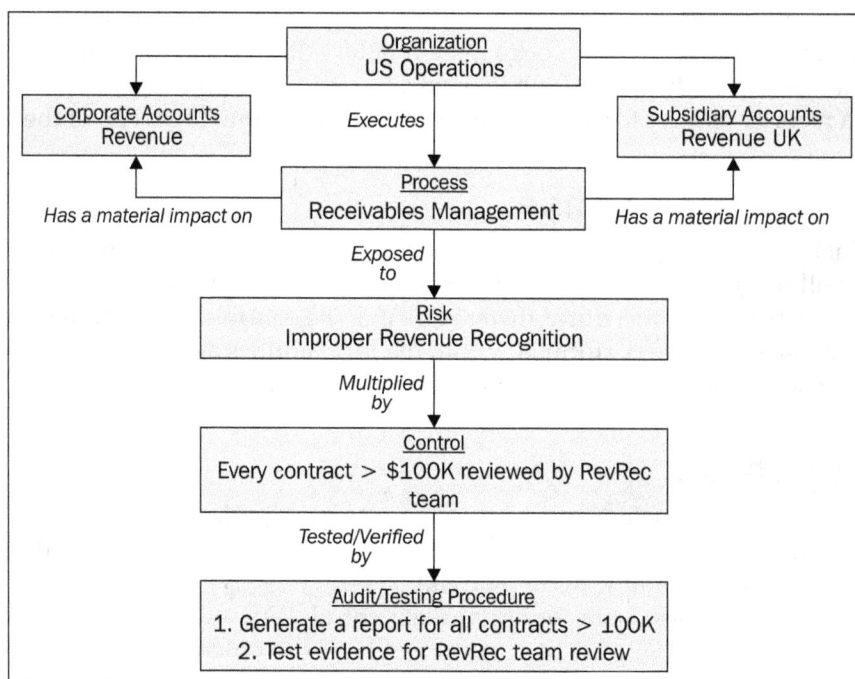

In this example, a subsidiary of Infission runs the U.S. Operations. Part of the results for the subsidiary is the revenue line. The receivables management process has a material impact on what is reported as revenue. There is an inherent risk that we may apply improper revenue recognition policies. For example, we may recognize revenue, even though we have written into the contract that the customer has right of return if the product does not perform as specified, within 90 days. The control may be that every contract with revenue over 100,000 dollars is reviewed by the Revenue Recognition Team. That control may be tested by generating a report of all contracts over 100,000 and testing for revenue recognition approval.

GRC Capability Maturity Model

The governance process itself can start small in a fairly ad hoc manner and can mature to where the governance processes are truly optimized. The IT Policy Compliance Group, an industry and advisory consortium adapted the **Capability Maturity Model** first published by The Carnegie Mellon Software Engineering Institute to the GRC Domain. It has provided a way for companies to measure where they are on the spectrum, and give themselves a sense of how far they have to go and the costs and benefits in getting there.

The following figure shows the levels in the Capability Maturity Model and the process characteristics at each of the levels:

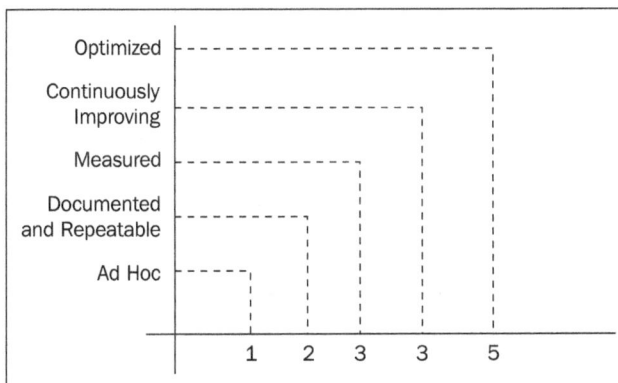

We will be revisiting the Capability Maturity Model to see how different pieces of our GRC solution help move us along the spectrum towards optimizing our controls footprint, minimizing the costs, maximizing the repeatability, and ensuring we have measurable results that can be expressed in terms of business value. The IT Policy Compliance Group provides standardized assessments to help companies measure where they are.

Summary

In this chapter, we have introduced the GRC Concepts and explained the breadth of tools that Oracle has, to address the GRC problems. We have introduced the fictional company with whom we will be taking the governance, risk, and compliance journey. We have also introduced the key roles that have a stake in the governance, risk, and compliance process and explained what that stake is. We have shown the overall risk management and compliance process at a very high level to see how the information comes together for the signing officers to certify to the investors in the enterprise that the risks are managed and the controls are effective. We have illustrated how a sample process, risk, and control are related to a financial statement line for a subsidiary within the enterprise and explained how the process can move from an ad hoc manual process to a repeatable, automated, and optimized solution over time.

In the next chapter we will introduce the Governance theme with Corporate Governance. We will take a look at key strategic issues that Infission faces as an enterprise and also how to craft and communicate the strategic intent of Infission.

2
Corporate Governance

The first domain of GRC that we will look at is Governance, and in particular, Corporate Governance. It is the area of GRC that has had least attention from the software vendors. In the *Chapter 1, Introduction*, we introduced the organizational structure of Infission at the top of the enterprise and we introduced the members of Infission that are most concerned with the governance problem.

We break the corporate governance chapter into the following areas:

- Developing and Communicating Corporate Strategy with Balanced Scorecard
- Communicating and Confirming Corporate Strategy with iLearning
- Managing Records
- Financial Planning and Analysis
- Monitoring Execution with Oracle Business Intelligence
- Risk Management
- Whistleblower Protections

Developing and Communicating Corporate Strategy with Balanced Scorecard

The first thing that we do for the management team is we help them bring their vision for the company to a set of measurable goals that they can justify to their investors. We use Oracle's balanced scorecard tools to do this. We develop the scorecard at the corporate level, and break it down for some senior executives to align objectives at divisional level. We then move the objectives into the executive's goals in the performance management applications that are part of **Human Capital Management** (HCM). Here we will show the reports and metrics that are delivered by Oracle Applications that allow these goals to be monitored and thereby the executive's performance measured.

Balanced Scorecard Theory

The rise of **Balanced Scorecard** was a reaction to the narrow definitions of performance that purely financial measures cause, measuring performance in terms of historical results, not keeping an eye on the needs of the customer, not planning for the future either in terms of people and processes. Balanced scorecard gathers together metrics from a broader base and groups them into perspectives that show the different dimensions of performance and stewardship. The balanced scorecard theory was popularized by the writings of *Kaplan* and *Norton* in their 1993 book *The Balanced Scorecard*.

The four perspectives

The touchstone of balanced scorecard is metrics gathered under four perspectives. The four perspectives are customer, financial, processes and learning and growth. The four perspectives are interrelated. In order to meet financial objectives you need to focus on customer needs. In order to improve financial results you need to find better, less costly, more efficient ways to work, and if you are going to have results, not just now but into the future, you need to make some investment in learning and growth.

The following screenshot shows the Perspective Definition UI in Oracle's Balanced Scorecard:

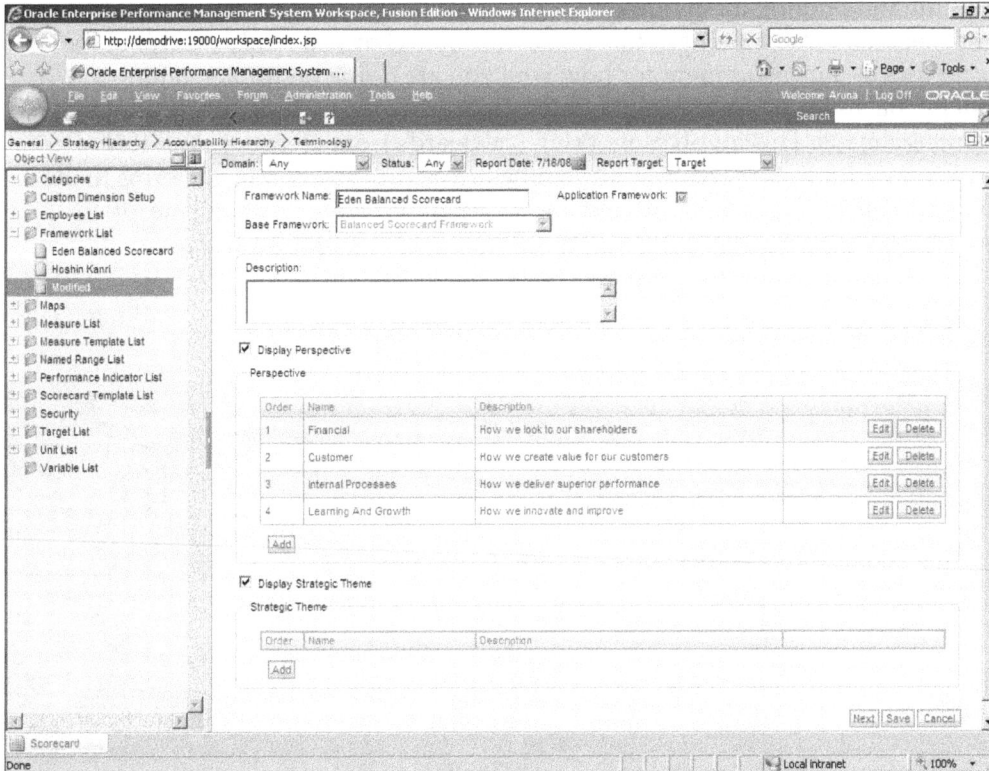

Measures

It is useful to fit the metrics into the different perspectives. For example, a company that manufactures high-tech equipment, probably needs to allow its customers to return products, this is clearly in the customer perspective. It may have a secondary channel for refurbished products. This is clearly in the financial perspective. In order to enable the customer to return the products it may need to improve its reverse logistics. This is clearly in the internal processes perspective. In order to improve the longevity of its battery technology and power management it needs to develop energy engineering disciplines. This is clearly in the learning and growth perspective.

Strategy Maps

Key performance Indicators (KPIs) are all very useful, but plucking them out of the air and pinning them down on a balanced scorecard does not measure your execution unless thought through carefully. What you really need is to see the metrics as a measurement for how well you are doing on implementing a strategy. Balanced scorecard methodology has grown to include the development of strategy maps. This involves working backwards from measures and Key Performance Indicators (KPI's) that signify success in broad financial terms to the customer centered, process centered and learning objectives that an enterprise needs to meet to accomplish them. The following is a sample strategy map drawn in Oracle's Balanced Scorecard tool.

The following is a sample strategy map from Balanced Scorecard:

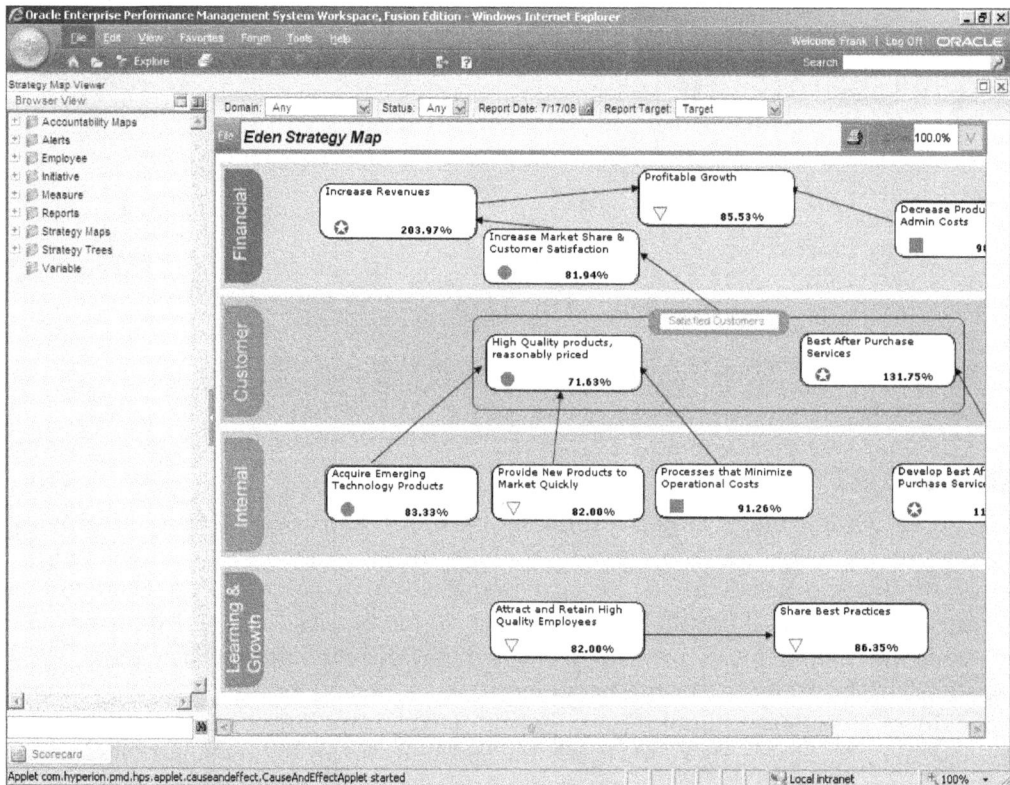

Infission's strategic initiative

In our case study, Infission is a home computer manufacturer. The market for computer equipment in both the consumer and corporate markets has been fairly stagnant in the past few years. The market has also changed significantly. The environmental consciousness of both its customers and shareholders has changed dramatically and as a consequence its strategy has had to radically change to incorporate these consumer and investor preferences.

Oracle's Balanced Scorecard

Of course the next thing is to show how this is expressed in Oracle's balanced scorecard product. The following diagram shows the strategic planning process:

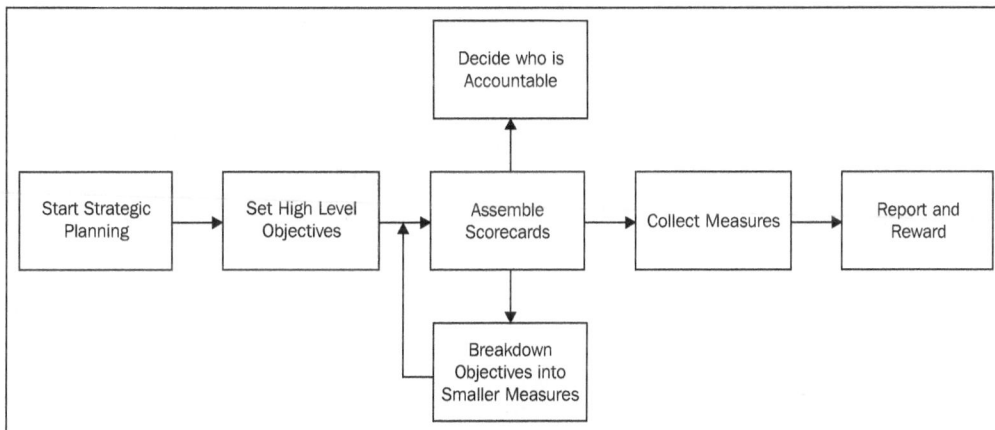

Accessing Oracle Hyperion's Balanced Scorecard

Balanced Scorecard is part of the Hyperion set of products. Scorecard is accessed solely through the Workspace. When you are in the Hyperion System 9 Workspace, from the **Applications** tab select **Performance Scorecard**.

The main components and how they are related

The following logical data model diagram shows the major components of the balanced scorecard system, and how those components are related:

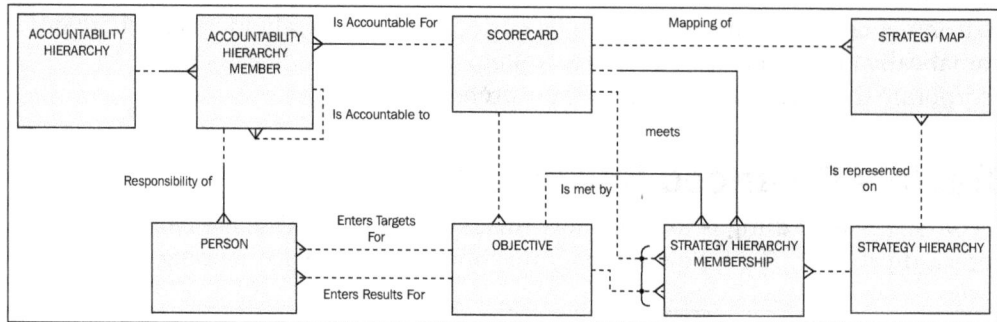

The key entities are explained as follows:

- **Scorecards**: A collection of scores against a set of objectives typically aggregated and weighted to a total possible score of 100.

- **Objectives**: Objectives are grouped under a scorecard. Some strategic goal against which the enterprise wishes to measure progress.

- **Strategy Hierarchy**: A way of organizing objectives to express how the results of one objective contribute to the results of another.

- **Strategy Hierarchy Membership**: Breaks-down an objective into smaller objectives and scorecards that contribute to the overall objective.

- **Strategy Map**: Displays a scorecard using the cause and effect relationships implicit in the hierarchy.

- **Accountability Hierarchy**: A collection of accountability elements that are typically departments, business units that have managers that will be held accountable for results.

- **Accountability Hierarchy Member**: The departments or business units that are assembled into a hierarchy.

- **Person**: Employees can have responsibility for an accountability hierarchy member, and therefore responsibility for the objectives in its scorecard. The manager of a department or business unit may be responsible for setting targets for his managers. The finance staff may be responsible for collecting results for the objectives.

Setting up measures

From the scorecard page, click on the browse icon at the top of the left-hand navigation panel and then click on **Measure Templates List**. The following UI is where you set up measures:

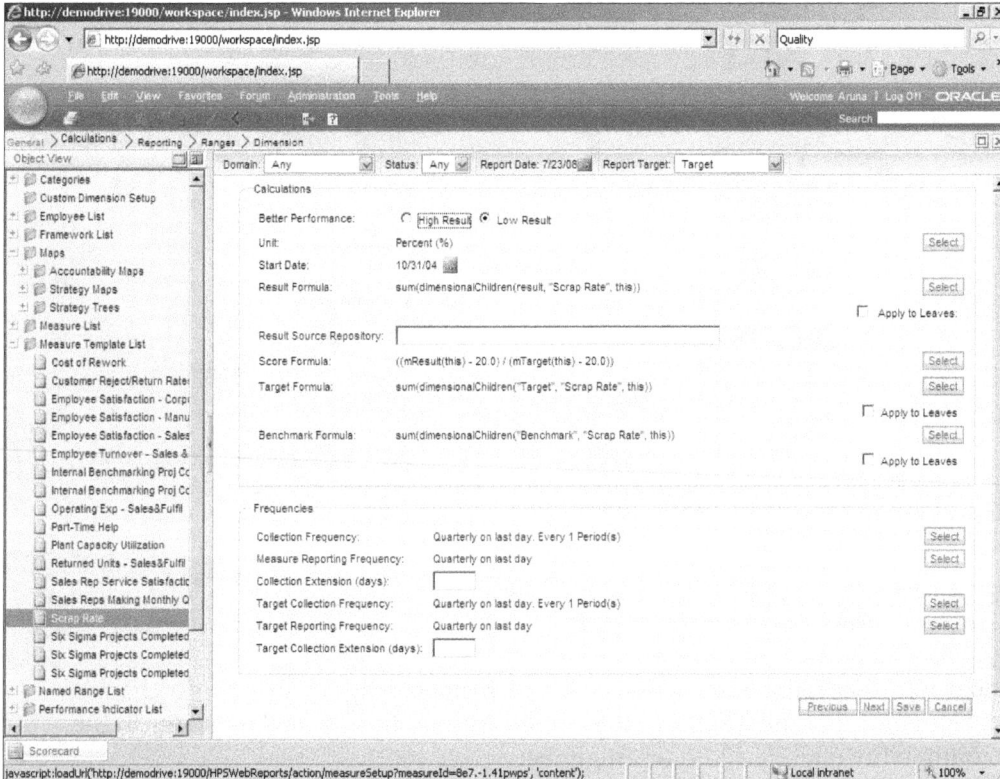

In this screen the user is setting up measures. You can set up whether you are trying to get a high result, (such as the percentage of production materials from post consumer content), or a low result, (such as energy per unit produced). You set up the formula to calculate the result.

Setting up an Accountability Hierarchy

From the scorecard page, click on the browse icon at the top of the left-hand navigation panel and then click on **Accountability Map**. The following UI is where you set up **Accountability Maps**:

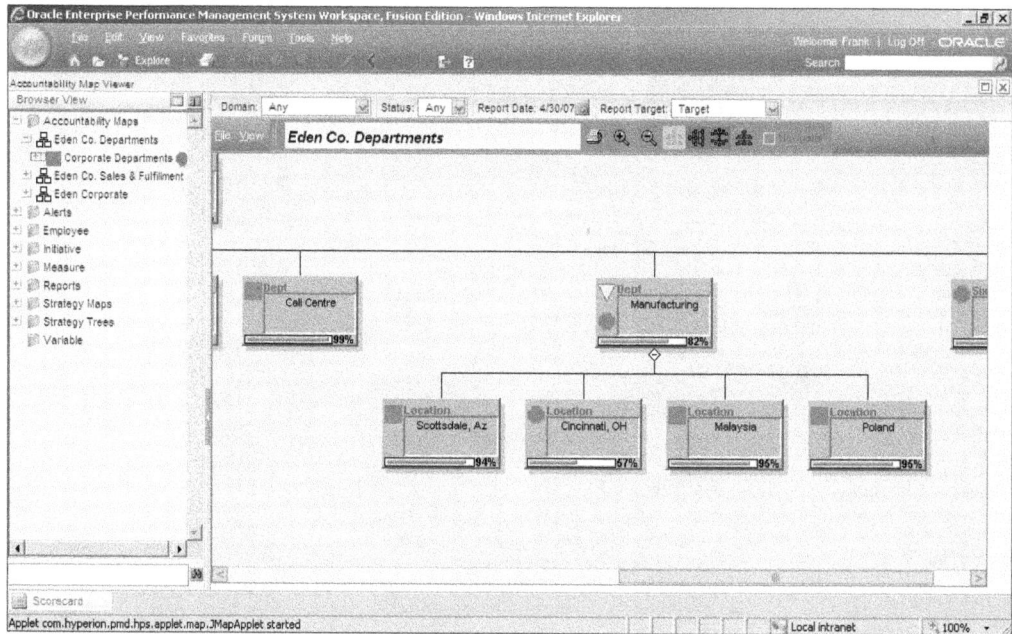

You can further refine responsibility for performance by constructing a chain of commands that must achieve the results. You do this by adding nodes to the accountability map. Such nodes might be:

- Subsidiary for compliance measures
- Business Unit for financial measures
- Department for functional measures
- Geographic region for sales measures
- Item Category for marketing measures

Assembling the Scorecard

From the scorecard page, click on the browse icon at the top of the left-hand navigation panel and then click on **Scorecard Template List**. The following UI is where you assemble the scorecard:

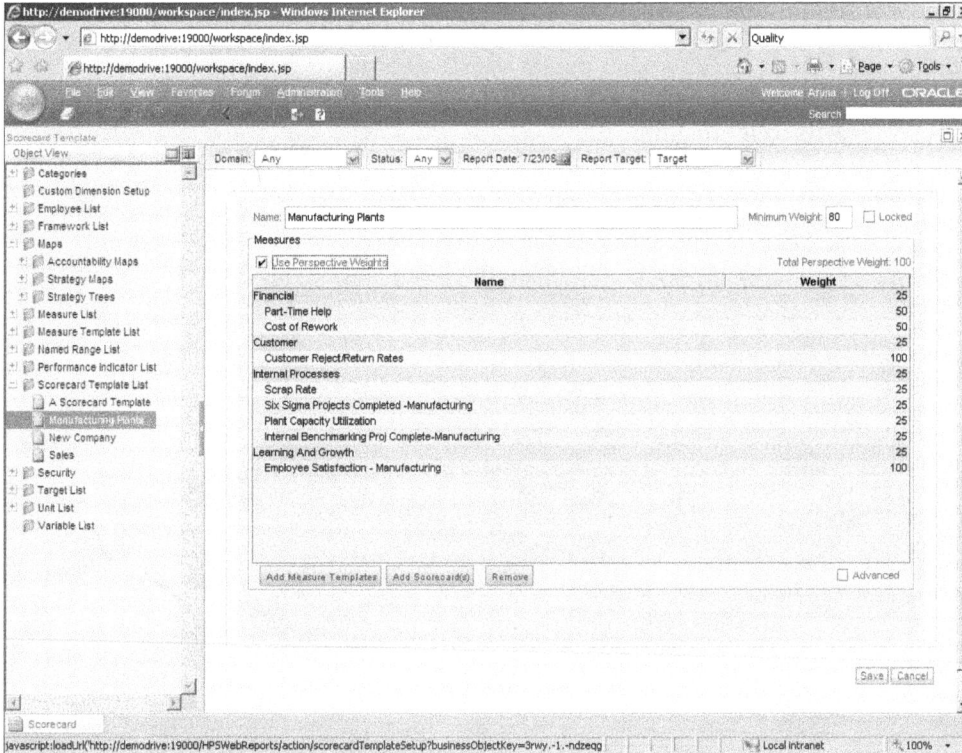

Measures are assembled into scorecards by assigning weights to the measures. This allows a weighted average to be calculated for all the measures in the scorecard. It gives you a measure of how well the strategy has been met.

Breaking down Measures and Scorecards into lower-level objectives

From the scorecard page, click on the browse icon at the top of the left hand navigation panel and then click on **Strategy Trees**.

Balanced scorecard allows you to break down the high-level strategic objectives into smaller tactical objectives. For example, you might have a strategic objective of minimizing environmental impact, but you will have to have tactical objectives for providing for customer returns at the end of the product's life. This intermediary objective may have its own scorecard for objectives such as understanding customer use patterns and engagement with waste management companies for pick up. Each objective on high-level scorecard can be broken down into smaller objectives and scorecards. It is the relationships between objectives, which is implicit in the hierarchy that is used to draw the strategy map.

Authorizing Managers to Scorecards

From the scorecard page, click on the browse icon at the top of the left-hand navigation panel and then click on **Employee List**. In the following UI you assign scorecards to managers:

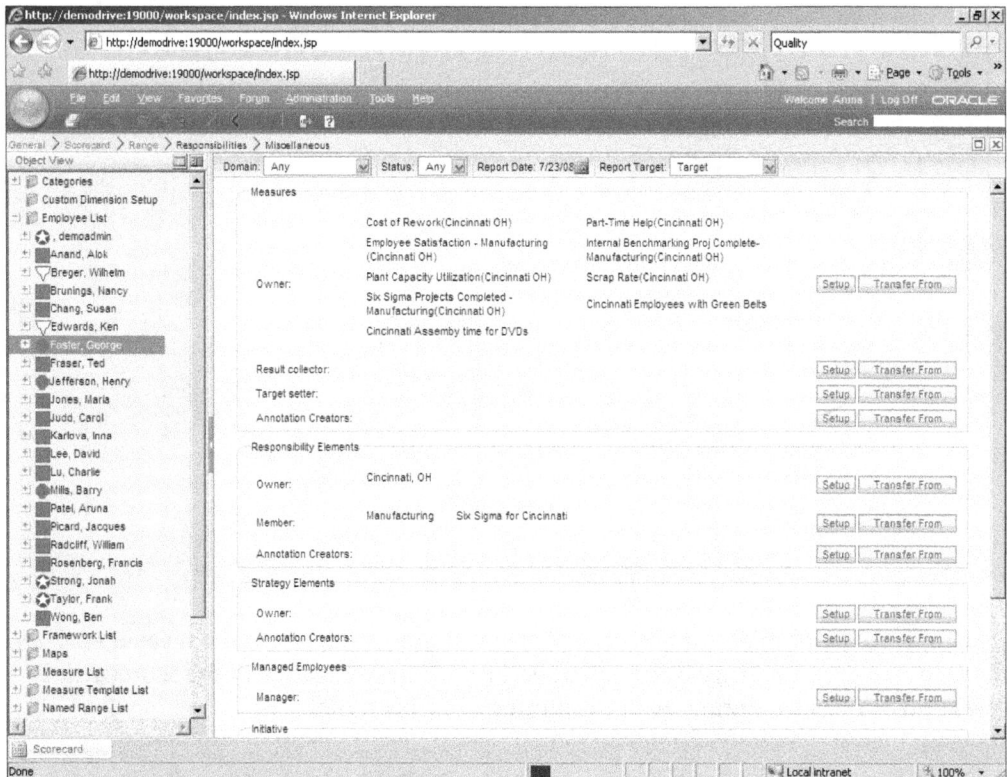

When you set up users within balanced scorecard, you also assign them to measures by setting up their relationship to those measures. Are they the owner, or are they responsible to collect the results, or are they responsible for commenting on the results as an annotation creator. You also state the dimensions that they are responsible for. For example, the geographies, plants, or business units.

Loading data

From the scorecard page, click on the browse icon at the top of the left-hand navigation panel and then click on **Reports**. In the following UI you can load scorecard data:

There are many different ways to get data into the balanced scorecard system. You can load the data in the following ways:

- Enter the data manually
- Transfer data from existing Essbase databases using **Extract Transform and Load (ETL)** tool
- Transfer data from existing data warehouse
- Transfer data from existing legacy systems
- Upload data using spreadsheets

Developing the Strategy Map for Infission and reviewing it with the Board

Given what we have discovered about the changes in the investors and customer sentiments regarding sustainability, the following strategy map can be used to explain to the board the new objectives for the enterprise and how those objectives contribute, ultimately to the survival of the enterprise:

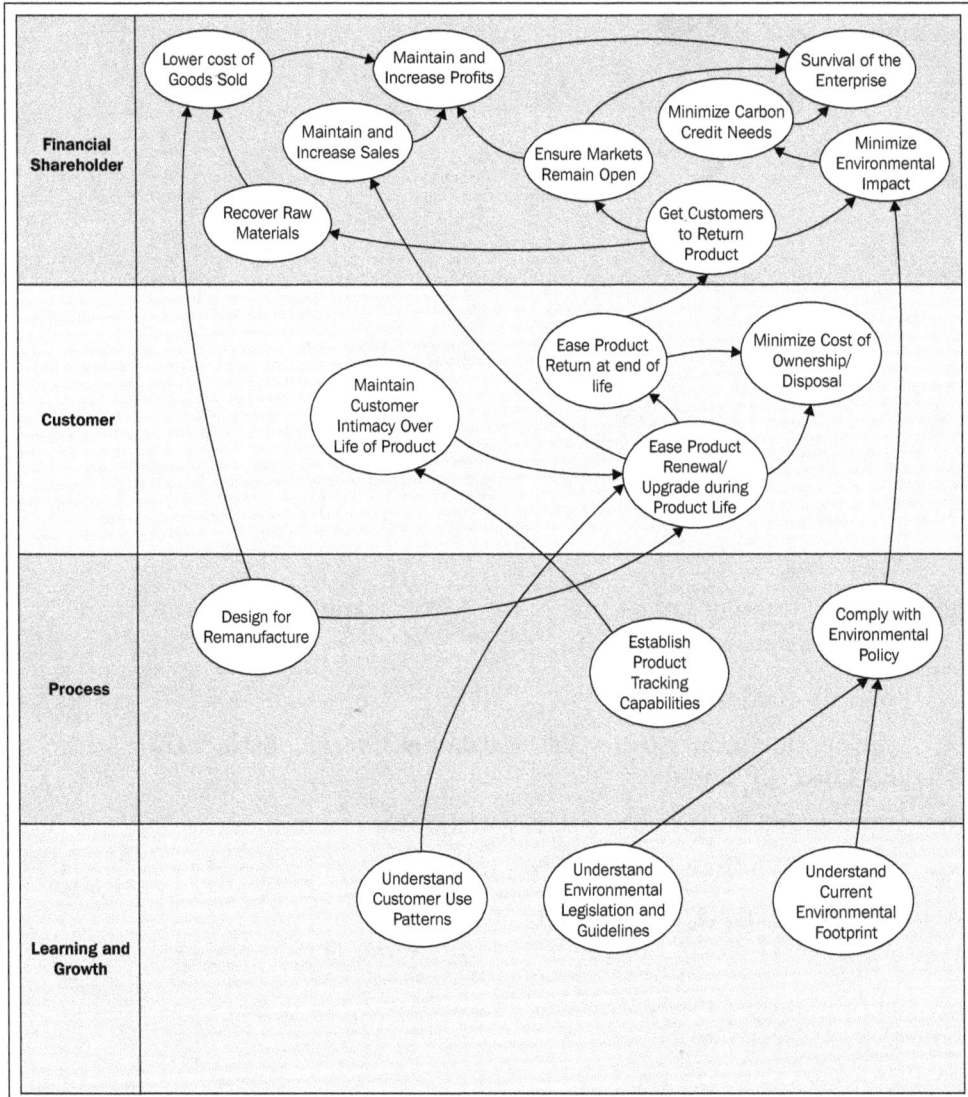

As you can see we have created an objective to minimize the costs of ownership and disposal and to minimize the carbon credits required for manufacturing. In order to lower the carbon credits required for manufacture, one piece of the strategy is to get customers to return product, which is required for market access in some markets, helps minimize the environmental impact, and helps the enterprise recover raw materials, thus lowering its cost of goods sold.

This strategy yields the following balanced scorecard very naturally:

Environmental Balanced Scorecard		Weighting Within Parent	Score	Weighted Score
	Total			
Financial / Shareholder			3.3	
	Maintain and Increase Profits	60.00%	4.5	2.7
	Lower Costs of Remanufacture	50.00%	6.0	3.0
	Lower Costs of Goods Sold	50.00%	3.0	1.5
	Minimize Cleanup Costs and Contingencies	30.00%	4.5	1.4
	Ensure Markets remain open	40.00%	4.0	1.6
	Maintain and Increase Sales	100.00%	5.0	5.0
	Minimize Carbon Credit Needs	30.00%	5.0	1.5
	Minimize Environmental Impact	100.00%	1.5	1.5
	Ensure Company Survival	100.00%	1.5	1.5
		40.00%	1.5	0.6
Customer				
	Minimize Cost of Ownership / Disposal	25.00%		
	Ease Product Return at end life	50.00%		6.0
	Maintain Customer Intimacy Over Life of Product	25.00%		
	Ease Product Renewal/Upgrade during Product Life	50.00%		6.0
Process				
	Establish Product Tracking Capabilities			
	Establish Reverse Logistics Capabilities			
	Design for Remanufacture			
	Design for Disassembly			
	Design for Recovery			
	Design for Disposal			
	Design for Minimal Impact			
	Comply with Environmental Policy			
	Audit Environmental Compliance			
Learning and Growth				
	Understand Current Carbon Footprint			
	Understand Current Environmental Footprint			
	Understand Environmental Legislation and Guidelines			
	Develop Environmental Policy			
	Understand Customer Use Patterns			

When you set up the measure you also need to state how you will measure progress towards it, in the form of a Key Performance Indicator. In this example, the objective of minimizing our required carbon credits is measured through the carbon footprint of our current manufacturing plan. Targets could be set in terms of total energy required.

Assigning objectives to Managers and creating goals in HCM

In order to assign objectives to managers, from **E-Business Suite Login** choose a manager responsibility and select **Appraisals**. In this UI, you assign people objectives for an appraisal period:

What we are showing here is really closing the loop between the measurement system in scorecard, and the incentive system in HCM. For good governance, the measures that managers agree to and are accountable for in the overall corporate strategy should also be reflected in **Management by Objectives (MBOs)** in the Appraisal System. Performance ratings should include objectives that are consistent with the scorecards and strategy.

Communicating and confirming Corporate Strategy with iLearning

The next thing we do for InFission is that we develop some training material to be delivered and confirmed through iLearning. Some of the training is to confirm understanding of corporate policies such as ethics standards and harassment policies. Some of the training material is to confirm understanding of the strategy that we helped develop in the previous section. An example might be a course entitled "Infission's Social Responsibility and Ethical Purchasing Strategies". Here we show the courses and reports from iLearning that help us confirm policy compliance and strategy comprehension.

Developing Learning Assets Flow

The following diagram shows the learning process:

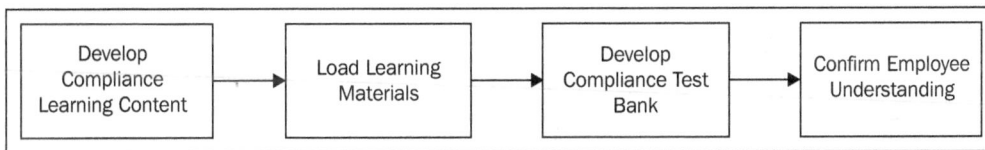

The steps for the learning assets flow are as follows:

1. Place compliance course in catalog.
2. Upload load learning content.
3. Create a question bank.
4. Review employee learning.

The major components of the Learning System

The major components of the Learning System can be seen in the following diagram:

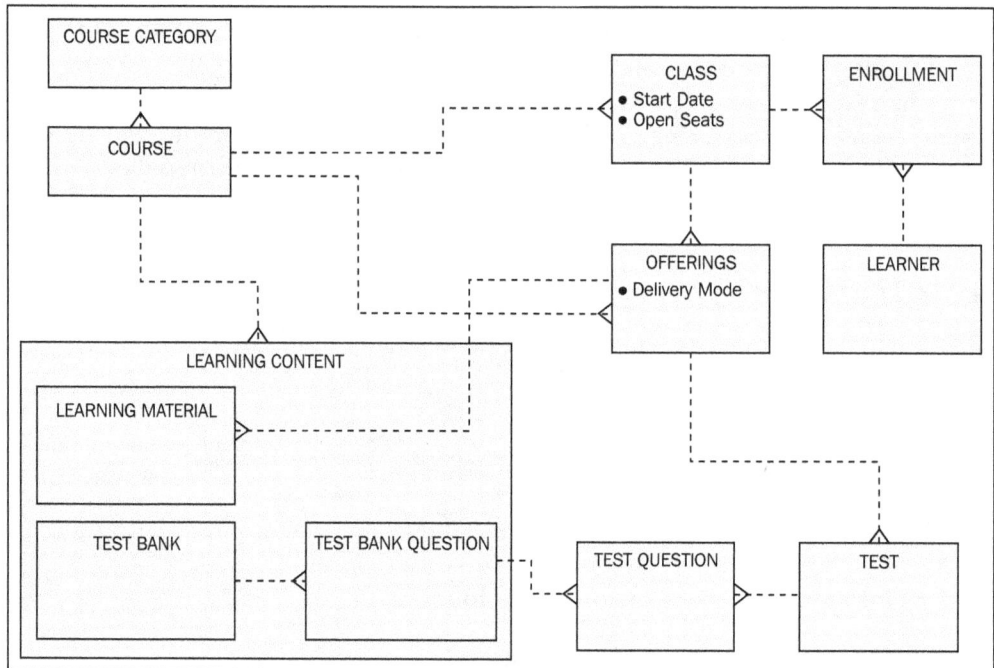

The major components of the Learning System are as follows:

- **Course Category**: For example, Governance and Compliance Courses
- **Course**: For example, Data Privacy Awareness training
- **Class**: For example, California Breach Laws training July 15th 2010
- **Enrollment**: For example, John Doe enrolled in California Breach Laws training on July 15th 2010
- **Learner**: For example, John Doe
- **Offering**: For example, California Breach Laws web-based training
- **Learning** Materials: For example, Data Privacy Awareness Training Courseware
- **Test Bank**: For example, questions on California Breach Law

Responsibilities

You use the Learning System with the following responsibilities:

- **Learning Management Administrator**: A Learning Management Administrator is responsible for setting up the course catalog, loading course materials, and constructing tests.

- **Learner Manager**: A Learner Manager is a manager that has subordinates whose development plans include learning. A learner manager is responsible for ensuring that the correct courses are included in the employee's development plan, and monitoring the successful outcome of those courses.

- **Learner Self Service**: A learner is an employee whose development plans include learning. A learner is responsible for enrolling in and attending classes, and performing tests and evaluations.

Adding an Entry in the Course Catalog

Navigate to the **Learning Management** | **Catalog**, as shown in the following screenshot:

Use this screen to add entries to the course catalog. The course catalog entries could be Course Categories, Courses, or offerings. Choose what to create from the drop down and click on the **Go** button.

Uploading Course Content

Navigate to the **Learning Management | Catalog**, as shown in the following screenshot:

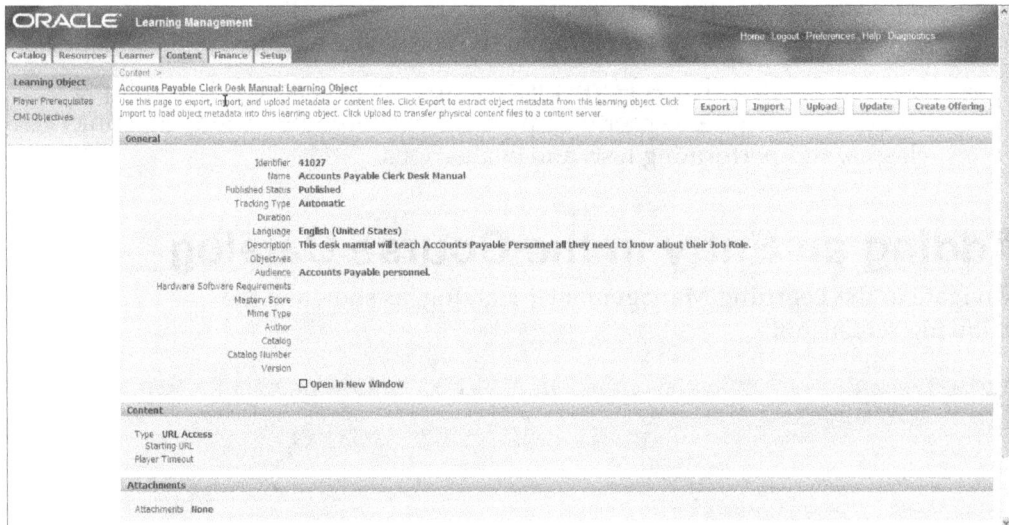

Use this screen to add content to the course catalog. Content could be learning materials or test materials. Course material might be a recorded presentation or slideware. Select what you want to upload from the drop down and click on the **Go** button.

> Note that the content must be published before it is available for learners.

Developing a question bank to confirm understanding

Navigate to **Learning Management Administrator | Content Administration**:

In order to add questions you need to create a question bank to hold them. To review or create question banks click on the **Question Bank** link in the `Catalog` folder. Create a question bank, for example, you might create a *compliance* question bank. You might add to the question bank questions on *Data Privacy Obligations* such as "Which of the following constitute a breach under the California breach law?". You can create a test for each offering. You may have a set of questions for self paced learning, and a different set of questions for instructor-led training.

Monitoring employee's understanding

Navigate to **Learning Management Administrator | Enrollment and Subscriptions**:

Use this screen to see how your learners have done on a class, or set of classes. You can orient your search by class to check for example, how employees are doing in absorbing the data privacy laws and regulations as part of your security awareness program. You can orient your search by learner to confirm that the business ethics course has been taken and successfully completed by a new sales manager.

There are also a number of reports to help you track the understanding that your learners have absorbed of compliance or strategic concepts. An example is the **Evaluation Master Report** that will show evaluations for a Course and Class name, with a summary of the questions.

The Infission Strategic Objectives Classes

At Infission we noted that we needed a sustainability strategy in the first chapter. To ensure that we have employees that have absorbed this strategy we have decided to set up a **Sustainability Course Category**. In the Sustainability Course Category we have created courses and question banks for waste and landfill reduction, design for disassembly and re-use, energy engineering principles, and ethical purchasing. We have created offerings for each course that are web-based training.

Managing Records Retention Policies with Content Management Server

The next thing we do for Infission is to talk to Chief Counsel to define and implement records categories of documents, and the periods for which the documents must be retained, and after which they must be destroyed. This is to aid discovery of documents during the period that they must be retained, and to remove the liability inherent in discovery when documents are no longer required to be retained. We define sensitivity levels and develop access control lists to grant appropriate access to sensitive documents. We then show how the records retention policies are implemented.

Note that as authors we debated whether to document **Oracle Files** or **Universal Content Manager** (**UCM**) as our baseline for documentation here in EBS 12.0. We decided that UCM is really the go forward content management system for Oracle.

Many companies deploying E-Business Suite may not be aware that the attachments capability can be more natively integrated with a document management system. Attachments can be simultaneously added to the document management system and attached to the object in EBS. For more information review this document at:

http://www.oracle.com/us/products/middleware/content-management/059442.pdf

Records Governance Process

The following is the diagram showing the records management process:

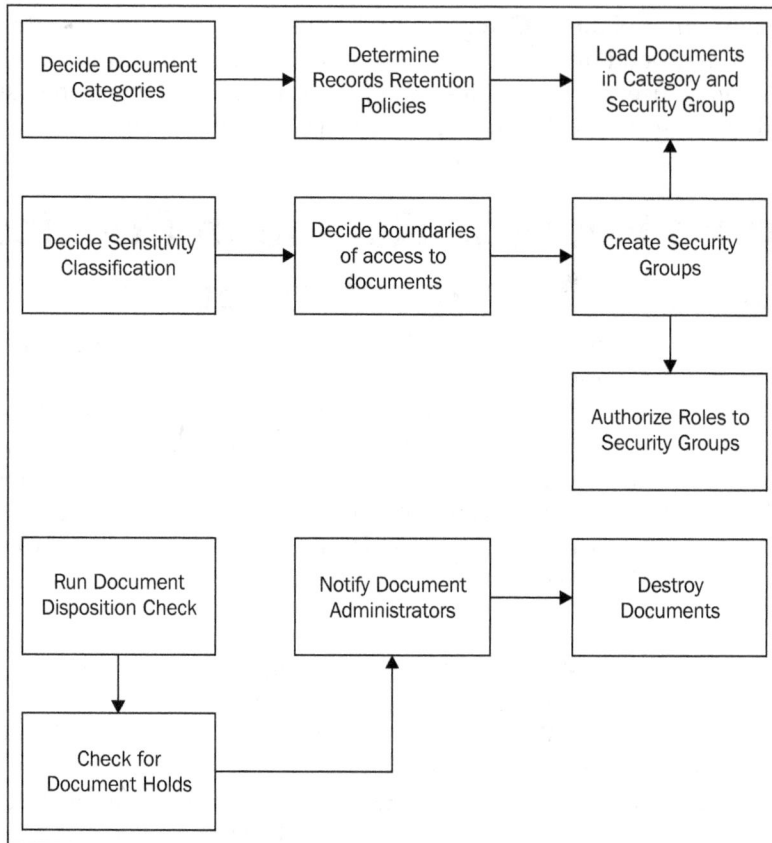

```
┌─────────────────┐      ┌─────────────────┐      ┌─────────────────┐
│ Decide Document │─────▶│   Determine     │─────▶│ Load Documents  │
│   Categories    │      │ Records Retention│      │ in Category and │
│                 │      │    Policies     │      │ Security Group  │
└─────────────────┘      └─────────────────┘      └─────────────────┘
                                                            ▲
                                                            │
┌─────────────────┐      ┌─────────────────┐      ┌─────────────────┐
│ Decide Sensitivity│───▶│ Decide boundaries│────▶│ Create Security │
│  Classification │      │   of access to  │      │     Groups      │
│                 │      │    documents    │      │                 │
└─────────────────┘      └─────────────────┘      └─────────────────┘
                                                            │
                                                            ▼
                                                  ┌─────────────────┐
                                                  │ Authorize Roles to│
                                                  │  Security Groups │
                                                  └─────────────────┘

┌─────────────────┐      ┌─────────────────┐      ┌─────────────────┐
│  Run Document   │      │ Notify Document │─────▶│    Destroy      │
│ Disposition Check│     │ Administrators  │      │   Documents     │
└─────────────────┘      └─────────────────┘      └─────────────────┘
         │                        ▲
         ▼                        │
┌─────────────────┐               │
│   Check for     │───────────────┘
│ Document Holds  │
└─────────────────┘
```

The steps in the records governance process are as follows:

1. Decide document categories.
2. Determine Records Retention Policy for each document category.
3. Decide document sensitivity classifications.
4. Decide boundaries of access to documents.
5. Create security groups.
6. Load documents into categories and security groups.
7. Assign roles to security groups.

Process for destroying documents is as follows:

1. Run document disposition check.
2. Check document holds.
3. Notify document administrators.
4. Destroy documents.

Records Governance Components and how they are related

The following diagram depicts the major components of the records and document management system and the relationships between them:

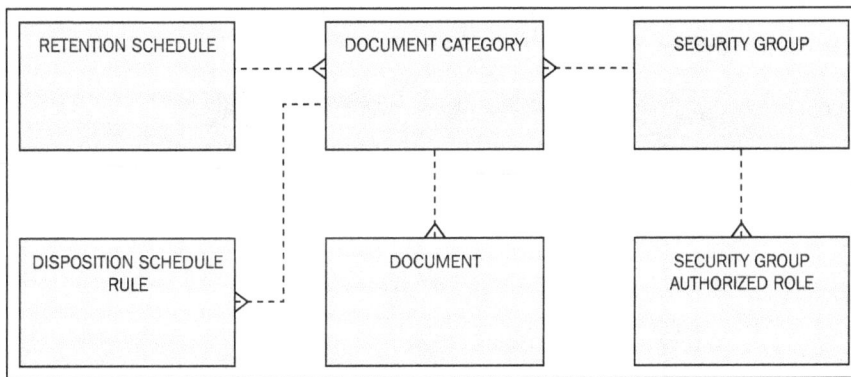

The following is a definition of the major components within the records governance process:

- **Retention Schedule**: You may have different retention schedules for different markets. For example, you may have a retention schedule for commercial markets and a different retention schedule for government markets.
- **Document Category**: Within the retention schedule different document categories are subject to different disposition rules.
- **Disposition Schedule Rule**: A disposition rule might be that a category of documents must be stored for seven years and then destroyed.
- **Document**: An example of a document might be an employee's employment records. A document is in a document category.

- **Security Group**: A security group is a boundary around a set of documents that are likely to be authorized together. For example, HR Records.

- **Security Group Authorized Role**: The authorization of a role to a set of documents is identified by a security group. For example, a Vice President of HR being authorized to HR Records.

Roles for accessing Universal Content Manager (UCM)

You can log in to the Universal Content Manager as an Administrator. The administrator designs the security for other users of the system. Other users are assigned roles. These roles are assigned specific permissions to groups of documents. Undefined users are assigned the guest role if they connect to the server. The following screenshot shows the Universal Content Manager Administration Applets:

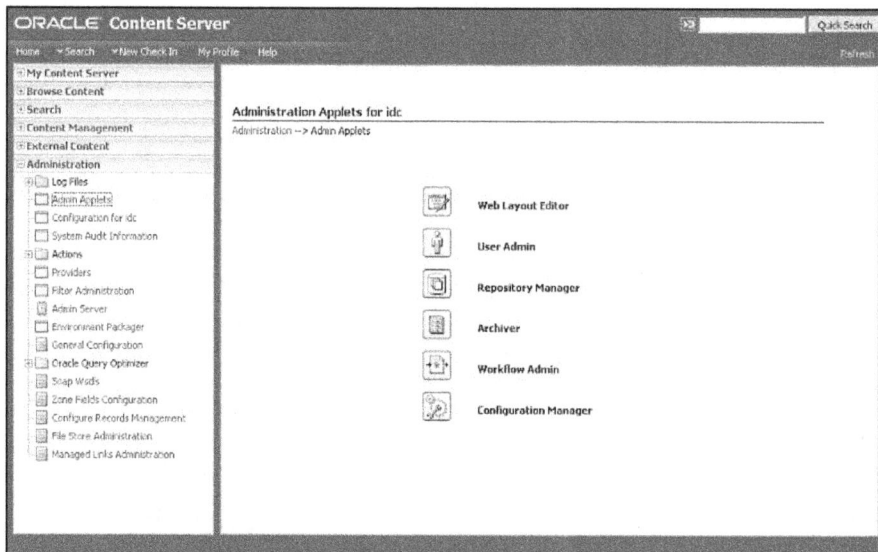

You can run this application by accessing it on the **Administration** page or in standalone mode. In the security menu you will find:

- **Permissions by Group**
- **Permissions by Role**

> Note that we have chosen to not delve deep into the hardcore technical considerations of how to integrate with an LDAP server, configure Secure Socket Layer, and so on. These are all worthy topics, but they are well covered in the *Universal Content Management Managing Security and User Access* guide.

Standard Sensitivity Classifications

Data classification is the act of placing data into categories that will dictate the level of internal controls to protect that data against theft, compromise, and inappropriate use. Information security is best managed when data is classified and the risks associated with each category are uniform and understood.

The IT Governance Institute has included data classification in COBIT 4.0:

> *"Establish a classification scheme that applies throughout the enterprise, based on the criticality and sensitivity (e.g., public, confidential, top secret) of enterprise data. This scheme includes details about data ownership, definition of appropriate security levels and protection controls, and a brief description of data retention and destruction requirements, criticality and sensitivity. It is used as the basis for applying controls such as access controls, archiving or encryption." – ITGI*

The following screenshot is the definition of standard sensitivity classifications in Oracle **Universal Records Management**:

The following are a set of sensitivity classifications that you may find useful in a typical commercial enterprise:

Sensitivity Classification	Definition	Typical Documents
Public information	Information that is suitable for public domain.	Brochures, company's public website.
Personal information	This is information belonging to a private individual, but the individual commonly may share with others for personal or business reasons. This generally includes contact information such as addresses, telephone numbers, e-mail addresses, and so on. It may be considered a breach of privacy to disclose such information to external parties.	Work address, work telephone number.
Private information	Information is private if it is associated with an individual and its disclosure might not be in the individual's best interests. This would include a broad range of information that could be exploited to cause a personal damage. Some types of private information, including records of a person's health care, education, and employment, may be protected by privacy laws in some cases. Disclosing private information can make the perpetrator liable for civil remedies and may in some cases be subject to criminal penalties.	A person's SSN, credit card numbers, and other financial information should be considered private, since their disclosure might lead to crimes such as identity theft or fraud.

Sensitivity Classification	Definition	Typical Documents
Confidential business information	Confidential business information refers to information whose disclosure may harm the business.	Such information may include trade secrets as described in the *Economic Espionage Act of 1996 (18 U.S.C. § 1831–1839)*. In practice, it may include sales and marketing plans, new product plans, and notes associated with patentable inventions. In publicly held companies, confidential information may include "insider" financial data, whose disclosure is regulated by the United States Securities and Exchange Commission.

Typical Security Groups that reflect Security Boundaries and Sensitivity Classifications

You want to ensure that sensitive documents are not available to people without a need to know. You will want to set up the boundaries for access to documents even if they are available to people within the enterprise. For example, accounting information may be company confidential and available to people working in the accounting department, but not available to people working in the sales department or research and development.

On the other hand, we do not want to overburden security administrators with too many security groups to associate to roles. The system will also slow down if a user is authorized to too many security groups. We want the coarsest grain of security classification that is consistent with the need to know.

The following are some illustrations that might help you think through your own installation:

Security Group	Authorized Roles
HR Public	Employee
HR Personal Information	HR Manager, HR Specialist, Vice President HR
HR Confidential business information	HR Manager, Vice President HR
FIN Routine business information	Accountant, Accounting Manager, Controller, Chief Financial Officer
FIN Confidential business information	Accounting Manager, Controller, Chief Financial Officer
Sales Routine Business Information	Salesperson, Sales Manager, Account Manager, Vice President of Sales
Sales Confidential Business Information	Sales Manager, Account Manager, Vice President of Sales

The following are some illustrative document categories that might fall into the security groups. They should help you think through the security groups and document categories in your implementation.

Security Group	Document Categories
HR Public	Job Postings
HR Personal Information	Company Directory
HR Confidential business information	Copies of Personnel Records
FIN Public	10Q and 10K Published Financial Reports
FIN Confidential business information	Profit Forecast
Sales Routine Business Information	Brochures
Sales Confidential Business Information	Bid Review Packages

Illustrative Retention Policies

There are both operational and regulatory reasons to keep hold of records, but there is also a corresponding risk in retaining records that are then subject to discovery longer than needed or required. If records exist, tampering with those records to avoid culpability has extreme consequences. For example, sections 802 and 803 of Sarbanes-Oxley.

Combining the sections of the ammended legislation with the sections from Sarbanes makes this very hard to read.

"Whoever knowingly alters, destroys, mutilates, conceals, covers up, falsifies, or makes a false entry in any record, document, or tangible object with the intent to impede, obstruct, or influence the investigation or proper administration of any matter within the jurisdiction of any department or agency of the United States or any case filed under title 11, or in relation to or contemplation of any such matter or case, shall be fined under this title, imprisoned not more than 20 years, or both.

(a)(1) Any accountant who conducts an audit of an issuer of securities to which section 10A(a) of the Securities Exchange Act of 1934 (15 U.S.C. 78j-1(a)) applies, shall maintain all audit or review workpapers for a period of 5 years from the end of the fiscal period in which the audit or review was concluded.

(2) The Securities and Exchange Commission shall promulgate, within 180 days, after adequate notice and an opportunity for comment, such rules and regulations, as are reasonably necessary, relating to the retention of relevant records such as workpapers, documents that form the basis of an audit or review, memoranda, correspondence, communications, other documents, and records (including electronic records) which are created, sent, or received in connection with an audit or review and contain conclusions, opinions, analyses, or financial data relating to such an audit or review, which is conducted by any accountant who conducts an audit of an issuer of securities to which section 10A(a) of the Securities Exchange Act of 1934 (15 U.S.C. 78j-1(a)) applies.

(b) Whoever knowingly and willfully violates subsection (a)(1), or any rule or regulation promulgated by the Securities and Exchange Commission under subsection (a)(2), shall be fined under this title, imprisoned not more than 10 years, or both.

(c) Whoever corruptly--

(1) alters, destroys, mutilates, or conceals a record, document, or other object, or attempts to do so, with the intent to impair the object's integrity or availability for use in an official proceeding; or

(2) otherwise obstructs, influences, or impedes any official proceeding, or attempts to do so, shall be fined under this title or imprisoned not more than 20 years, or both.

It's important for employers to be familiar with all relevant federal and state record retention laws. Under the Americans with Disabilities Act (ADA) and Title VII of the Civil Rights Act of 1964, for example, covered employers must retain personnel or employment records they made or keep them for one year from the date the record was made or from when an action was taken (e.g., termination), whichever is later.

The Age Discrimination in Employment Act (ADEA), also has separate retention standards for records containing specific employee information. To further complicate things, separate rules also apply for different categories of employers. Employment agencies for example, must keep records on placements, referrals, job orders by employers, applications, test papers completed by applicants as part of the selection process, and advertisements or notices relating to job openings.

The Fair Labor Standards Act (FLSA) and the Family and Medical Leave Act (FMLA) also have separate, rigid requirements for retention of certain documents relating to an individual's employment, such as payroll slips, timesheets or others documents on which wage computations are based, any records relating to any leave time the employee has taken, and documentation of employee benefits.

The Lilly Ledbetter Fair Pay Act, which changed the statute of limitations on when an employee can file a pay discrimination claim, does retain some limits on employer liability by restricting back-pay awards to two years, but employer questions and concerns will still arise, particularly regarding record retention requirements since claims can be filed based on decisions made years earlier.

The following are some of the federal employment laws that employers should look at to make sure they are keeping documents long enough to meet the laws' requirements or to cover the period of time in which an employee can file suit under the laws: Health Insurance Portability and Accountability Act (HIPAA), COBRA, Uniformed Services Employment and Reemployment Rights Act (USERRA), Occupational Health and Safety Act (OSH Act), National Labor Relations Act (NLRA), Employee Retirement Income Security Act (ERISA), Immigration Reform and Control Act (IRCA), Equal Pay Act (EPA), and the Fair Credit Reporting Act (FCRA).

There are also record retention requirements for documents such as EEO-1 (Equal Employment Opportunity) reports and tax records.

The following table shows some illustrative Records Retention Policies:

Document Category	Retention Policy
Copies of Personnel Records	72 months
General Matters Correspondence	1 month
Audit Committee Binders	84 months
Audit Planning	84 months
Bid Review Packages	60 months

Records retention management is handled through a component of Universal content manager called **Universal Records Management**. It can manage the retention and disposition of content within UCM and external content.

In order to navigate to the retention policy definition, expand the retention schedule, and then the file plan. Choose a document category. The right-click menu will reveal the retention policies and other category information such as the security group that is authorized to this category.

The following screenshots show how the disposition rule is established. The first screenshot shows selecting a category of documents:

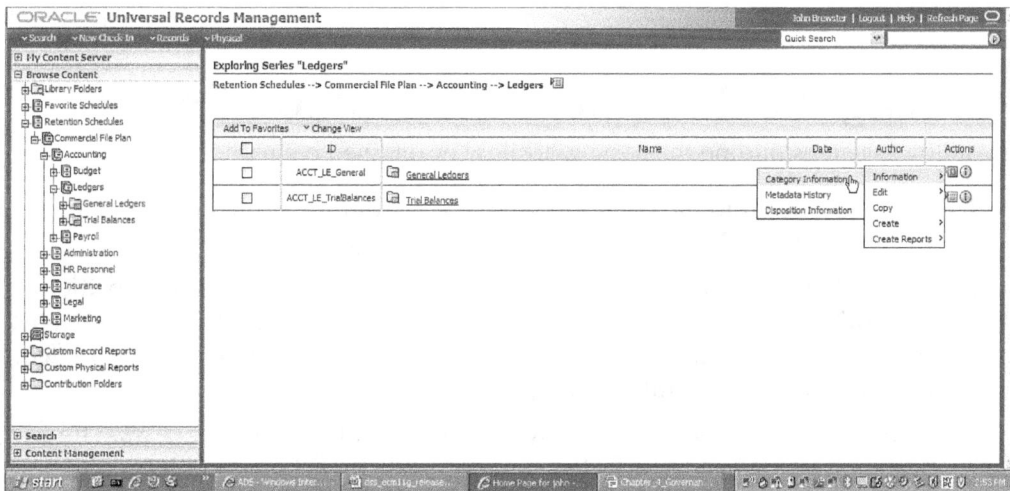

Once you have selected a document category you can create its disposition rule. In the following example captured in the screenshot, the disposition action is that employee records should be destroyed after a period of three years:

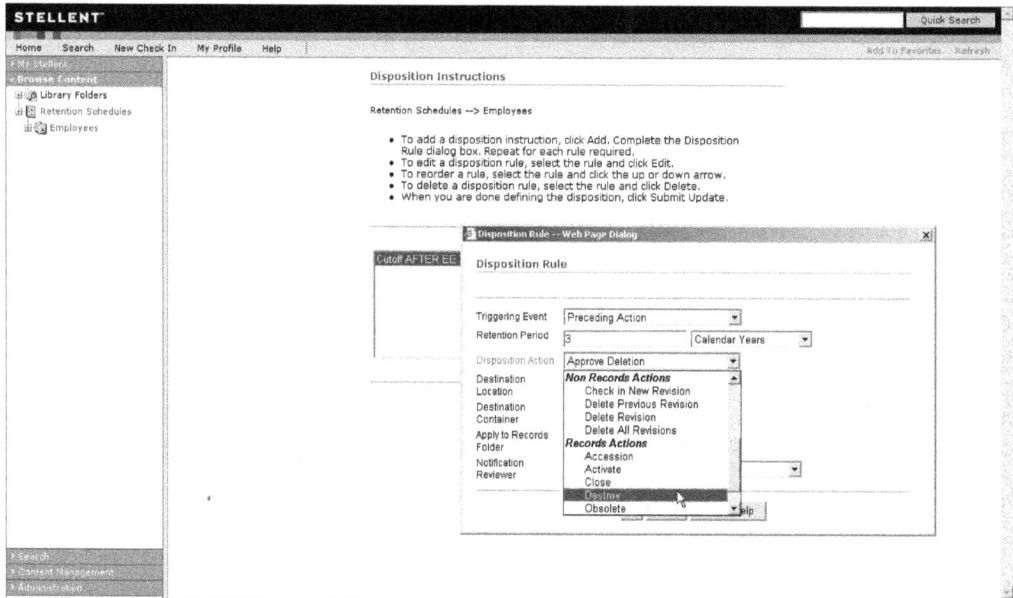

Running the Document Disposition Check

The following steps outline the basic workflow of retained content:

1. Items are filed into the retention schedule by users. The filed items assume the disposition schedules of their assigned category.

2. Disposition rules are processed in accordance with the defined disposition schedules, which usually have a retention period. The processing is activated by either a system-derived trigger or custom trigger. The trigger could affect one or more items simultaneously.

3. Content is often filed then destroyed after a certain number of years. The system tracks when the affected content is due for action. Notification e-mail is sent to reviewers with links to the pages where reviewers can review and approve content, and folders that are due for dispositions.

4. In contrast, time-event and event-based dispositions must be triggered with a non- system-derived trigger (a trigger that was defined for a particular scenario). For example, when a pending legal case starts litigation, the Records Administrator must enable the custom trigger and set its activation date, because the start date information is external. Custom triggers can define event and time-event based disposition actions based, on the occurrence of a particular event.

By taking advantage of these records management features, compliance and legal teams can easily apply litigation and audit holds to both records and non-records, thus preventing the accidental or intentional deletion of information needed for litigation or audits. When you run the checks for document disposition, legal holds will ensure that this content is not flagged for destruction.

The following screenshot shows the user interface in which you schedule the document disposition check:

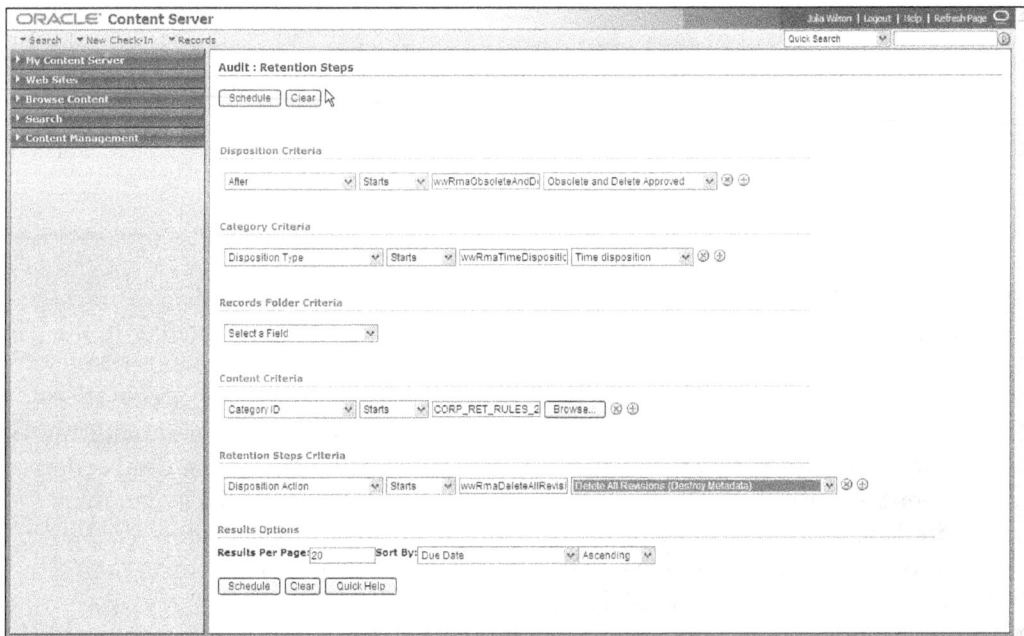

Whenever a disposition event is due for action (as activated by a trigger), an e-mail notification is sent to the person responsible for processing the events. The pending events and reviews are displayed in the pages accessed from the **Retention Assignments** links within the user interface. The Records Administrator processes the disposition actions in the pending events pages. This is a manual process.

The following screenshot shows the disposition notifications being shown in a dashboard:

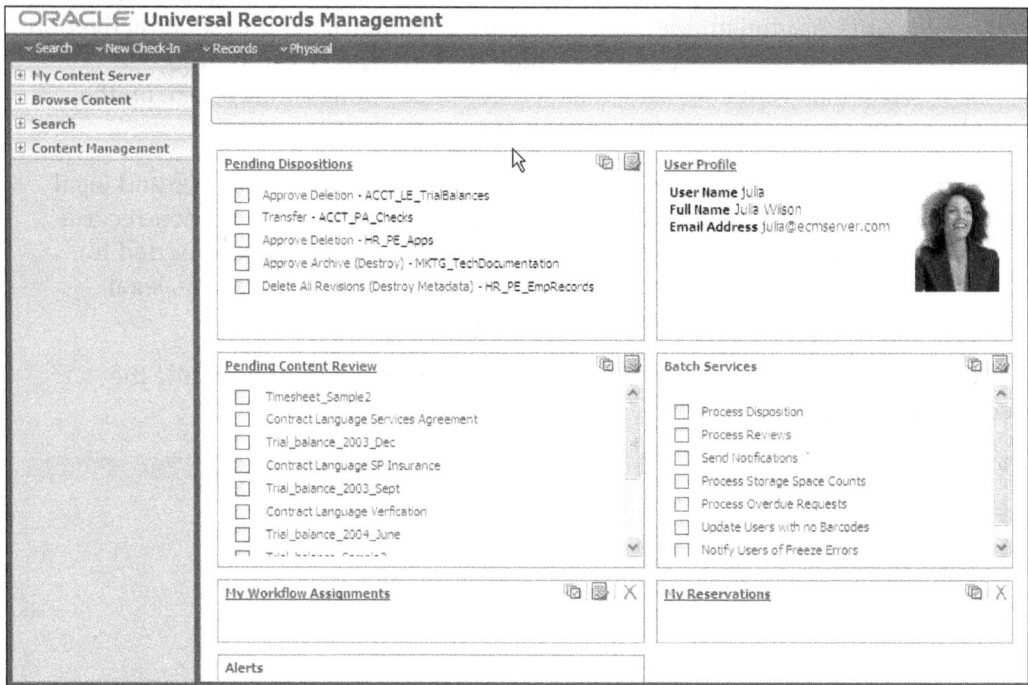

In the federal trade commission's recent $50,000 dollar settlement with an Illinios mortgage firm for discarding personal information without first destroying it, the regulatory agency cited the absence of the required written policies and procedures as a basis for the penalty. Similarly, the failure to have the required written policies and procedures was cited by the attorney general of Texas with two national firms when it was discovered that they were violating the state's information destruction requirement. According to the Texas Attorney General's office the fines amounted to hundreds of thousands of dollars and required the retailers to develop written information destruction programs (Source: National Association of Information Destruction Press Release, June 10, 2008).

According to Robert Johnson, National Association of Information Destruction's Executive Director, *"For some organizations, the policy on information destruction amounts to a single sentence, advising employees to destroy sensitive information properly before it is discarded. In today's social and business climate, that simply does not provide sufficient direction to employees who are dealing with many forms of media"*. Johnson adds *"Because of the consequences of improper disposal, regulators, auditors, courts of law, the media and public sentiment are insisting on a more thorough approach to information destruction."*

Destruction can take many forms. *Disk-wiping* software can prevent unauthorized recovery by overwriting entire drives/disks (or particular sections of them) before these magnetic media are discarded or reused. Overwritten areas must be unreadable to comply with the Department of Defense standard for permanent erasure of digital information (U.S. DoD 5220.22).

To erase magnetic media, there are several types of degaussers, which remove all recorded information in a single pass, allowing hard drives, diskettes, audio and video tapes, and data cartridges to be reused many times with no interference from previous use. Hand-held degaussing wands erase both floppy and hard computer disks.

Financial planning and analysis with Hyperion FR

The next thing we do for Infission Corporation is talk to the CFO and controller about how to turn the strategic plan that we have developed into a financial plan. This plan may form the guidance that we issue when we review the Management Discussion and Analysis in the annual results, or guidance that we are issuing on a quarterly basis. We show the various Oracle tools used in collating and communicating the plan. We will also show how to test the assumptions on which the plan is based.

Financial Planning and Analysis Flow

The following diagram shows the flow through the financial planning and analysis process:

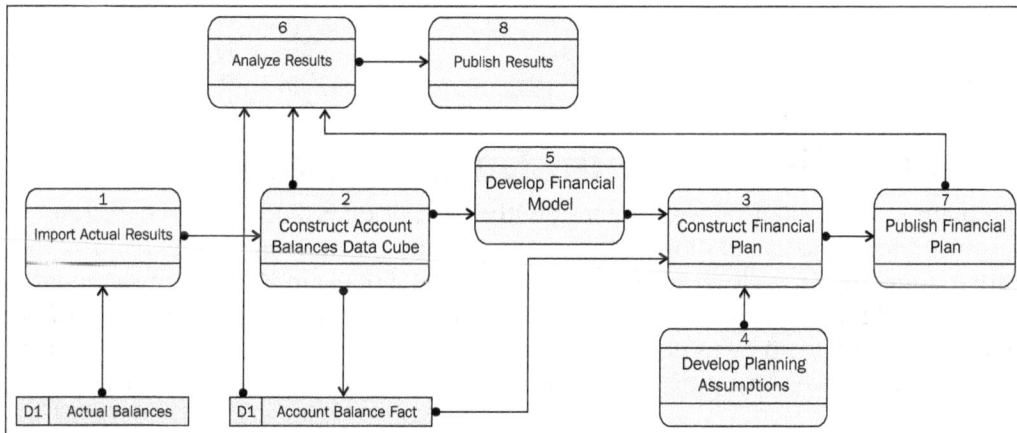

Accessing the Financial Planning and Analysis tools

With the acquisition of Hyperion, Oracle acquired the leading financial planning tool in the market, **Hyperion FP**. This tool was integrated in the field to the leading Financial Management Applications.

The following screenshot is the homepage of the **Enterprise Performance Management** (**EPM**) product:

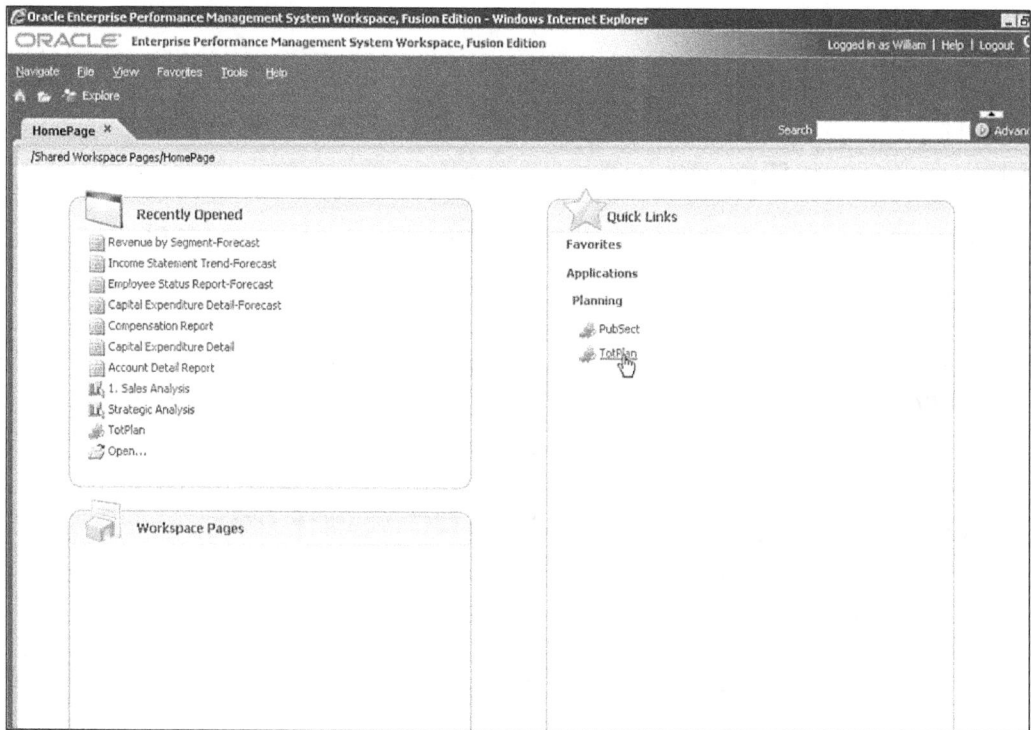

Constructing Account Balance Data Cube

The planning and analysis environment within Hyperion is a dimensional design optimized for rapid calculation and presentation along a number of dimensions. The transactional model is closer to a normalized model. For example, the transactional model might have a reporting calendar. A transaction has a **General Ledger Posting Date** that links it to an accounting period in a calendar, which is the period in which to update a balance. Any entity may be linked to any entity. There is no center.

In the dimensional model the account balance fact can be analyzed in a period dimension, as well as the scenario, company, business unit, cost center, and account dimensions. The information is pre-aggregated for analysis at multiple levels in multiple dimensions. The fact is at the center, and dimensions radiate out.

If you take a flip forward to the section on the components of the financial planning and analysis (*Financial Planning and Analysis Components and how they are related* section) there is a diagrammatic comparison between these two representations.

Developing the Financial Model

Some of the lines in the financial model are going to be based on directly entered new planning assumptions such as sales volume or number of people. Some lines in the financial model will be derived based on those numbers. For example, the marketing and promotion costs may be projected to be 15 percent of the revenue line.

In order to navigate to this Revenue Driver's page, log onto **Hyperion Financial Planning** and choose the **Planning Application**:

Users can also view planning data forms from within Microsoft Excel with the same functionality as the web-based interface.

Using **Smart View**, you can view, import, manipulate, distribute and share data in Microsoft Excel, Word, and PowerPoint interfaces.

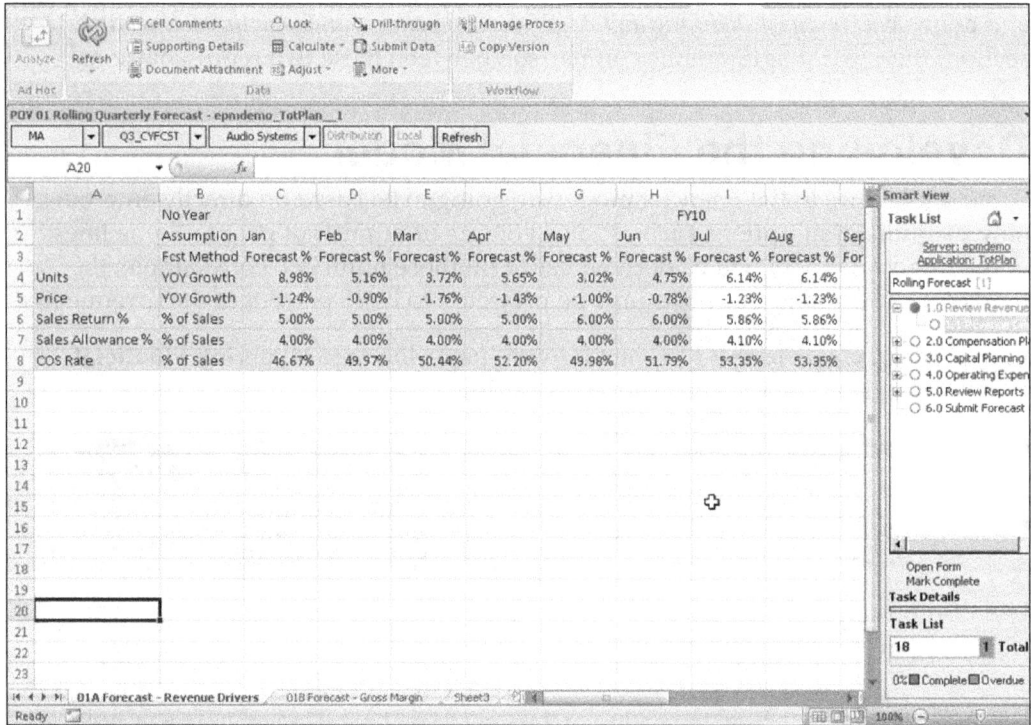

We can open this form in Smart View simply by clicking a button. Click on the **Open in Smart View** icon.

Developing planning assumptions

Some of the lines in the financial model are based on a set of planning assumptions gathered in the planning process. For example, for a commercial company the sales volume projections are likely to be at least confirmed back with the sales organizations.

In another example, growth in material costs may be estimated to be the current standard costs extended by the projected volumes and adjusted for an inflationary index of 2.5 percent. With the Hyperion product the collection and collation of the planning assumptions is a highly collaborative process.

In order to enter planning assumptions click on the **Supporting Detail** icon on the tool bar.

Constructing the Financial plan

When the previous year's data has been collected, the financial model established and the planning assumptions have been gathered, you can construct the new financial plan, as well as challenge the assumptions on which it is based.

The following screenshot shows a rolling forecast in Enterprise Performance Management:

The primary ways of testing assumptions are sensitivity analysis and variance analysis. For example, for a clothing manufacturer, the financial plan may be based on pricing that assumes manufacturer's recommended price can be held for six weeks before the change of season forces the price point to drop to 50 percent of **Manufacturer's Suggested Retail Price (MSRP)** within four weeks and that 80 percent of manufactured volume can be sold at MSRP. The sensitivity analysis may show that if less that 60 percent of manufactured volume is sold at MSRP the season fails to break even. Variance Analysis would demonstrate the change in margin that is due to changes in the planning assumptions individually.

Publishing the Financial plan

The publication of the financial plan is needed to ensure that it is a tool to guide and motivate managers. Some aspects of the plan may also be communicated to investors as part of revised earnings guidance or in the management discussion and analysis in the annual accounts.

You move the profit forecast through its approval process for publication by clicking on the **Submit Forecast** link in the left-hand panel. You can also submit your forecast or plan from within Excel. The following screenshot shows the promotion work:

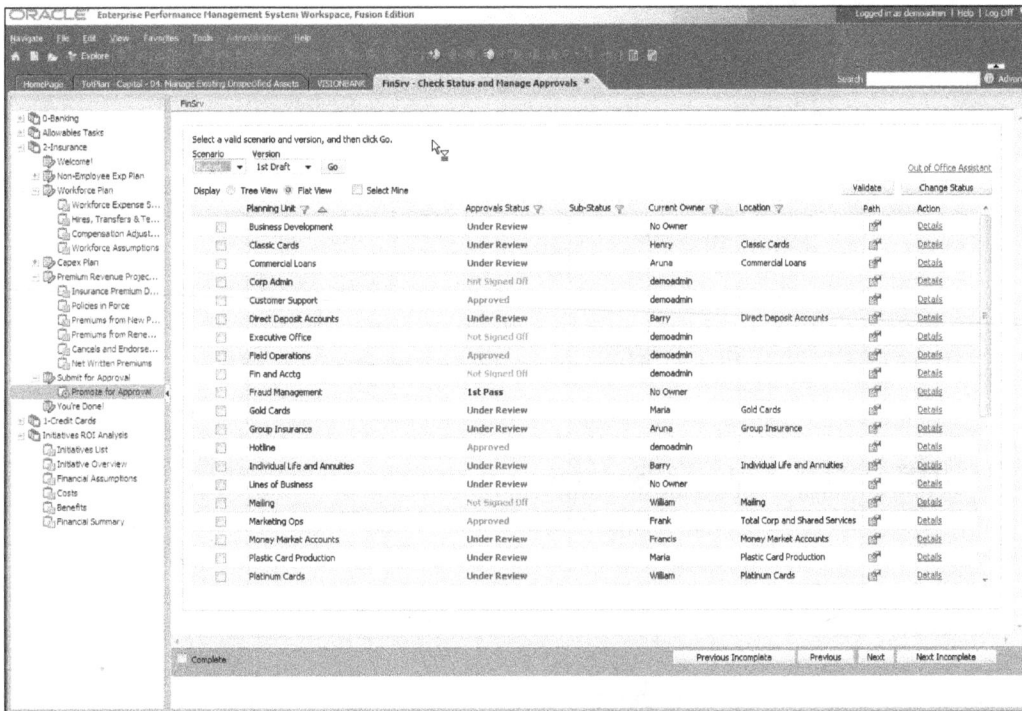

Analyzing the results

When a period closes and the result collated, it must then be explained through variance analysis and partitioned out for responsible managers along various dimensions. For example, cost center managers

You can navigate to **Variance Analysis** from the left-hand task pane:

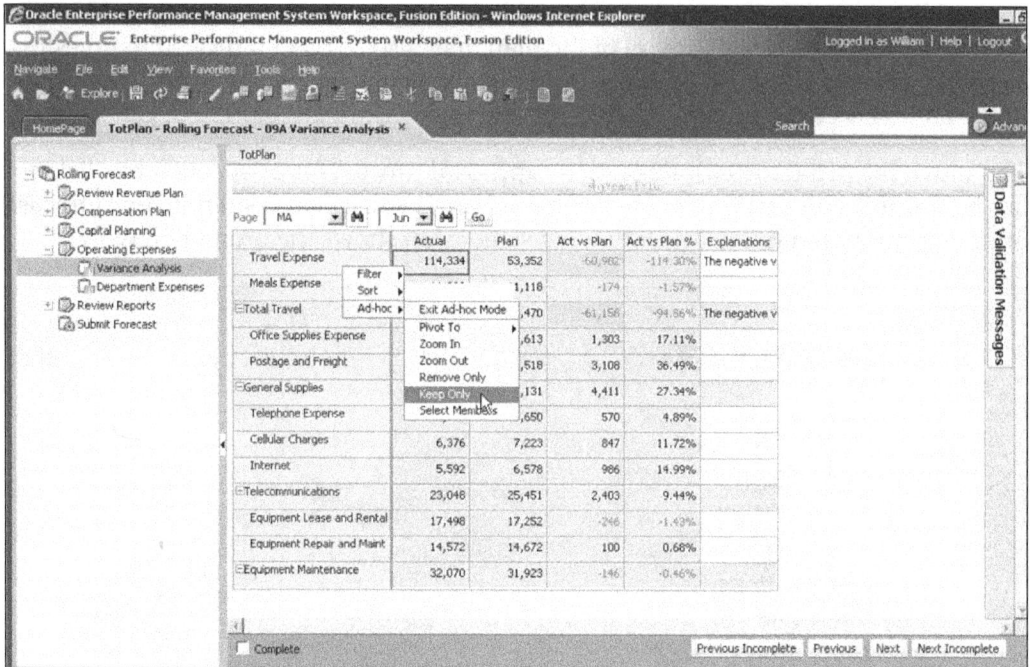

Publishing the results

Finally when the results can be explained the results can be published both internally and externally. The following screenshot shows the reports available:

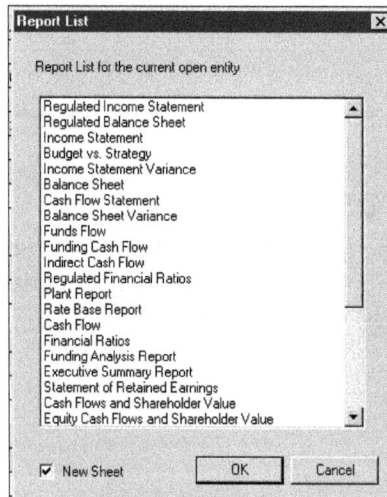

Oracle Hyperion Planning offers highly formatted, production-quality reports in real time and a user-friendly interface that doesn't require IT intervention. Reports can be easily created and run by end users, providing flexibility and saving time for data analysis instead of model maintenance. Reports can be run on demand or scheduled for delivery.

In order to run a report click on the **Explore** icon at the top of the view and navigate to a report. Launch a report in PDF format by right-clicking and selecting **Open In | PDF Preview**.

Financial Planning and Analysis Components and how they are related

The following is a diagram of the main components of the Hyperion Financial Planning and Analysis system and shows how they are related. On the left, the diagram shows a relational model and on the right it shows a dimensional model.

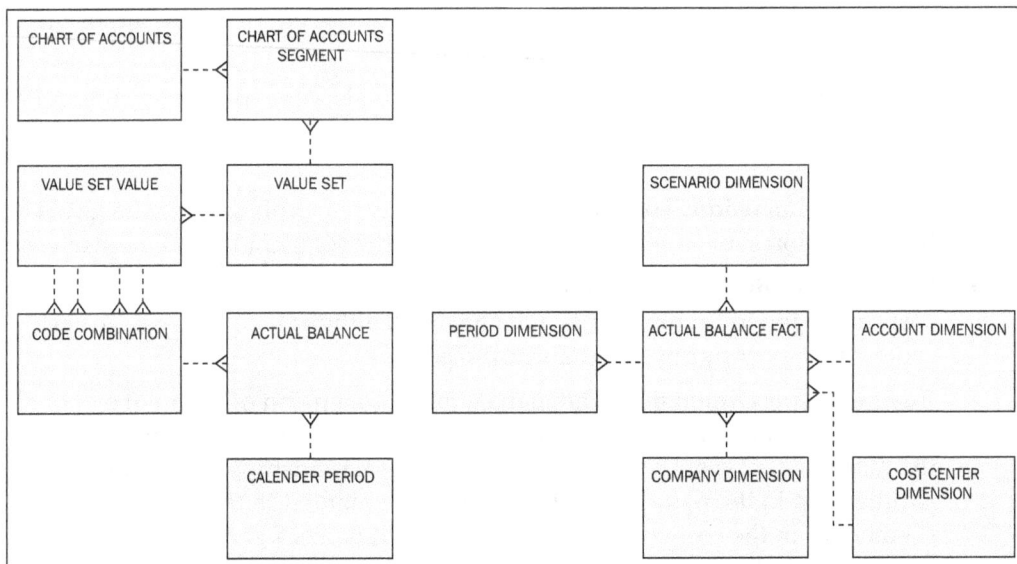

- **Actual Balance**: This is the actual balance from the transactional system. In our case E-Business Suite 12.1.

- **Code Combination**: The account balance is the balance for a combination of segment values. The combination is held in the code combinations table that is the actual chart of accounts.

- **Calendar Period**: The account balance is the balance for a particular period in the accounting calendar.

- **Value Set Value**: The code combination has a value for each segment in the chart of accounts. The value must be a valid value in the value set for that segment. The value set could be reused in other charts of accounts.

- **Account Balance Fact**: Next we work with the dimensional side of the components. The center point here is the Account balances fact. These may be actual values imported from the transactional system, official budgets, or forecasts that may be created under a different scenario.

- **Period Dimension**: The account balance fact may be analyzed and summarized by many dimensions. An important dimension is the period dimension. Costs and revenues for the same period can be gathered to create a projected Financial Statement for that period or collection of periods.

- **Scenario Dimension**: The financial planning process will test many different scenarios before one of those scenarios is selected to be the plan that will drive the enterprise and may be communicated. However, being able to see the development of the final plan through various scenarios is an important capability in being able to defend the final plan.

- **Company Dimension**: The company dimension is self explanatory. It is very likely to be linked to the balancing segment in the transactional systems chart of accounts.

- **Account Dimension**: The account dimension is self explanatory. The levels of the dimension should reflect the hierarchy in the segment values themselves.

- **Cost Center Dimension**: The cost center dimension is self explanatory. The cost center generally represents a department, although you may have cost centers that exist purely for analysis purposes.

- **Business Unit Dimension**: The management dimension of your cube may be a business unit or a division dimension that is closely aligned to the management responsibility and reporting relationships. This could be a dimension in its own right or it may be implemented in the balancing segment or in the cost center segment. It would be very good practice to break it out in the transformation to the cube.

- **Ledger Dimension**: The Ledger dimension is the boundary within which the additivity of balances in the cube can be guaranteed. You have to think very carefully if you want to add balances from different ledgers as to whether the results will be meaningful or not.

Monitoring Execution with Oracle Business Intelligence

To close the loop on the corporate governance we will show how the strategy is tracked in Business Intelligence. We show a few of the financial and non-financial goals that we agreed at the start of the corporate governance process and how we can measure progress towards those goals with various business intelligence tools.

With its new release of Business Intelligence, Oracle has created a common data warehouse structure and extracts, transforms, and loads data from many of its acquired applications product lines into this data warehouse. Oracle Business Intelligence Applications includes dashboards that deliver performance metrics directly to executives, managers, and analysts in the form of easy-to-read charts, graphs, and tables. The complete environment contains over 500 dashboard pages.

The business intelligence content is decomposed into a number of business intelligence applications.

- Oracle Financial Analytics
- Oracle Procurement and Spend Analytics
- Oracle Supply Chain and Order Management Analytics
- Oracle Project Analytics
- Oracle Human Resources Analytics
- Oracle Sales Analytics
- Oracle Price Analytics
- Oracle Marketing Analytics
- Oracle Loyalty Analytics
- Oracle Service Analytics
- Oracle Call Center Telephony Analytics

Oracle Financial Analytics

Log in to BI analytics and choose the **Financial Interactive Dashboard** link at the top of the browser:

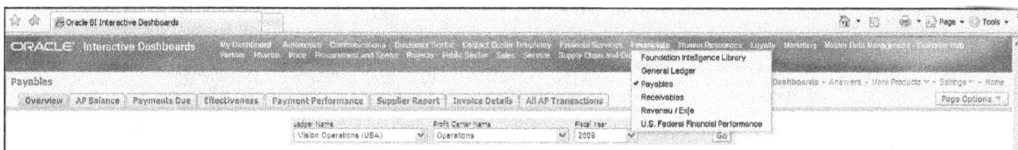

You can choose a dashboard for:

- **General Ledger**
- **Payables**
- **Receivables**
- **Profitability**

Click on the **General Ledger** link. You will get to the following dashboard:

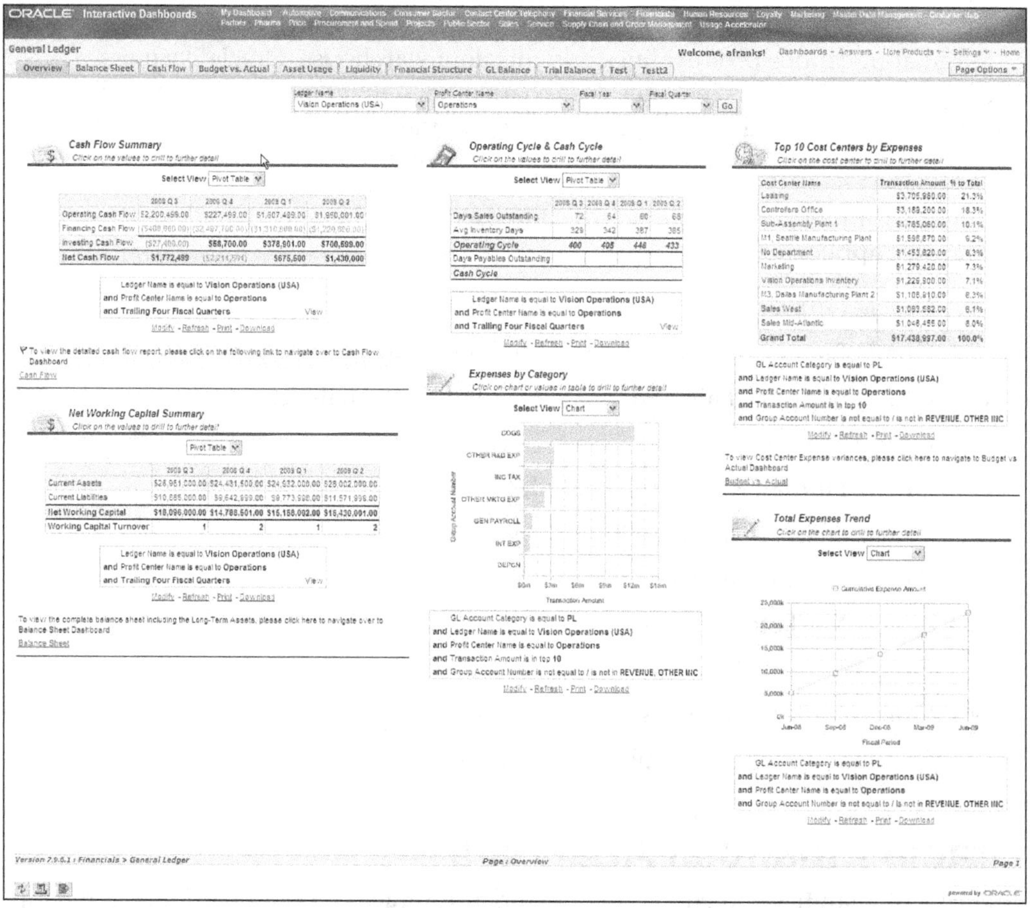

In this dashboard you can see the following metrics:

- **Cash Generated**
- **Cash to Cash Cycle Time**
- **Highest Spending Cost Centers**

- **Highest Category of Expenses**
- **Expenses Trend**

These are the kind of objectives that you should have in the Financial Section of your balanced scorecard. These metrics are available to be analyzed along the following dimensions:

- Ledger
- Profit Center
- Fiscal Year and Quarter

Other dashboards in Financial Analytics

The **Profitability dashboard** gives various measures of Return on Investment including, return on equity and return on assets, flagging in red, yellow, or green whether the return percentages are on target. It also uses measures of profitability such as gross margin and operating margin. It provides a cost breakdown as a percentage of sales as well as gross margin breakdown by customer category and product hierarchy. These are the kind of objectives that you should have in the Financial Section of your balanced scorecard.

The **Payables dashboard** gives you a snapshot of metrics in the payables function, such as average days left to pay the suppliers, days late, amounts coming due and amount outstanding as well as efficiency of the invoice registration and disbursements process. Each of the metrics is expanded in its own tab.

The **Receivables dashboard** is symmetrical with the Payables dashboard. It gives a snapshot of metrics in the receivables function, such as days of sale outstanding, invoices created and payments received. Again, each of the metrics is expanded in its own tab.

These are the kind of metrics you should have in the internal process perspective in your balanced scorecard.

Oracle Sales Analytics

Log in to BI analytics and choose the **Sales Interactive Dashboard** link at in the top of the browser:

You can choose a dashboard for:

- **Competitors**
- **Customers**
- **Demand Generation**
- **Pipeline**
- **Sales Effectiveness**

Click on the **Demand Generation** link. You will get to the following dashboard:

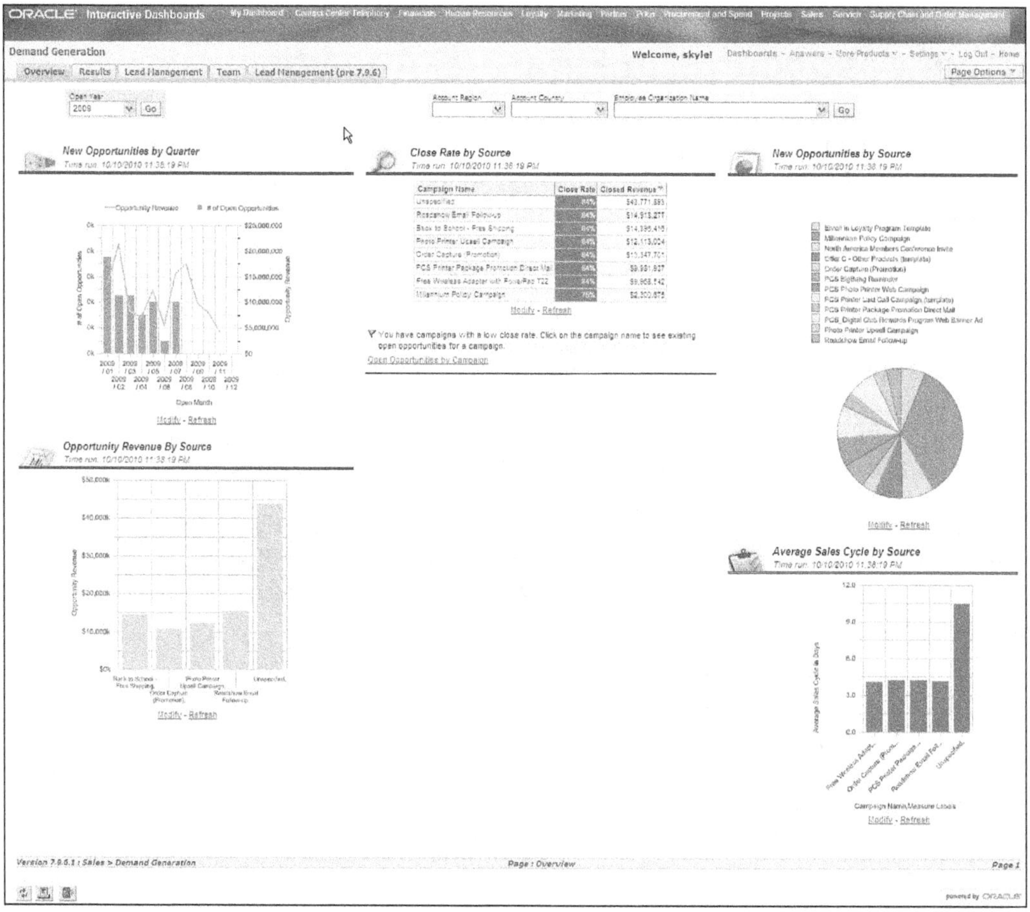

In this dashboard you can see the following metrics:

- New opportunities
- Opportunity revenue (opportunity revenue is expanded in the **Results** tab)
- Opportunity closure rates
- Sales cycle time

These metrics are available to be analyzed along the following dimensions:

- **Time**: For example, period, quarter, and year.
- **Region**: Region is a grouping of countries. Examples of regions are groupings such as Latin America or Europe, Middle East, and Africa.
- **Country**: For example, United States, Chile.
- **Employee Organization**: Employee organization is the organization to which the employee is assigned to work. This is very likely to be the sales department.

The **Lead Management** tab is not really an expansion of the metrics on the main dashboard, but gives great metrics of the flow into the opportunity management process.

Other dashboards in Sales Analytics

The **Competitors dashboard** focuses on win/loss analysis. It shows a win/loss analyzed by customer, over time, both in terms of number of opportunities as well as the value of the opportunity. It analyzes wins by reason and loss by reason as well as listing recent competitive wins. It expands these metrics by competitor, by team member, and by product, each in a dedicated tab. The last subtab provides a heat map by product line and competitor to surface quickly whether you are winning or losing in these two dimensions.

The **Customers dashboard** shows the account activity over time in terms of both number of accounts and number of activities. It shows the top customer accounts as measured by both opportunity revenue and realized revenue. It shows the number of accounts with activities as well as an analysis of accounts by geography and industry. The dashboard has an **Account Summary** tab that presents key metrics for a customer account. It also has a **Products** tab that lets you know the products that are most often quoted, where you already have penetration and where you have whitespace in the market.

The **Pipeline dashboard** shows an analysis of the pipeline by sales stage, current forecast revenue versus quota as well as a breakdown of pipeline between opportunity revenue and revenue forecast to close.

The **Sales Effectiveness dashboard** shows metrics such as days from quote to order, average order size, top performing sales people based on their sales cycle time, deal size and win rate. The Sales Effectiveness Dashboard has tabs dedicated to measuring forecast accuracy, seeing the sales effectiveness of your team as well as how well the products are doing in terms of win rates and excessive discounts.

These are the kind of objectives that you might have in the Customer or Internal Processes perspective of your balanced scorecard.

Oracle Procurement Analytics

Log in to BI analytics and choose the **Procurement and Spend Interactive Dashboard** link at the top of the browser, as shown in the following screenshot:

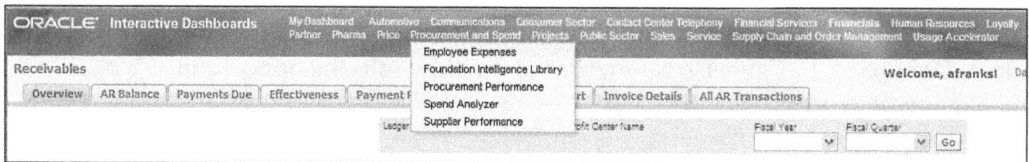

You can choose a dashboard for:

- **Employee Expenses**
- **Procurement Performance**
- **Spend Analyzer**
- **Supplier Performance**

Click on the **Spend Analyzer** link. You will get to the following dashboard:

In this dashboard you can see following metrics:

- **Total Spend**: The total amount spent overall.
- **Payables Leakage Rate**: (Leakage Amount/Invoice Amount)*100. This is the Invoice amount for invoices that did not match to a purchase order or receipt, as a percentage of the total invoice amount. Use this KPI to identify how much of your invoice amount has not gone through your procurement organization. A lower rate is desirable.
- **Non-Contract Purchases Rate**: (Non-Contract Purchases Amount/ PO Purchases Amount)*100. Percent of non-contract purchases to the total purchase amount. Non-contract purchases occur when, for an item purchased on a standard purchase order, there was no negotiated pricing (no blanket purchase agreement in place. Use this KPI to measure the percentage of purchases made without any contract being in place. A lower rate is desirable.
- **Contract Leakage Rate**: (Leakage Amount / PO Purchases Amount) * 100. This is percentage of contract leakage to the total purchase amount. Contract leakage occurs when, for an item purchased on a standard purchase order, a blanket purchase agreement was in effect that could have been used instead. Use this KPI to measure the percentage of purchases that are made off-contract. A lower rate is desirable.
- **Spend by Category**: The total amounts spent in each procurement category.
- **Spend by Supplier**.
- **Savings Potential**: The difference between the average amount paid for an item and the lowest amount paid for an item.

These metrics are available to be analyzed along the following dimensions:

- Time
  - Year
  - Quarter
  - Month
- Business Unit
- Cost Center
- Top Level Item Category
- Supplier

Other dashboards in Procurement Analytics

The **Employee Expenses** dashboard is really targeted at running the expenses reimbursement operation. It gives a cycle time breakdown of expense reports among Filing cycle time, Approval cycle time, and Reimbursement cycle time. It has an analysis of expenses over time, by cost center and by expense category. It has a page dedicated to review of costs by person, useful for supervisors. It also has a page dedicated to review of expenses by and for a cost center, as well as a page dedicated to the flow and backlog of the expense reports.

The **Supplier Performance** dashboard is targeted at the procurement operation. It gives an aggregate supplier scorecard, which covers On-time Delivery, Quality, Cost, and Disbursements. It also gives the supplier scorecards for individual suppliers as well as showing the number of suppliers for each product category.

The **Procurement Performance** dashboard is targeted at the person running the procurement function. It shows a collection of procurement metrics including Non-Agreement Purchase Rate, Contract Leakage Rate, and On-time Delivery. It also shows the trend in the value being purchased as well as an analysis of deliveries after the requested date on the requisition. It also shows the trends for the percentage of purchase value made without a contract in place, and the trend for purchases made where a contract exists, but was still purchased off-contract.

These are the kind of objectives that you should have in the Internal Processes Perspective of your balanced scorecard.

Oracle Human Resources Analytics

Log in to BI analytics and choose the **Human Resources Interactive Dashboard** link at the top of the browser:

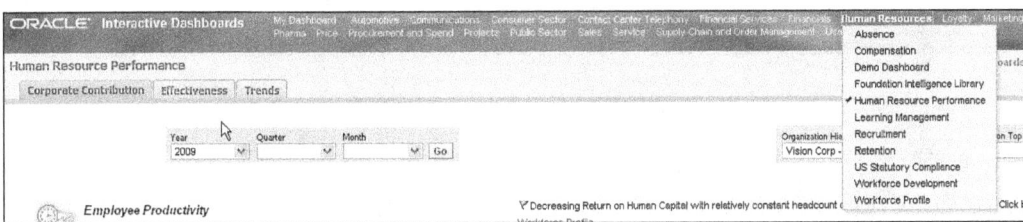

You can choose a dashboard for:

- **Absence**
- **Compensation**
- **Human Resource Performance**
- **Learning Management**
- **Recruitment**
- **Retention**
- **Workforce Development**
- **Workforce Profile**

Click on the **Human Resource Performance** link. You will get to the following dashboard:

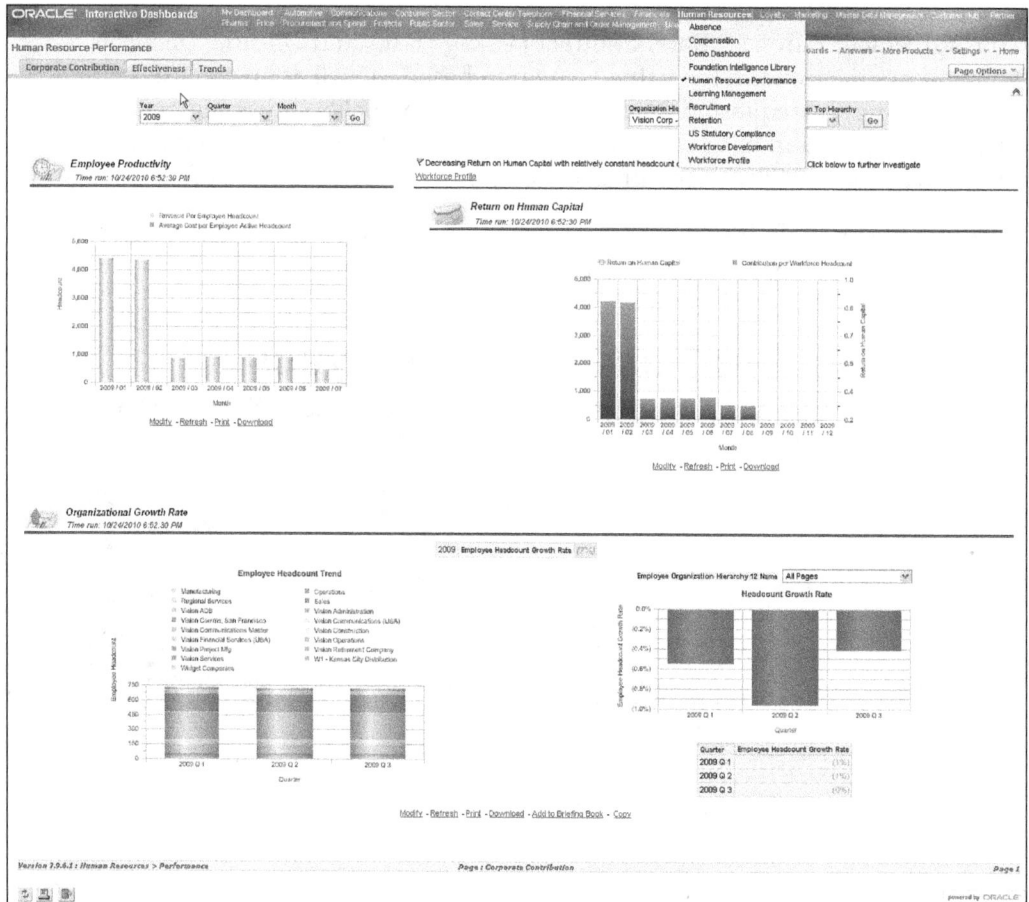

In this dashboard you can see following metrics:

- **Employee Productivity** as revenue per employee and cost per employee
- **Return on Human Capital** as measured by contribution per employee and return on human capital
- **Return on Human Capital** is defined as contribution per employee divided by cost per employee
- **Organizational Growth Rate** as a percentage and by organization

These metrics are available to be analyzed along the following dimensions:

- Time
  - Year
  - Quarter
  - Month

- Organization Hierarchy Name
- Organization Top Hierarchy

Other Dashboards in Human Resources Analytics

The **Absence dashboard** shows some Key Performance Indicators for absences, as well as a breakdown of absences by organization, by reason, and over time.

The **Compensation dashboard** shows compensation by organization and over time. It has a tab that shows compensation analysis, breaking down salary between standard and overtime, fixed and variable. It has a tab dedicated to pay for performance that shows correlation between salary and performance, and promotion and performance.

The **Learning dashboard** shows enrollments in classes and successful completions.

The **Recruitment dashboard** shows key recruiting KPI's such as vacancy rate, vacancy fill rate, applicant hire rate. It has many tabs dedicated to different aspects of the recruiting process including Quality of Hire that measures both the retention and performance of the new hires.

The **Compliance dashboard** allows you to measure conformance with mandates such as Equal Opportunities and Affirmative Action.

The **Retention dashboard** allows you to see where people are leaving the organization and why.

The **Workforce Development dashboard** allows you to see how you are rating the performance of the organization and where your best and worst performers are.

The **Workforce Profile** dashboard gives a description of the organizational make up in such KPIs as headcount growth, turnover, average span of control, supervisor ratio, and number of managers.

These are the kind of objectives that you should have in the Internal Processes and Learning and Growth perspectives of your balanced scorecard.

Enterprise Risk Management

Next, we open our dialogue with the Chief Audit Executive for InFission Corporation.

We help him develop the Audit plan to confirm the risks to the enterprise mission and ensure that the controls that mitigate for those risks are effective.

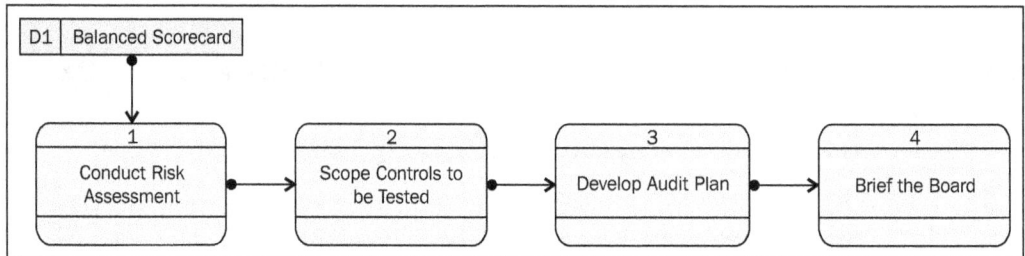

Within Oracle this is really the realm of GRC Manager and GRC Intelligence. This topic will be covered in detail when we get to the risk management section of the book. The reason that we also touch on it in the governance section of the book is to point out the overlap between the strategic direction setting for the enterprise and the risk management activities of the enterprise. Part of direction setting needs to be risk assessment.

As the Institute of Risk Management in the UK puts it as "The Board has responsibility for determining the strategic direction of the organization and for creating the environment and the structures for risk management to operate effectively. This may be through an executive group, a non-executive committee, an audit committee or such other function that suits the organization's way of operating and is capable of acting as a 'sponsor' for risk management". Or as put by the International Organization for Standardization (ISO), "Risk Management is a key business process within both the private and public sectors around the world. Effective risk management and the resulting controlled environment are central to sound corporate governance and for this reason, much of the law that has been created in response to corporate collapses and scandals, now requires effective risk management."

And lastly as put by the committee of sponsoring organizations of the Treadway commission, "Aligning risk appetite and strategy – Management considers the entity's risk appetite in evaluating strategic alternatives, setting related objectives, and developing mechanisms to manage related risks".

Verifying and quantifying risks and bringing them back to the board of directors is the job of the Chief Audit Executive. The vehicle he uses to verify and quantify the risks to which the enterprise is exposed in the Audit Plan. The Audit Plan is the set of controls to be tested in the planning period. These are made visible in the GRC Manager.

Conducting a Risk Assessment

The risks assessment at this level is really conducted through a workshop or a guided interview process. The output of the risk assessment is the catalog of risks. At the end of this process, the risks will be strategic risks such as:

- Competitor movement
- Technology changes
- Mergers and acquisition integrations
- Legal environment changes

Scope Controls to be Tested

In order to bring controls into scope of the audit plan, navigate to **Administrative Tools** option from the GRC Manager main menu. You can update the **In Scope** attribute on process and controls. You can select the controls to scope in by: Organization, Process, Financial Statement Line, or a specific control. The following screenshot shows the user interface in which you can mark a set of controls to be "In Scope":

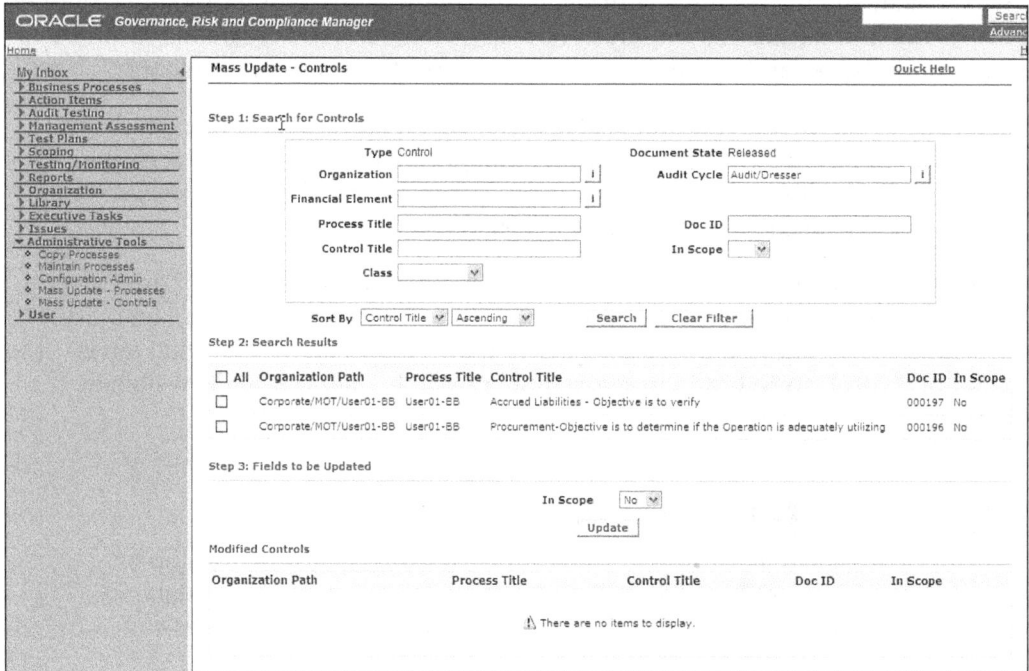

You can change the **In Scope** field to **Yes** for selected processes and/or controls and click on the **Update** button. The process of initiating testing and assigning the evaluation of controls to testers is expanded greatly in the risk management chapters.

Develop Audit Plan

In order to review all the processes or controls that are in scope for audit, click on the **Scoping** option from the GRC Manager main menu. The following screenshot shows controls that are scoped for IC Admin. You can filter the listing of controls by organization or owner depending on who the assignment of testing work will be done.

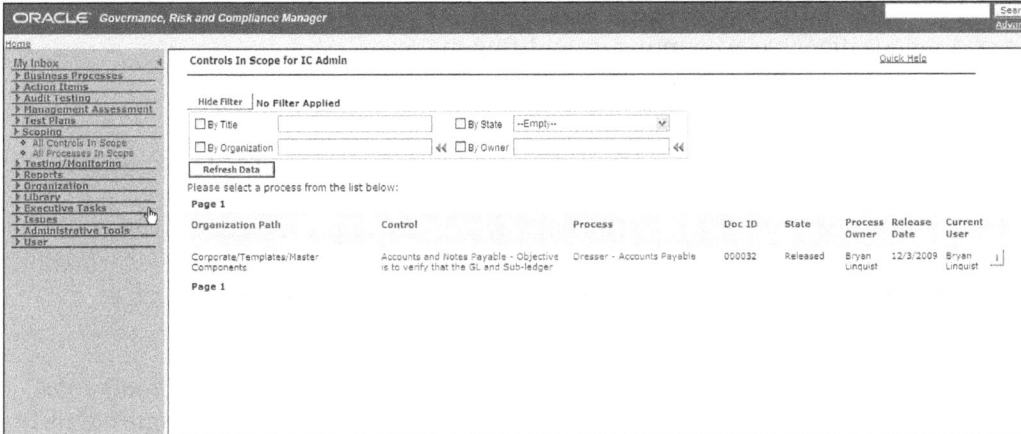

Briefing the Board

The following is a heat map. It is a well-accepted style of graph that lets executives very quickly see the risk inventory and the sense of the aggregate impact and likelihood of the risks that the enterprise faces. To navigate to the heat map, click on **Executive Tasks** in the menu and then click on **Dashboard**:

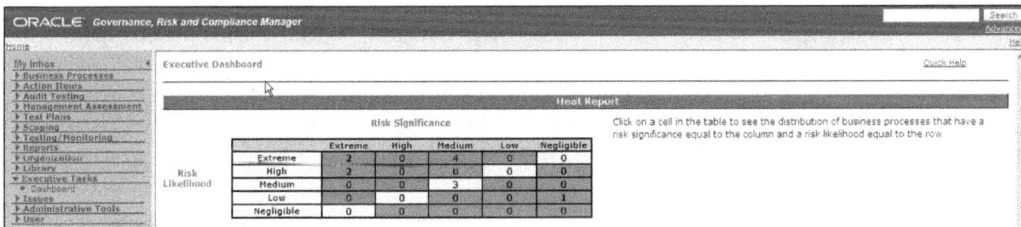

Whistle-blower protections

We circle back with the Audit Committee of the board to ensure that they have a system for concerned employees and other stakeholders to report their concerns confidentially and without fear of prejudice.

Section 301 of the Sarbanes-Oxley states:

"(4) COMPLAINTS- Each audit committee shall establish procedures for--

(A) the receipt, retention, and treatment of complaints received by the issuer regarding accounting, internal accounting controls, or auditing matters; and

(B) the confidential, anonymous submission by employees of the issuer of concerns regarding questionable accounting or auditing matters."

Section 806 states:

"No company with a class of securities registered under section 12 of the Securities Exchange Act may discharge, demote, suspend, threaten, harass, or in any other manner discriminate against an employee in the terms and conditions of employment because of any lawful act done by the employee to provide information regarding any conduct which the employee reasonably believes constitutes a violation of the Securities and Exchange Commission."

There are a number of ways to support Whistle-blower reporting. Some companies choose to outsource to a third party. Some have a hotline. You may configure **Oracle Survey** to allow for anonymous submission of a survey to capture whistle-blower issue. You can configure the issue logging in GRC Manager to serve as the log of whistle-blower issues. However, we have chosen to explain a little more about the set up of the **iService** product and how it might be configured to provide whistle-blower incidents with anonymous creation, the ability to track progress for the reporter and the board. It is in its nature, intended to be able to be used by people who are not logged in, and it is intended to give them a number by which they can track their problem.

The following diagram shows the process for processing whistle-blower complaints:

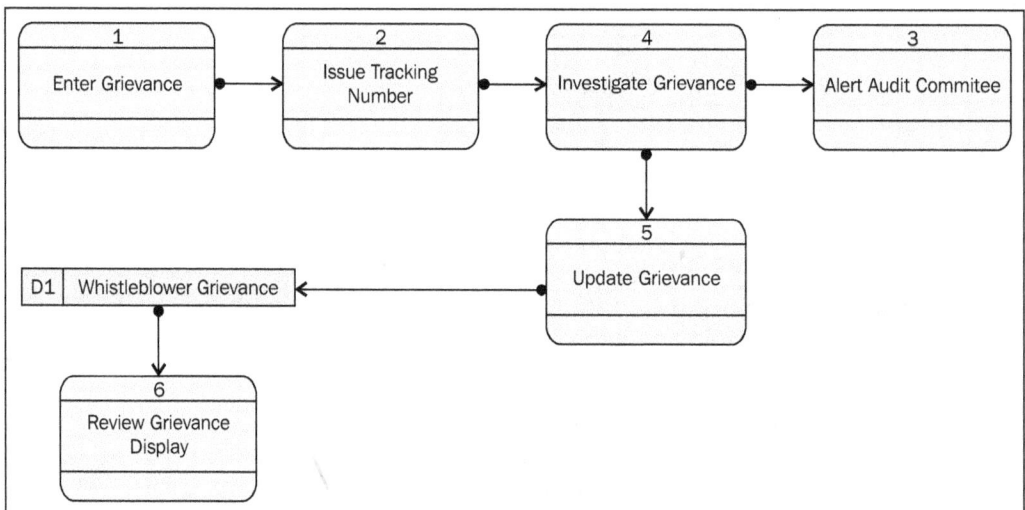

Setting up iSupport for anonymous access

In order to set up anonymous access to the iSupport product you need to run through the following steps. These are creating users and profiles in the System Administrator responsibility of Oracle:

1. Create the user.

2. Set the guest username and password with the profile option **GUEST_USER_PWD** in the format `<user_name>/<password>`.

3. Set the appropriate value in the profile option **Oracle iSupport: Authenticated Guest User Responsibility Name**, (default value is **iSupport Guest Responsibility**).

4. Set the appropriate value for the guest user in the profile option **JTF_DEFAULT_RESPONSIBILITY**.

5. Add the responsibilities **IBU_GUEST_USER_RESP** and **IBU_AUTH_ GUEST_USER_RESP** to the guest user.

6. Assign the proper role to the guest user. The role IBU_GUEST_USER is shipped out of the box.

7. iSupport uses the home page, `ibuhpage.jsp`. You need set this URL in order to access the **Whistle-blower incident reporting** page.

Configuring for recording whistle-blower complaints

Within iSupport you can create service requests. If you are using service request to capture a whistleblower complaint it is advisable to create a template to help guide the complainant. Service request templates provide a structured, formatted method of gathering information during Service Request creation.

The information gathered from the templates assists in:

- Routing the complaint for appropriate investigation
- Determining the severity of the complaint

Creating a template for whistle-blower complaints

Use the following steps to begin creating a new service request template:

1. Log in to the **Applications login** as Oracle iSupport Administrator.
2. Navigate to **Administration | Support | Request Management | Template**.
3. You might create a template called **Whistle-blower Complaints**. You can create effective dates, as well as an urgency level with the template.
4. Next, you start defining questions to help gather the information about the complaint. Each question will have an answer type: Choice or Free Text.

For example, the first question might be "Please state the nature of your complaint". It might have an answer type of "Choice". This is a pick-list type answer and can be used in scoring. Scoring is used for determining the severity of the Service Request.

Your next question might be "Please describe your complaint". It might have an answer type of "Free Text". This answer cannot be used in scoring.

To set up answers for a choice question, in the **Template Detail** area, click the underlined hyperlink of a question. The answers you set up here becomes a pick-list for the end user, and the answer you select as a default appears as the default answer on the user side. For example, the choice types for stating the nature of your complaint might be:

- Fraud
- Accounting misrepresentation
- Discrimination
- Sexual harassment
- Management practice
- Informational

For each choice-type answer, set a severity value of 1-9. After the end user answers the questions, the application will add up these values and the final score will be used to determine the severity of the Service Request, based on the Severity Thresholds you set.

You set up severity thresholds for the template. The system takes the average of all of the questions for which you set a severity value and compares it to the severity threshold.

For example, if the question "Please provide the nature of your complaint" has an answer "Bad Management" with a severity value of 3, it may break the threshold of important, but not break the threshold of "seriousness". You may choose that all serious complaints are investigated by internal audit, whereas important complaints are investigated by human resources.

Summary

In this chapter, we have looked at issues surrounding corporate governance. We have looked at the problem from the perspective of the Board of Directors and very senior management. We have taken a cursory glance at the array of corporate governance problems and given an insight into some candidate applications from Oracle that address those problems. What we have covered here should be enough to open a dialogue with senior management and to explore the value of these tools.

In the *Developing and Communicating Corporate Strategy with Balanced Scorecard* section, the first domain of the Governance part of GRC, we have looked at corporate governance. We have seen the job titles of those charged with governing the corporation, from the board and through the executive level. We introduce the members of Infission that are most concerned with the governance problem. We used Oracle's Balanced Scorecard to help turn the mission of the enterprise into a set of goals. We brought the senior management team into the discussion and developed objectives for our divisional managers that are consistent with the enterprise scorecard. We took the objectives for our most senior managers and ensured that the objectives that we agree form the basis of performance appraisal. We took the metrics from the Business Intelligence system that measured performance against these objectives.

In the *Communicating and confirming Corporate Strategy with iLearning* section, we discussed how the strategic objectives and compliance priorities can be suffused throughout the enterprise using a learning tool such as iLearning. We showed the overall flow of creating these learning assets. We ran through the major components of the learning system and showed how those components are related. We showed what a strategy class and a compliance class for Infission might actually look like, and we showed how management and the board can review the proportion of people who have taken the class and the number that have demonstrated competence.

In the *Managing Records Retention Policies with Content Management Server* section, we demonstrated the best way to organize the storage of documents in the document management system. We demonstrated the folder structures that best reflect the sensitivity levels and the access control lists that protect them. We demonstrated typical document categories and showed reasonable records retention policies for those document categories given the legislative constraints and discovery requirements. We showed how the records retention policies are implemented for each document category for how documents are destroyed at the end of their retention period. We reinforced the need to ensure that documents can truly not be discovered at the end of their document retention period.

In the *Financial planning and analysis with Hyperion FR* section, we turned the strategic plan into a financial plan. We showed how the assumptions on which the plan is based are brought into the planning environment, where scenarios are built, assumptions are tested, and the plan is routed for approval. We showed the analysis of the actual results against the budget and then finally showed how the results might be reported.

In the *Monitoring Execution with Oracle Business Intelligence* section, we examined how we could trace execution of the strategy that we had laid out in out balanced scorecard through Business Intelligence. We sat with the Board and showed how the objectives in the balanced scorecard that we agreed with the investors can become a Key Performance Indicator on the dashboards that monitor and drive management. We took a look at just a few of the dashboards that make up the Oracle Business Intelligence application and showed where the metrics, which they expose, should be represented in the balanced scorecard.

In the *Enterprise Risk Management* section, we gave a brief introduction to the topic of risk management. We explained the overlap between the strategic management activities and risk management activities. We introduced the Chief Audit Executive to the Board. We also introduced two of the vehicles that he uses to brief the Board on the risks to the enterprise: the Risk Assessment and the Audit Plan. We gave a glance at Oracle's Governance Risk and Compliance Manager as the application in which this process is run.

In the *Whistle-blower protections* section, we worked with the Audit committee on their whistle-blower system. We explained the important provisions of Sarbanes-Oxley with respect to the need to provide employees with a way to report their concerns confidentially and without fear of prejudice. We showed how to set up the guest account in iSupport and showed how to configure a support request template to be able to capture whistle-blower complaints.

In the next chapter, we examine the next domain of governance—IT Governance.

3
Information Technology Governance

The next domain of GRC that we look at is **IT governance**. The audit committee of Infission has been asked by their auditors what their IT governance processes are. They have asked us to work with the CIO to craft a response. First, we go through a bit of education but then we break IT governance down into the following sections:

- **IT governance balanced scorecard**: Recording and communicating the strategic objectives for Information Technology

- **Portfolio planning**: Ensuring work is authorized and valuable, and aligned with objectives for IT

- **Configuration management**: Ensuring that changes made to code or the settings for the applications are authorized and appropriate

- **End user support**: Ensuring requests from users are recorded and responded to in a timely fashion

We can look at a few quotes on how the world views the IT governance problem.

> *"Governance processes are designed to help companies use limited resources wisely. However, several Fortune 500 CIOs recently told me that business units in their companies have used the recession as an excuse to circumvent virtually all [IT] governance. Projects have bypassed the executive steering committee, skipped the priority setting process, and headed toward implementation with flimsy business cases and incomplete project plans. When IT protests, the business units claim that they needed to fast track the projects in order to respond to competitive threats. In fact, they have ceded ground to their competitors by avoiding virtually all disciplines necessary for project success."*

Bart Perkins, Dec 21, 2009, Computer World

Lapses in IT governance and subsequent IT failures can lead to significant losses at otherwise successful companies. The following are just random selection of recent IT failures, which have hit the headlines:

- **Cedar Sinai** (a hospital): Decommissions 70 million dollar application after mandating its use by all Cedar practitioners, because physicians revolt against the unwieldy system (Source: CIO.com, `http://www.cio.com/article/29736/Health_Care_IT_A_Big_Rollout_Bust`)
- **Green Giant** (a frozen food processor): Trucks 40 railroad car loads of fresh produce to land fill every day for a month due to failing to adequately implement the SAP system (Source: The CGEIT Exam IT Governance Foundations. Tunita Group and Professional Assurance LLC.)
- **Marin County:** Sued its ERP Implementor for 30 million dollars for the deployment, which is still not working four years after it initially went live (Source: ZD Net, `http://www.zdnet.com/blog/projectfailures/marin-county-sues-deloitte-alleges-fraud-on-sap-project/9774`)
- **Lumber Liquidators**: Attributes a weak third quarter to a complex SAP implementation, saying the project imposed a significant drain on worker productivity (Source: PC World, `http://www.pcworld.com/businesscenter/article/209886/erp_woes_blamed_for_lumber_companys_bad_quarter.html`)

ISACA, the **Information Systems Audit and Control Association**, (the professional institute for IT governance), defines the governance of enterprise IT in the following domains (Source Privacy Rights.org):

- Strategic Alignment
- Value Delivery
- Risk Management
- Resource Management
- Performance Management

ISACA has put together a new governance framework and supporting publications, addressing the governance of IT-enabled business investments called **Val IT** that addresses the strategic alignment and value delivery aspects.

The **Val IT Framework** is supported by publications and operational tools and provides guidance to:

- Define the relationship between IT and the business and those functions in the organization with governance responsibilities
- Manage an organization's portfolio of IT-enabled business investments

- Maximize the quality of business cases for IT-enabled business investments with particular emphasis on the definition of key financial indicators, the quantification of "soft" benefits, and the comprehensive appraisal of the downside risk

Val IT addresses assumptions, costs, risks, and outcomes related to a balanced portfolio of IT-enabled business investments. It also provides a benchmarking capability and allows enterprises to exchange experiences on best practices for value management.

Information on Val IT is available from the ISACA website at:

```
http://www.isaca.org/Knowledge-Center/Val-IT-IT-Value-Delivery-/
Documents/Val-IT-Brochure.pdf.
```

Developing and communicating IT strategy with balanced scorecards

The whole notion of aligning with corporate strategy means that the corporate strategy must be known and documented. In the previous chapter, we introduced balanced scorecard as the vehicle for developing and communicating corporate strategy. The next step is to develop a balanced scorecard for the governance of the enterprise IT.

The following figure is a map of an IT strategy:

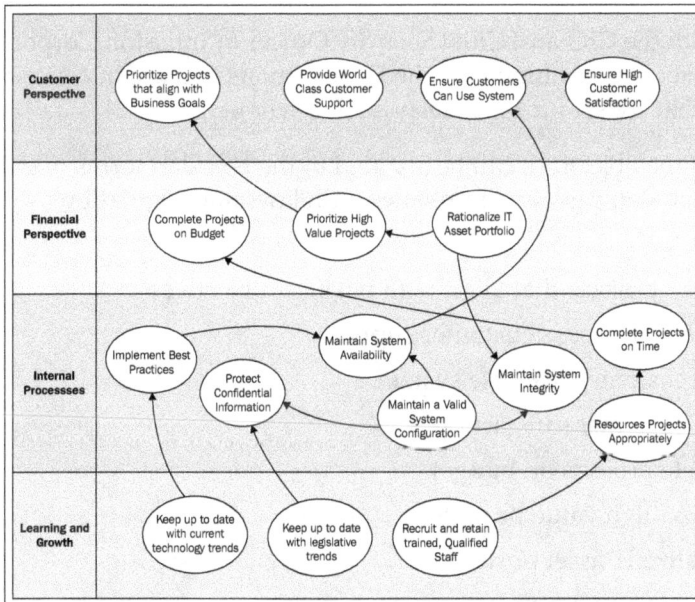

The following table shows an IT-balanced scorecard:

Information Technology Balanced Scorecard
Customer
Prioritize Projects that Align with Business Goals Provide World Class Customer Support Ensure Customers Can Use System Ensure Customer Satisfaction
Financial Perspective
Complete Projects on Budget Prioritize High Value Projects Rationalize IT Asset Portfolio
Process
Implement Best Practice Protect Confidential Information Maintain System Availability Maintain a Valid System Configuration Maintain System Integrity Complete Projects on Time Resource Projects Appropriately
Learning and Growth
Keep up with Current Technology Trends Keep up with Legislative Trends Recruit and Retain Trained Qualified Staff

Next, we sit with the CIO and Chief Security Officer of Infission Corporation. We establish a set of goals tuned for the IT operations that are in concert with the objectives that we set for the enterprise as a whole.

We ensure that the objectives can be justified to the board in terms of either ability to meet strategic goals, compliance with laws and regulations, or efficiency of operations.

- Prioritize projects that align with business objectives
- Provide world class customer support
- Ensure customers can use system
- Ensure customer satisfaction
- Complete projects on budget
- Prioritize high value projects
- Rationalize IT asset portfolio
- Implement best practices

In the managing information security management aspects of the CIO's responsibility, we can leverage some standard references, for example, ISO 27000, the International Standards Organization's standard on information security management systems and Federal Information Security Management Act, which requires each federal agency to develop, document, and implement an agency-wide program to provide information security for the information and information systems that support the operations and assets of the agency, including those provided or managed by another agency, contractor, or other source (for more information, see `http://csrc.nist.gov/ groups/SMA/fisma/overview.html`). These standards will be looked at in more detail when we look at security governance but are mentioned here to point out that security governance is part of IT governance.

IT project portfolio planning

Next, we establish the alignment of the projects running within the IT Department with the IT balanced scorecard that we have developed with the CIO and the Chief Security Officer. We will use Oracle's **Project Portfolio Analysis tool** to gather the project portfolios from the IT Directors, and then score, prioritize, and rank the projects. We will show where the cut-off point for the ranked projects is the limit of what is achievable with the available resources and funding. The following diagram shows the process for prioritizing a project portfolio:

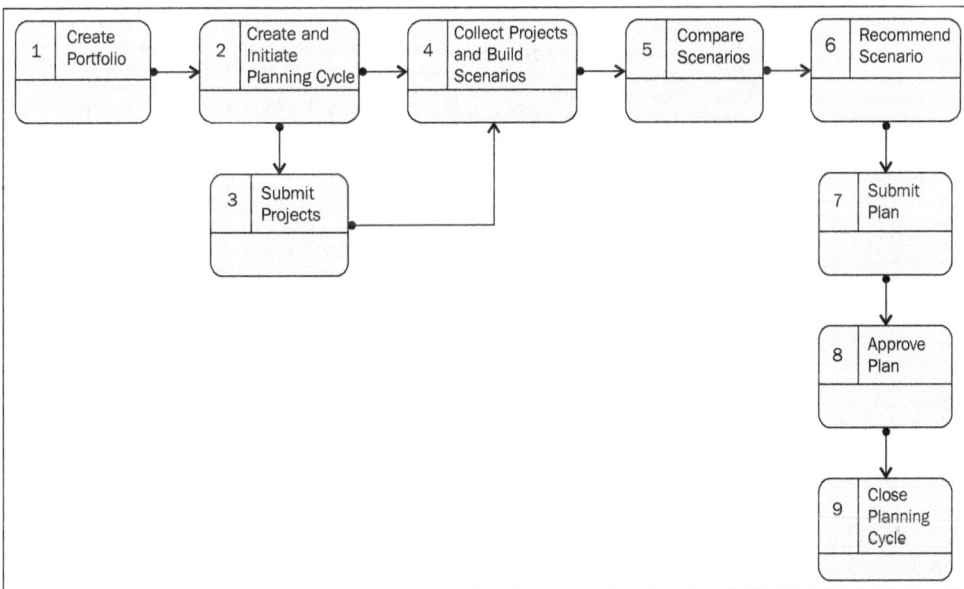

The following objects make up the **Portfolio Planning System**:

- **Portfolio**: Portfolio is merely a collection of projects.
- **Project**: It is a project in Oracle projects
- **Project Scenario**: A Project Scenario is the project within Portfolio Analysis for the planning cycle. There can be many occurrences of the project within the planning cycle, one for each scenario.
- **Scenario**: A scenario is one possible future that might be planned for. The planning cycle will probably consider many scenarios.
- **Planning Cycle**: A planning cycle is a process by which the Portfolio of projects is ranked, prioritized, and a scenario is approved for implementation.
- **Project Scorecard Objective Score**: Projects can be scored against objectives that are consistent with the IT balanced scorecard and the overall enterprise scorecard.
- **Project Scorecard Objective**: A project scorecard may have a number of objectives.
- **Project Scorecard**: Each project can have its own scorecard within each scenario.
- **Portfolio Plan**: An approved scenario within an approved planning cycle is the plan for that portfolio.

The objects and their relationships are illustrated in the following data model:

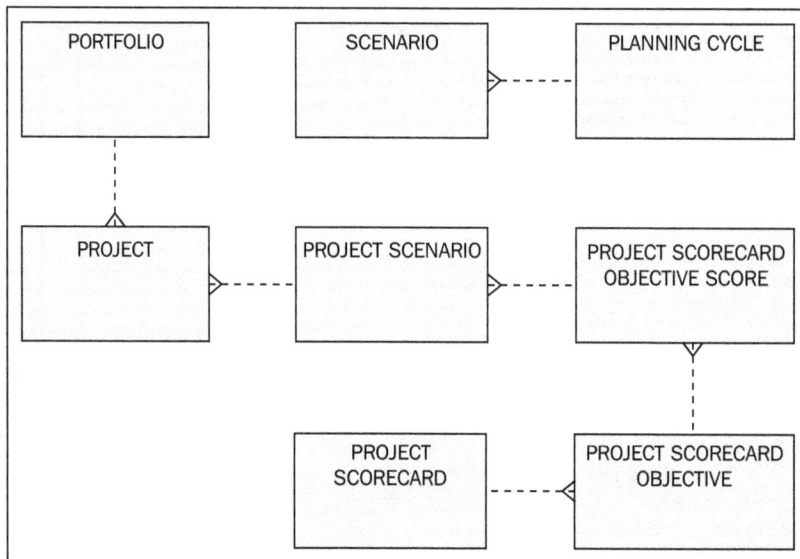

Roles for accessing portfolio analysis

Oracle provides the following roles to access portfolio analysis:

- **Portfolio Approver**: A portfolio approver can view portfolios and their submitted scenarios and can approve or reject the submitted scenarios and portfolio plans

- **Portfolio Analyst**: A portfolio analyst can create, view, and update portfolios; create, initiate, and close planning cycles; collect projects, build and recommend scenarios, and submit portfolio plans for approval

- **Portfolio Owner**: A portfolio owner has all of the above abilities and is the default portfolio approver

Decide investment criteria

The first thing to do in evaluating a set of projects is to decide the investment criteria. Each project will be scored against these criteria. Each criterion is weighted to ensure that a weighted average score for a project can be calculated. Criteria are split into financial criteria such as Return of Investment and / or Net Present Value, and non-financial criteria such as degree of fit with strategic objectives or technical risks.

In order to set up investment criteria, click on the **Setup** tab within **Portfolio Analysis**. The following screenshot shows the **Setup Investment Criteria** screen:

Create portfolio

A portfolio is a set of ongoing projects and project proposals that are evaluated for funding together. In Oracle Project Portfolio Analysis, you can create what-if scenarios for your portfolios in the planning cycles. For example, you may provide funds for a project proposal by canceling an ongoing project.

There can be many portfolios in the enterprise. Marketing may have a portfolio for marketing projects and IT may have a portfolio for IT Projects. Within IT there may be portfolios at the regional or departmental level that roll-up to an overall enterprise IT project portfolio.

If you are using the portfolio planning processes for the first time, you will need to pull projects into a portfolio for planning. In order to create a portfolio, open the **Create Portfolio** page and enter the portfolio name, a class code for the unique portfolio selection class category, and the name of the portfolio owner.

Portfolio analyzer uses the class category and class code structures within Oracle Projects to select projects into a portfolio, for example, a class code of "IT Projects". Optionally, you can enter a start organization from the portfolio organization hierarchy, for example, Corporate IT Department. You also define the portfolio access by entering the names of additional users with the portfolio approver and portfolio analyst roles.

Initiate planning cycle

A portfolio planning cycle is a series of activities that are dedicated to examine and approve a set of projects. During a planning cycle, you can decide which projects to fund, based on the strategic and financial goals of your company.

You can create a planning cycle whenever a business change occurs or a periodic review process takes place. For example, you might re-evaluate your IT portfolio in response to a change in privacy legislation. You might re-evaluate your IT Portfolio as part of your capital budgeting cycle.

In order to create a planning cycle, open the **Planning Cycle** tab and enter the planning cycle name and description:

You can optionally enter the details for the planning cycle:investment class category, discount rate, targets for internal rate of return and payback period, and a distribution list for planning cycle communications.

Submit new projects for inclusion in portfolio

After the Portfolio Analyst initiates a planning cycle, Oracle Workflow sends notifications to the Oracle Projects users, defined on the distribution list, asking them to submit projects to the planning cycle.

Oracle Project Portfolio Analysis collects the cost and benefits information from the approved baseline versions of cost and revenue financial plans of portfolio projects.

Oracle Project Portfolio Analysis uses the financial plan information to calculate the net present value, return on investment, internal rate of return, and payback period.

Score projects

Portfolio Analysis also allows the managers to evaluate and score projects based on the company's strategic criteria. You can access the project scorecard from the **Project Setup** page in **Oracle Project Management**:

The entered scores are weighted based on the weighting in the investment criteria. You can view and change the scores on the **Project Details** page in a planning cycle, but such changes are part of a planning scenario and do not affect the scores in the project system.

Create and compare the scenarios

A scenario is a possible future that is being planned for. Good governance and good risk management means that many possible futures are being planned for and each possible future may have a different set of projects that will help meet the enterprise objectives in that scenario. For example, in one scenario the company may unify subsidiaries IT processes under a corporate IT function to maximize processing efficiencies. In another scenario, the company may devolve management of IT to the subsidiaries to maximize local accountability and prepare for spin offs. Projects that are eligible to be included in the portfolio are collected in the initial scenario of the planning cycle.

In order to create a scenario, click on **Scenarios** to open the list of scenarios for the planning cycle and open the **Create Scenarios** page. Enter a scenario name and a description:

You can create a scenario by copying an existing scenario and then changing its information as per the needs (such as discount rate and funds available). When you copy a scenario, all the projects, including their project scores and funding approval statuses are copied into the new scenario. You can also add the proposed projects by selecting the scenario that should contain the new project, clicking on the **Add Projects** button and entering the project search criteria.

When you add a project to a scenario, the project is also added to the initial scenario.

You can compare scenarios to determine, which scenario best fits the financial metrics and strategic objectives of the planning cycle. In developing the scenario you may find that you can make a scenario achievable, you may increase funding, exclude or delay projects.

In order to compare scenarios, access the **Scenarios** page and select and open a scenario. Click on the **Compare Scenarios** button to access the **View Comparisons** page where you can select up to three scenarios for comparison.

The **View Comparisons** page contains graphical measures of the strategic objectives and financial metrics of the selected scenarios. The scenarios that you selected for comparison are displayed together in the graphs to help you select the scenario that best meets your organization's objectives.

Recommend and approve the scenario

A portfolio approver can perform the following actions:

- Review the recommended scenarios.
- Approve a scenario.
- Approve or reject both the portfolio plan and the scenario. This marks the end of the planning cycle.

When the portfolio analyst recommends a portfolio plan for approval, Oracle Workflow changes the planning cycle status to **Submitted** and sends a notification to the portfolio approvers and portfolio analysts. The notification contains the name of the planning cycle that is ready for review and approval.

After careful examination of the recommended scenarios, the portfolio approver can approve a scenario and portfolio plan separately or together.

In order to approve a scenario or a scenario and portfolio plan together, open the **Scenarios** page of the current planning cycle, and select the scenario that you want to approve.

In order to approve a portfolio plan after you approve the scenario, open the **Planning Cycle** page, and click on the **Checklist.** Select the **Approve Plan** task in the checklist.

After you approve the portfolio plan, Oracle Workflow changes the planning cycle status to **Approved** and sends a notification to the project managers and project owners that a planning cycle has been approved or rejected.

Close planning cycle and implement scenario recommendations

The approval of a portfolio plan automatically changes the project funding approval status of projects that are included in the approved scenario to Approved.

Oracle Project Portfolio Analysis also creates a project set in Oracle Projects.

The project set is named after the portfolio and the planning cycle. For example, for a portfolio plan named "IT Governance" containing a planning cycle that is named "2010 Strategic IT Plan", the project set name would be "IT Governance – 2010 Strategic IT Plan".

Project sets enable project managers to review and monitor projects that belong to a portfolio. Two project sets are created during the lifecycle of a portfolio plan:

- Submitted Project Set
- Approved Project Set

Oracle Project Portfolio Analysis automatically creates a second project set after the portfolio plan is approved.

The following screenshot shows the **Funding Approval Status** of the projects within a scenario:

Maintaining a valid configuration

Next, we will work with the IT Director to show how the configuration of the business systems is documented within Oracle Applications Manager. We will show how authorized changes to that configuration are reflected in the patch tracking system. We will also show how we can ensure that a developer or any other unauthorized person cannot directly update the approved configuration of the production systems. An Oracle Applications customer can manage the configuration from either Applications Manager within the E-Business Suite or use the Management Pack for E-Business Suite within the Enterprise Manager. It really depends on whether E-Business Suite is the dominant application in your deployment as to whether you choose Application Manager or Enterprise Manager to manage your configuration.

Managing the configuration using Applications Manager

In order to access the **Applications Manager**, you can choose the System Administrator responsibility and access the **Applications Manager** page. From the home page you can see a snapshot of the system status, and changes to the configuration in terms of patches, profile options, context file, as well as the status of the web components:

Clicking on the **Software Updates** tab you can see the patches that have been recently applied and can search for a specific patch:

Maintaining a valid configuration using Enterprise Manager Application Management Pack for E-Business Suite

Application Management Pack for Oracle E-Business Suite extends **Enterprise Manager 10g Grid Control** to help monitor and manage an Oracle Applications system more effectively. The pack integrates **Oracle Applications Manager with Grid Control** to provide a consolidated, end-to-end E-Business Suite management solution.

Configuration Management capabilities within Enterprise manager include:

- Configuration management database
- Automatic discovery
- Configuration snapshot
- Change audit trail
- Configuration compare

Application Management Pack for Oracle E-Business Suite provides administrators with the ability to collect, compare, and search Oracle E-Business Suite configuration details, including application system summary, patches applied, application context files and related configuration files, technology stack inventory, concurrent processing configuration, workflow configuration, user activity, and custom configuration.

The following screenshot is the Oracle Applications page in **Enterprise Manager 10g**:

Service desk administration through Oracle Enterprise Manager

Next, we will work with IT Managers to ensure that user issues are recorded and surrounding documentation is captured to ensure rapid resolution. We will show how to create service requests, problems reports, and contact Oracle Support with these details:

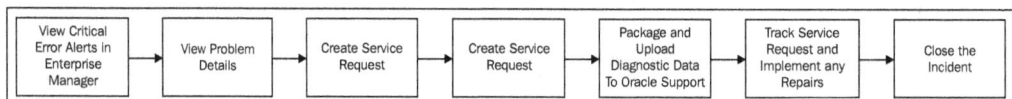

The framework that sets the best practices for support management is known as **Information Technology Infrastructure Library** (ITIL). ITIL is a set of guidelines that describes an integrated and process-based best practice framework for managing IT services. It was developed in the late 1980s by the British government in response to the growing dependence on Information Technology. Over time, ITIL has evolved to become the *de facto* standard for service management.

The ITIL framework provides broad service management recommendations as well as common definitions and terminology. By adopting ITIL guidelines, businesses can achieve significant benefits in areas such as risk management, change management, and service provisioning.

In ITIL terminology, an **incident** is defined as an event, which is not part of the standard operation of a service, and which causes, or may cause, an interruption to, or reduction in, the quality of that service.

The goal of **Incident Management** is to restore normal service operation as quickly as possible and minimize the adverse impact on business operations.

Oracle provides a number of out of the box best practice capabilities to support the ITIL Incident Management process.

Oracle Enterprise Manager (EM) proactively detects events that could lead to incidents by monitoring business applications from the real end-user experience of the application down through its underlying technology stack, applications, middleware, database, storage, and servers. EM can raise alerts for many things that may interest an administrator including incidents and other significant activities that may not be failures. These can be visually monitored using the **EM System Dashboard** and notifications for these can also be sent to the appropriate administrators. EM's notification system enables the mapping of the specific alerts to specific administrators thus ensuring that the administrators with the appropriate skills are notified when such incidents are detected. Alerts that have well-known solutions can be automatically resolved using **corrective actions**. Corrective actions enable administrators to specify the corrective tasks that should be executed if the alert is detected (for example, restart a process if it becomes unavailable). This eliminates the need for operator intervention and thus enables the timely resolution of the incident before it impacts end users.

Support workbench

In order to access **Support Workbench** after logging into Oracle Enterprise Manager, click on the **Software and Support** tab on the database home page and then click on **Support Workbench** under the **Support** section on the **Software and Support** page.

> Note that Support Workbench and incident creation is not available for the whole application stack. It is available only for problems that occur in the RDBMS for EBS.

Any problem may give rise to many incidents. For example, an end user may have an incident with his PC freezing. The problem may be caused by unauthorized software installation. Such a problem, in turn may cause many other incidents.

The following screenshot shows the **Support Workbench** interface in EM:

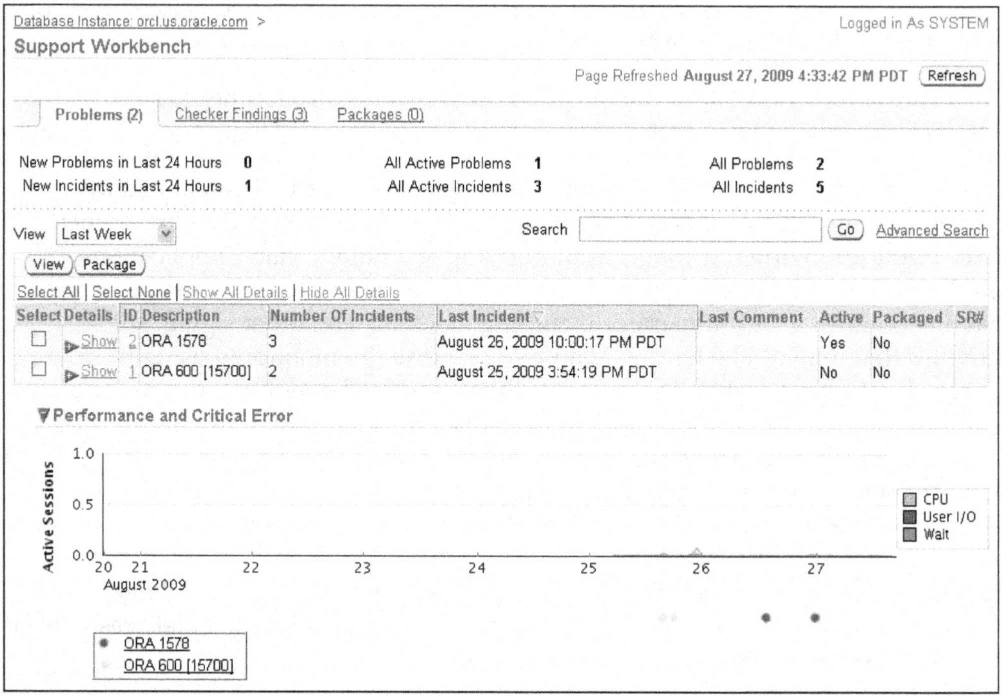

From this page, you can see problems that have occurred over a selected period and the count by error code.

Problem details

You can view additional details for a problem by selecting a problem on the **Problems** tab, and then clicking on **View** to view the details:

From here you can see the **SR#** (Service Request Number) and the **Bug#** (Bug Number) if it has been raised. You can also raise the service requests with Oracle Support and package the diagnostics from here.

Packaging problem details

In order to create a package, select an incident and click on **Package** on the **Support Workbench Problems** page. This packages all of the diagnostics files to be sent to Oracle Support.

Quick Packaging: Create New Package

Cancel Step 1 of 4 Next

Target +ASM_dadvmn0652.us.oracle.com   Logged in As **sys**
Problems Selected ORA 7445 [_kernel_vsyscall()+2]

Use quick packaging to generate an upload file for a single problem and send it to Oracle with default options. If Oracle Configuration Manager set up, the upload file will still be created but it will not be sent to Oracle.

* Package Name	ORA7445___20090722090952
Package Description	Oracle ASM test problem
Send to Oracle Support	⦿ Yes ◯ No
My Oracle Support Username	oracle
My Oracle Support Password	••••••••
Customer Support Identifier (CSI)	
Country	United States
Create new Service Request (SR)	⦿ Yes ◯ No

Summary

In this chapter, we examined the area of IT governance. We sat with the CIO and Chief Security Officer of Infission Corporation. We reviewed the corporate strategy with them, helped them in developing an IT strategy that is consistent with it, and documented this strategy in Oracle's balanced scorecard.

Next, we took an inventory of the current and proposed IT projects, and went through a portfolio analysis. We also looked at the financial projections of the projects and reviewed the alignment between the projects and the scorecard that we helped develop. We helped the CIO see the ranking of the projects with respect to both financial and non-financial metrics using Oracle Portfolio Analysis. We also saw where the funding for those projects runs out, canceling those projects, or otherwise identifying what funding would be needed in order to pursue those projects.

Next, we sat with the IT Director to ensure that the configuration of the systems is base-lined at an agreed state and that configuration is under an effective change management process using Oracle's Application Manager and the E-Business Suite Configuration Management Pack within the Enterprise Manager.

Lastly, we worked with the IT Director to ensure that Infission has good processes for support in accordance with the IT strategy in balanced scorecard. We showed him how problems and incidents can be identified using Enterprise Manager. We also illustrated how the time to resolution can be dramatically reduced through the packaging of diagnostic information and integration into Oracle Support.

In the next chapter, we will tackle the next domain of governance that is, Security governance.

4
Security Governance

In this chapter, we will talk to the Chief Security Officer of the company and get an understanding of his sense of security risks that the company faces and the security posture that it adopts. We will help him express his priorities and objectives in the form of a balanced scorecard and ensure that the objectives are in concert with the corporate strategy. We will show him how to limit the access to systems only to authorized users and how to ensure that such authorization is based on specific needs. We will show how some of the security policies limit the duties of any individual so that privileges required to commit a fraud are separated. Next, we will show how to follow the guidance for hardening the system. Finally, we will guide him through setting up the security incident management and security incident response through the capabilities provided in Oracle Service.

> Note that it is beyond the scope of this book to advise you on security for the E-Business Suite. This chapter aims to put security into a governance perspective and take you through some general themes in security management. For a detailed review of E-Business Suite security, the book "Oracle E-Business Suite Security(in italics)", Oracle Press(in italics), written by John Abel is a great resource.

Security balanced scorecard

The following figure shows an illustrative scorecard of security objectives arranged with relationships between them:

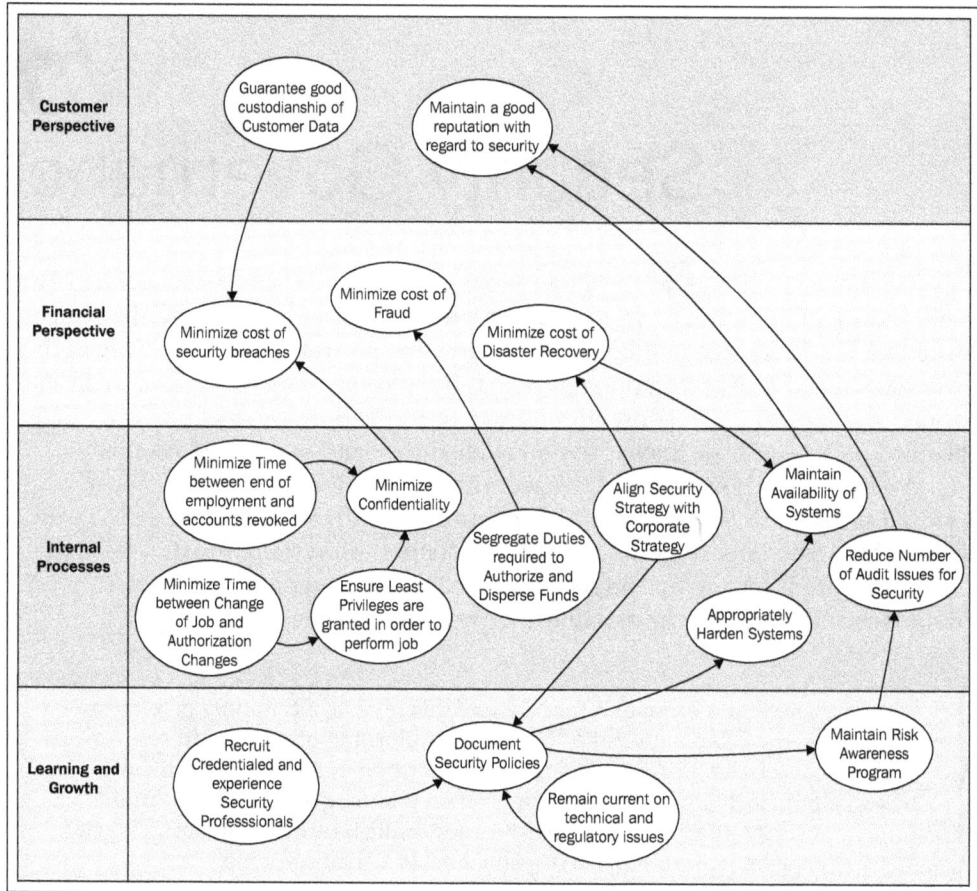

The first thing that we will do when working with the Chief Security Officer is to work on a balanced scorecard for the security function. We will help him come up with metrics that show, how well he is doing in addressing both the objectives of the company as well as the information risks. In this example the objectives are as follows:

- Customer perspective:
    - ○ Guarantee good custodianship of customer data
    - ○ Maintain a good reputation with regard to security

- Financial perspective:
    - Minimize the cost of security breaches
    - Minimize cost of fraud
    - Minimize cost of disaster recovery

- Process perspective:
    - Maintain confidentiality
    - Minimize the time between a job change and authorization changes
    - Minimize time between End of Employment and Revocation of Accounts
    - Segregation of Duties required or authorize and dispense funds
    - Align security with corporate strategy
    - Appropriately harden systems
    - Maintain availability of systems
    - Reduce number of audit issues for security

- Learning and growth perspective:
    - Recruit credentialed and experienced security professionals
    - Document security policies
    - Remain current on technical and regulatory issues
    - Maintain a Risk Awareness program

Relationships between the objectives

The following bullets explain the relationships between those objectives:

- Customer perspective:
    - If you demonstrate good governance over customer data you will reduce the cost of security breaches
    - If you maintain the availability of systems you will maintain a good reputation for security
    - If you ensure that you reduce the number of audit issues for security, you will maintain a good reputation for security

- Financial perspective:
    - If you maintain confidentiality you will minimize the cost of security breaches.

- ° If you appropriately segregate duties you will minimize the cost of fraud. The following screenshot shows an Oracle Balanced Scorecard implementation with a drill-down on the reduce fraud objective to a GRC Intelligence report on Segregation of Duties violations:

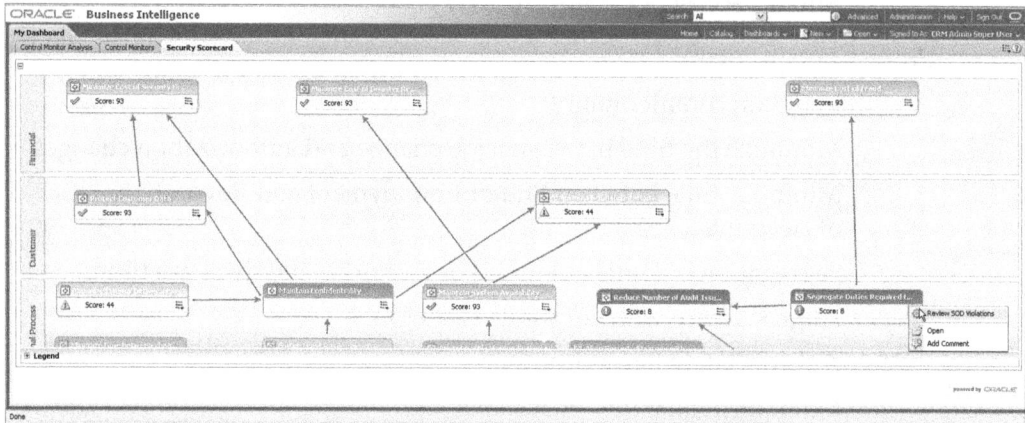

- • Process perspective:
    - ° If you minimize the time between change of job and authorization changes, you will ensure that least privileges are granted and thus you will maintain confidentiality
    - ° If you minimize the time between end of employment and revocation of accounts, you will maintain confidentiality
    - ° If you align security strategy with corporate strategy it will force you to document you security policies
    - ° If you have minimized the cost of disaster recovery you will maintain the availability of systems
    - ° If you appropriately harden systems they will be protected against threats and availability will be maintained
    - ° If you maintain a security awareness program, you will reduce the number of security issues

- • Learning and growth perspective:
    - ° If you recruit credentialed and experienced security professionals, you will be able to remain current on technical and regulatory issues and thus keep appropriate security policies documented
    - ° You will need to document appropriate security policies to maintain a risk awareness program

Metrics for the objectives

A few example metrics that would allow you to see whether you are meeting the objectives might be as follows:

- Guarantee good custodianship of customer data. You would count security incidents involving customer data to measure success in this objective.

- Maintain a good reputation with regard to security. You would count incidents and findings that could cause reputational harm to measure and maintain success in this objective.

- Segregation of Duties required to authorize and disperse funds. You would count the number of Segregation of Duties violations.

- Minimize time between End of Employment and Revocation of Accounts. You would measure the latency between the HR transaction and the transaction in the security system.

Perspectives from standard bodies and professional institutions

As part of briefing the security executives, it is worth reviewing how this domain is described by their peers and professional institutions.

IT Governance Institute

In 2001, ITGI published **Information Security Governance: Guidance for Boards of Directors and Executive Management**.

> *Information Security governance is a subset of enterprise governance that provides strategic direction, ensures objectives are achieved, manages risk appropriately, uses organizational resources responsibly, and monitors the success or failure of the enterprise security program.*

ISO 17799

Information security is characterized within ISO 17799 as the preservation of:

- **Confidentiality**: Ensuring that information is accessible only to those authorized to have access to it

- **Integrity**: Safeguarding the accuracy and completeness of information and processing methods

- **Availability**: Ensuring that authorized users have access to information and the associated assets when required

It suggests that you introduce performance measures to determine if information security is succeeding. For example, metrics for information security include:

- No incidents causing public embarrassment
- Number of critical business processes that rely on IT and have adequate continuity plans
- Number of critical infrastructure components with automatic availability monitoring
- Measured improvement in employee awareness of ethical conduct requirements, system security principles, and performance of duties in an ethical and secure manner
- Full compliance or agreed-upon and recorded deviations from minimum security requirements
- Percentage of IT-related plans and policies developed and documented covering IT security mission, vision, goals, values, and code of conduct
- Percentage of IT security plans and policies communicated to all stakeholders

ISO 17799 also breaks our specific objectives:

- Management should identify responsibilities and procedures for defining, agreeing on, and funding risk management improvements. A reality check of the security strategy should be conducted by a third party to increase objectivity and should be repeated at appropriate time intervals.

- Critical infrastructure components should be identified and continuously monitored. Service level agreements should be used to raise awareness and increase co-operation with suppliers for security and continuity needs.

- Management endorses and should be demonstrably committed to the information security and control policies, stressing the need for communication, understanding and compliance. Policy enforcement should be considered and decided upon at the time of policy development. A confirmation process should be in place to measure awareness, understanding, and compliance with policies. Information control policies should be aligned with the overall strategic plans. There should be a consistently applied policy development framework that guides formulation, roll-out, understanding, and compliance.

- There should be an awareness that, although insiders continue to be the primary source of most security risks, attacks by organized criminals and other outsiders are increasing.

- Proper attention should be paid to data privacy, copyright, and other data-related legislation.

Quotes from prominent Security managers

IT security provides the management processes, technology and assurance to allow business management to ensure business transactions can be trusted; ensure IT services are usable and can appropriately resist and recover from failures due to error, deliberate attacks or disaster; and ensure critical confidential information is withheld from those who should not have access to it.

—Dr. Paul Dorey, Director, Digital Business Security, BP PLC

Directors have a responsibility to protect shareholder value. This responsibility applies just as stringently to valued information assets as it does to any other asset. Boards must recognize that securing that information is not just an investment; it is essential for survival in all cases and for many it can even create competitive advantage.

—Ronald Saull, Chief Information Officer and Senior Vice President, Great-West Life Assurance Company/London Life/Investors Group

It is also worth reviewing some cases of the very real consequences of not adequately governing information security:

Company	Exposure	Cause
Bank of America	1.3 million consumers exposed	Lost Backup Tape
DSW retail	1.2 million consumers exposed	Hacking
Card Services	40 million consumers exposed	Hacking
TJX Stores	45 million consumers exposed	Internal theft
UCLA	800,000 consumers exposed	Human error
Fidelity	196,000 consumers exposed	Stolen laptop

Source: Todd Fitzgerald, CISM, CISA, CISSP, ITILV3, 2008 ISACA Chapter Briefing

Account provisioning and identity management

Next, we will show how the identity management and provisioning systems ensure that each action in the system can be traced to an individual who is accountable for it. We will also show, how efficiently we can react to events in the human resources system and make the appropriate changes in the identity management and provisioning system to ensure that the access is always appropriate and principles of least privilege are maintained.

If you are using E-Business Suite, your security is administered through **responsibilities, top-level menus, submenus**, and **menu exclusion rules**. The responsibilities seeded by Oracle do not always represent a consistent metaphor. In some cases, the responsibility is seeded to represent a Job. For example, the collections product seeds a responsibility of Collections Manager. In some cases, the responsibility is seeded with all functionalities for a product. For example, Oracle seeds a responsibility "Financial Intelligence". In other cases, a duty that you might find listed on a job description is a responsibility. For example, supervising employees is under the Manager responsibility.

The E-Business suite has its own identity store in FND_USERS. However, it does allow integration with a LDAP service. This allows a single user to be identified and accountable across all systems. In order to do this, Oracle Internet Directory and the FND_USER table must be kept synchronized. Synchronization events are raised via the workflow-based Business Event System whenever users are added or modified.

Designing roles

Next, we take the principle of least privilege and we show how to reflect that in a set of roles. We will show how to make those roles reflective of real world jobs and duties. We will also show how these roles are implemented in the security system. The following is part of a role definition for an Accounts **Payable Manager**, showing the mapping between the real world *job, duty, and entitlement* as you might find on a job description with the **Top Level Menu**, **Sub Menu**, and **Functions** in the E-Business Suite:

| | | Top Level Menu | Accounts Payable Manager | | | Job |

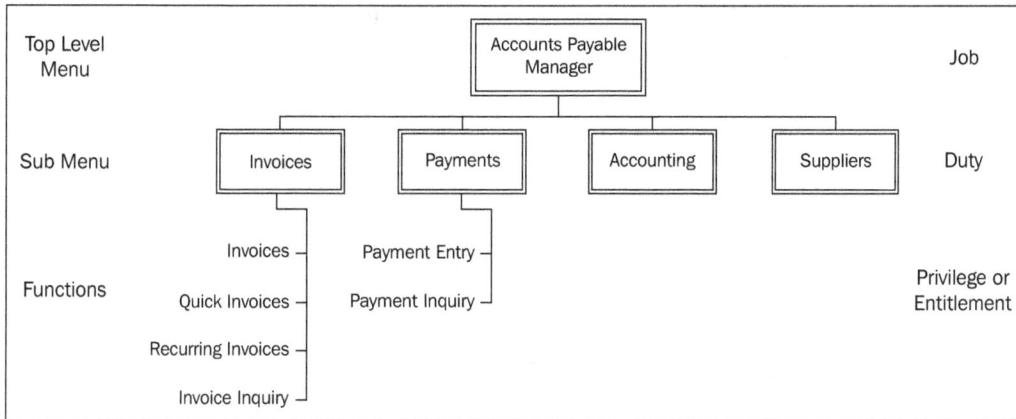

Function Security

The following screenshot shows the top-level menu and its submenus for the **Accounts Payable** system:

In order to navigate to the menu definition, log in using a System Administrator responsibility and choose the **Application** submenu and click on **Menu**.

In the simplest case for an E-Business Suite deployment, all of the functionality required for someone with a given job should be gathered together in a menu. If there are duties that are common to a number of jobs, for example, supplier management may be a duty that is common to Accounts Payable Managers and Buyers, it may be useful to group that functionality into a submenu. In an E-Business Suite, such security considerations also have navigation consequences.

The following screenshot shows the same menu structure represented as a tree, which is how the user sees it:

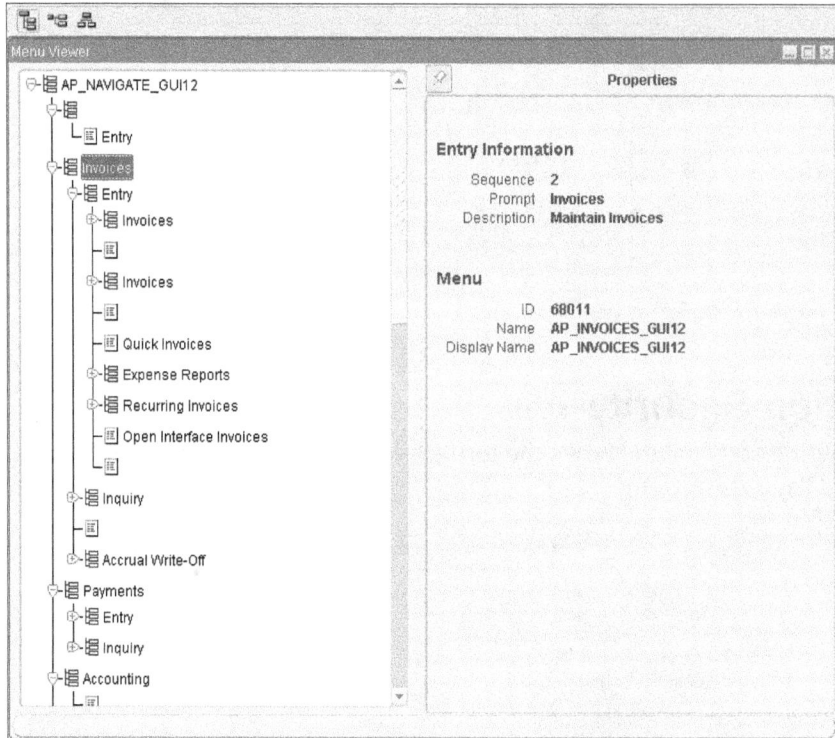

At the lowest level, the tasks in the real world are represented by **Form Functions**. (In EBS, a function may be reused with different parameters. A function with a set of parameters is a Form Function).

Data security

To authorize a user to a set of operating units, ledgers, inventory organizations, people, you set **Profile Options** that are specific to a responsibility. Some example responsibility level profile options that influence data security are as follows:

- **HR**: Security Profile to limit the people information that is available to a responsibility
- **GL**: Security Profile to limit what companies accounting data is available to a responsibility

- **AMS**: Security Profile to limit the set of items that are available to a responsibility

- **MO**: Security Profile to limit the list of operating units that are available to a responsibility

The set of data is generally defined in profile options that are related to a responsibility. If a job needs access to different sets of data, then you need different responsibilities. For example, an HR Professional that also manages people may be reviewing competencies for their own staff in one responsibility and the competencies for the employees of their client managers in another responsibility. You will need two responsibilities, each with their own security profile. The following is a screenshot of the responsibility for a **Payables Manager** showing a top-level menu:

In order to define a responsibility, sign in using a System Administratior's responsibility and choose the **Security** submenu and choose **Responsibilities**. You can also remove authorization to entries in the menu for a responsibility by clicking on the **Menu Exclusions** tab and entering **Menu Exclusions**:

Aggregating responsibilities into roles

Since 11.5.10, E-Business Suite has had a product called **User Management** (**UMX**) that allows for grouping responsibilities together into a role. You may find that any given user had to be given many responsibilities. For example, if you were a manager in the HR Department, you would have one responsibility for your work as a manager, and another for your work as an HR Professional. Your work as an HR Professional may be to provide HR Support for the Sales Department. You may have access to the same screens in both these responsibilities. When logging in with a "Manager" responsibility, you get access to your subordinates. When logging in with an "HR Professional" responsibility you get access to the HR records of people in the Sales Department. The following is a screenshot showing the role inheritance:

In order to navigate to the role definitions, log in using a User Management responsibility and click on the **Role and Role Inheritance** tab.

What is the difference between a role and a responsibility? The **MetaLink Note 290525.1** states:

"Responsibilities can now be considered a special type of role that represents the set of navigation menus contained within an application. Therefore, responsibilities loosely represent an application itself, whereas roles can be used to determine what parts of that application (and data therein) a user has access to. This represents a shift in the definition of a responsibility in Oracle Applications. Previously, a responsibility has been used not only to define the application navigation menus, but also to confer privileges and permissions within that application.

Using this definition of responsibility, it was often necessary to create several similar responsibilities in order to effectively carve out data and functional security access for a group of users. This has increased the overall cost of ownership as the number of responsibilities has grown."

This means that both the vagaries of the delivered responsibilities and the need to have roles that span distinct sets of data to it are catered for.

Role provisioning

UMX also has the capability to request a role using Oracle Workflow.

The following is the Role Request UI through which users can request roles in a self-service manner:

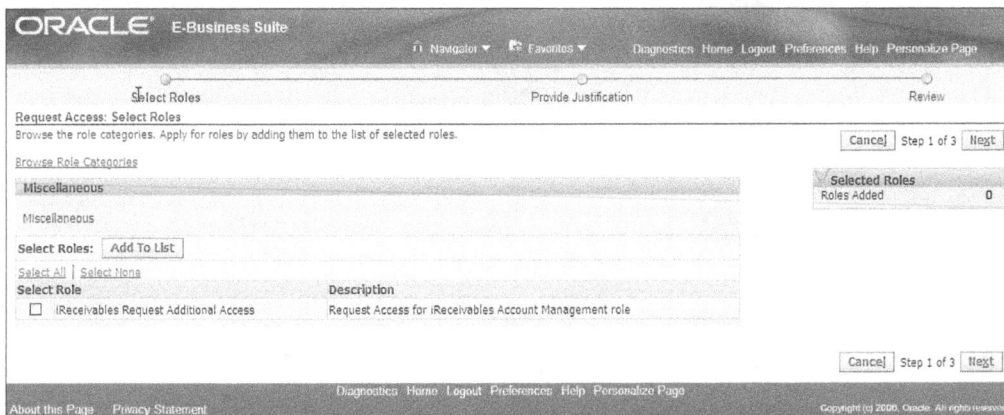

Oracle User Management supports three types of registration processes:

- **Self-Service Account Requests**: If you have ever made an online transaction, you probably did a self-registration and created an account to tie the order to your account. This registration process type is very similar in that the system provides a method for persons to request a new user account. This type of registration process also offers identity verification, which confirms the identity of the requester (via an e-mail notification that requires a response) before the registration request is processed. If the recipient does not reply within a predetermined amount of time, the request will be automatically rejected.

- **Requests for Additional Access**: Oracle UMX provides an Access Request Tool that enables existing users to request additional roles. Users can only request the additional roles that have been defined as appropriate based on their current roles. Users can request additional access through the Oracle User Management Access Request Tool (ART), available in the **Global Preferences** menu.

- **Creation by Administrators**: While the name of this registration process does not sound all that intriguing, the reason it exists presents a much more interesting point for discussion. In UMX, the definition of an Account Administrator is changing from that of one or two select individuals working in IT or on the helpdesk to users in the Business Units. With the concept of delegated administration, the ability to create user(s) can be extended beyond the traditional confines of an organization's IT department into the business, and even beyond the organization to business partners and clients, because each account creation registration process can be made available to select administrators.

The following is a set of role provisioning workflows from UMX:

Identity management

E-Business Suite is now certified with connectors from Oracle Identity Management (OIM). EBS Employee Reconciliation connect treats E-Business Suite HR store and in particular the PER_ALL_PEOPLE_F table, as an authoritative source for identities. OIM has two adapters. The first treats E-Business Suite HR as a trusted source of identities and allows two-way synchronization between HR_PERSON table and identities in OIM. The second reconciles FND_USER accounts along with the UMX Role and responsibilities.

Account provisioning is also preconfigured to provide real time validation against Segregation of Duties policies defined in Oracle Applications Access Controls Governor for any responsibility or role assignments.

The connector also detects all major worker lifecycle events including on-boarding, job changes transfers, and terminations. This tighter integration with people's movements within the Human Capital Management applications will help to minimize the latency between an HR event and representing its consequence in security. It automates the security administration and allows security professionals to concentrate on threats, vulnerabilities, and appropriate policies rather than assigning and revoking roles and accounts.

Limiting access to administrative pages

Limiting functional access of administrators is also important. There are several kinds of administrative forms that are security sensitive. As a security administrator, you need to limit the number of people that have access to the pages:

- **Functional security administrative pages**: These are the pages that control the security infrastructure, such as the UMX pages or the define responsibility pages.

- **Design-time at runtime pages**: These are the pages that allow users to define metadata that controls the application. Examples include the flexfield pages or personalization pages. As these pages often allow SQL or HTML fragments to be added, they allow an unscrupulous administrator to effectively design a SQL injection or Cross-site Scripting vulnerability into the application. We recommend that these pages should not be assigned to any users during normal operation of a production system.

Segregation of Duties Policies

Next, we will look at how we can alert management to combination of privileges that may present an opportunity for fraud. Segregation of Duties is well examined in *Chapter 9, IT Audit*. Here, we examine how the segregation of duties policies influence role design, and how they are reported within the GRC Intelligence.

A segregation of duties policy is generally implemented to ensure that a person cannot authorize a disbursement (or commitment) of funds as well as actually make the disbursement. For this reason, the policies tend to be in the financial applications. They are mentioned here to give you a complete picture of role design. The following is a screenshot of a set of segregation of duties policies in **Oracle Application Access Controls Governor**. The topic of segregation of duties and how such policies are implemented is fully explored in *Chapter 9, IT Audit*.

Violations of segregation of duties can be monitored through GRC Intelligence. The following screenshot is of the **Control Monitors** tab showing security incidents by application and by control:

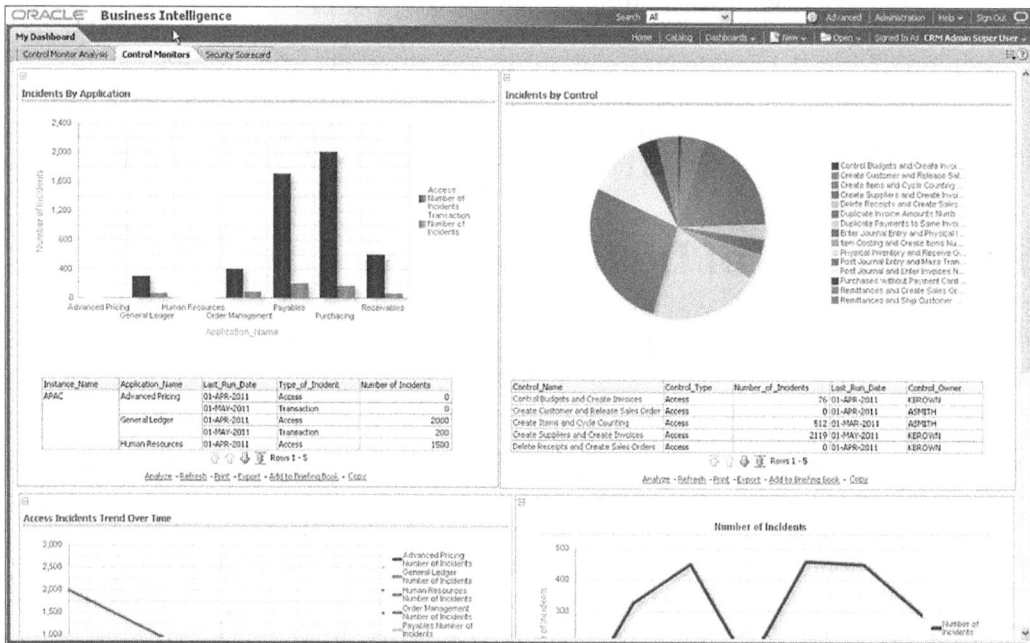

Server, applications, and network hardening

Next, we focus on reacting to threats, and ensure that the components on the network are all configured to resist those threats at the perimeter and also ensure that any threats that have penetrated or originated inside the perimeter are discovered, contained and eliminated. The following is a brief example of a **Threat and Vulnerability Matrix**. We will expand the practitioners' guidance when we get to our compliance chapters. What we have for you here is the end result of the risk analysis for information assets.

Relevance of control as a countermeasure to a Threat 9 Highly Relevant 0 Not relevant Threats in Y axis Controls in X Axis	Security Policy	Hardening of Environment	Firewalls	Configuration of Architecture	Employee Training	Auditing & Monitoring	System Administration Due diligence	Demilitarized Zone	Single Sign On	Prevent external spyware load	GPS tracking system
Intrusion (Hacking, Password Attacks)	9	9	9	1	9	3	3	3	1	1	0
Server Failures	1	3	9	9	1	9	1	9	1	1	0
Physical Damage to Hardware	1	9	3	9	0	3	1	3	0	1	0
Extortion	9	1	3	1	3	1	3	3	9	1	1
Insider Attacks	9	9	1	3	3	3	3	0	3	3	1
Spoofing	9	1	9	1	3	9	3	3	9	9	1
Denial of Service	3	3	1	9	1	3	3	1	1	1	0
Human Error	3	3	3	1	9	3	9	3	1	0	1
Theft of Computers	3	9	1	1	3	3	3	0	1	1	9
Malicious Code	9	3	1	0	3	3	3	0	0	1	9
Buffer Overflow Attacks	1	3	1	9	3	3	3	0	0	1	0

The preceding table shows the **Threat and Countermeasures matrix**.

It is not the ambition of the authors to document the security hardening steps. Oracle does a great job of this through **Metalink Note 189367.1: E-Business Suite Security Best Practices**. It is our ambition to make risk management practitioners aware of the problems, where the remedies are documented and illustrate the nature of a few of those remedies.

System wide advice

Some advice applies to the entire E-Business deployment and the infrastructure in which it operates.

- **Keep software up to date**: One of the principles of good security practice is to keep all software versions and patches up to date. For many reasons including good security practice, move to the latest version of **Autoconfig and Patch Tools (AD)**.

  Apply **Critical Patch Updates (CPUs)** as quickly as possible. These contain fixes to high priority security vulnerabilities, and go through rigorous testing before their release.

- **Restrict network access to critical services**: Keep both the E-Business application middle-tier and the database behind a firewall. In addition, place a firewall between the middle-tier and the database. The firewalls provide assurance that access to these systems is restricted to a known network route, which can be monitored and restricted, if necessary.

- **Follow the principle of least privilege**: The principal of least privilege states that users should be given the least amount of privileges to perform their jobs. Overambitious granting of responsibilities, roles, grants, and so on, especially early on in an organization's life-cycle when people are few and work needs to be done quickly, often leaves a system wide open for abuse. User privileges should be reviewed periodically to determine relevance to current job responsibilities.

- **Monitor system activity**: System security stands on three legs that is, good security protocols, proper system configuration, and system monitoring.

  Auditing and reviewing audit records address the third requirement. Each component within a system has some degree of monitoring capability.

  Two ways to monitor the appropriateness of the system configuration and any updates that Oracle recommends is using Applications Manager or the Application Management Packs within Oracle Enterprise Manager.

The following is a screenshot of the **Applications Manager** security page:

The tightening of controls should be done at all levels of the IT Infrastructure.

- Database Tier
- Applications Tier
- Operating Environment Tier

Database tier

We can implement better controls at the database tier by restricting the other network nodes that the database listener will listen to and restrict the port numbers on which it will listen.

Oracle TNS listener security

You can improve the security of the database by restricting the IP addresses or the network nodes that the database communicates with. Valid node checking allows or denies access from specified IP addresses to Oracle services. In order to enable valid node checking, set the following parameters:

```
$TNS_ADMIN/sqlnet.ora:
tcp.validnode_checking = YES
tcp.invited_nodes = ( X.X.X.X, hostname, ... )
tcp.excluded_nodes = ( hostname, X.X.X.X, ... )
```

The first parameter turns on valid node checking. The latter two parameters respectively specify the IP addresses or hostnames that are permitted to make or are denied from making network connections to Oracle services. Replace x.x.x.x with the IP addresses of middle-tiers. Middle-tier applications include web servers, forms servers, reports servers, concurrent managers, and discoverer.

> Note that you can also turn this on via Autoconfig and it will do it for you.

Oracle database security

It is always a good database hardening step to remove services and ports that are not needed and other mechanisms to reach the database. Some examples include:

- **Disable XDB**: In order to support XDB, the TNS Listener process listens on two additional TCP ports: 2100 for FTP access and 8080 for accessing HTTP. Oracle E-Business Suite does not require these services; they should be disabled.

  In order to disable XDB, remove or comment out the line in init.ora that reads as follows:

  ```
  *.dispatchers='(PROTOCOL=TCP) (SERVICE=sidXDB)'
  ```

- **Review database links**: Review database links in both production and development environments.

Application tier

At the applications tier, we can harden the system by restricting access to the administrative web pages and changing and or disabling the seeded accounts.

Protect administrative web pages

Within **Oracle Application Server**, a number of web pages provide administrative and testing functionality. These pages offer information about various services, the server's state, and its configuration. While useful for debugging, these pages must be restricted or disabled in a production system.

Use the configuration files `httpd.conf` and `httpd_pls.conf` to limit web page access to a list of trusted hosts. In order to do this, create a file `trusted.conf` and include it in the `httpd.conf` and `httpd_pls.conf` files.

This new file contains the following content. The following is an example code snippet:

```
<Location ~ "/dev60html/run(form|rep).htm">
Order deny,allow
Deny from all
Allow from localhost <list of TRUSTED IPs>
</Location>
```

There are many such location tags in the file, each one pointing to a particular service. The preceding snippet is the authorized IP Addresses for the Forms and Reports service.

The `order deny, allow` tells the system how to judge the precedence when combining allows and denies to determine if the IP Address is authorized.

Replace `<list of TRUSTED IPs>` with host machines from which administrators may connect.

E-Business Suite security

Change passwords for seeded application user accounts. Oracle comes with seeded user accounts having default passwords. You should change the default passwords immediately.

Note that Oracle DB provides a script, which checks accounts for all default passwords that are shipped with Oracle products, including the E-Business Suite. E-Business Suite also ships a script, which checks for default passwords of E-Business Suite users (`FND_USERS`). Both the scripts should be run after a major upgrade to ensure there are no database or E-Business Suite user accounts with default passwords.

Also, note that the Oracle E-Business Suite supports both encryption and hashing of the E-Business Suite user passwords. **Hashing** means that the password itself is not stored, but that the "hash" that is some transformation of the password is stored. This transformation is one way, meaning that you cannot recreate the password from the hash. The default is to use encryption, but you should switch this over to hashing at the first opportunity. Be aware that the operation of switching the accounts over is non-reversible, so be sure to test and back up before performing this change.

Depending on product usage, some seeded accounts may be disabled. Do not disable the SYSADMIN or GUEST user accounts.

Account	Product/Purpose	Change	Disable
AUTOINSTALL	AD	Y	Y
CONCURRENT MANAGER	FND/AOL: Concurrent Manager	Y	Y
FEEDER SYSTEM AD	Supports data from feeder system	Y	Y
GUEST	Guest application user	Y	N
IBE_ADMIN	iSupport Admin user	Y	Y
IBEGUEST	iSupport Guest user	Y	N
IEXADMIN	Internet Expenses Admin	Y	Y
INITIAL SETUP	AD	Y	Y
IRC_EMP_GUEST	iRecruitment Employee Guest Login	Y	Y
IRC_EXT_GUEST	iRecruitment External Guest Login	Y	Y
MOBILEADM	Mobile Applications Admin	Y	Y
OP_CUST_CARE_ADMIN	Customer Care Admin for Oracle Provisioning	Y	Y
OP_SYSADMIN	OP (Process Manufacturing) Admin User	Y	Y
STANDALONE BATCH PROCESS	FND/AOL	Y	Y
SYSADMIN	Application Systems Admin	Y	N
WIZARD	Application Implementation Wizard	Y	N

You should also set some profile options to appropriate values, which have an impact on the security:

Profile Option	Default	Recommended Setting
Signon Password Failure Limit	None	3
Signon Password Hard to Guess	No	Yes
		Oracle defines a password as hard-to-guess if it follows the following rules:
		The password contains at least one letter and at least one number.
		The password does not contain repeating characters.
		The password does not contain the username.
Signon Password Length	5 characters	8 characters
Signon Password No Reuse	None	180 days
Signon Password Case	None	Sensitive: This will allow case-sensitive passwords.

Desktop security

At the desktop layer, we can harden the system by changing some of the browser security and convenience settings.

Turn off auto-complete in browser settings

For kiosk machines, change the browsers **AutoComplete** settings. For example, Internet Explorer can automatically show previous values entered in the same form field. Although desirable for frequently accessed pages, this feature should be disabled for privacy and security reasons.

In order to turn off the **AutoComplete** feature in Internet Explorer, navigate to **Tools | Internet Options | Content**. From the **Content** tab, click on the **AutoComplete** button, uncheck the **Forms** and **User names and passwords on forms** checkboxes. Also, do not use the **Remember password** function, as this is a known security vulnerability.

Operating environment security

At the operating environment level, you can harden the system by limiting communications to known components and ports only.

Firewall configuration and filtering of IP packets

IP filtering helps to prevent unwanted access. On the internet or large network, use a firewall machine or router with firewalling capabilities.

A firewall machine sits between the Internet and the Intranet or the Intranet and the internal servers. It provides a point of resistance by protecting the internal systems from external users. A firewall machine can filter packets and/or can be a proxy server. Firewalls may be software or hardware. For software, dedicate a machine to be the firewall. Do not assume that using Network Address Translation (NAT) substitutes for a firewall. Filtering out unused services at the firewall or router level stops infiltration attempts earlier in the process. Unless running NFS between networks, turn off all Remote Procedure Call (RPC) ports on the router. Better yet, enable only specific ports in use, adding new ones as needed.

Security incident response through Oracle service

The following screenshot shows the user interface from which you create a service request. The different types of service requests are shown in the following screenshot with the **IT-Security Incident** link highlighted:

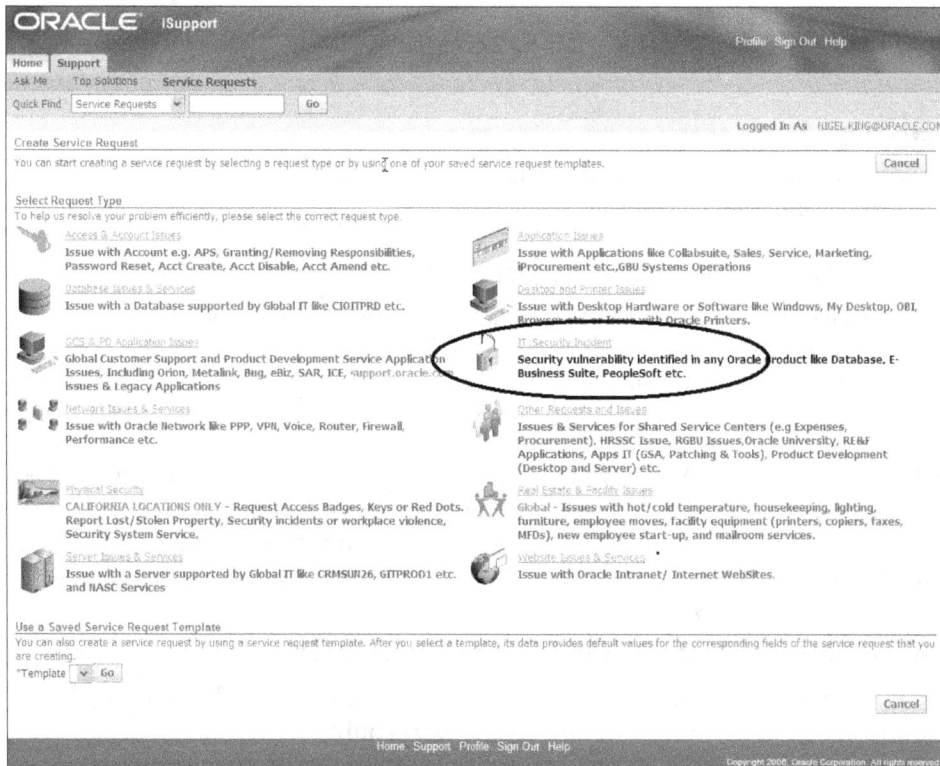

The next screenshot shows the details of a security incident being entered:

We ensure that the security incidents are also captured. We take special attention to the configuration of the service product when capturing security incidents. The security incidents themselves should not become a broadcast mechanism to advertise the discovered vulnerability. There may be many alternative ways to capture security incident with the E-Business Suite. We recommend using the Service Request system. The service request system was designed to record service requests for products that you sell, but it is well suited to this task with a bit of configuration. In order to configure the service request, log in to the **applications** as an **Oracle iSupport Administrator**. From here, you can configure the service request types, task flows, and pages that capture the security incident information and the request templates that guide and speed data entry for the service request. Details of how to configure different types of service requests is explained in *Chapter 2, Corporate Governance*, in the context of whistle-blower reporting.

Summary

In this chapter, we included the Chief Security Officer(CSO) in our governance discussions. We helped him construct a Security Balanced Scorecard with objectives for security management that are in concert with the overall corporate objectives. We then demonstrated how principles of least privilege are implemented through role design in responsibilities and the user management (UMX) application. We looked at how the principle of accountability is implemented in the standard FND_USER tables and glanced at Oracle's Single Sign On (SSO). We explained how employee on-boarding, off-boarding, transfers, and promotions must be reflected in the security system to meet the security objectives in our scorecard. We showed the CSO how the policies of the duties that must be segregated are articulated and how they are enforced through Oracle Access Controls Governor, and reported in GRC Manager. Next, we explained to him the threats, vulnerabilities, and countermeasures that are available. We further explained how to harden the system to address those threats, also counseled him on the costs of doing so, and helped him understand that a completely secure system is not realistic or cost effective. Lastly, we took the CSO through security incident tracking and response.

5

Risk Assessment and Control Verification

In the previous chapters, we have discussed the governance program at InFission. We have provided information about the governance approach, processes, and systems that the board of directors and management can use to set strategy and establish governance guidelines. Once the management, with the approval of the board of directors, has established the strategic objective, and corporate governance policies, the Chief Audit Executive prepares the annual internal audit risk assessment plan to assure that the enterprise can meet its strategic objectives. Control verification activities follow risk assessment to obtain management verification of internal controls design and operating effectiveness. **Risk Assessment** and **Control Verification** enable organizations to maintain good governance, monitor operational effectiveness, and comply with applicable laws and regulations.

Risk assessment is typically conducted based on a framework that applies at all levels—enterprise, function, and business unit—of the organization. In recent years, many well-managed organizations have adopted an **Enterprise Risk Management (ERM)** framework. Risk assessment is a key component of this framework and it can provide a more holistic risk management's approach that is closely aligned with management view of the organization. Many organizations use a *qualitative* approach by periodically asking managers to rate risks based on likelihood of occurrence and impact on the business. Some organizations with a mature risk management program also implement a more rigorous *quantitative* assessment program using probabilistic and non-probabilistic models by monitoring internal risk incidents, such as transaction errors and external risk incidents, such as loss events within their industry peers.

Control verification requires the management to assess the internal controls design and operating effectiveness at the beginning of the fiscal year. Many organizations send quarterly control assessment surveys to process owners and control owners to identify any changes in the control environment.

The results of management risk assessment and control verification are reviewed and evaluated by the Chief Audit Executive to select the business units, significant processes, control activities, and technology infrastructure for the annual audit plan. The Audit Committee approves the Audit plan based on the control verification approach, resource budget, and testing schedule. In general, the control verification approach is based on the risk rating and tolerance. For example, controls that mitigate low risk activities are assigned to employees that own the controls for self-assessment, whereas, higher risk controls are verified by independent auditors to assure the effectiveness on internal controls. We will discuss audit planning and controls testing in *Chapter 7, Managing Your Testing Phase: Management Testing and Certifying Controls; Chapter 8, Managing Your Audit Function*; and *Chapter 9, IT Audit*.

We will begin this chapter with an approach for risk assessment and control verification that InFission has adopted. Next, we will show how InFission Audit and Compliance team perform risk assessment and control verification activities independently within Oracle GRC Manager and GRC Intelligence to manage risk and verify controls across the enterprise. We will address the following topics in this chapter:

- Describe a **Program Office** that should include executive management leadership to ensure the *tone at the top* and necessary sponsorship for achieving risk management objectives

- Provide an overview of the risk management frameworks commonly used by publically traded companies to assure internal controls over financial statements

- Illustrate the activities to gather qualitative and quantitative data and rate risks based on the data collected and tolerance for risk

- Explain management control verification activities and representation of evidence of control design and operating effectiveness

- Show how to create a Qualitative Risk Assessment in Oracle GRC Manager and rate risks using Oracle GRC Intelligence to analyze qualitative risks as well as quantitative risks

InFission approach for Risk Assessment and Control Verification

At InFission, our Compliance Director is responsible for setting up the program office and selecting the controls framework, conducting management interviews, and reviewing prior year control documents.

The global process owners are ultimately responsible for identifying the inherent risk exposure, as well as the certification of control effectiveness in their process. However, many process owners also require their staff to identify any risks and verify the controls for which they are responsible.

At InFission, the Chief Financial Officer (CFO) has also appointed a Compliance Director as the head of Compliance Program Management Office (PMO) in order to assist the management to complete the risks assessment and control verification activities. The Compliance PMO team uses Oracle GRC Manager and Oracle GRC Intelligence to obtain qualitative risk rating by creating risk assessment questionnaires that provide management response to financial, operational, and IT risks.

The Chief Audit Executive (CAE) maintains independence throughout the management assessment process. Once the risk assessment results are submitted by the Compliance PMO in GRC Manager, the CAE reviews the management risk rating using GRC Intelligence dashboards and prepares the Audit plan in Oracle GRC Manager to include internal controls that require verification by independent auditors as well as management.

The internal audit team performs independent, top-down risk assessment using a quantitative approach. This approach includes a probabilistic model that measures both the likelihood and impact of risk events, as well as non-probabilistic models that include sensitivity analysis and scenario planning. Non-probabilistic models are relied upon when available data is limited. The data model for quantitative risk assessment is maintained in Oracle GRC Intelligence and the data is periodically extracted from Hyperion Financial Management (HFM), Oracle GRC Manager, and Oracle E-Business Suite.

The following figure displays the risk assessment and controls verification approach at InFission:

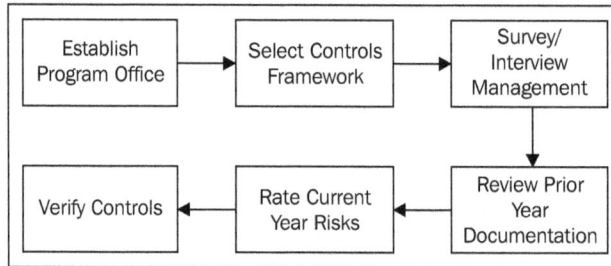

```
┌──────────────────────────────────────────────────────────────────┐
│  ┌──────────────┐      ┌──────────────┐      ┌──────────────┐     │
│  │  Establish   │ ───▶ │Select Controls│ ──▶ │   Survey/    │     │
│  │Program Office│      │  Framework   │      │  Interview   │     │
│  └──────────────┘      └──────────────┘      │  Management  │     │
│                                               └──────────────┘     │
│                                                      │             │
│                                                      ▼             │
│  ┌──────────────┐      ┌──────────────┐      ┌──────────────┐     │
│  │              │ ◀─── │ Rate Current │ ◀─── │ Review Prior │     │
│  │Verify Controls│      │  Year Risks  │      │     Year     │     │
│  └──────────────┘      └──────────────┘      │Documentation │     │
│                                               └──────────────┘     │
└──────────────────────────────────────────────────────────────────┘
```

Establishing Program Office

InFission Program office is critical for achieving risk management objectives. First and foremost, the program office has the executive management leadership that provides the sponsorship, authorization, and ensures the *tone at the top*. The program office establishes the controls framework, conducts the risk assessment, manages the test plan for control verification, assigns the resources, and monitors all activities to ensure the appropriate oversight necessary for internal and external communication.

The InFission Risk Program Office consists of the steering committee, full time internal control managers, and part-time field control coordinators. The GRC Manager and Intelligence applications enable the program office to establish a well-structured approach to support key functions to manage risk assessment plans and track control verification activities through workflows, as well as provide reporting and dashboards to monitor and communicate progress.

InFission Program Office is responsible for regulatory compliance risks such as misstatement of financial results under the US Sarbanes Oxley Act of 2002 (SOX), operational risks such as manufacturing defects, financial risks such as duplicate vendor payments, IT risks such as unauthorized access to ERP systems, and enterprise risks such as market risks. While this structure requires more resources and costs dedicated to managing enterprise risks, there are many benefits that justify such an approach where all management risk assessment, and control verification activities can be managed more effectively by a single authority, the **Compliance Program Management Office (CPMO)**. In such a structure, the CPMO relies on the management control self assessment, to keep executive management appraised of any control deficiencies using a consistent risk management framework.

Selecting controls framework

An essential task of the program office is to establish a framework that will be used to assess organizational risks and verify the controls mitigating those risks. There are a number of well-established controls frameworks that can be selected based on the overall control objectives of the organization. For example, InFission has selected the Committee of Sponsoring Organization of the Treadway Commission (COSO) framework that is most prevalent among publically traded companies. This framework is implemented to provide assurance of internal controls over financial statements. InFission has selected the COBIT (Control Objectives for Information and related Technology framework), which is commonly used for IT controls. These two frameworks are described as follows:

The COSO framework

The COSO framework consists of five interrelated components: Control Environment, Risk Assessment, Controls Activities, Information and Communication, and Monitoring. These are derived from the way management runs a business, and are integrated with the management process. Although the components apply to all entities, small and mid-size companies may implement them differently to large ones. Smaller organizations may have controls that are less formal and less structured, yet such an organization can still have effective internal control.

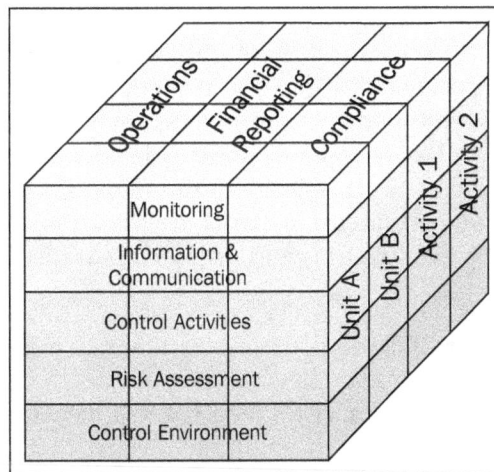

According to COSO "Every entity faces a variety of risks from external and internal sources that must be assessed. A precondition to risk assessment is establishment of objectives, linked at different levels, and internally consistent. Risk assessment is the identification and analysis of relevant risks to achievement of the objectives forming a basis for determining how the risks should be managed. Because economic, industry, regulatory, and operating conditions will continue to change, mechanisms are needed to identify and deal with the special risks associated with change."

Effective risk assessment requires:

- Defined business objectives
- Identification of risks for achieving objectives
- Risk rating method
- Actions to mitigate risks

If any one of these factors is absent, an unsatisfactory rating is generally warranted. Furthermore, audit inquiries and tests should be designed to determine if there are key risks, which are not contemplated by the management. If such risks are identified and deemed critical, an unsatisfactory rating should be rendered on that basis alone, even if all the other factors listed are present.

Holistic risk assessment—COSO ERM

Organizations that have adopted a more holistic view of risk assessment have included an Enterprise Risk Management (ERM) into the risk assessment plans. COSO defines ERM as, "A process, affected by an entity's board of directors, management, and other personnel, applied in strategy setting and across the enterprise, designed to identify potential events that may affect the entity, and manage risks to be within its risk appetite, to provide reasonable assurance regarding the achievement of entity objectives." Implementation of controls is one common method management can use to manage risks within its risk appetite. Internal auditors audit the key controls and provide assurance on the management of significant risks.

Risk managers and auditors include two fundamental risk measurement concepts, when conducting a risk assessment. They measure and track inherent risk and residual risk (also known as current risk). Inherent risk measurements assess the susceptibility of information or data to a material misstatement, assuming that there are no related mitigating controls. The IIA's International Standards for the Professional Practice of Internal Auditing (Standards) define residual risk as, "the risk remaining after the management takes action to reduce the impact and likelihood of an adverse event, including control activities in responding to a risk". Current risk is often defined as the risk managed within existing controls or control systems.

The COBIT framework

COBIT 4.1 has 34 high-level processes that cover 210 control objectives categorized in four domains: Planning and Organization, Acquisition and Implementation, Delivery and Support, and Monitoring and Evaluation. COBIT provides benefits to managers, IT users, and auditors. Managers benefit from COBIT as it provides them with a foundation upon which IT-related decisions and investments can be based. Decision making is more effective because COBIT aids management in defining a strategic IT plan, defining the information architecture, acquiring the necessary IT hardware and software to execute an IT strategy, ensuring continuous service, and monitoring the performance of the IT system. IT users benefit from COBIT because of the assurance provided to them by COBIT's defined controls, security, and process governance. COBIT benefits auditors because it helps them identify IT control issues within a company's IT infrastructure. It also helps them corroborate their audit findings. In *Chapter 10, Cross Industry Cross Compliance*, we will go into more details regarding this framework.

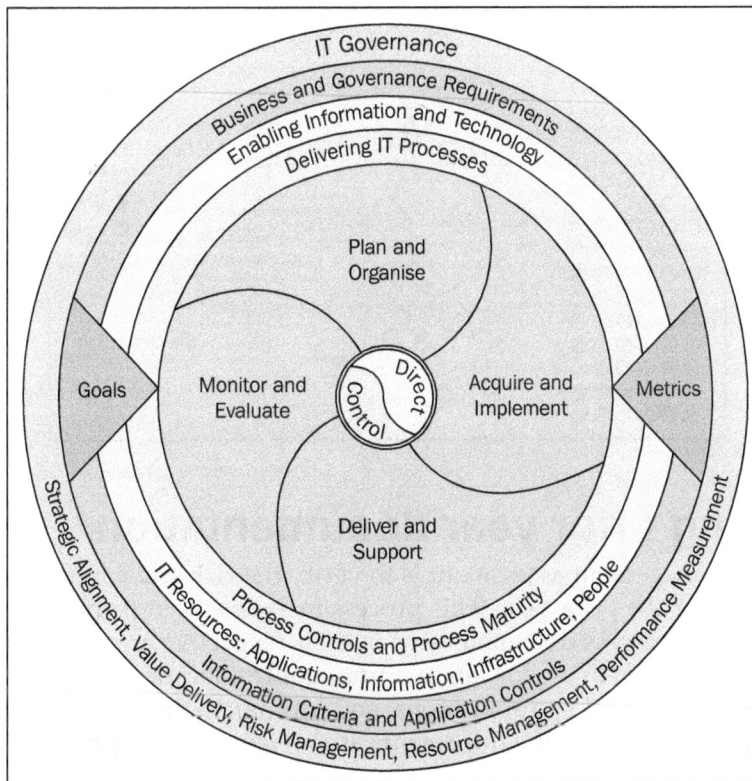

Survey and interview management

InFission Compliance PMO facilitates management surveys and interviews to determine the inherent risks based on management assessment on the impact and likelihood of key events that can negatively impact InFission's business model and assets. An anonymous annual management survey is initiated to identify significant areas of risk. Managers are encouraged to provide opinions and exchange information. The survey results are tabulated and evaluated by risk managers to identify the top risks to the company. Next, the executive management interviews are conducted to select the risk based on strategic objectives and business performance targets.

The following figure depicts the survey and interview process:

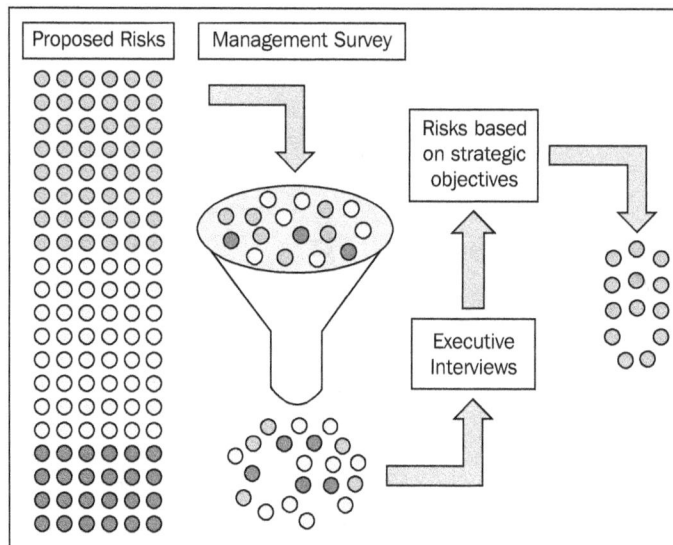

Reviewing prior year documentation

A key step in management assessment is to verify the risk and control documentation for the prior year. This process includes input from process owners regarding process documentation in their respective areas. In addition, it includes the selection of significant accounts, control locations, key business processes, mission critical IT applications, and ultimately the enterprise control verification plan. The following documents are reviewed in the process:

- Prior Year Consolidated Balance Sheet
- Prior Year Consolidated Income Statement
- Prior Year Account-Process Matrix
- Prior Year Risks-Control Matrix (RCM)
- Prior Year Key Process List by Location
- Prior Year Issue Log
- Prior Year IT Application and General Computer Controls (ITGC and Application) Matrix

The spreadsheet shown in the following screenshot is used to review control documentation:

Rating current year risk

Once the risks are reviewed with executive management, the risk managers categorize the risk response and treatment.

The following map is created to identify the top risks with all impacted business processes based on the organization's tolerance for risk as indentified by the management:

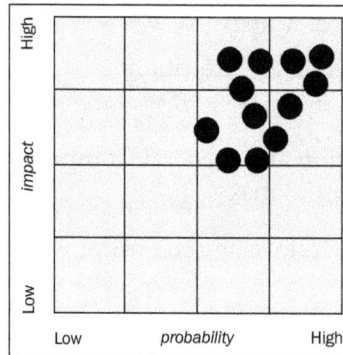

Verifying controls

InFission Compliance PMO facilitates manage control verification by preparing a control self-assessment survey with specific questions regarding key controls. The key controls are determined by reviewing the results for risk rating, financial statements, and control documentations which include:

- Key Process List by Location
- Account-Process Matrix
- Risks-Control Matrix
- IT General Computer Controls and Application Matrix

The Compliance PMO selects the key controls to be included in the control self-assessment survey by selecting the internal controls, which mitigate risk with high likelihood and impact using the input from the risk assessment, shown as follows:

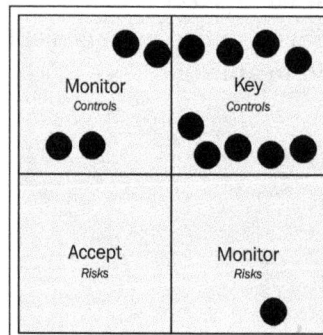

The survey is distributed to process owners and control owners every quarter with deadlines for each control location. The survey also shows the results of the current year's risk assessment conducted pursuant to the risk assessment framework. The Compliance PMO also has the option, during the year, to initiate additional surveys to address any changes to the control environment.

The survey includes questions regarding significant processes, risks, and key controls that require mandatory response by the process owners. Process owners are also asked to identify any control deficiencies at this point and action plans are developed to ensure that these deficiencies get remediated before the control testing phase.

Oracle's GRC Manager and Intelligence—risk assessment and control verification system

InFission has selected Oracle GRC Manager and Intelligence (GRCMI) application to support the risk assessment and control verification process based on GRCMI functionality to meet business requirements.

Oracle GRC Manager is a comprehensive enterprise risk management application that offers web-based risk and compliance management features. The module can be used by executives, controllers, internal audit departments, and public accounting firms to document and test internal controls and monitor ongoing compliance.

With Oracle GRC Manager, InFission can increase internal control management efficiency, improve risk assessment confidence, and lower external audit verification costs. You can use the application's intuitive workbench to organize, execute, and manage audit activities, which can be similar to the following:

- Define standard business processes
- Set up risks to which processes are exposed
- Set up controls that can mitigate process risk
- Set up the Organization Structure (Auditable Units) and map processes to this structure
- Record assessment of the organization's compliance with established controls and regulations
- Assess risk and verify controls design and operating effectiveness
- Review the compliance of your business processes/systems and record audit results.

Oracle GRC Manager is independent of the applications that it tests and validates, and can be successfully deployed in any environment (Oracle or non-Oracle).

Oracle GRC Intelligence provides business process risk and control analytics with the flexibility to drill down into transaction systems from high-level dashboards. The solution provides prebuilt key performance indicators (KPIs) that show the progress of risk and control activities, and highlights specific areas of concern, such as unmitigated risks and ineffective controls. These indicators enable you to effectively analyze GRC activities to identify potential issues earlier, and to take more timely and effective corrective actions. Oracle GRC Intelligence is also fully extensible, allowing users to create new KPIs and reports based on both Oracle and non-Oracle data sources.

Assessment workflow in Oracle GRC Manager

Oracle GRC Manager Assessment workflow is used to route a business process for the assessment of its risks and verification of controls. This assessment workflow enables you to record assessment of the organization's risks and controls. The amount of control testing work performed in an audit depends to a large measure on this up front assessment.

The following figure shows the assessment workflow:

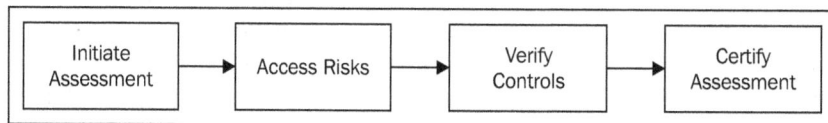

| Initiate Assessment | → | Access Risks | → | Verify Controls | → | Certify Assessment |

Assessment workflow is activated whenever a user with permissions wishes to have one or more processes assessed. The workflow progresses are explained in the following sections.

Initiating assessment

The Compliance PMO employs a qualitative risk assessment technique to determine the inherent as well as residual risks, which are rated in terms of likelihood and impact on the screen page in GRC Manager.

A management assessment survey is created in Oracle GRC Manager to identify risks and verify controls. In this survey, the management evaluates events that can impact organizational objectives based on the understanding of the internal operations, industry trends, and external factors. The risks are also linked to the business processes and the controls that mitigate the risks and are linked to the corresponding controls.

The assessment is routed to the business process owner, who assesses risks and verifies the controls to complete the survey.

The workflow is initiated by a user with rights to the business process and authorized to initiate assessment. The initiator creates an assessment cover that specifies the assessment title, reviewers, assessment types, and the risks and controls to be assessed. The document is in the *prepare* state.

In order to start an assessment of risks within a single business process, for example, Account Payable, open a business process by navigating to **Business Processes | Released Processes**, then click on the title **Accounts Payable** that contains a risk named **Accrued liabilities are not properly supported or booked in the correct period**. Then, click on **Initiate Assessment**. Enter a title for the **Assessment Cover** document. Specify a **Fiscal Period** for the assessment (required) on the **Basics** tab.

Selecting assessment type

Once the assessment is initiated, you can specify the type of the assessment by completing the information regarding **Test Period** (fiscal), **Assessment Type**, which is set to **Operational and Design** here, survey, **Due Date**, and assessor(s), as shown in the following screenshot:

Management Assessment Selection Wizard	Quick Help

Select the type or types of assessments that you would like management to complete.

Assessment Type:	Operational Design

Test Period	2012 Q4 ▼
Due Date:	3/30/2012 ◀◀

Management Assessment

Control Owner Reviewer:	AdilKhan	i
Reviewer:	AdilKhan	i
Executive Reviewer:	AdilKhan	i

Back	Next	Finish	Cancel

Selecting risks in scope

The **Management Assessment Selection Wizard** is displayed when you click on the **Prepare Assessment** button. When you use the wizard, you can back up steps to change selections if needed, or you can cancel the wizard and return to the assessment cover document.

> Note that the **Prepare Selection** button is enabled only when the management assessment cover document is in a **Prepare** state. If the document tabs are being edited, the button will not be displayed.

Specify the risks that should be included in the assessment. By default all the risks in the process should be included. All risks are displayed. If the **Assessment Type** is a **Survey**, you can select a survey from the list:

All	Risk	Title	Significance	Likelihood	Rating	Release Date	Related Control(s)
☑	000305	Accrued liabilities are not properly supported or booked in the correct period	3 Medium	Extreme	15	3/11/2012 10:48:16 AM	Accrued Liabilities - Objective is to verify
☑	000306	Approval authorities are not documented	1 Low	Medium	3	3/11/2012 10:48:16 AM	Disbursements are carried out in accordance
☑	000307	Intercompany transactions are not recorded valued correctly or reconciled	2 Med Low	Low	4	3/11/2012 10:48:16 AM	Inter-company Transactions-Obj is to verify that all inter-company accounts
☑	000308	Operations not leveraging purchasing power	3 Medium	Medium	9	3/11/2012 10:48:16 AM	Procurement-Objective is to determine cost savings or ROI putforth in CapEx AR
☑	000309	ROI not realized	2 Med Low	Negligible	2	3/11/2012 10:48:16 AM	Procurement-Objective is to determine if the Operation is adequately utilizing, Three-way match is completed and exceptions are investigated
☑	000310	Reconciliations are not performed timely reviewed and approved	2 Med Low	High	8	3/11/2012 10:48:16 AM	Accounts and Notes Payable - Objective is to verify that the GL and Sub-ledger, Cash / Bank Accounts - Objective is to verify

Selecting control in scope

Specify the controls that should be included in the assessment. By default all the controls that mitigate the risk in the process should be included. Select the controls in scope for this assessment and specify if they are required, optional, or excluded. GRC Manager provides the option to scope **Key**, **Monitoring**, **Secondary**, and **Subordinate** controls, as shown in the following screenshot:

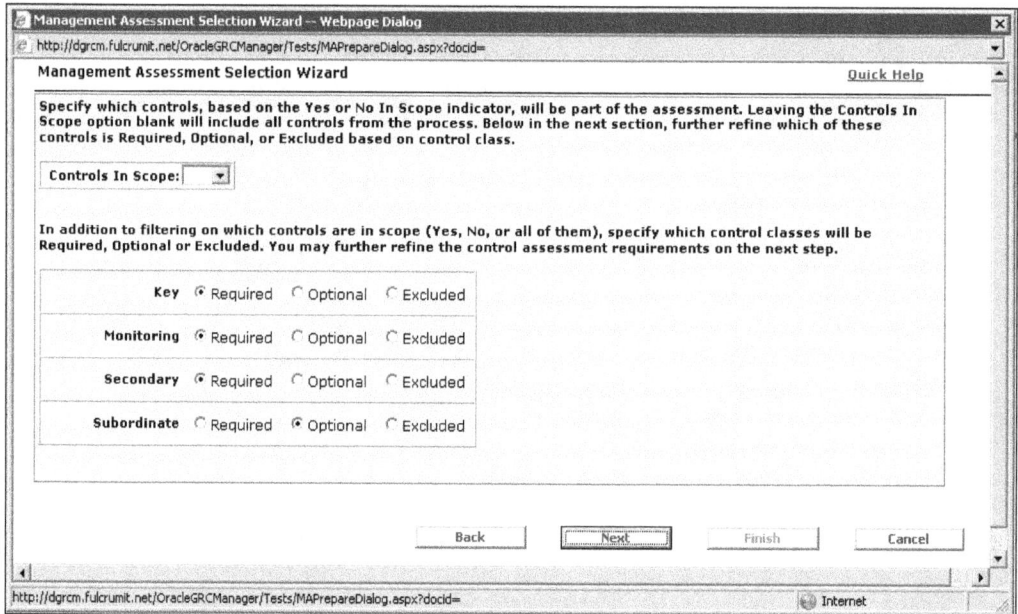

Starting assessment

Once you have prepared the assessment, you can send it to the management by selecting the **Start Assessment** button to kick off the Assessment workflow and send an e-mail notification to the process owners. The processes are now in and the **Owner Assessment** state and the assessment documents are automatically assigned the name of the business unit and a number (in sequential order), shown as follows:

Management Assessment: Assessment - P2P - Accounts Payable

| Close | Edit | Prepare Selection | Start Assessment | Cancel Assessment |

Organization: Corporate/InFission Corp   **ID:** 000750

Process: P2P - Accounts Payable | Process Profile | **Release Date:**

Title: Assessment - P2P - Accounts Payable   **Version:** 1

State: Prepare   **Due Date:** 3/30/2012

Basics   Comments   Controls   Risks   Process   Certification   Attachments   Issues   History

General		Workflow	
Period:	2012 Q4	**Process Owner:**	AdilKhan
Assessment Type:	Operational Design	**Control Owner Reviewer:**	AdilKhan
		Reviewer:	AdilKhan
		Executive Reviewer:	AdilKhan
Percent Complete	0	**CMS Status:**	Review
		Current User:	AdilKhan

Description:

Assessing risks

In order to assess and pass or fail risks included in a management assessment of one or more business processes, navigate to **My Inbox** or **Management Assessments | Assessments Inbox** to see a list of assessments assigned to you. Select the title of an assessment and open it. Select the **Management Assessment Risks** tab to view the risks. In order to assess a risk, click on a button to perform the type of assessment for the risk as specified on the **Risks** tab.

The **Risk Assessment** page will be displayed, as shown in the following screenshot:

Management Assessment: Assessment - P2P - Accounts Payable

| Close | Edit | | Complete Assessment | | Fail Assessment | |

Assessment Steps
- Controls 0%
- Risks
- Process
- Certification

Organization: Corporate/InFission Corp
Process: P2P - Accounts Payable | Process Profile |
Title: Assessment - P2P - Accounts Payable
State: Owner Assessment

ID: 000750
Release Date:
Version: 1
Due Date: 3/30/2012

Basics Comments Controls **Risks** Process Certification Attachments Issues History

* - Required

Risk Information	Class	Control Information	Assess	Assessment Result	Release Date
Accrued liabilities are not properly supported or booked in the correct period					3/11/2012
*	Key	Accrued Liabilities - Objective is to verify			3/11/2012
Approval authorities are not documented					3/11/2012
*	Key	Disbursements are carried out in accordance			3/11/2012
Intercompany transactions are not recorded valued correctly or reconciled					3/11/2012
*	Key	Inter-company Transactions-Obj is to verify that all inter-company accounts			3/11/2012
Operations not leveraging purchasing power					3/11/2012
*	Key	Procurement-Objective is to determine cost savings or ROI putforth in CapEx AR			3/11/2012
ROI not realized					3/11/2012
*	Key	Procurement-Objective is to determine if the Operation is adequately utilizing			3/11/2012
*	Key	Three-way match is completed and exceptions are investigated			3/11/2012
Reconciliations are not performed timely reviewed and approved					3/11/2012
*	Key	Accounts and Notes Payable - Objective is to verify that the GL and Subledger			3/11/2012

Reviewing risks

In order to review the current risk rating and provide new risk information, click on the risk to see the risk details, as shown in the following screenshot:

Complete an assessment for a risk and click on **Save**. When you have finished assessing all required documentation, click on **Complete Assessment**.

Verifying Controls

After the risks are evaluated, navigate to the **Control Verification** page to evaluate the control for operating and design effectiveness. You will also be required to complete a survey, which then certifies the results after you complete the control evaluation.

The document is in the **Owner Assessment** state, as shown in the following screenshot:

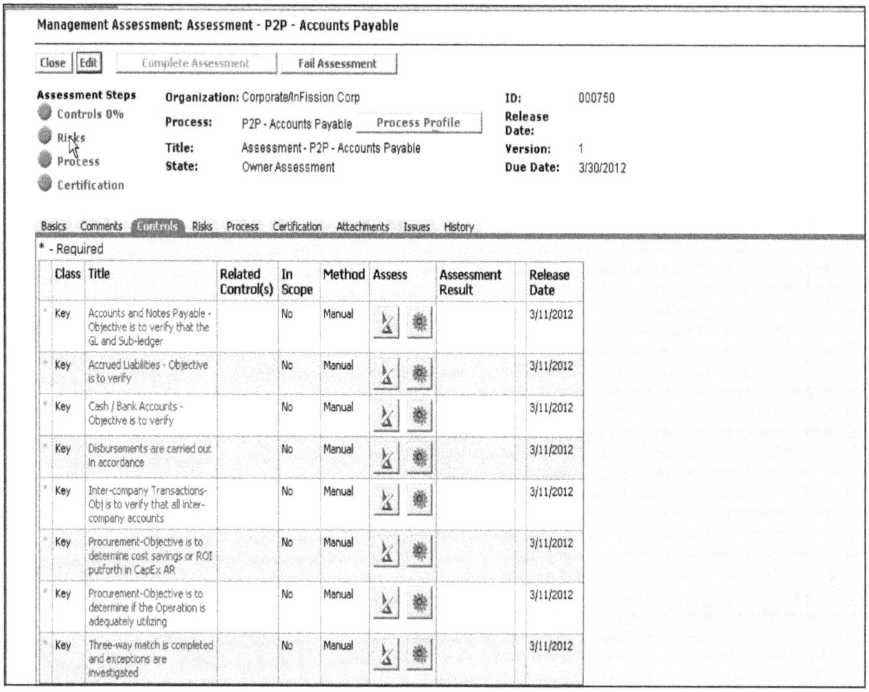

Select the design icon corresponding to the control to verify the control on the screen, as shown in the following screenshot:

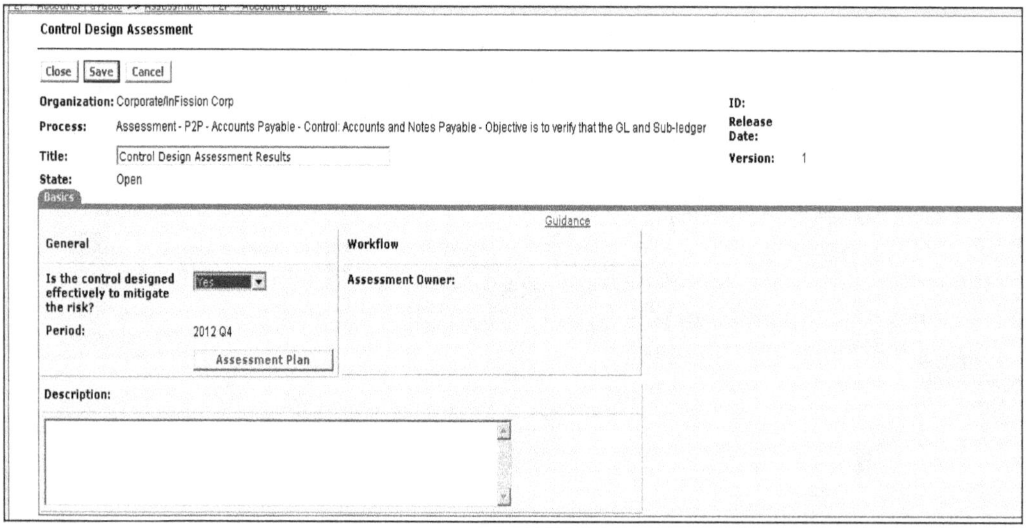

In order to view and print the assessment plan, select the **Assessment Plan** button on the **Control Design Assessment** page to see the details, as shown in the following screenshot:

Certifying assessment

Optionally, the assessment is routed to the first (if more than one) executive reviewer, who reviews the results and its documentation, passes or fails the assessment, and certifies the results on the page shown in the following screenshot:

If there is a second executive reviewer, the assessment is routed to the user, who reviews the results and its documentation, passes or fails the assessment, and certifies the result.

When all specified assessors have completed their tasks, depending on the results of the assessments, the workflow ends.

Evaluating assessment

Once the risk assessment and control verification is completed by the process owner, the Compliance PMO analyzes the risks that were identified by the management and rates each risk in terms of likelihood and impact to operations and financial statements.

The risk rating is submitted to the CAE to determine the risk treatment. The CAE prepares the audit test plan based on the risks identified and rated to provide reasonable assurance.

In order to ensure risks are identified, analyzed, and treated effectively, the approach to risk assessment is systematically structured in Oracle GRC Manager. All risk documentation is stored in a risk register within Oracle GRC Manager. This documentation includes risk description, inherent and residual risk rating, and mitigating controls. Risks are classified as global, regional, and local, and they are directly linked to the InFission organization structure. Each risk is quantified in terms of **impact** and **likelihood** described in the risk registers.

The GRC Manager Risk Register is reviewed by the CAE to include inherently high risks in the internal Audit plan. However, only a limited number of low risks are periodically included in the internal audit activity's plan to give them coverage and confirm that their risks have not changed. Also, the internal audit plan establishes a method for prioritizing outstanding risks not yet subject to an internal audit. The residual risks remain unchanged where the inherent risks are ranked low and not included in the audit plan. The CAE provides an independent risk assessment report to the Audit Committee including the details of the risk analysis and causes of the lack of or ineffectiveness of internal controls.

Assessing quantitative risks in Oracle GRC Intelligence

During the risk assessment phase, InFission uses Oracle GRC Intelligence to review the risks and evaluate the potential effects on the financial statements using quantitative analysis. The risks that have been identified *qualitatively* by the management are linked to the financial statement account considering the pervasiveness and magnitude of the effect on the financial statements and the likelihood that they will occur (inherent risk). Additionally, the risk that any mitigating controls might fail (control risk) are tracked by associating the prior year issue log in Oracle GRC Intelligence Application. Collectively, these two components represent the risk that a material misstatement of the financial statements would occur. Thus, InFission can track this combination of risks, commonly referred to as the Risk of Material Misstatement (ROMM) in Oracle GRC Intelligence. Based on the assessment of inherent risk and control risk, InFission can arrive at an assessment of misstatement risks.

The risk assessment can be conducted at both the overall financial statement level and the account balance/transaction class/entity level utilizing Oracle GRC Intelligence dashboards.

Risk assessment is performed at least once a year by InFission Chief Audit Executive to determine the scope of audit activities

Conduct quantitative risk assessment

Oracle GRC Intelligence provides a number of out of the box dashboards to conduct quantitative risk assessment. A few commonly used dashboards are included in this section.

Risk rating is determined by reviewing the prior year's Risk and Controls status by Account and Process. You can navigate to the **Risk Mitigation by Risk and Process Type** dashboard in Oracle GRC Intelligence, and select the account dimension and chart view to view the risk by account. In the following example, **Account Level 2 Name** may represent the **Current Liabilities** account on the balance sheet where the risk rating for **Accrued Liabilities**, **Breach of Security**, and so on can be analyzed based on impact and likelihood. **Process Count**, **Key Control Count**, and **Subordinate Control Count** are displayed in the following dashboard to adjust risk rating based on previous year's risk of control failure:

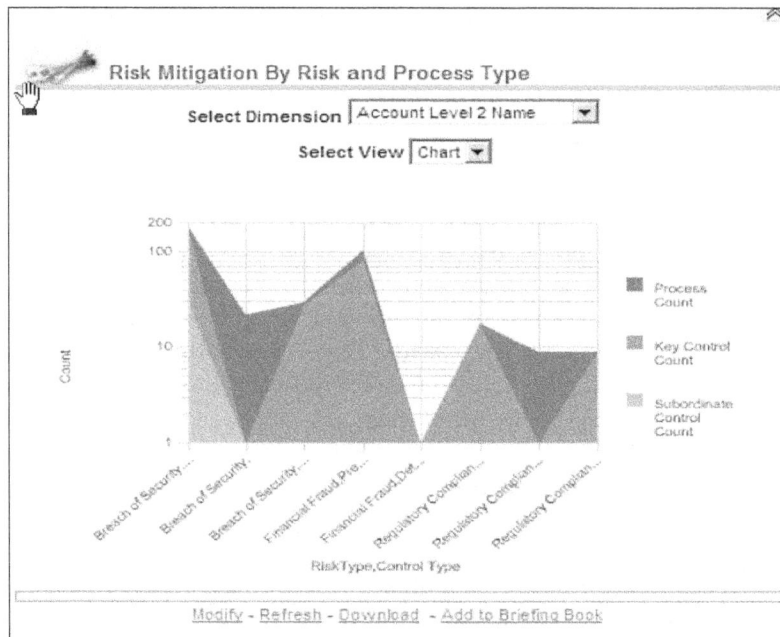

Next, risks can be further analyzed by navigating to the **Number of Controls Failures By Risk Type** dashboard, selecting the same account dimension and viewing the **Failed Control** % by account, process, control type, risk type, and financial period in table and chart format, as shown in the following screenshot:

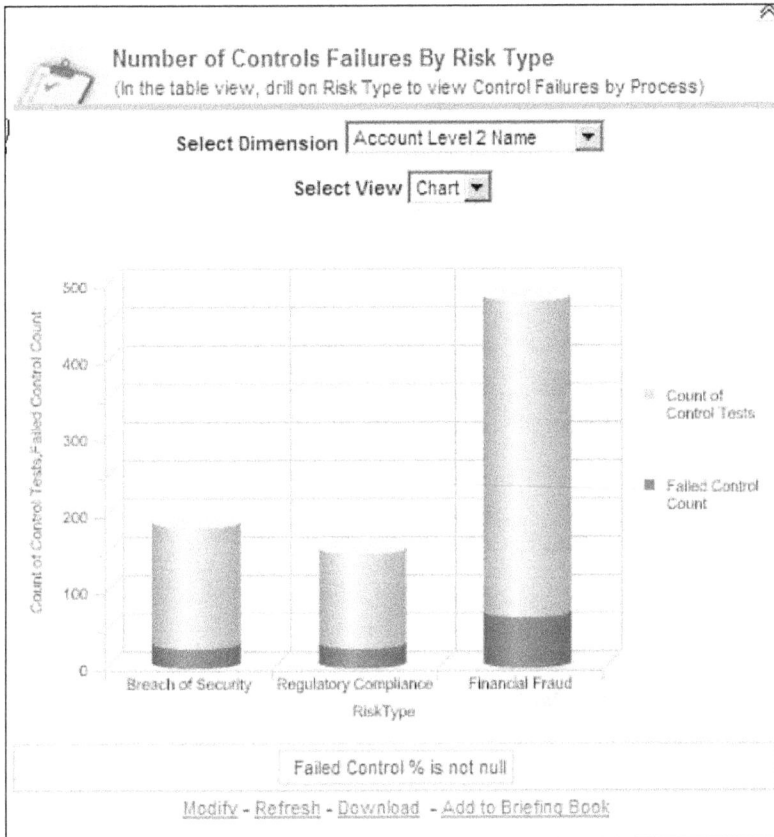

Additional risk analysis is performed by navigating to the **Number of Controls by Risk Type and Significance** dashboard, in order to select which locations, processes, and controls should be included for verification in the Audit plan, as shown in the following screenshot:

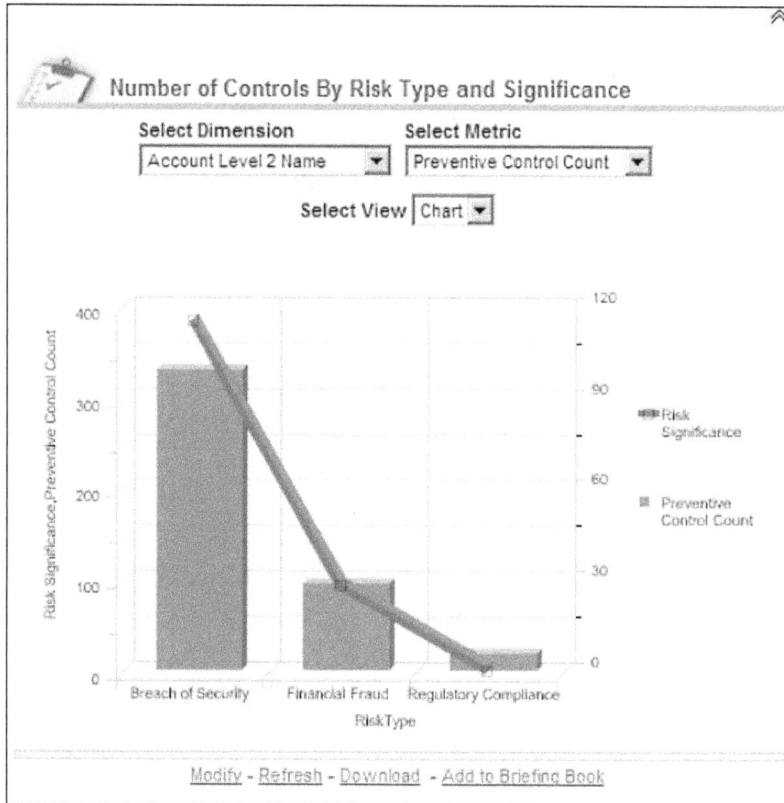

Once the risk assessment is completed, the Chief Audit Officer prepares the Audit Committee report, which includes a summary of enterprise risk, which can be displayed by navigating to the **Risk Heat Map** dashboard, as shown in the following screenshot:

Risk Heat Map - Business Processes

Risk Significance	Low Likelihood Number of Processes	Medium Likelihood Number of Processes	High Likelihood Number of Processes	Extreme Likelihood Number of Processes
Med-Low	2	6		
Medium		4		
Med-High	2	1	3	
High		1		2

Request contains **no** filters

Modify - Refresh - Download - Add to Briefing Book

Summary

Risk Assessment and Control Verification activities are critical for the management to ensure that the organization achieves its objectives. These activities require executive management sponsorship, a structured framework, workflow-based systems, and business intelligence tools.

Most organizations perform risk assessment at least once a year to evaluate enterprise risks for many different perspectives, such as strategic risk, operational risk, compliance risk, IT risk, and frauds. The management also checks and verifies the controls, which mitigate the risks to an acceptable level for the organization. Organizations subject to Sarbanes-Oxley law require the management to assess and certify that the internal controls over financial statements are design and operating effectiveness every quarter as the financial results are disclosed publically.

Generally, the internal controls management function is managed through a Program Management Office established by the Chief Financial Officer. The Chief Audit Executive and the Audit Department review the results of the assessment, and perform their risk assessment and audit independent of the management assessment.

In recent years, many organizations have adopted the Enterprise Risk Management (ERM) framework, established by COSO for risk assessment and controls verification. IT organizations also utilize the COBIT framework to assess IT risks and controls. These frameworks provide a more holistic view of the risks and control activities that are required to mitigate the inherent risks to a residual level that is acceptable to the organization.

Oracle GRC Manager enables organizations to implement a holistic approach to assess risks and verify controls by initiating an assessment workflow that is distributed through e-mail to those managers who are responsible for significant business processes. Once the managers receive the e-mail notification, they can access the pages to review risks, evaluate controls, and identify any issues, which must be remediated to meet the risk management and compliance guidance provided by the board of directors.

Oracle GRC Intelligence is a specialized business intelligence tool that enables chief audit executive and the internal audit department to collect transactional data from various internal and external sources to develop a model that can enable a quantitative risk analysis. This technique is utilized by leading audit teams to develop an optimum internal audit plan that takes into account the qualitative risk assessment from the management as well as other key probabilistic and non-probabilistic factors.

6
Documenting Your Controls

Documentation of your internal controls should clearly describe the process and procedures, as well as risks, which expose the process and controls that mitigate the risks. The accuracy of control documentation is critical to verify the controls, identify control gaps, and remediate any issues. In this chapter we will:

- Describe the approach and techniques to assist you to streamline the control document management process

- Discuss how to create effective process and procedure manuals to understand the internal controls

- Provide examples of documenting business processes using Oracle Tutor and instructions for maintaining key components of control documentation such as control locations (business units), process definitions, risk ratings and controls attributes using Oracle GRC Manager

- Show how to keep the control documentation current by requesting the process owners and control owners to periodically provide updates to their respective processes and controls using data collection workflow

Process and procedure documents

Many organizations maintain business processes and procedure manuals using narratives and flowcharts, which clearly describe the responsibilities of employees based on their roles. Process and procedure manuals help to ensure that the managers responsible for the processes (business process owners), and internal auditors share a common understanding of a process. Process and procedure manuals should be updated periodically, as and when required. The accuracy of these documents is essential for risk assessment and controls verification.

The process narratives should include all the subprocesses and procedures that are performed by employees responsible to ensure that there is a complete picture of how the process is actually executed. Process narrative should describe manual procedures as well as procedures enabled through software applications, such as ERP systems that enable the process. Process documentation may also include scope of the process, reference to company policies, such as authorization levels and supervisor review, and references to related processes. Process narratives that include procedures performed in an application should also reference the application access controls, segregation of duty policies, configuration controls, and transaction integrity.

The process flowcharts should provide a graphical representation of all the procedures, conditional steps, and inputs/outputs that describe the process and procedures. The graphical representation should also include a legend of shapes, conditions, and data. Flowcharts can be reviewed more effectively if the charts also include complete and accurate lists of the risks and controls that correlate to the process flow. Many organizations separate procedures within a process by lines or "swim lanes" to represent the employee roles that are responsible for performing, reviewing, and approving each step in the process.

Process owners and audit staff should use flowcharts to walk-through the process and gain a clear understanding of the process, as well as control activities that will mitigate the risks exposure.

InFission approach for managing process and procedure documents

At InFission, each department manager is responsible for maintaining the process and procedure documentation. The audit team reviews the narratives and process flow diagrams with each department biannually, as well as whenever any changes are made to a significant process. Each auditor is assigned to review one or more process narrative and flowchart documents. The review is initiated by the auditor obtaining the latest documentation from the designated employees in each department. Once the auditor receives the process documentation, she or he verifies the documents based on InFission standards and governing business policies. Next, the auditor schedules a process walkthrough session with the process owner(s) in the department.

During this session, the auditor and process owner review inputs and outputs to the process along with the responsibilities for individual employees in the department. Any changes to the process, personnel, or enabling information technology are identified and documentation is revised to reflect the changes. InFission uses Oracle GRC Manager and Oracle Tutor to manage process documents.

Managing process documents in Oracle GRC Manager

Oracle GRC Manager Application is designed to help reduce the cost and complexity of the document management process by enabling the organization to create and manage documentation efficiently. GRC Manager ensures that the business process documents are maintained accurately and change controls are enforced so an organization can comply with industry and government regulations.

InFission uses GRC Manager to support the following process management requirements:

- Manage the synchronization between where business processes are executed and where business processes are monitored.

- Link documentation for business processes to accounts, and track risks, controls, and issues for each business process.

- Enables users to monitor, evaluate, and report on the status of processes whenever necessary.

- Enable users to associate controls in GRC Manager to control automations by implementing control automation integration.

- Oracle GRC Manager includes content management services to manage business process documents that must be monitored to ensure accurate risk assessment and control verification. All business processes are linked to business units (folders) in organization maps. For example, a business process document can be created for a payroll unit in the organization map, and the process will contain documented information on assertions, risks, controls, attachments, and test instructions. The following screenshot displays the InFission folder structure to maintain documents by process and maintain folders for each business unit where the process is performed:

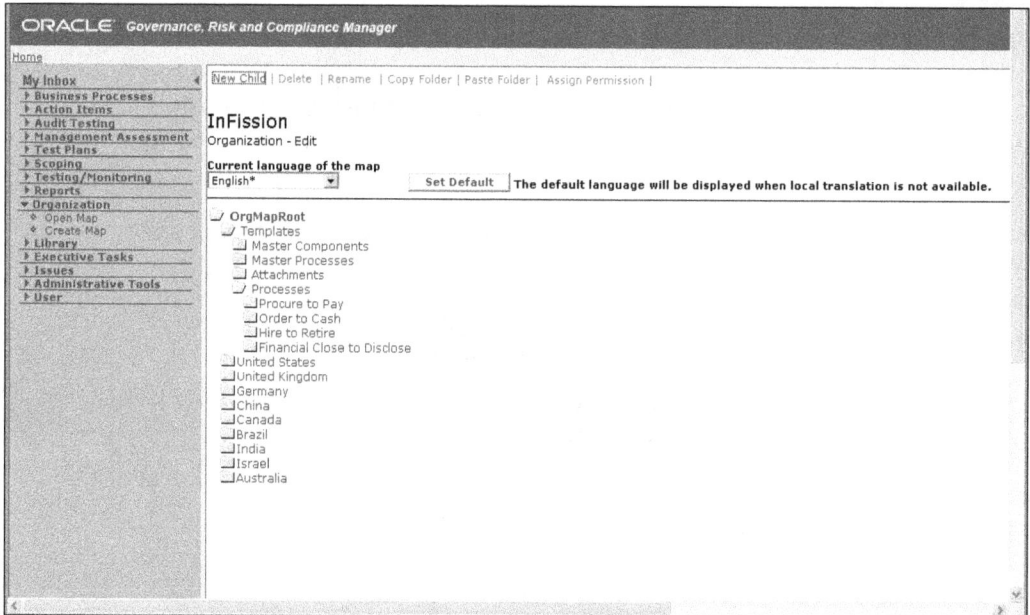

The user who creates or owns the business process can specify assertions, risks, controls, test instructions, and file attachments (flowcharts). Reviewers can review and approve the information, and testers can test the controls and save the test results in the business process documentation. All the information is tracked through the business process, which is linked to a unit in the organization map. When a user creates a report, the documents stored and tracked for an organization's business processes are searched to compile the required information.

All document types can be managed through Oracle GRC Manager. Documents are stored in a central repository (via Oracle Content Server) that provides version control, security, and automated actions that help to preserve, protect, and notify key individuals in the organization to ensure business process continuity. The document types are linked as follows:

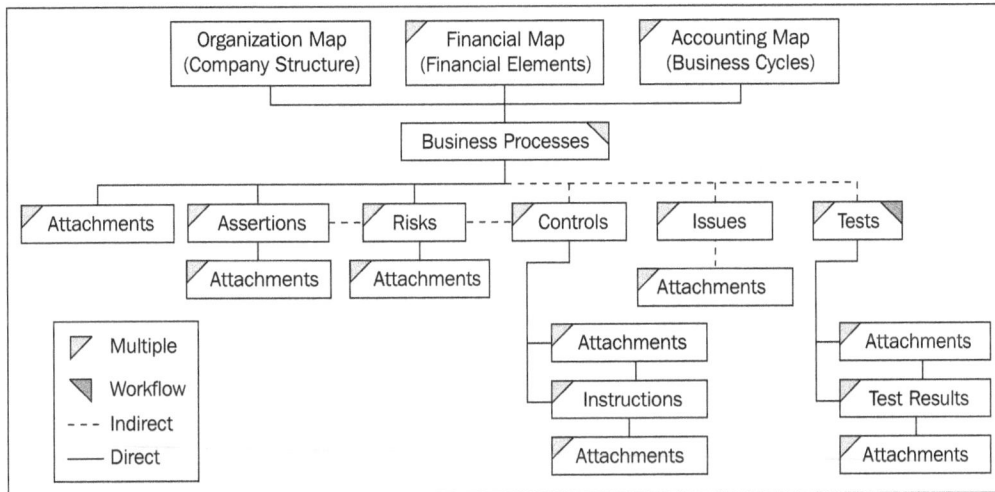

Creating a Business Process in Oracle GRC Manager

In order to create a business process in Oracle GRC Manager, carry out the following steps:

1. Select the **Business Processes** tray, and click on **Add New Process**.
2. The **Business Process Page** will be displayed with the **Basics** tab enabled.
3. Enter a title for the new business process.
4. Select the organizational location for the business process by clicking on the **Info** icon located next to the **Organization** textbox.
5. The **Organization map** screen will be displayed.
6. Select a location by navigating to the organization map and clicking on the appropriate location folder.

7. Click on the **OK** button.

8. Enter appropriate information for the fields in the **Basics** tab, as shown in the following screenshot:

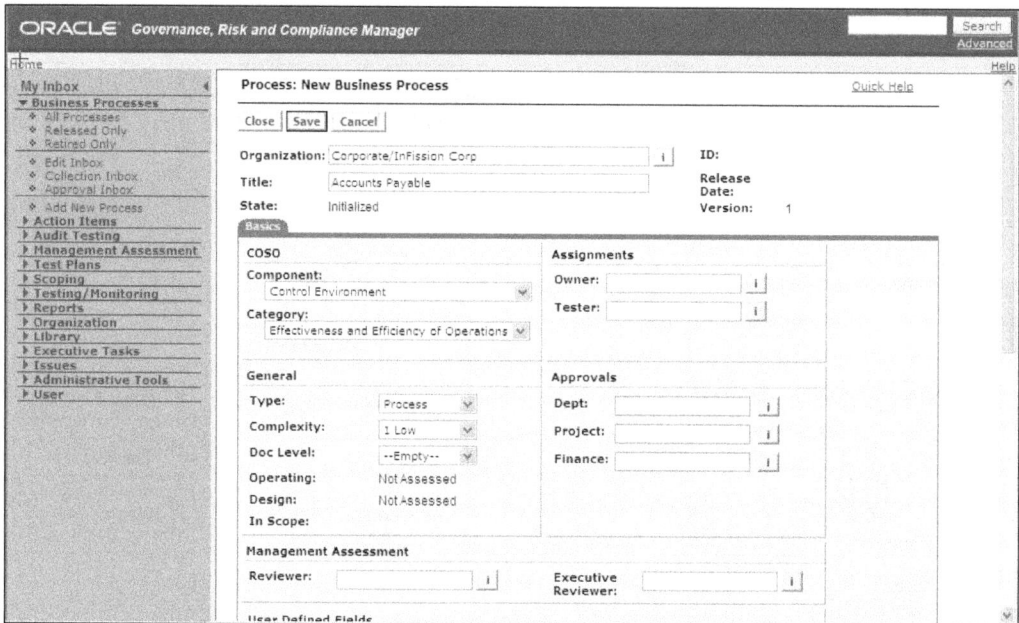

Document process narrative in Oracle Tutor

InFission uses Oracle Tutor to document process narratives. This tool automatically generates flowcharts when the narrative information is updated.

Oracle Tutor is used to document an organization's "people to people" activities, and the "what and when" level that is above how to use a business application. Oracle Tutor is a MS Word based suite of products that streamline writing, deploying, and maintaining procedures and supporting process documentation. By using Tutor pre-built model content during the blueprinting phase, process owners can collaborate and quickly document current state business practices, ensuring all aspects of each process are addressed.

Business process documentation developed with Tutor provides auditors with a transparent sustainable architecture of information that supports compliance.

A process narrative, authored in Oracle Tutor, provides necessary structure for audit walkthrough. The key components of the process narrative are shown in the example of the Accounts Payable – Month End Close process. The following screenshot shows the scope and policy that governs the process:

Scope

This procedure covers activities performed by the accounts payable department at the end of each fiscal month. These activities comprise:

- verifying accounts payable transactions posted to the general ledger

- purging records more than two years old

- estimating accrued accounts payable

> This procedure also covers all activities performed by the accounts payable department at the end of the fiscal year.
>
> This procedure does not cover reconciling accounts payable accounts. Refer to *Accounts Payable Month End Reconciliation [PR770220]*.

Policy

> **Standard costs** are used to determine inventory values.
>
> **Vendor invoices** reflecting prices that exceed purchase order prices will not be vouchered or paid.
>
> **Proof of delivery documents**, for example, vendor packing lists or purchase receipt tags, are filed and maintained by the receiving department only; they are not forwarded to the accounts payable department for filing and reference.
>
> **Purchase order** copies are filed by the purchasing department only; they are not forwarded to the receiving department or the accounts payable department for filing and reference.
>
> **Purchase price variances** are calculated and posted to the appropriate accounts as individual receipts are processed, rather than at the end of the month.
>
> **Financial liability** is recognized at the time materials and services are received, not when their corresponding invoices are vouchered; that is, inventory and expense accounts are debited at the time the receiving department enters a purchase order receipt transaction into the database.
>
> All **payment requests** including invoices

Next, the Tutor document provides the responsibilities of the **Accounts Payables Supervisor**, listing of roles that are included in the distribution of any changes to this document, and ownership of the process document:

Responsibility

The Accounts Payable Supervisor is responsible for

- preparing all journal vouchers pertaining to accounts payable transactions, accrued accounts payable, and adjustments for accounts payable aging reconciliations

- posting accounts payable transactions to the general ledger

- verifying current accounts payable aging

- updating vendor information

- deleting inactive vendors from the database

The Accounts Payable Clerk is responsible for

- locating and voiding missing checks

- correcting account distribution errors

The Controller is responsible for approving journal vouchers.

Distribution

Accounts Payable Clerk'

Accounts Payable Supervisor'

Controller'

Ownership

The Accounts Payable Supervisor [list@YourCompany.com?Subject=Accounts Payable Month End Close PR770219.doc] is responsible for ensuring this document is necessary, reflects actual practice, and supports corporate policy.

The **Ownership** section is followed by **Activity Preface**, **Prior Activity**, and the step by step activity for the process as follows:

Activity Preface

This activity is performed at the end of every fiscal month.

This activity is completed during the preliminary postings phase of the month end close of the general ledger.

This activity assumes that accounts payable journal transactions are automatically posted to the temporary general ledger. Accounts payable journal vouchers are posted in the general ledger according to the Close Schedule and the Standard Journal Voucher Log.

The Accounts Payable Transactions journal voucher is posted by the end of the first day following month end. The Accrued Accounts Payable journal voucher and the Adjustment for Accounts Payable Aging Reconciliation journal voucher are posted by the end of the third day following month end.

The Close Schedule shows the overall plan for closing the general ledger. The Standard Journal Voucher Log shows the specific journal vouchers to be posted and when they are posted. The Journal Voucher Responsibility Table shows who is responsible for each journal voucher. The standard journal voucher instructions show the requirements for completing each journal voucher.

Prior Activity

Establishing the Close Schedule [PR770314]

Accounts Payable Clerk

1. Determine whether any checks are unaccounted for.

Application Module Name
Report any checks unaccounted for.
Window Name

If checks are missing, goto task #2. Otherwise, goto task #4.

2. Locate the missing checks.

3. Void the missing checks.

4. Notify the Accounts Payable Supervisor that all checks are accounted for.

The flowchart for the **Accounts Payable Month End Close** process is automatically generated by Oracle Tutor, which is shown in the following figure:

Accounts Payable Month End Close

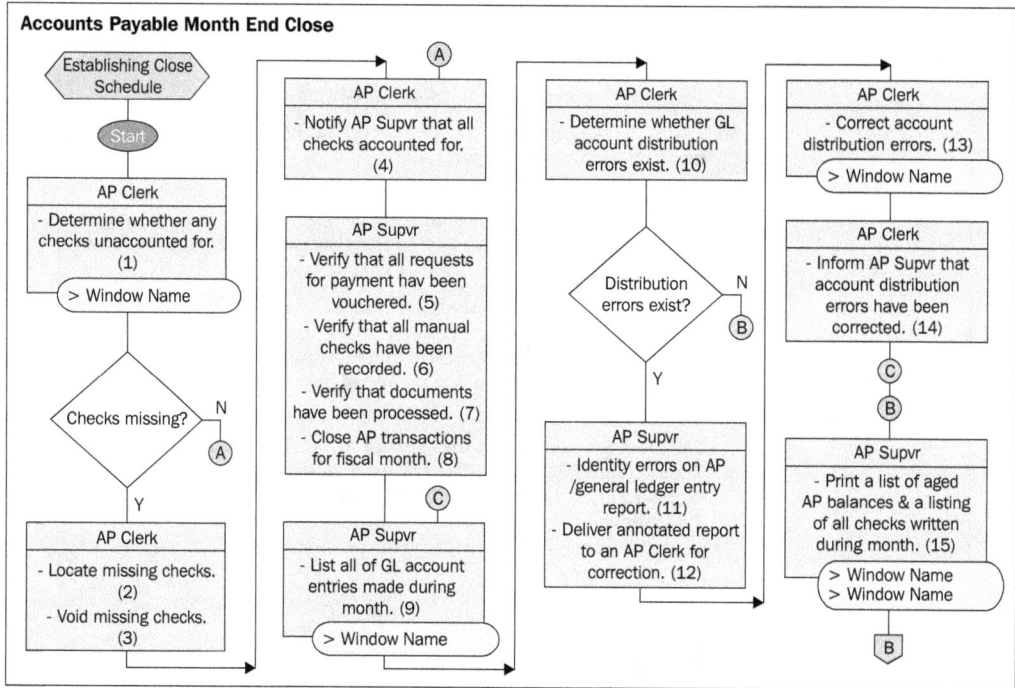

Risks and controls documents

A risk is a possibility of acts or events that could adversely impact an organization's business process. Risks also provide the source for designing the controls that mitigate damage, which could be caused by the risks and a control mitigates the potential damage from a risk for a specific business process. For each risk documented for a process, there must be a documented control. Controls provide a safety mechanism to ensure that all risks are addressed by documented responses that mitigate the risks.

Risks and controls documents are generally maintained as a matrix of each business process that link the risks to the business process and describe who, how, and when the controls mitigate risks. The matrix also contains detailed risk characteristics—such as likelihood, impact, and type—as well as controls characteristics—such as control objectives, frequency, type, and method. Control documents required for compliance with Sarbanes-Oxley Act also include control assertions that are linked to the Committee of Sponsoring Organization's (COSO) Integrated Internal Control Framework.

For example, the control elements of completeness, accuracy, authorization, safeguarding of assets, rights/obligations, and so on can be incorporated into activities within a process. The SOX compliance audit plan ensures the verification of controls incorporated into the processes being documented, mitigates the associated risk of financial statement misstatement, and ensures consistency with GAAP.

InFission approach to risk and controls documentation

Each department manager is also responsible for maintaining the risks and controls documentation in a similar manner as it is done for the Process and Procedure documents. However, the audit team provides risks and controls templates to the process owners who ensure that the controls are designed to meet InFission risk tolerance and control objectives. The biannual walkthrough of control documentations with each department also includes the review of the risks and controls matrix. In addition, as required by Sarbanes Oxley Act section 302, each process owner certifies that the controls are operating effectively and reports any issues to the audit team.

During the biannual control documentation walkthrough, the auditor and the process owner review any changes to the risk ratings, controls, and control test plans. Risk rating is a relative ranking of risk value, calculated as a product of the numeric values (1 through 5) from the **risk significance** and the **risk likelihood** values. InFission classifies risks into the following categories:

- Financial fraud
- Theft of assets
- Theft of services
- Regulatory compliance
- Breach of security

InFission auditor marks a control as a **key** if a failure of that control could cause a reasonable likelihood of a material error in the financial statements, which may not be prevented or detected on a timely basis.

Controls of lesser importance are classified as **secondary controls**. The secondary controls help the process owners mitigate a risk in the process in case the key control fails. InFission controls have the following frequency levels:

- Multiple times per day
- Daily
- Weekly
- Biweekly
- Monthly
- Quarterly
- Annually

InFission employs a continuous controls monitoring approach. The auditors also review the monitoring controls. Monitoring controls are a class of controls that track the status of one or more related controls. It is used for management assessment, for example, assessing a monitoring control and not assessing its related key control or related secondary control.

Managing risks in Oracle GRC Manager

Risks can be added to a business process when a process is initially created and also later when additional risks are identified. For each risk, there should be a control to mitigate the risk.

In order to create a risk, carry out the following steps:

1. Verify that the business process is in one of the following states **Initialized** or **Edit**.
2. Open the business process and click on the **Risks** tab.
3. A list of risks for the business process will be displayed. If there are no risks, the list will be empty.
4. Click on **Add Risk**.
5. The **BP Risk** page is displayed with the **Basics** and **Comments** tabs enabled.
6. Enter a title for the risk.

7. Select the appropriate attribute information in the fields for **Risk Significance**, **Risk Likelihood**, and **Risk Type**.

> Note that risks can also have file attachments.

8. Enter a description of the risk.

9. Enter the titles for any pre-existing assertions related to this risk in the **Related Assertion(s)** field, or by clicking on the **Info** icon next to the field to view a list of assertions that you can select.

10. If appropriate, click on the **Comments** tab and enter comments about the risk.

11. Click on **Save**.

If some fields are required and have not been filled in, a message will be displayed, informing you what fields are required. If all required fields have been filled in, or there are no required fields, the risk is entered into the system. If you do not want to save the changes, click on **Cancel** to undo the changes. If you click on **Close**, you will be prompted to save changes, and then the document is closed. The following screenshot will help you understand the steps we just discussed:

Managing controls in Oracle GRC Manager

Any user with permission to create or edit a business process can create a control. If the control ownership is enabled and a user has permission, a control owner can be assigned to a control. Controls can be created when a process is created, or added later as risks are identified and controls for those risks are required. Once a control has been documented, users can view the control and its values, description, comments, and documentation history.

You can specify that a control can be related to a specific risk in the same business process, using the **Related Risks** feature. Also, a control can be related to another control through the **Related Controls** feature on a **Control** page. This enables you to specify the type of relationship between controls (such as one control is a secondary control to another control).

One or more controls should exist for each documented risk in a business process.

In order to create a control for a business process, carry out the following steps:

1. Verify that the business process is in one of the following states **Initialized, Edit**, or **Collection**.
2. Open the business process.
3. The **Business Process** page will be displayed.
4. Click on the **Controls** tab.
5. A list of controls for the business process will be displayed. If there are no controls, the list will be empty.
6. Click on **Add Control** to open a new control document, as shown in the following screenshot.
7. The **BP Control** page is displayed with the Basics and Description tabs enabled.
8. Enter a title for the control.
9. Enter information in the fields.

> Note that controls can also have file attachments and references.

10. Click on **Save**:

For each control, test instructions are added to inform the user who tests the process controls about what test or tests to run on the control to check its accuracy and validity, and to verify that the control functions are documented. Test instructions can be created by any user with rights to the business process.

In order to add test instructions to controls, carry out the following steps:

1. Open the business process that has the control that you want to test.
2. Verify that the process is in one of the following states **Initialized**, **Edit**, or **Collection**.
3. If the process is in an **Edit** or **Collection** state, then verify that you are the current user.
4. Click on the **Controls** tab.
5. A list of controls for the business process will be displayed. If there are no controls, the list will be empty.
6. Select a control title.
7. The **Control** page will be displayed.
8. Click on the **Test Instructions** tab.
9. A list of test instructions for the control will be displayed. If there are no test instructions, then the list will be empty.

10. Click on **Add Test**.

11. The **Test Instructions** page is shown in the following screenshot with the **Basics**, **Comments**, and **Details** tabs enabled:

Managing control documentation lifecycle in GRC Manager

Control documentation must be reviewed periodically to evaluate the accuracy and completeness of business processes, narratives, flowcharts, risks, controls, and test plans. GRC Manager enables this review process through a **data collection workflow**. The Data Collection workflow provides the ability to route the process to specified users to update control documentation. Reviewers can also be added to this workflow to examine and approve updates to control documentation. In this section, we will describe the data collection workflow. There are additional workflows that support the control documentation lifecycle, which will be described in the subsequent chapters. A brief overview of these basic stages is as follows:

1. A GRC Manager Administrator or Business Processor Author creates a business process, documenting assertions, risks, controls, test instructions, attaching appropriate files, and assigning workflow reviewers for the process.

2. The business process is sent through a data collection workflow, where the process is routed to the process owner and reviewers to examine and to add or edit the documentation and provide data.

3. The business process owner revises the process documentation based on reviewer feedback. The owner then sends the process through an **approval workflow**, where the process is routed to reviewers to approve or reject the process. When the process is approved, it is released into the system and becomes active.

4. The business process is sent through a **testing workflow** to test the controls for the risks associated with the process. If any revisions to the process are necessary, then the process is sent through the approval workflow.

5. The business process owner can send a process through an **assessment workflow**, where the process, and its controls and risks are reviewed, and if appropriate, modified to improve its design and operational effectiveness.

6. If a business process or parts of a process become obsolete, the process owner or GRC Manager Administrator can retire a process or certain process documentation.

Workflows can be initiated for reasons and at times not included in this general lifecycle description. For example, a process test could result in an issue that the process owner would remediate then the process owner could initiate an approval workflow for the revised process or initiate an assessment workflow because the revised process has changed significantly. These additional workflows are explained in the subsequent chapters on management assessment and internal audit.

The following figure provides an overview of the basic stages of control documentation:

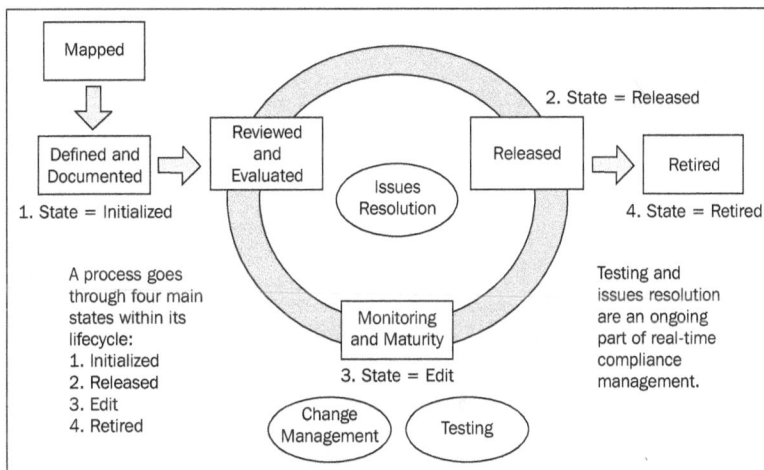

Use Data collection workflow to update documents

When a user with appropriate permission to a business process initiates data collection, the data collection workflow is started. The workflow routes the business process to users in the following order:

1. The process is initiated by the user with rights to the business process.

2. The process owner contributes documentation and approves or rejects the process.

3. The process reviewers examine the process documentation, and approve or reject the process.

4. A compliance reviewer examines the process documentation, and approves or rejects the process.

5. You can send a business process that is in the **Released** state for data collection by clicking on the **Data Collection** button on the process page, as shown in the following screenshot:

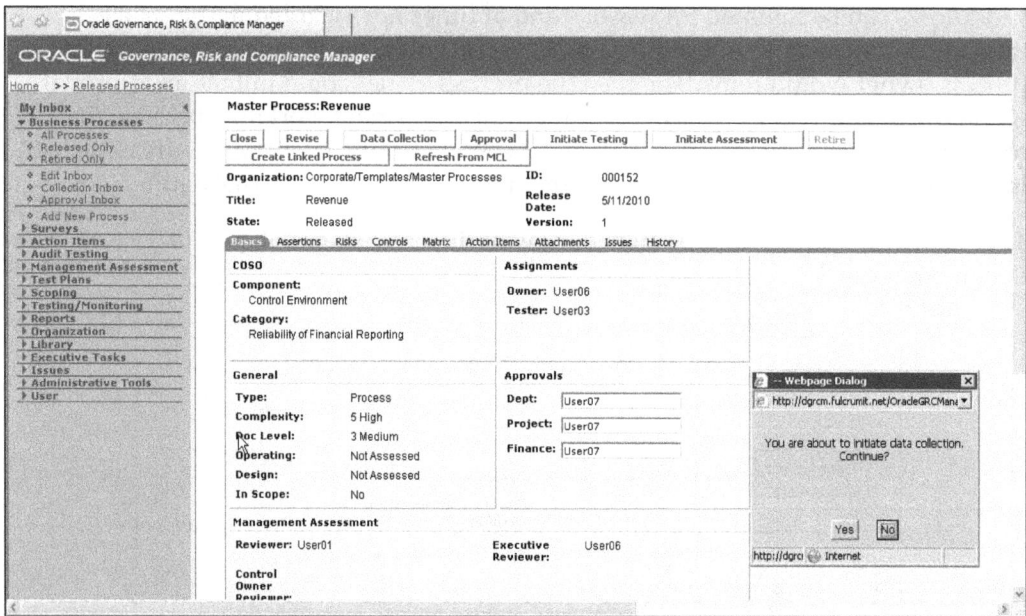

The following list summarizes the workflow steps:

1. A user with rights to a business process, usually an administrator (or someone in the audit department), initiates data collection.

2. An e-mail notification is sent to the assigned process owner, notifying the owner to enter the system and check their **Inbox**. The e-mail notification includes a link to the system that takes the user to the application login page.

3. The process owner opens the business process and contributes data for assertion, risk, control, test instruction, and attachment documentation. Then the owner either approves the process or rejects the process, which is shown in the following screenshot.

4. If the process is approved, it is removed from the process owner's **Inbox** and sent to the next step.

5. If the process is rejected, an e-mail is sent to the user who initiated the data collection, notifying them of the reason for rejection. The initiator can then choose to restart the workflow or delete the workflow.

6. An e-mail notification is sent to the assigned reviewer(s) who are responsible for reviewing data for assertion, risk, control, test instruction, and attachment documentation for the business process. The e-mail notification includes a link to the system that takes users to the application login page.

7. The users review each assertion, risk, control, test instruction, and attachment document. When finished, reviewers either approve or reject the process.

8. If the process is approved, it is removed from the reviewer's **Inbox** and sent to the next step.

9. If the process is rejected, the reviewer enters a message explaining why the process was rejected, and the message is sent to the process owner to modify the process documentation.

10. An e-mail notification is sent to the workflow initiator (usually an administrator or someone in the audit group), notifying the user to enter the system and check their inbox. The e-mail notification includes a link to the system that takes the user to the application login page.

11. The workflow initiator is the final reviewer. The user reviews the assertion, risk, control, test instruction, and attachment documentation, and approves or rejects the business process. The user can change any of the documentation to ensure its integrity and validity.

12. If the process is approved, its status is changed to **Released**, the system is notified, and the process is removed from the data collection workflow.

13. If the process is rejected, the user enters a message explaining the reason for the rejection, and the message is sent to the process owner to modify the process documentation.

Contributing to a process

When a data collection workflow is initiated, an e-mail is sent to the business process owner with a notification to log in to the system and check their **Inbox**. A link is provided from the e-mail to the system. Clicking on the link takes the user to the application login page.

The business process owner can now add and edit documentation for processes, risks, controls, test instructions, and attachments, such as flowcharts and narratives, for a process.

In order to contribute documentation to a process, complete the following steps:

1. From the application navigation panel, select **My Inbox** or **Business Processes**.

2. Click on the title of the process to which you want to contribute data.

3. Select the tab for the assertion, risk, control, or attachment that you want to add and enter or edit the information. Enter or revise as many assertions, risks, controls, or attachments as needed.

4. When you are finished entering data for the process, click on **Approve**.

5. A confirmation prompt is displayed.

6. Click on **Yes**.

7. The data for the process is saved in the system and the business process page is displayed.

8. Click on **Close** to close the process page.

The process is removed from the business process owner's **Inbox** and sent to the next step in the workflow.

Reviewing data for a process

After the data collection workflow has gone through the process owner contribution step, it is then routed to reviewers. One or more users are notified by e-mail, one at a time, to review the business process and documentation. The number of reviewers depends on how many reviewers have been set up and assigned for the business process. A link is provided from the e-mail to the system. Clicking on the link takes the user to the application login page.

Each reviewer can perform the following actions:

- Review a process in data collection review
- Approve a process in data collection review
- Reject a process in data collection review

Reviewing a process in data collection review

Reviewers of a business process can review documentation for the process, risks, controls, test instructions, and attachments, such as flowcharts and narratives of a process.

In order to review a process and its documentation in the data collection workflow, complete the following steps:

1. From the application navigation panel, select **My Inbox** or **Business Processes**.

2. Click on the title of the process that you want to review, as shown in the following screenshot:

3. Review the process and its documentation. Select tabs to view the process details, risks, controls, and attachments.

4. When you are finished reviewing the process and its data, you have two choices, either click on the **Approve** button to approve the changes to the process or click on the **Reject** button to reject the changes to the process, as shown in the following screenshot:

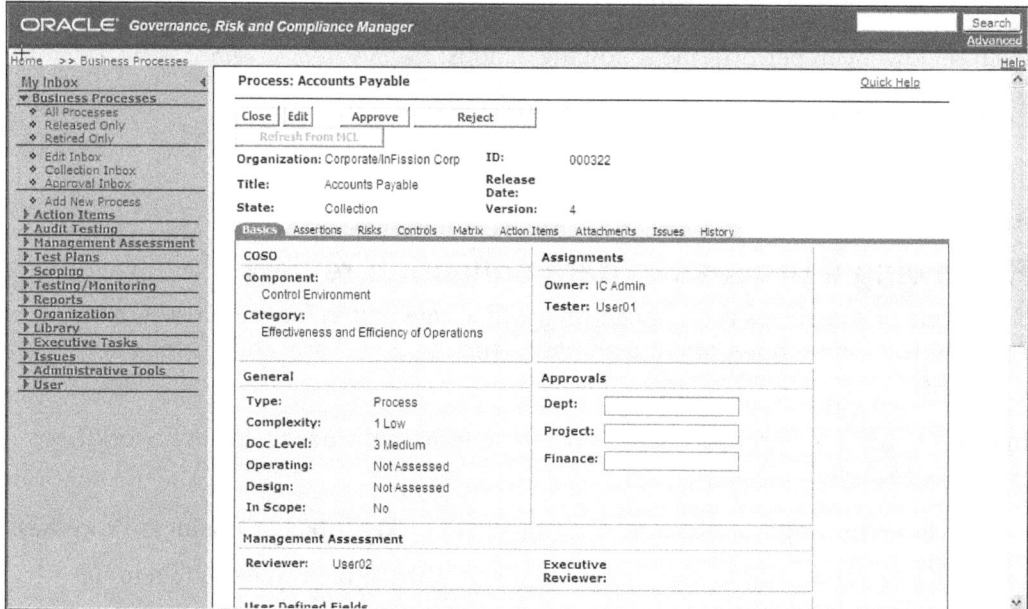

The preceding screenshot shows a process **Accounts Payable** that is currently in the **Collection** state waiting to be reviewed and approved (or rejected) by the owner.

Approving a process in data collection review

After the reviewer has finished reviewing the business process and its associated documentation, the reviewer can click on the **Approve** button to notify the system that the reviewer approves of the business process and its documentation.

In order to approve a business process in the process collection workflow, complete the following steps:

1. On the **Open Business Process** page, click on **Approve**. A confirmation prompt is displayed.

2. Click on **Yes**. The process is removed from the user's **Inbox** and sent to the next step in the workflow.

Rejecting a process in data collection review

After the reviewer has finished reviewing the business process and its associated documentation, the reviewer can notify the system that the user has rejected the business process and its documentation.

In order to reject a business process in the process collection workflow, complete the following steps:

1. In the open process page, click on **Reject**.
2. A reject message window is displayed.
3. Enter a reject message.
4. Click on **Yes**.

An e-mail is sent to the process owner within the workflow notifying them of the reason for rejection.

Canceling changes to a process

If the process is rejected by the owner back to the workflow initiator, the initiator can reset the process and all its supporting documentation (including assertions, risks, controls, and attachments) back to the original version before it entered the data collection workflow.

In order to cancel changes in a business process in the data collection workflow, complete the following steps:

1. On the **Open Business Process** page click on **Delete Workflow**.
2. A confirmation prompt is displayed.
3. Click on **Yes**.

The Data Collection workflow is canceled, all new revisions of documents are restored to their previous version, and the process and its supporting documentation are set to their previous state (Initialized or Released).

Summary

In this chapter, we have provided details to help you create and maintain control documentation by following best practices to manage key components of control documents such as process, procedures, risks controls, and business units. We have explained how Oracle GRC Manager and Oracle Tutor can be used to streamline this key process that is critical for internal audit, risk management, and compliance.

You can determine the accuracy and completeness of your organization's control documentation by starting with the review of process narratives, policies, and flowcharts. Next, you can examine the risks, and register for processes and controls that mitigate these risks. Many organizations maintain a **Risk and Controls Matrix** to make the association with each significant process easier. There may be variances in business process, risks, and controls by the business unit that are important to understand. These variances can occur due to regional business practices, variations in the business segments, or differences in systems. Your control documentation should be organized by business units to ensure that these variations can be managed for audit and compliance.

GRC Manager can enable you to track and manage control documents by providing content management function to check-in check-out functions with audit history and secure workflows to ensure that the documents are reviewed and updated periodically. Many organizations prefer to use a content management system because spreadsheets and word processor documents are prone to errors and inaccuracies when multiple employees have to share and maintain the documents. Oracle Tutor can help you improve the time it takes to create process documents by automatically generating the flowcharts based on the process narratives. This feature alone can save you hundreds of hours in creating and maintaining process documents. When a process is changed, you simply edit the narrative in your word-processor and Tutor will reflect the change in the flowchart.

7
Managing Your Testing Phase: Management Testing and Certifying Controls

In the previous chapter, we learned the techniques used to develop and maintain the controls documentation that is essential to test and certify controls. After completing the controls documentation as described in the previous chapter, you can begin testing the design and operating effectiveness of internal controls. There are two major methods for testing internal controls: **Management testing** and **Independent testing**. In this chapter, we will describe the Management testing uses, approach, and techniques that are a critical phase of a governance, and risk and compliance-program. Management testing is often included in the audit plan for control self-assessment. Management testing is also required by compliance regulations, such as Sarbanes-Oxley for asserting controls over financial statements, and it is an important part of the Enterprise Risk Management program.

Management testing for internal audit program

Many organizations start the control testing phase of the audit plan by asking process owners and controls owners to assess the risks and evaluate the internal controls before conducting the independent audit. This process, commonly referred to as the **Control Self-Assessment (CSA)**, is defined by the **Institute of Internal Auditors (IIA)** as "A process through which internal control effectiveness is examined with the objective of providing reasonable assurance that all business objectives are met."

The assessment process can help auditors to improve the effectiveness of overall audit plan. Employees that manage the process and monitor related control activities have deeper knowledge of risks and controls. The auditors can facilitate the management self-assessment of the risks and controls within a business process without comprising the independence as long as the auditor maintains the management testing records as the evidence of the process, risks, or controls assessed by management.

In addition to evaluating many aspects of the internal control system, auditors can use CSA to gain a better understanding of the organizational policies and procedures, which helps gain a better understanding of the internal control system, and to assess all types of risks such as inherent risks and residual risks.

Management testing for Regulatory Compliance Audits

The growing regulatory compliance requirements have set higher expectations for management evaluation of internal controls. For example, under the Sarbanes-Oxley act of 2002, Public Company Accounting Oversight Board (PCAOB)'s Auditing Standard (AS) 2 was established, which gives guidance of special interest contained in the document named as "An Audit of Internal Control over Financial Reporting Performed in Conjunction with an Audit of Financial Statements." The AS 2 audit requires that financial statement auditors audit and attest to the fairness of management's assessment of their internal control system over financial reporting.

Many organizations have implemented the Committee of Sponsoring Organizations (COSO) controls framework to comply with this audit standard. Management plays a key role in the effective implementation of all aspects of this framework's controls including environment, risk assessment, control activities, information and communication, and monitoring. For example, management can help evaluate the control environment by assessing entity level controls such as tone at the top and code of conduct. Such controls are often reflected in an employee's perception of management's behavior and attitudes that can only be evaluated using employee interviews and surveys.

Management testing can improve the quality and efficiency of compliance audits. For example, an employee survey of internal controls questionnaire can produce a highly corroborated evidence of controls effectiveness when many employees responsible for the business process can identify changes in policies, procedures, and control activities over the period under audit. The independent auditors can use the survey results to better assess risks due to procedural problems, identify ineffective controls, and processes.

This can help in developing an effective test plan for evaluating significant processes and key control activities at the selected locations within the organization in order to meet compliance audit objectives. Control self-assessment improves the efficiency of independent controls testing by enabling the independent auditors to use the control testing work papers obtained from the management testing. This testing approach is supported by AS2, which states that the higher the degree of **competence and objectivity** is reflected in the work of others, the greater the auditor may make use of that work. AS2 specifically groups **self-assessment programs** with the activities of the internal audit function and the audit committee as controls designed to monitor and evaluate other internal controls. Therefore, independent auditors can increase the efficiency of their testing activities by utilizing a CSA program to obtain control evaluations from the employees that are directly involved in monitoring the control activities. Such employees are often referred to as **Control Owners** and have a better understanding of the control for which they are responsible. The aggregate results of this larger group of control owners can help auditors form a more objective opinion of the overall control environment.

Management testing for Enterprise Risk Management

The **Enterprise Risk Management (ERM)** is an integrated framework, which was also developed by Committee of Sponsoring Organizations of the Treadway Commission in 2004 (COSO 2004). Unlike COSO Internal Controls framework, management takes a top down view of the risks, which guide the business unit's heads and department managers to set objectives, rate risks, and determine responses to risk. Under this framework, top management sets the objectives to achieve the desired outcomes, for example, be recognized as a market leader in innovations, achieve certain income level from operations, comply with laws and regulations, and provide a nurturing workplace to employees. Many organizations that have adopted this framework require management to test the controls, once the risks are assessed and mitigating controls are identified. The Enterprise Risk Management process is applied across the organization and it is designed to help identify risks to provide reasonable assurance that an entity is able to meet its business and financial reporting objectives. Once the objectives are established, management identifies both internal and external events that could prevent the organizations from achieving these objectives, such as emerging global competition, customer credit risks, or employee theft, that have a likelihood to negatively impact the organization's ability to achieve its objectives. Next, the management determines its options to respond to the risks by establishing the appropriate level of controls that can mitigate these risks. Once the controls are designed, periodic management testing provides the assurance that the operations within specific business units and departments have necessary controls to meet the business objectives.

InFission's approach to management testing

InFission utilizes management testing to support the internal audit, compliance, and Enterprise Risk Management programs.

The internal auditor team uses the findings management testing to develop the scope for the independent audit plan. A control self-assessment questionnaire is distributed to the management that identifies the status of controls effectiveness over the audit cycle. The auditors only facilitate this process and never participate in responding to this survey to preserve their independence. While the auditors do not rely solely on the results of the survey to determine the effectiveness of the controls, the results of the survey are used to determine the scope of the audit plan to focus on significant process changes, emerging risks, organizational changes, and other issues reported by management. Auditors also use the results of the control self-assessment to determine the qualitative assessment of controls such as the complexity of process activities, fraud risks, the spreadsheets that are used to record accounting information, the need for employee training to perform their jobs, and factors that affect the financial statements.

The auditors establish the inherent risk levels based on the evidence obtained from management responses to the controls survey. This approach enables the auditors to optimize the effectiveness of independent controls testing and efficient use of audit resources.

As a publically listed company on NASDAQ, InFission complies with the Sarbanes-Oxley Act (SOX). As a part of the SOX 404 compliance program, management testing approach is used to evaluate the overall control environment including the code of conduct and the tone at the top. An internal controls survey is distributed to management to obtain information such as the effectiveness of communications with the board of directors and the audit committee, management style, organization culture, employee competency, and human resources policies and practices.

In addition to including management in the testing of controls for internal audit and SOX compliance, InFission has also implemented a controls testing program to support its ERM initiative. The management has adopted the COSO-ERM framework to improve the overall strategic planning process. Once the enterprise risk assessment is completed based on the survey of management and a series of workshops facilitated by the internal audit team, management control testing is performed by business process owners and management that includes an in depth review with marketing, engineering, product development, and production operations.

The internal controls are assessed by the employees within each functional area of the business that is included in the scope of management testing. Upper management reviews and certifies the controls assessed by employees. The company uses electronic survey tool, which includes the questionnaires to elicit data about controls, risks, and processes. This process helps in improving the management's visibility to risks and controls throughout each business unit and improves the efficiency and effectiveness of business operations.

Management testing using Oracle GRC Manager

InFission utilizes the **survey and assessment** tools in Oracle GRC Manager to perform all management testing of internal controls. The **GRC Survey tool** is used to assist the internal audit team to determine the scope of an independent audit plan. The **GRC Assessment tool** is used to obtain the evidence of key controls over financial statements to comply with Sarbanes-Oxley Act. The assessment tool in GRC Manager also enables business process owners and management reviewers to assess the validity and effectiveness of controls that mitigate enterprise risks under the ERM framework established by management.

Using GRC Survey tool to determine the scope of audit plan

The audit team uses the survey tool in GRC manager to assist in gathering the evidence of controls to help build an effective audit plan. Surveys are created from survey templates. Surveys include the following components:

- A set of users (called **Responders**) who must respond to the survey
- The time frame during which users can respond
- Instructions on how to respond

Managing surveys in GRC manager includes the following tasks:

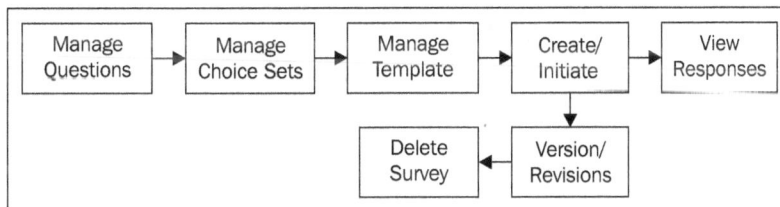

```
┌─────────────────────────────────────────────────────────────────────────┐
│  ┌──────────┐   ┌──────────┐   ┌──────────┐   ┌──────────┐   ┌──────────┐ │
│  │ Manage   │→  │ Manage   │→  │ Manage   │→  │ Create/  │→  │ View     │ │
│  │ Questions│   │ Choice   │   │ Template │   │ Initiate │   │ Responses│ │
│  │          │   │ Sets     │   │          │   │          │   │          │ │
│  └──────────┘   └──────────┘   └──────────┘   └──────────┘   └──────────┘ │
│                                      ↓                                    │
│                 ┌──────────┐   ┌──────────┐                               │
│                 │ Delete   │←  │ Version/ │                               │
│                 │ Survey   │   │ Revisions│                               │
│                 └──────────┘   └──────────┘                               │
└─────────────────────────────────────────────────────────────────────────┘
```

Managing survey questions

Carry out the following steps, in order to manage survey questions:

1. From the **Navigation** menu, select the **GRC Tools** menu and click on the **Manage Survey Questions** link.

2. Enter a question **ID** and select the format of the question. Now enter the question text in the **Question Text** textbox and set the **Status** to **Active**, as shown in the following screenshot:

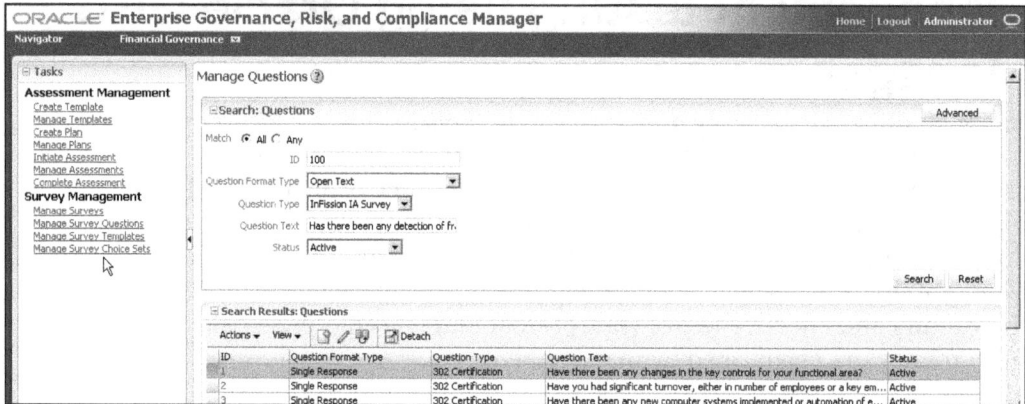

The format type for the question identifies how the responses to the question are presented. Your choices will be as follows:

- **Single Response**: These are radio buttons that present multiple options, only one of these can be chosen.

- **Single Response with Other, Please Specify**: These are radio buttons that present multiple options, only one of these can be chosen. One of the options is **Other, Please Specify**, which includes a text field where the respondent can enter an alternate choice.

- **Single Response Drop Down List**: A list of values that presents multiple options, only one of which can be chosen.

- **Multiple Choices**: These are checkboxes that present multiple options, from which respondents can select multiple options.

- **Multiple Choice with Other, Please Specify**: These are checkboxes that present multiple options, from which respondents can select multiple options. One of the options is **Other, Please Specify**, which includes a text field where the respondent can enter an alternate choice.

- **Multiple Choice List Box**: A scrolling list box that allows users to select multiple values.

- **Rating on a Scale**: These are radio buttons that represent a range of values. For example, if the question is, "How often do you use this tool?". The values might range from always to never.

- **Numeric Allocation**: This presents multiple options to which the respondent enters a number to quantify each option for the question. For example, if the question is, "What percentage of your monthly minutes do you allot for the following features on your cell phone?", then the answers must be equal to 100 percent. The values might be e-mail, texting, voice, and GPS, and the user is expected to enter a number for each option.

- **Open text**: This is a textbox into which the respondents can enter free-form text.

The GRC Manager Survey Tool provides choice sets which contain appropriate answers to the questions. You can specify an existing choice set or create a new one. If you choose an existing choice set, you can edit it to suit your needs. For example, you can select a choice set that contains the values **Yes** and **No**, and create your own value of **Maybe**, or you could select the choice set of **High**, **Medium**, and **Low** and delete **Medium**. You can then save any new combination of answers as another choice set for use in the future.

Managing survey choice sets

Choice sets are a collection of answers to be used as a shortcut for completing questions. For example, a choice set could contain the answers: **I agree**, **I Disagree** or **High**, **Medium**, **Low** or **Yes**, **No**. The answers could be appropriate for a very large number of questions. Using choice sets provides reusability of answers as well as consistent recognition to the same answer across questions.

1. From the **Navigation** menu, select the **GRC Tools** menu and click on the **Manage Survey Choice Sets** link.

2. Select the **Create** option from the **Actions** menu, as shown in the following screenshot:

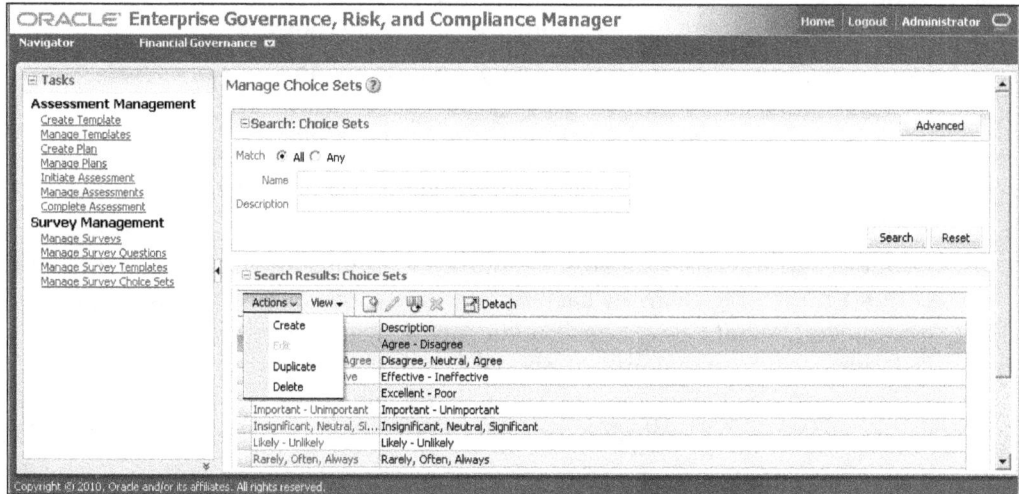

3. Enter the **Choice Set Details**: Enter the **Name**, **Description**, and **Choices**:

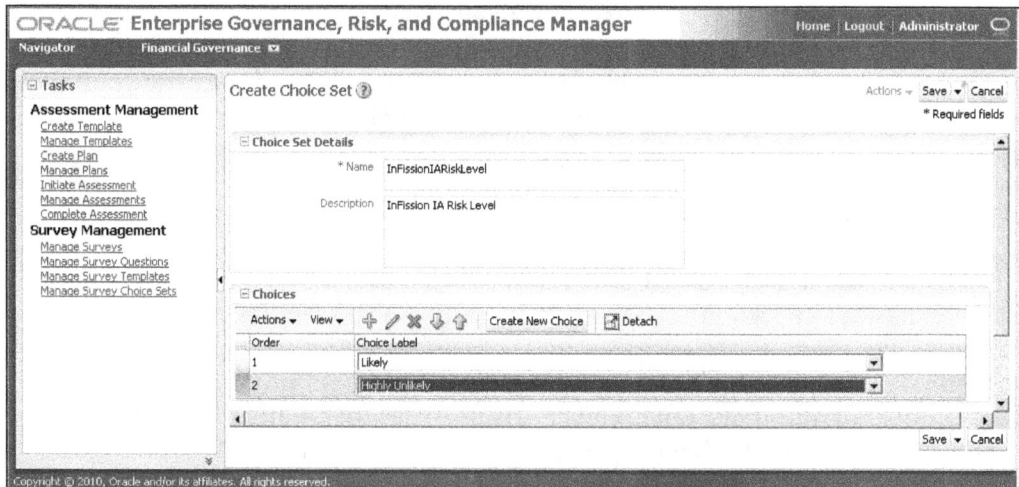

Managing survey templates

Survey templates are used to help maintain reusable survey questionnaires. InFission maintains templates for all recurring surveys including SOX 302, Fraud Risks, and ERM assessment. These templates ensure consistent survey results across the InFission enterprise.

Carry out the following steps in order to create templates in GRC Manager:

1. From the **Navigation** menu, select the **GRC Tools** menu and click on the **Manage Survey Choice Sets** link. Select the **Create** option from the **Actions** menu, as shown in the following screenshot:

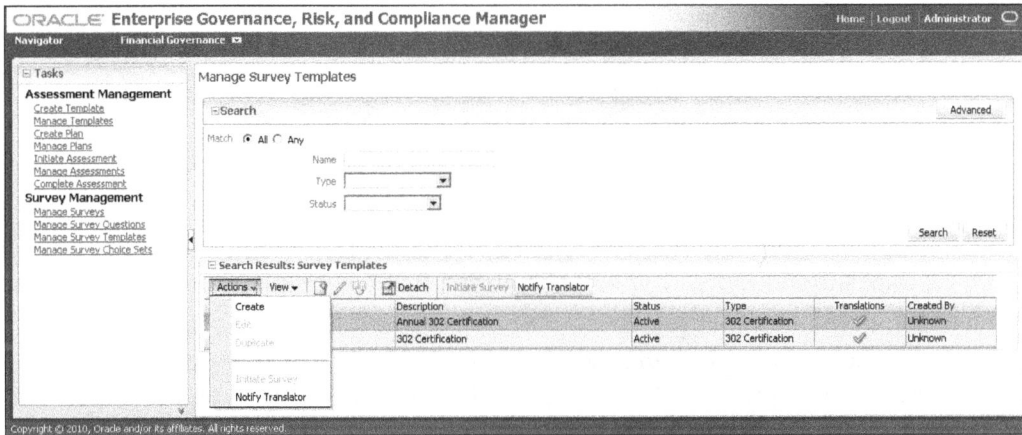

2. Next, enter the **Name**, **Description**, and **Type** for the template and enter the **Respondent Instructions** in the **Details** tab, as shown in the following screenshot:

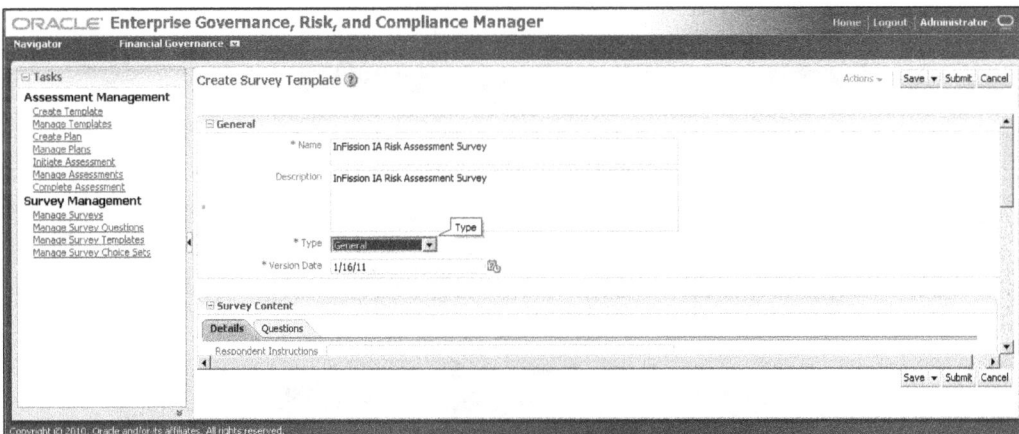

The **Type** of the survey will determine what the survey will be used for. For example, the survey types may include financial compliance, SOX 302 certification, internal audit, ERM, general, or any other types that you may need to create.

The survey type will also determine:

- Do respondents require any special instructions for filling out the survey?

- Will the template have to be translated, and, if so, into what languages?

- Options include the languages that your installation is using. Note that this field is informational only, translation is not automated, and it is a manual task performed by the translators.

- What questions are parts of the survey? You can create new questions or reuse existing questions.

- How do you want the survey displayed? You can format the survey by inserting page breaks at any point.

- Which delegates are required? For surveys templates, you can specify a translator delegate, who will be notified that the template needs to be translated.

- Is the survey template what you expect it to be? Use the **Preview** button to verify that the format and layout of the questions are as you intended.

Adding questions to a survey template

You can add questions to a survey template by following the given steps:

1. Click on the ⊞ icon under the **Questions** tab, as shown in the following screenshot:

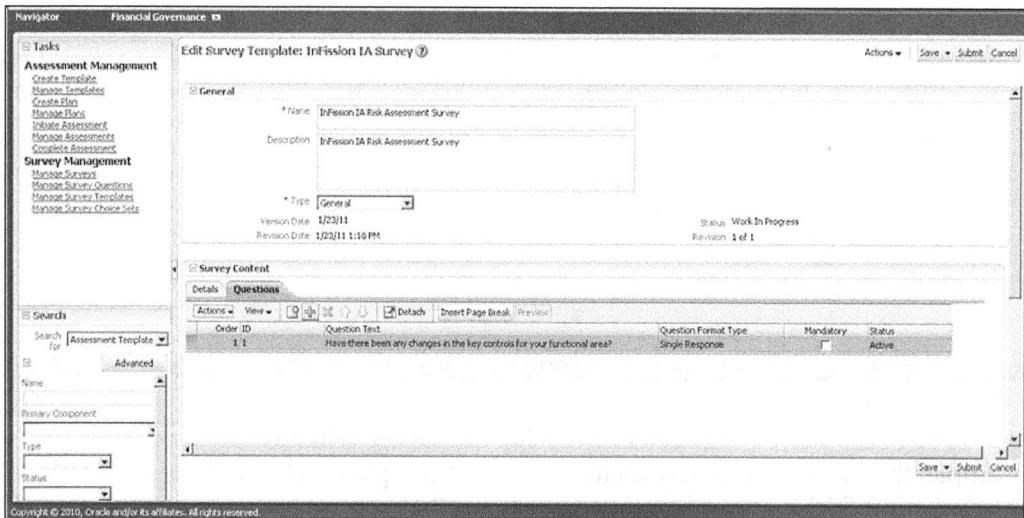

2. Add the question from the list.

3. You can make the questions mandatory by checking the **Mandatory** flag.

Once the template is created, you can save it by clicking on the **Save** button. Changes can be made to the survey template by selecting the **Edit Definition** option under the **Actions** link next to the **Save** button.

You can also preview the survey by selecting the **Preview** option under the **Actions** link next to the **Save** button.

Deleting a survey template

You can only delete a survey template when it is in a **new** state. Once the survey is **active**, it cannot be deleted. When a survey template is deleted, the template is no longer available. However, the questions that are associated to it are not deleted and all historical data remains.

Survey templates can be retired while they are active. However, you cannot retire a survey template if there are surveys that use the template that are open to collect responses. Once a survey template is retired the assessment owner (and any other upstream delegates who have some type of an association to the survey) receives a notification that is displayed in the **Pending Activities** section of the dashboard or **Overview** pages. For example, if a survey owner retires a survey, any business owners who are using the survey for an assessment are notified.

Survey translations

You can specify that a survey template, including the questions associated to the survey, should be translated. Once a survey is translated, the system displays the survey based on the respondent's language preference. If the survey is not translated into the respondent's preferred language, it is presented in the base language of the installation.

Creating and initiating a survey

Carry out the following steps in order to create a survey:

1. From the **Navigation** menu, select the **GRC Tools** menu and click on the **Manage Survey** link. Select the **Create** option from the **Actions** menu, as shown in the following screenshot:

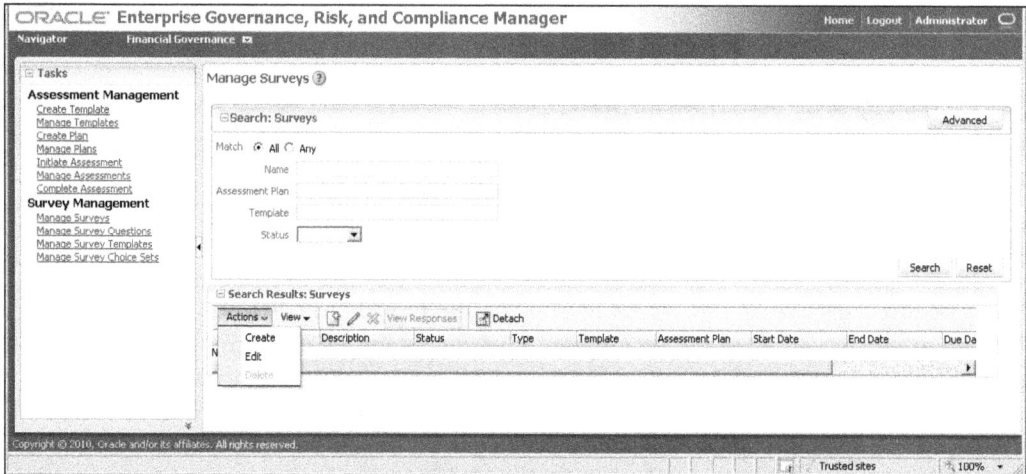

2. Next, select a template. (Insert after the InFission survey template is active):

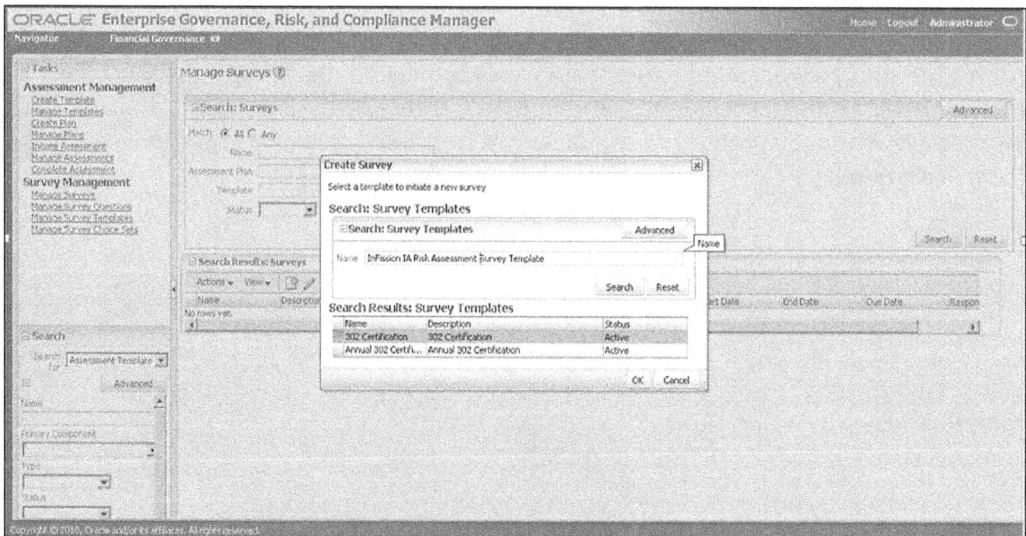

3. Enter the **Survey Name** and **Component Name** (Risk Controls, Process, and so on) and select the **Start Date**, **End Date**, and **Component Type**.

4. Select the **Respondents**.

When initiating the survey, you must decide the following things:

- When should this survey be completed? An end date is required, but you can edit the date and extend the survey period if needed.

- Is this survey associated with a component type?

- Is this survey associated with a specific component?

- Which users need to respond to this survey? You can choose individual users or you can select from an existing list. You can also save the respondents list for future use.

Once you have submitted your survey, the only edits you can make to it are the end date and respondent list.

Completing a survey

If you are designated as a survey respondent, the survey appears in your work-list. In order to complete the survey, select the survey and click on the **Edit** icon. Once you have submitted the survey, the originator can view your responses via the **Survey Management** page.

GRC Manager assessments

InFission utilizes the Oracle GRC Manager Assessment tool to obtain the evidence of key controls over financial statements to comply with Sarbanes-Oxley Act. The assessment tool in GRC Manager also enables business process owners and management reviewers to assess the validity and effectiveness of controls that mitigate enterprise risks under the ERM framework established by management.

Components such as risks and controls require periodic review of how they are defined and implemented to ensure that the appropriate levels of documentation and control are in place.

Assessment Management in GRC Manager includes the following tasks:

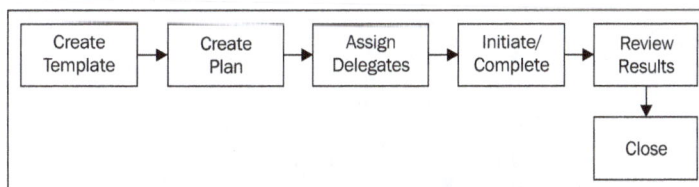

```
Create      Create      Assign       Initiate/     Review
Template -> Plan   -> Delegates -> Complete -> Results
                                                  |
                                                  v
                                                Close
```

Creating the assessment templates

An **assessment template** is a collection of assessment activities. Assessment templates also display user-defined component relationships and their related assessment activities.

Carry out the following steps in order to create an assessment template:

1. From the **Navigation** menu, select the **GRC Tools** menu and click on the **Create Template** link under the **Assessment Management** task.

2. Select the **Create** option from the **Actions** menu.

    When creating an assessment template, consider the following aspects:

    ° For which application module will the template be used?

    ° What is the primary component that will be assessed?

    ° What type of assessment will be performed? For example, you might need to prepare financial year end or financial SOD assessments.

    ° What activities will be performed during this assessment?

    ° Who will be responsible for performing each activity?

3. Select the activities as per your requirement.

    Depending on the component you have added, you can choose activities such as **Audit Test**, **Operating Assessment**, **Design Assessment**, or **Certify**.

4. Now, assign the **Delegates** to the template:

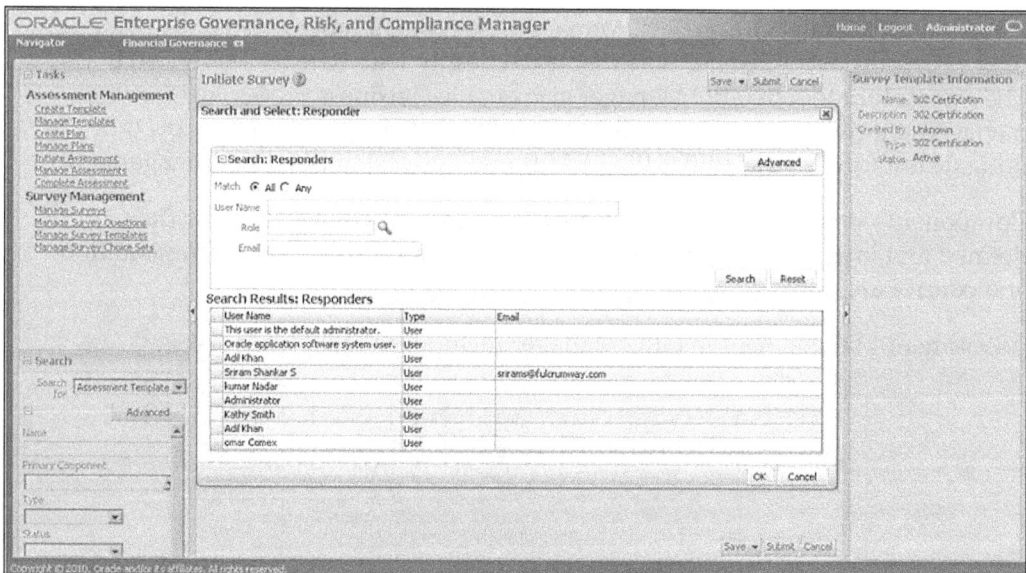

For risks, controls, and GRC components, **Delegation Responsibility** can be selected for the assessor. The reviewer and approver are determined by the delegation model that is associated with the object. **Assessor Responsibility** is a required field. The list of available assessor responsibilities are determined by the delegation model assigned to the object. For example, the **Risk Delegation Model** may have separate assessor responsibilities for each activity such as:

- Audit assessments
- Risk assessment
- Certify

Creating an assessment plan

Carry out the following steps in order to create an assessment plan:

1. From the **Navigation** menu, select the **GRC Tools** menu and click on the **Create Plan** link under the **Assessment Management** task.

2. Select the **Create** option from the **Actions** menu, as shown in the following screenshot:

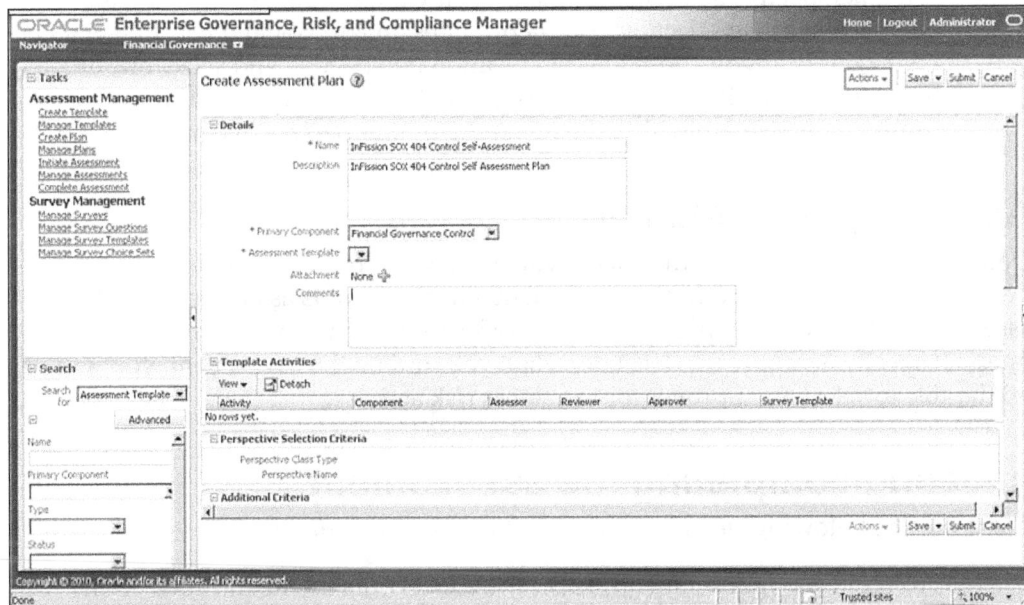

An assessment plan is used to specify, which components will be used in an assessment. The assessment plan references the assessment template, which is a collection of assessment activities to be used, including additional assessment criteria. Templates can be applied to multiple assessment plans. When you initiate an assessment, you can indicate, which plan to use. You can use assessment plans repeatedly to initiate and complete new assessments.

When creating an assessment plan, consider the following:

- With which component will this plan be associated?

- Which assessment template will this plan use? The options that you have to choose from are dependent on the component that you choose, and you can only select active templates.

- Does this plan require a survey template to be attached? A survey template can be included on any assessment activity for components.

- What selection criteria do you want to specify? This determines what will be assessed for the component that you chose. If you do not select any criteria, everything associated with your component will be assessed. However, selecting criteria limits what will be assessed.

- What perspective selection criteria do you want to specify? Entering a perspective in the selection criteria provides an additional filter of the data. For example, if you chose the organization perspective and select one of the child items within it, the assessment will only include the assessment components that are within the hierarchy of that perspective node.

Assigning the delegate

Delegates are assigned from the list of available **owner**, **reviewer**, and **approver** delegates that are specified in the assessment template that is associated with the assessment plan. For example, if the assess risk activity in the associated template does not specify an approver delegate, when you initiate the assessment, you will not be able to select an approver for the assess risk activity.

Initiating/completing the assessment

Carry out the following steps in order to initiate an assessment:

1. From the **Navigation** menu, select the **GRC Tools** menu and click on the **Initiate Assessment** link under the **Assessment Management** task. Select the **Create** option from the **Actions** menu.

When you initiate an assessment, you select an active assessment plan and choose the assessment activities that will be performed. If a survey template is associated with assessment activity, a survey is initiated. You can schedule an assessment's due date and modify the delegates that have been assigned to the assessment activities during the creation of the assessment plan. You can also review and override individual objects from the assessment plan selection criteria.

When initiating an assessment, consider the following:

   ° Which assessment plan will be used for this assessment? The assessment plan contains the criteria for the assessment activities that are associated with the assessment template.

   ° What activities need to be performed? For example, will this be an audit test or an operating assessment?

   ° What selection criteria are needed for this assessment? The assessment administrator who initiates the assessment can refine the plan selection criteria.

   ° What components will be assessed? The components that you can choose from are based on the information model's primary component and are filtered depending on the application module.

   ° What delegates are required? If the activity is of type Survey, the owner is the component owner, not the assessor.

Initiating an ad-hoc assessment

As part of managing objects such as risks, controls, and GRC components, you can create ad-hoc assessments. Depending on the object you are creating, you can perform some or all of the following assessment activities:

- **Operational assessment**: Enables the reviewer to determine if the object is operating effectively and as designed. It answers the question: "Is the object operating effectively and as designed?"

- **Certification**: Certification is part of the assessment process. All resources that have an active role in the accuracy of the assessment are typically required to provide an answer to the certification statement and provide supportive comments to their answer. It answers the question: "Is the information in this assessment accurate and complete to the best of my knowledge?"

- **Design review**: Enables the reviewer to determine if the object is designed effectively and meets the objectives. It answers the question: "Is the object designed effectively and does it meet the objectives?"

- **Audit test**: Enables the reviewer to test if the object meets audit guidelines. Resources follow the audit guidelines that have been defined by the corporation. It also answers the question: "Does this object meet audit guidelines?"

- **Documentation update**: It enables the reviewer to determine if the object has the appropriate documentation required.

Completing the assessments

You can complete an assessment by selecting **Complete Assessment** task from the task list on the **GRC Tools** page. This invokes the **My Assessments** page, from which you can:

- Create an issue for the assessment

- View the hierarchy associated with the assessment

- Drill on the component to view details

- Click on the **Complete** button to complete the assessment

You can also complete an assessment via the **Manage Assessments** page, from the **Assessments** tab of an object, or from the work list on your home page.

Assessments are displayed as long as the assessment plan is active, even if you have completed it. The owner is the only person who can close an assessment.

Reviewing the assessment results

The following assessment options are available to the reviewer for design, operating, and audit test assessments:

- **Pass**: The object is operating properly to mitigate the risks.

- **Pass with exception**: The object is operating properly to mitigate the risks with noted exception.

- **No Opinion**: The reviewer has reviewed the object but does not have a definite answer of pass or fail.

- **Failed**: The object does not operate properly to mitigate the risk. The assessment fails and you are presented with the option to create an issue within the workflow.

The following options are available to certify assessments:

- **I agree with this statement**: The delegate completing the certification agrees that the information in the assessment is accurate
- **I agree with this statement with the noted exception**: The delegate completing the certification agrees that the information in the assessment is accurate with noted exceptions
- **I do not agree with this statement**: The delegate completing the certification does not agree that the information in the assessment is accurate
- **No Opinion**: The delegate completing the certification either cannot or chooses not to make a statement regarding the assessment

The following options are available to reviewer for documentation update assessments:

- **Complete**: The required documentation is complete
- **No Action**: The documentation is sufficient and no additional action is required

Closing an assessment

Only the assessment owner can close an assessment. In most cases, this happens either when the due date is reached or when all of the individual assessments within the initiated assessment batch are completed.

Summary

In this chapter, we have described the management testing process, approach, and automation. Management testing is a key component of the governance, risk and compliance programs at many organizations. Management testing can improve audit plan effectiveness, make regulatory compliance more sustainable, and align Enterprise Risk Management with strategic objectives. Managers of a process and related controls can be included in developing the scope of the annual audit plan by asking them to assess the risks and evaluate the internal controls based on their deep knowledge of risks and controls. Employees can be interviewed and surveyed to support many aspects of growing regulatory compliance requirements, such as Sarbanes-Oxley, by asking them to share their perception of management's behavior and attitudes towards company level controls such as tone at the top and code of conduct. Management testing can also help identify risks and provide reasonable assurance that an entity is able to meet its business and financial reporting objectives under an Enterprise Risk Management (ERM) framework.

8
Managing Your Audit Function

An **audit function** is essential in providing an independent opinion, as to the effectiveness of the internal controls to the board of directors and stockholders. Managing internal audit function requires a combination of internal and external audit resources. Many organizations establish an independent internal audit department headed by the Chief Audit Executive (CAE), who directly reports to the chairperson of the audit committee. In addition, the board of directors also retains the external auditors to provide an independent audit opinion. The audit management function includes planning, design walkthrough, testing, reporting, issue/remediation, and close activities. In this chapter, we will describe the key activities of the audit management process, share an approach for management of audit activities, and provide examples to automate the audit management function.

Audit planning

The planning phase includes establishing the scope and objectives of each audit engagement. The plan document also includes budget, timeline, and resources assignments to perform the audit.

Once the audit plan is established and approved by the audit committee, the CAE communicates the audit scope and objectives to the business manager.

This communication also outlines the key audit tasks, such as a formal meeting with the managers, controls documentation requests, and other necessary audit steps.

InFission audit planning approach

At InFission, the CAE establishes the audit plan, which is approved by the Audit Committee. The CAE ensures that the internal audit resources are appropriate, sufficient, and effectively deployed to achieve the approved plan by communicating the resource needs to senior management and the board in the audit plan. The CAE is responsible for maintaining the audit standards, policies, and procedures.

InFission audit plan includes several audit engagements to address the audit objectives, such as:

- Independent opinion of internal controls based on risk assessment
- Management assertions of controls over financial statements to comply with Sarbanes-Oxley Act
- IT audit to provide assurance over management information systems

The CAE communicates the audit plan objectives, guidelines, and standards to the Audit Directors. Each Audit Director is responsible for managing audit engagements, reviewing the audit activities, and approving the audit results. The CAE requires formal documentation from the audit directors, which includes management interview responses from risk assessment meetings, risk rating criteria, and audit tasks details for work plans within the scope of the engagement.

Each Audit Director prepares a detailed engagement work plan, which includes the objectives of the engagement, scope of the engagement in terms of risks, processes, controls, and test plans. The audit work plan describes the audit task details and procedures for gathering, analyzing, and documenting test samples. An opinion framework is established to interpret the test results and categorize the findings. The Audit Director also determines the audit period covered and estimated completion dates.

The work plan also includes resource level requirement details for the engagement to identify the auditors that will perform specific audit tasks based on the complexity of the audit, internal audit activities, and requirement for direct supervision. The auditors are assigned to the work plan based on their audit experience, understanding for the business area, technical knowledge, language skills, and accounting as well as audit expertise. Audit resources include employees, external auditors, financial managers, and GRC software tools for testing IT-enabled controls.

The CAE ensures that the skills, experience, and technical knowledge of the resources assigned to the each audit engagement are appropriate for the planned activities before approving the engagement. The CAE also ensures that resources are deployed effectively to audit the geographically dispersed business units based on the localized risk ratings.

Once the audit engagement is approved by the CAE, any modifications, as appropriate, during the engagement require a formal approval by the CAE.

Next, the Audit Director communicates the audit engagement information to the managers that are responsible for risks, processes, and controls within the scope of the engagement. The managers need to know about the engagement targeting their area of responsibility so that they can prepare the necessary documentation and participate in the scheduled audit meetings. The management is informed of the engagement objectives, scope of work, resource requirements, and timelines. Management is notified of any key factors impacting conditions and operations of the business area within the audit scope, including any changes in internal and external environment.

The level and frequency of communications during the audit engagement is based on the audit communication and reporting policies established by the CAE.

Managing audit plan using Oracle GRC Manager

The InFission Chief Audit Executive (CAE) and Audit Directors use Oracle GRC Manager to manage audit plans. GRC Manager supports key audit management activities, such as documenting the objectives of the engagement, selecting the controls, mitigating risks within each business process in scope, and so on. Audit Directors create detail audit work plans in GRC Manager to document the audit task details for collecting, reviewing, and documenting test samples. The test evaluation framework is also maintained in the application to manage the test results and categorize the findings. All audit plans are approved by the CAE using the workflows in GRC Manager.

Managing audit plans in GRC Manager consists of the following steps:

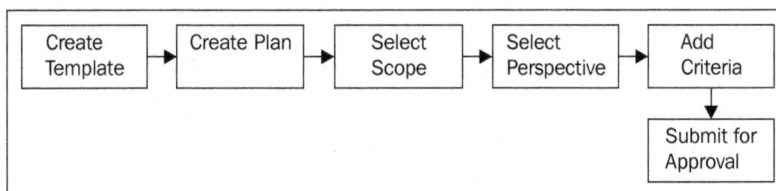

Create Template → Create Plan → Select Scope → Select Perspective → Add Criteria → Submit for Approval

Creating the audit template

Audit templates are useful in maintaining a library of reusable audit plans. Before you create an Audit Plan, you can create an Audit Template in GRC Manager as follows:

1. From the **Navigation** menu, select the **Assessment Management** menu and click on the **Create Template** link, as shown in the following screenshot:

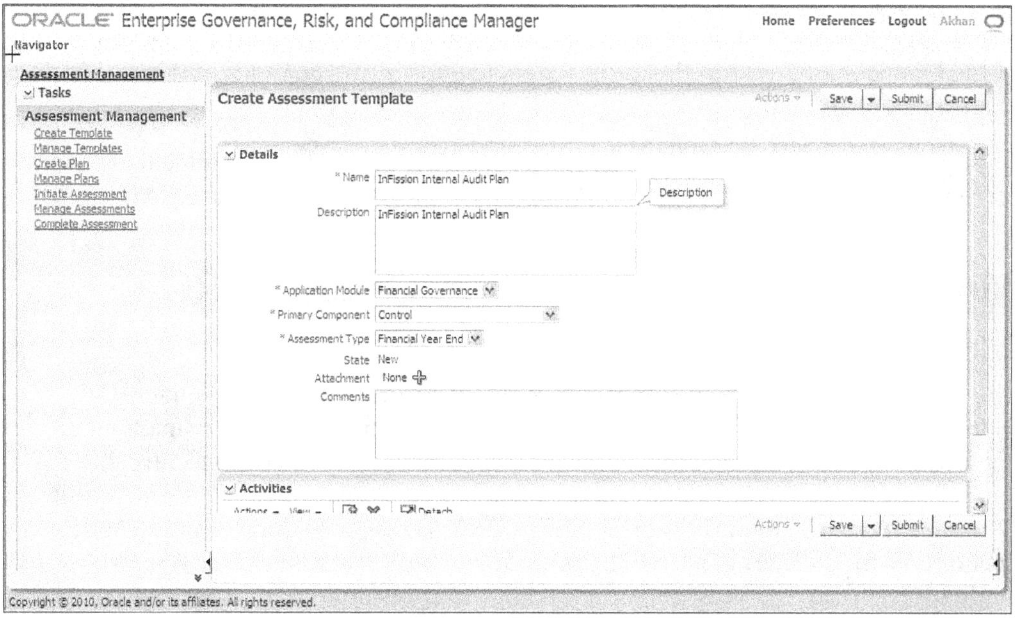

2. Enter the name and description in the respective textboxes.

3. Select the module that is appropriate for the type of the audit. For example, the Financial Governance module contains all the necessary components for the COSO framework that support common internal audit programs.

4. Select **Financial Year End** as the **Assessment Type** for this audit template. This option will enable the necessary GRC component for controls testing.

5. Select **Audit Test** as the activities to support the controls testing work plan, as shown in the following screenshot:

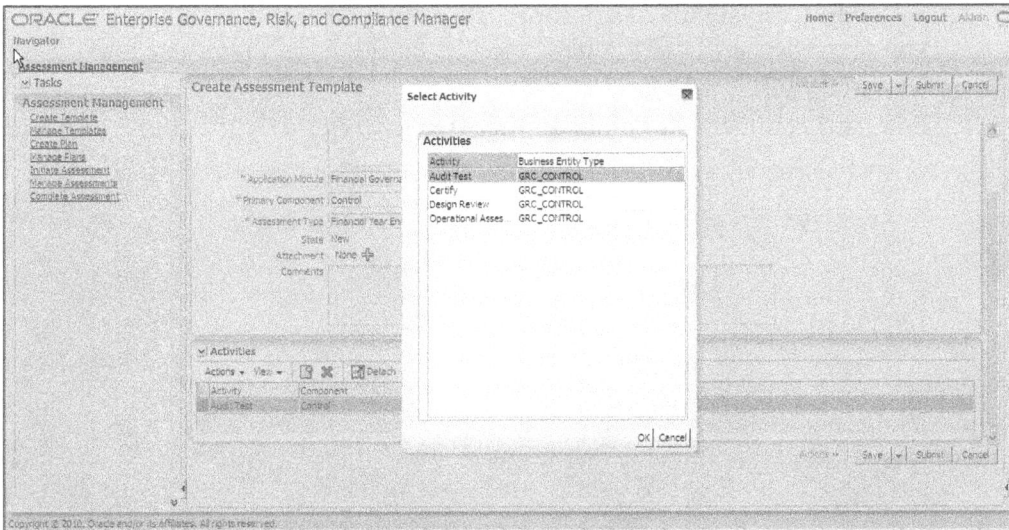

Creating the audit plan

1. From the **Navigation** menu, select the **Assessment Management** menu and click on the **Create Plan** link, as shown in the following screenshot:

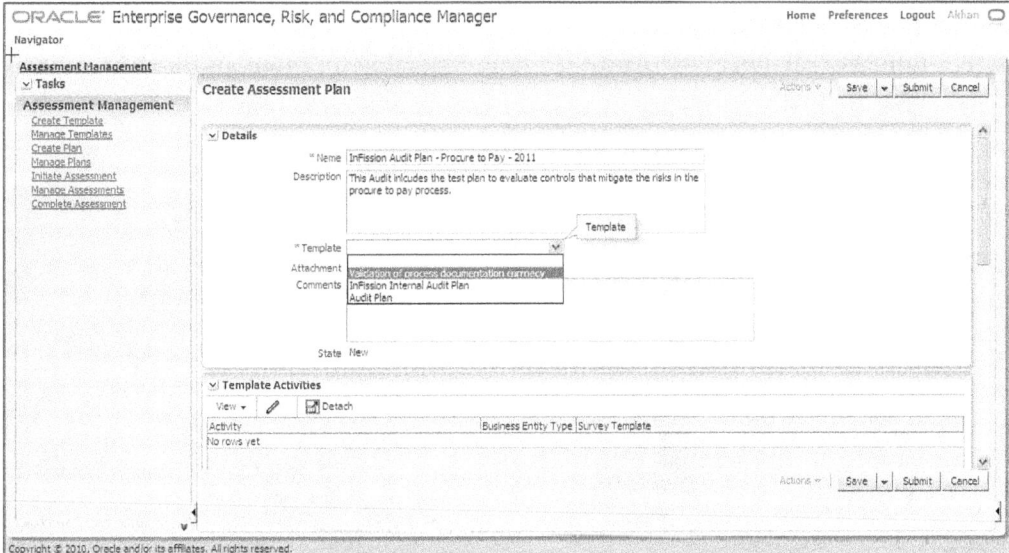

2. Enter the name and description in the respective textboxes.

3. Select the template that is appropriate for the type of the audit. For example, you may select a COSO template for SOX audits, and IT template for IT General Controls testing.

4. Enter any comments for other auditors to view regarding this audit.

5. Select controls in scope by clicking on the **Selection Criteria** section.

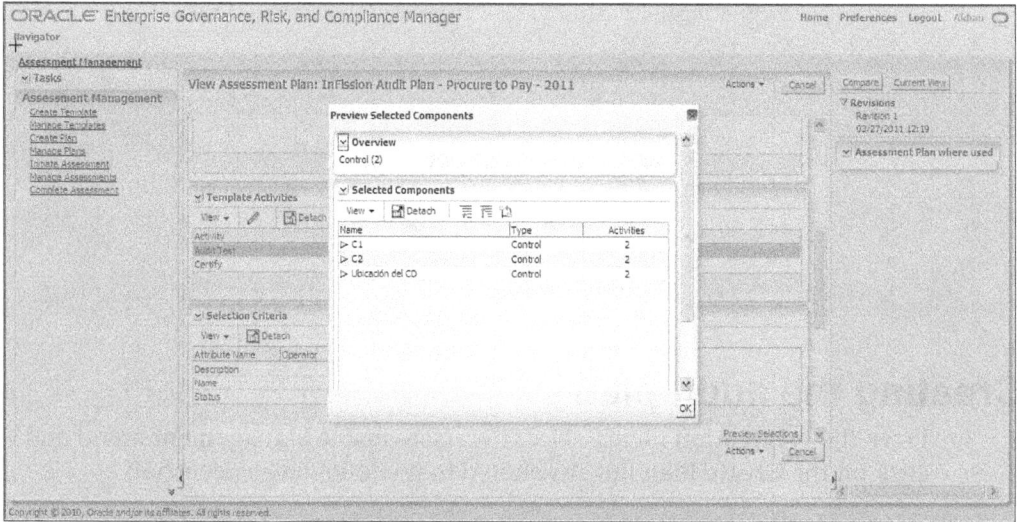

6. Enter comments in the **Audit Comments** dialog for other auditors to view them:

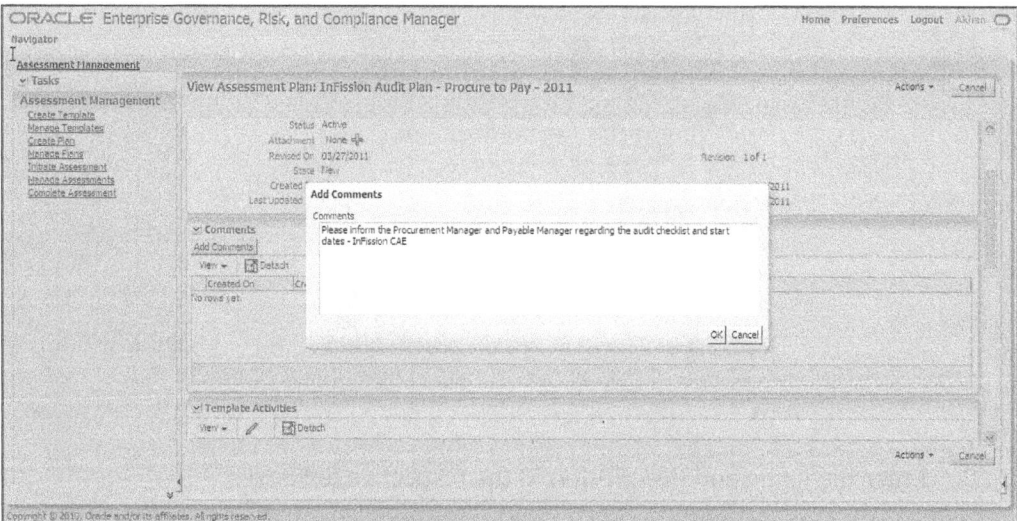

7. Select the *perspectives* that will be used as the framework for the audit plan. For example, select the COSO components for financial statement audit:

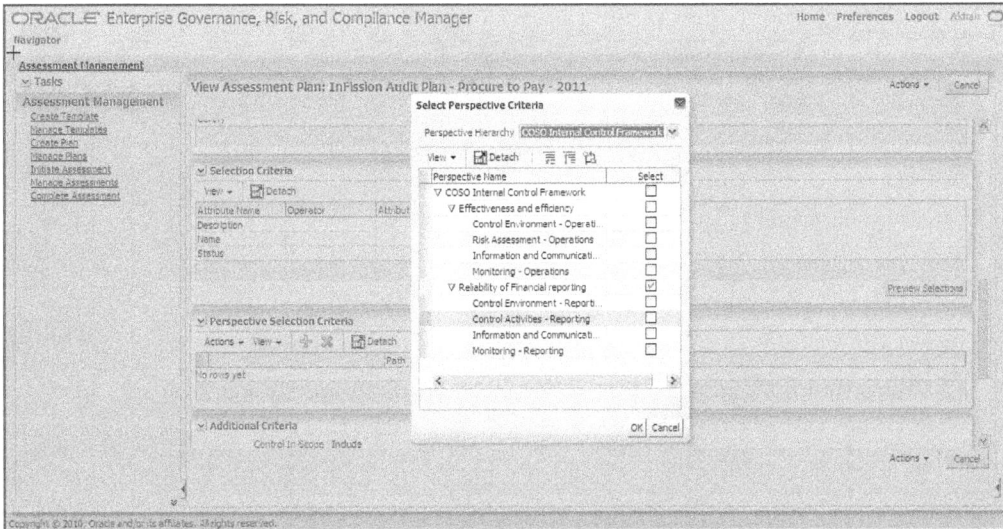

8. Specify any additional selection criteria as needed to further scope what controls will be assessed or audited based on the audit objectives. For example, you can use the selection criteria to select just the key controls for a SOX audit. If you do not select any criteria, all control will display for selection into the assessment scope:

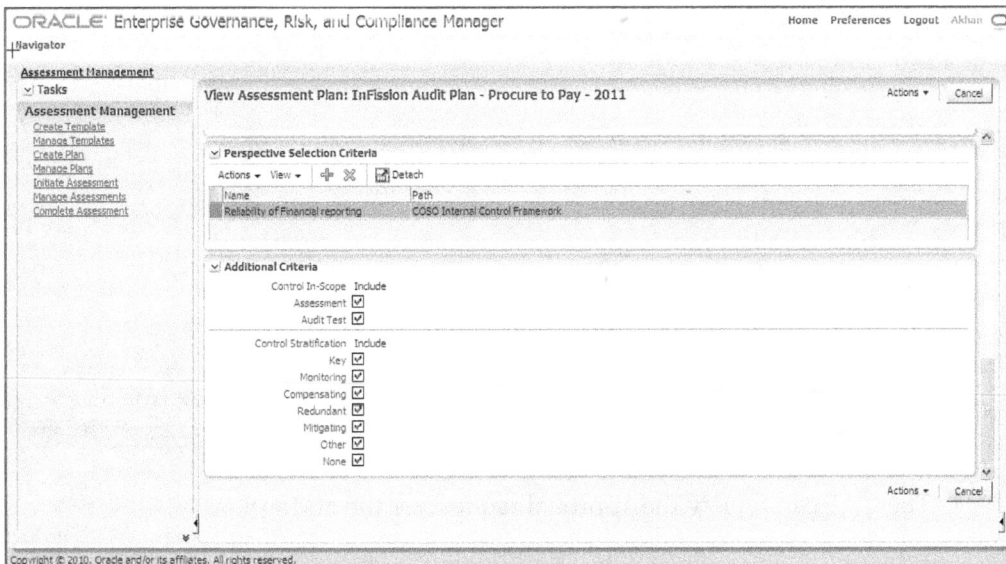

9. Save and submit the audit plan for approval:

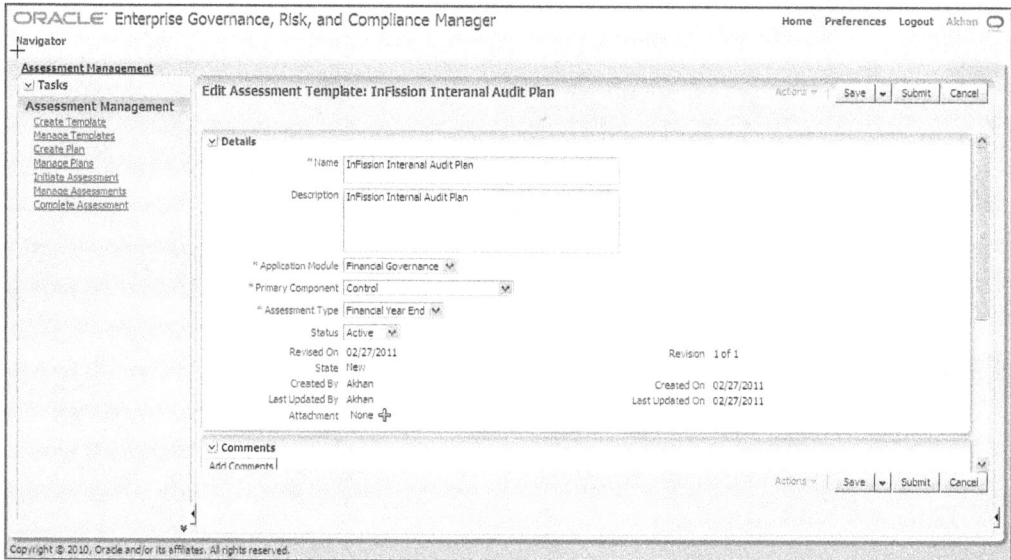

10. The CAE will receive the approval request in the worklist, as shown in the following screenshot:

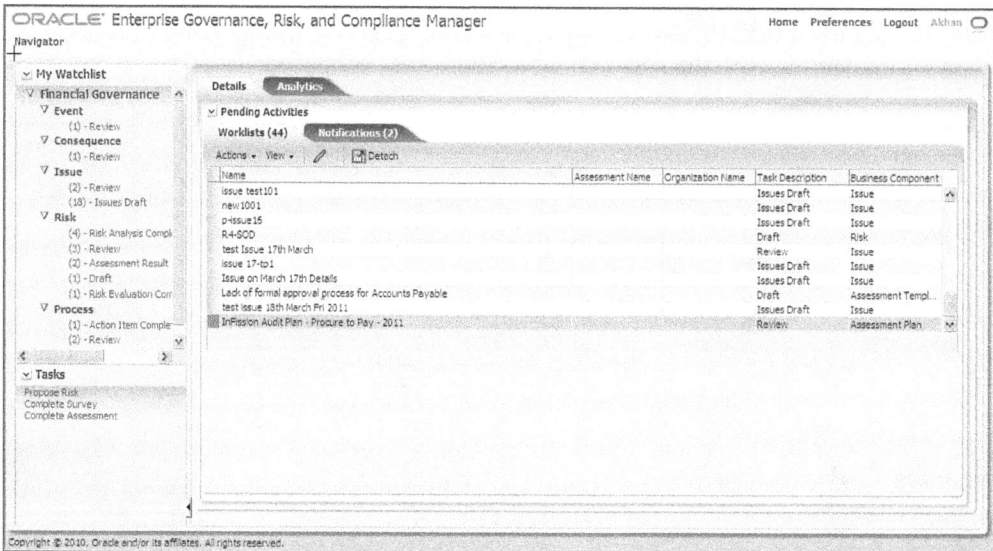

11. The CAE can review the approval request for the audit plan:

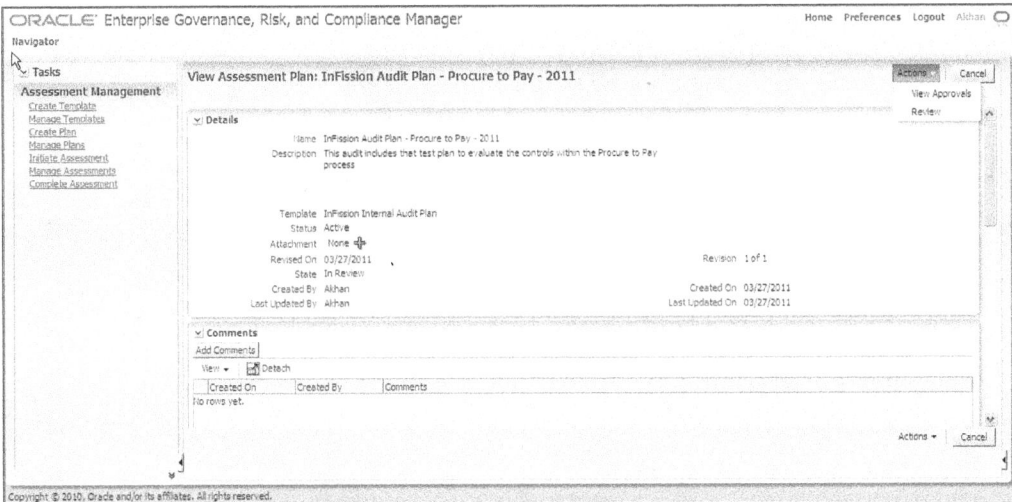

12. The CAE selects the **Accept** option from the **Actions** drop-down and enters his comments to approve the new audit plan:

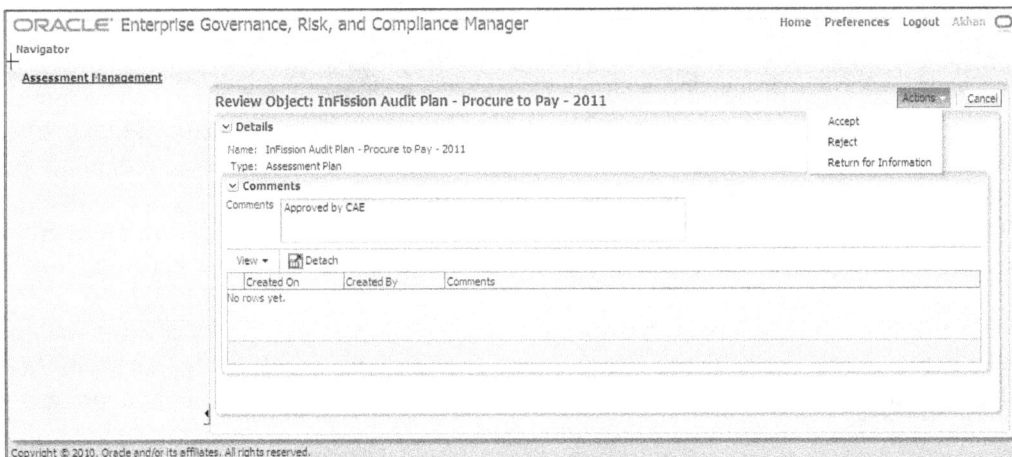

Internal controls assessment

Once the audit plan is developed and approved, the fieldwork begins with the evaluation of internal controls included in the scope of the audit plan. The assessment phase enables the organization to maintain controls effectiveness, identify opportunities for business improvement, and communicate findings. Controls assessment supports audit objectives, such as compliance with laws and regulations, safeguarding of assets, the reliability of financial statements, operational effectiveness, and enterprise risks identified by the management.

The audit findings provide independent audit opinion regarding the design and operating effectiveness of controls to the managers responsible for their controls over the business process within the scope of the assessment plan.

InFission internal controls assessment approach

InFission internal controls assessment objectives include:

- Financial governance controls
- IT governance controls
- Operational controls
- SOX Compliance controls

The CAE oversees the testing, administration, and assessment of the controls that are included in the scope of the audit plan. InFission process owners are responsible for updating and providing control documentation for their respective areas. The audit directors manage the fieldwork assigned to internal auditors. Internal auditors perform control documentation walk-through with the control owners to obtain control test samples which provide evidence of the effectiveness of controls, and also document the effectiveness of risk management and control activities in the assigned processes. The auditors also perform transaction testing to gather control evidence that the control is operating as described by the control owner. For example, to collect the evidence for the control over the **duplicate vendor payment** risk in the **Procure-to-Pay** process, InFission auditors obtain the supplier invoice and payment records from Oracle E-Business suite payables and purchasing modules using Oracle Transaction Controls Governor. (Refer to *Chapter 9, IT Audit* for further details). For manual and spread-sheet controls where the evidence requires independent examination to controls documents and work papers such as adjusting entries in the financial-close process, the auditor follows the procedures in the audit engagement. The auditor also communicates the initial findings and prepares the draft of the audit report.

The audit directors review the internal auditor findings and document their opinion about the adequacy and effectiveness of the control processes.

All audit opinions are reviewed and approved by the CAE based on sufficient audit evidence obtained through the completion of audits. The CAE also reviews the entire management's self-assessment of risks, processes, and controls, as well as the audit work performed by external auditors who provide assurances to the board of directors and the audit committee.

The CAE provides the management and the board of directors' periodic updates during the assessment phase.

The audit engagements are completed once the audit team has obtained sufficient and appropriate audit evidence about all business processes performed within the business units included in the audit plan. The audit engagements also include testing subprocesses, as well as a review of the mega processes operating across the organization. The auditors have the flexibility to adjust the test plans during the audit cycle, which is a result of changes in operations, external factors impacting the business, or change in management objectives. For example, due to the increase in output at a computer manufacturing plant in China, the sample size of evidence may no longer be sufficiently relative to the payment transaction volume to establish effectiveness of control over the three-way match in the vendor payment process for the Procure-to-Pay cycle (mega process). In such a case, the auditor may increase the number of random purchase orders, invoices, and receiving vouchers required to satisfy the audit procedure.

The audit engagements are revised based on events that impact the risks within the business processes, and controls that mitigate risks. Risks events can be external, such as marketplace or investment conditions, as well as internal, such as acquisitions and divestitures, joint ventures, organizational realignments, and information system upgrades. For example, when InFission acquired computer operations of a Chinese manufacturer, the audit engagement was revised to include the controls, which mitigate the risks in significant processes such as product manufacturing, inventory management, procurement, and distribution.

Assessing internal controls using Oracle GRC Manager

InFission audit team utilizes the **GRC Manager Assessment Workflow** tool to test the design and operating effectiveness of internal controls in order to ensure that the appropriate levels of documentation and control are in place. This assessment tool can also be implemented to evaluate the validity and effectiveness of risks, perspectives, and other base object components with a GRC module.

Assessing internal controls includes the following steps:

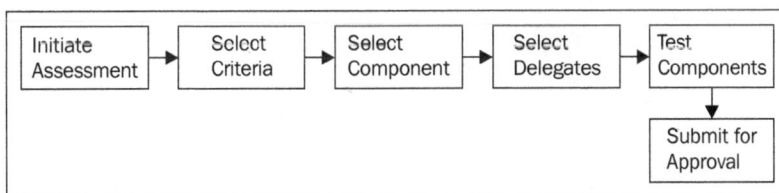

Initiating the assessment

Once the assessment plan is approved by the CAE, the Audit Director selects the active assessment plan and chooses the assessment activities that will be performed. The audit director also schedules the assessment's start date, a due date, and modifies the delegates that have been assigned to the assessment activities during the creation of the assessment plan. The InFission Financial Controls Assessment is initiated as shown in the following screenshot:

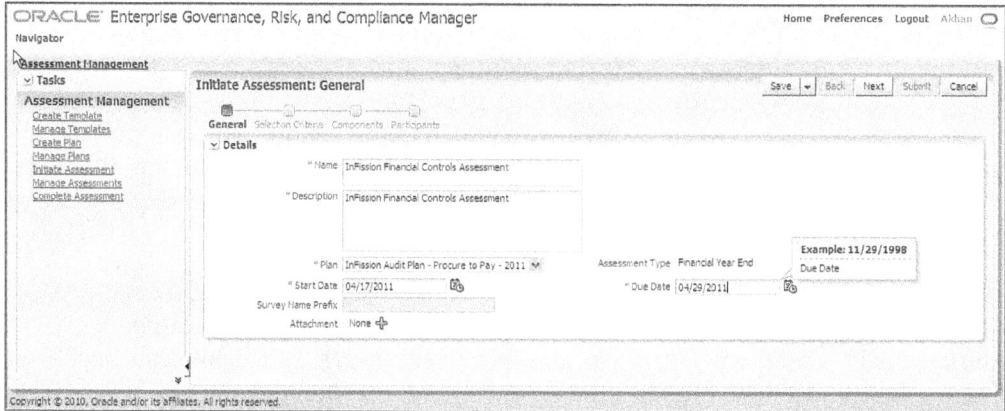

Selecting criteria

Next, the audit director reviews the assessment criteria and, if required, overrides individual objects from the assessment plan selection criteria, as shown in the following screenshot:

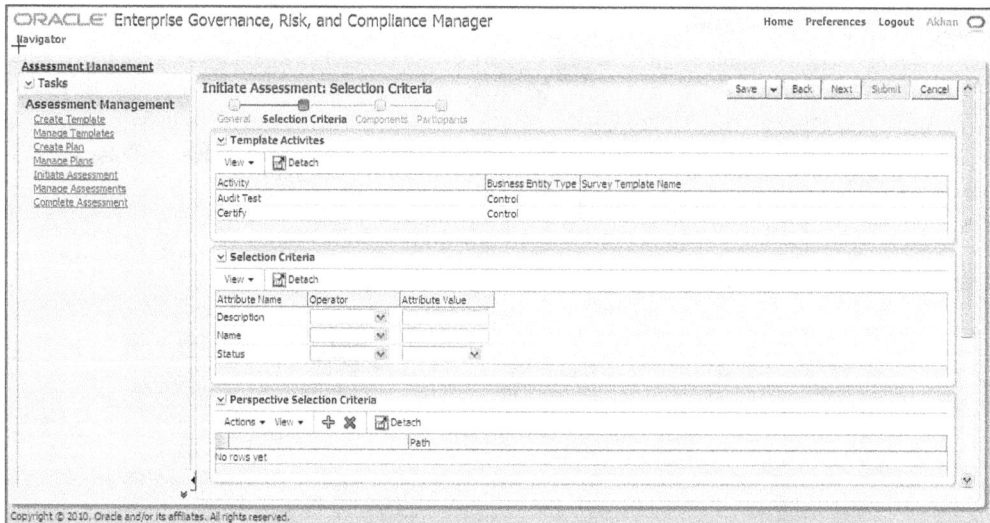

Selecting the components

Audit Director can also review the components (controls) and if required, override these components in scope for the assessment plan, as shown in the following screenshot:

Selecting the participants

Audit Director reviews the participants (owner, reviewer, and approver) and if required, overrides the participant for the assessment plan:

Controls assessment

After the assessment is initiated, it is assigned to the auditor to complete each assessment activity for the controls that are in scope. After the auditor completes the assessment, it is assigned to the reviewers and approvers. If the approver fails the assessment, an issue is created.

The following figure shows the **Controls Assessment Workflow**:

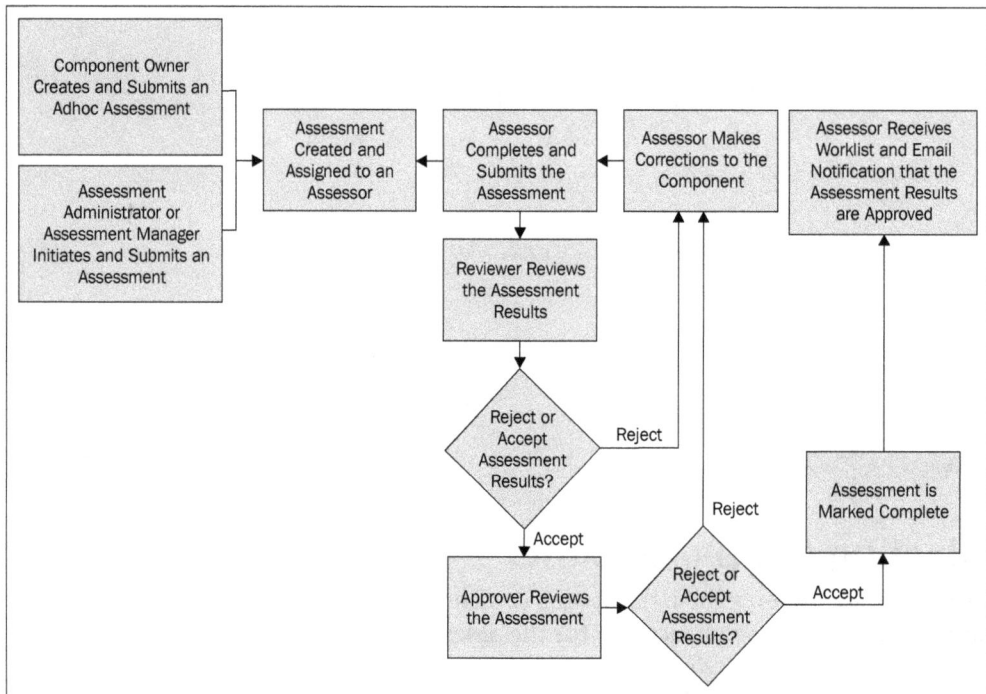

The auditors can assess controls or other GRC components, such as risks, processes, and so on assigned to them using any of the following methods:

1. Select the assessment from the worklist and click on the **Edit** icon.

2. From the object's **Assessments** page, select **Assessments**, and then click on the **Complete** or **Review/Approve** button, depending on your role and the status of the assessment.

3. From the **GRC Tools** page, click on the **Complete Assessments** link.

4. On the introduction screen, select a name from the list that you are presented with in the **My Assessments** page, as shown in the following screenshot:

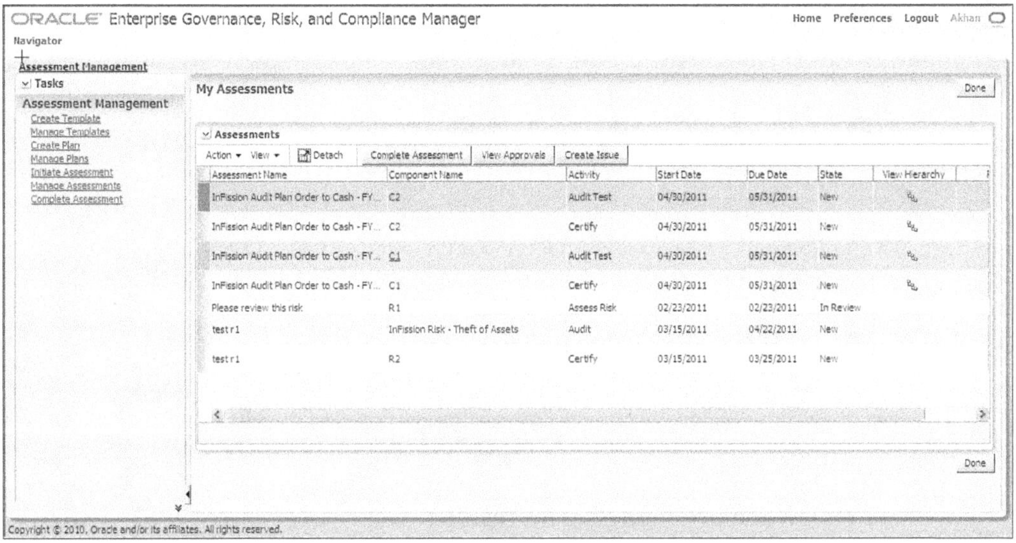

5. On the **Prior Results** screen, the results from prior assessments are displayed. The status of assessments can be:

   ° **New**: The assessment has been initiated but not started.

   ° **In progress**: The assessment is being performed by the assessor delegate.

   ° **In review**: The assessment is being reviewed by the assessment reviewer delegate.

   ° **Awaiting approval**: The assessment is being reviewed by the assessment approver delegate.

   ° **Rejected**: The assessment has been rejected at either the review or approval stage.

   ° **Complete**: The assessment has been completed, reviewed, and approved. An assessment is considered valid only if it is in **Complete** status.

6. On the **Assessment Management** page, review the assessment details:

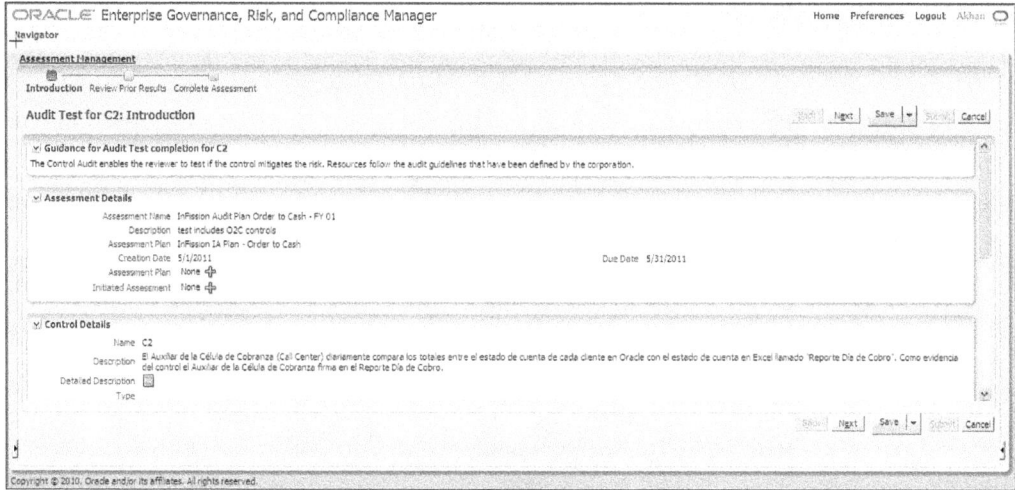

7. Next, review the prior assessment results:

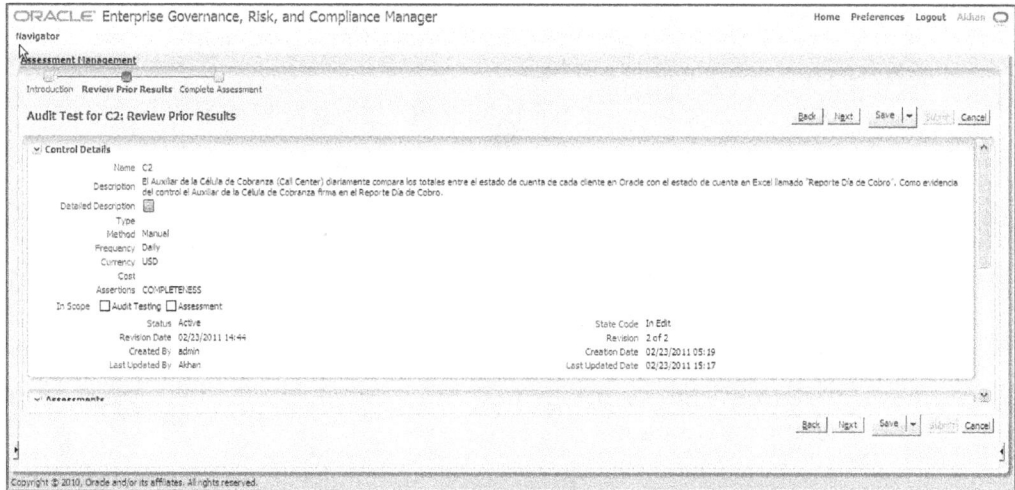

8. Enter the assessment results and complete the assessment:

The **Results Summary** options for design, operating, and audit test assessments are as follows:

- **Pass**: The control (GRC object) is operating properly to mitigate the risks.

- **Pass with exception**: The object is operating properly to mitigate the risks with noted exception.

- **No opinion**: You have reviewed the object but do not have a definite answer of pass or fail.

- **Failed**: The object does not operate properly to mitigate the risk. The assessment fails and you are presented with the option to create an issue within the workflow.

If the **Assessment Action** includes a **Certify** action, you can select from the following certification options:

- **I agree with this statement**: The information in the assessment is accurate
- **I agree with this statement with the noted exception**: The information in the assessment is accurate with noted exceptions
- **I do not agree with this statement**: The information in the assessment is not accurate
- **No opinion**: You either choose to make a statement or not make a statement regarding the assessment

If the **Assessment Action** includes a **Documentation Update** action, you can select from the following certification options:

- **Complete**: The required documentation is complete
- **No action**: The documentation is sufficient and no additional action is required

Managing issues

Issues are defects or deficiencies that are detected for controls or any other GRC component. Issues can be created against a control on GRC component such as business process during the assessment or audit. Issues can be created by auditors, process owners, control owners, or other users assigned as **Delegates** in the GRC Manager Security setup for the control or GRC component. Issue lifecycle in GRC Manager is as follows:

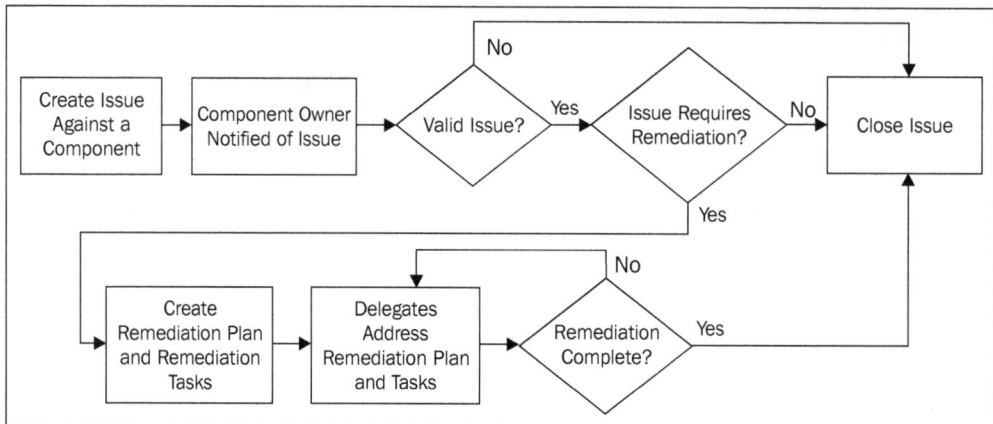

Carry out the following steps in order to manage issues in the GRC Manager:

1. In order to create a new issue, select the **Create New issue** link from the **Navigation** menu, enter the issue name, description, type, and severity, as shown in the following screenshot:

> When the issue is created, the issue owner is set to the owner of the control (or other GRC component) against which the issue is raised.

2. The issue owner, (who may or may not be the component owner) receives the issue notification in the **Worklists** window. The issue owner selects the issue to validate and determines the disposition of the issue. The issue owner can determine if the issue is valid, close the issue, or put it on hold:

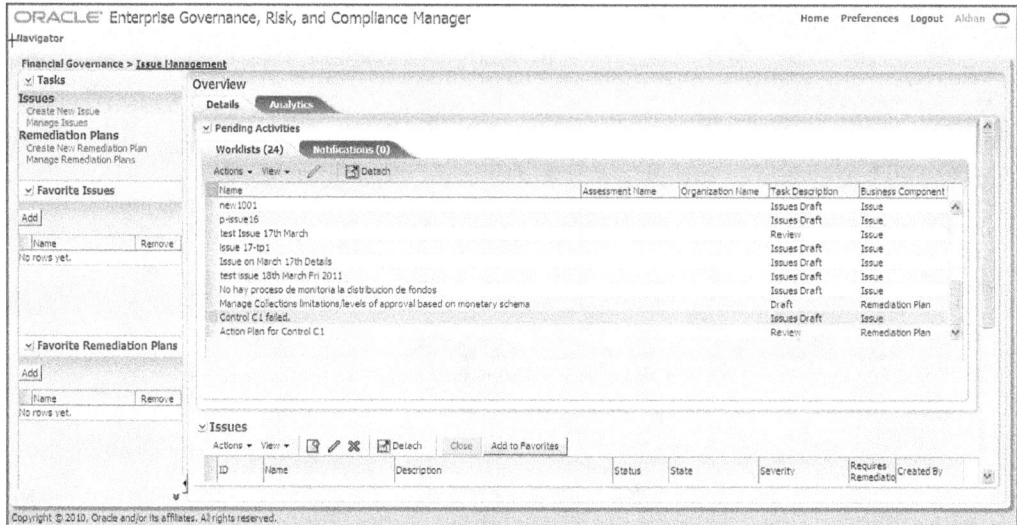

3. If the issue is valid, the owner can create a remediation plan required to address the issue.

   The remediation plan is to correct the control test plan definition, and the remediation tasks may also include the steps needed to test this control, as well as update the test plan instructions.

   You can enter a remediation plan by viewing the issue under the **Remediations** tab:

4. Define the remediation plan details. Enter the name and description. Specify how much it would cost to implement the remediation plan. Enter priority, estimated date, progress, and status details. Optionally, enter comments regarding this remediation plan:

5. Task details are created by entering task name, start date, status, due date, description, estimated date, and progress code details.

6. The delegates who are assigned the remediation task receive a notification:

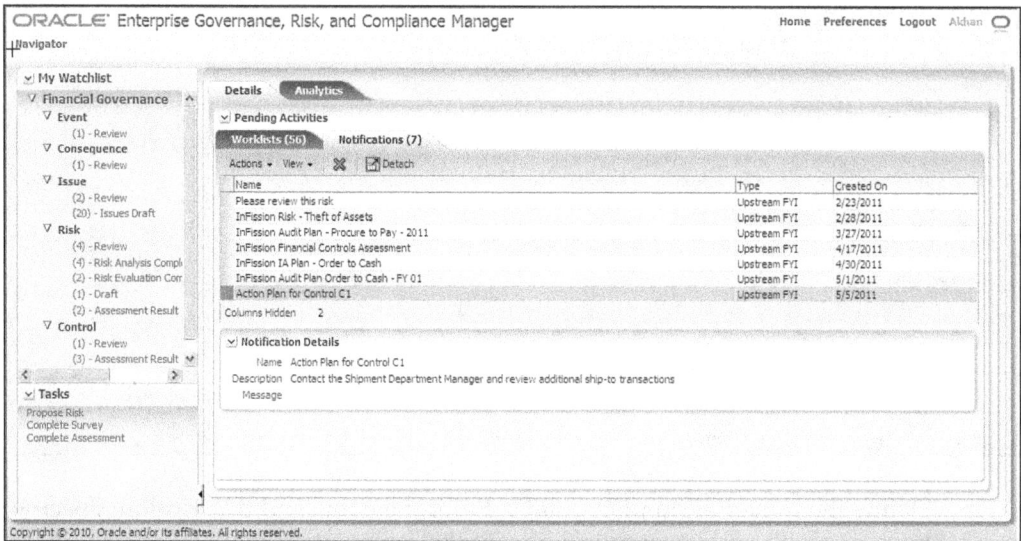

7. The delegates complete the remediation tasks:

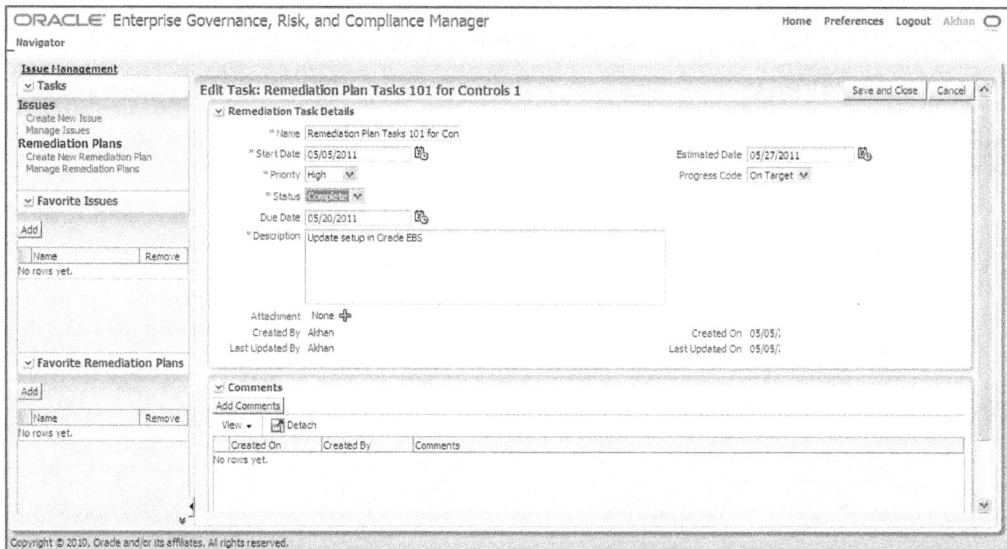

The **Priority** flag can be set to **High**, **Medium**, or **Low** by the user creating the task for a remediation plan.

The status is marked as **Complete** when all tasks are completed. After the remediation plan is completed, this issue is closed.

As the progress is made on the tasks for a remediation plan, the user can update the progress status: on schedule (**On Target**), not on schedule (**Delayed**), or are you unable to make progress due to external forces (**Blocked**). Progress for the remediation plan is derived from the status of the tasks. Progress for the issue remediation is derived from the status of the tasks for all remediation plans for the issue.

The **Due Date** is set when the task is created by the owner of the remediation plan, and is the date by which the activity should be completed. **Target Completion Date** is entered by the user assigned to do the work as when they expect to complete the work. This is used to report the progress of the activity. For example, if problems occur, an assignee can report their progress as **Blocked** and update the **Target Completion Date**. However, assignees cannot change the **Due Date**.

Closing an assessment

The audit director responsible for the assigned assessment reviews and approves the assessment as follows:

1. From your worklist, select the assessment results and click on the **Edit** icon or from the **Assessment** tab on the object, select the assessment and click on the **Review/Approve** button.

2. Review the assessment results and either pass or fail the assessment as appropriate. If the audit director does not agree with the assessment results, he/she can fail the assessment, which returns it to the original assessor's worklist:

Audit report

Once the auditor has completed the fieldwork and documented the preliminary findings, the next step is to prepare the audit report and provide conclusive opinion and recommendations with the evidence of supporting work papers.

The audit report is the final deliverable of the audit program that includes the independent opinion of the auditor and provides recommendations for improving the control environment. Before the audit report is finalized, a draft is presented to the management in order to facilitate the discussions regarding internal controls. The step provides the management with the opportunity to review and acknowledge the audit findings.

InFission's approach to audit report

At InFission, the CAE is responsible for issuing the final audit report. The CAE prepares a formal draft, taking into account any revisions resulting from the audit assessment and discussions with management during the audit. The CAE reviews all the audit findings including significant deficiencies or weaknesses as well as the remediation plans that are reported by auditors based on the evaluation of the overall effectiveness of InFission's control processes. The conclusion in the final audit report includes all findings with an unacceptable level of risk

Each Audit Director provides assessment reports to the CAE that include internal audit activity covering the audit director's overall evaluation of the effectiveness of the organization's control processes based on the aggregation of all audit assessments with the audit engagement. The assessment reports take into consideration internal audit engagements, as well as reviews of management's self-assessments. The audit directors deliver these reports to the CAE on a periodic basis, during the audit cycle as the findings are shared with the appropriate levels of management. This is done so that prompt action can be taken to correct or mitigate the consequences of discovered control discrepancies or weaknesses.

The final audit report is issued after management input is received.

The final audit report is distributed to the audit committee, executive management, and head of each business unit. This report is primarily for internal management use. The approval of the CAE is required for release of the report outside of the organization.

The existence of a significant deficiency or weakness does not necessarily lead to the judgment that the risk is unacceptable and it must be remediated. The internal auditor considers the nature and extent of risk exposure, as well as the level of potential consequences in determining whether the deficiency or weakness of the control increases the risk which is outside the acceptable threshold.

The CAE's report on the organization's control processes is normally presented to the executive management and the board once in a year. The report includes the audit findings based on the audit plan approved by the InFission Audit Committee and the board of directors. The report includes sections on Compliance such as SOX, Enterprise Risks Management such as reputational risks, credit risks, market risks as well as section of IT Governance such as IT security and disaster recovery plans.

The report states the critical role played by the control processes in the achievement of the organization's objectives. The report also describes the nature and extent of the work performed by the internal audit activity and the nature and extent of reliance on other assurance providers in formulating the opinion.

Obtain audit report in Oracle GRC Manager

Audit reports can be obtained by selecting the **Report Center** from the Oracle GRC Manager's **Navigator** menu and carrying out the following steps:

1. Select the report, for example, **Controls Assessment Report** from the **Tasks** menu:

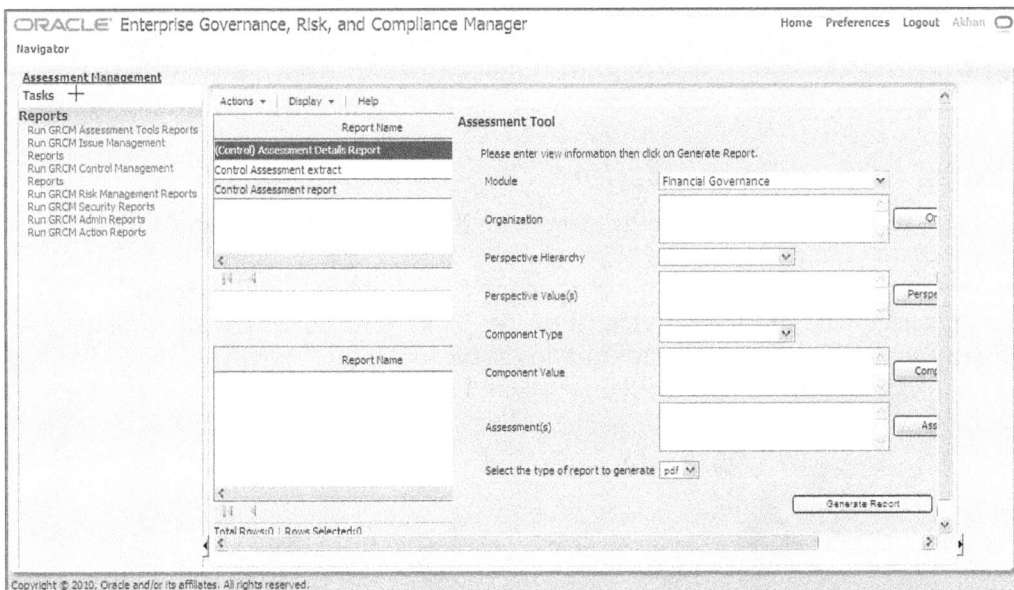

2. Select the report parameters, for example, **Financial Governance** for **Module** and click on the **Generate Report** button to review the report. The report is shown in the following screenshot:

ORACLE
Enterprise Governance, Risk and Compliance Manager

Control Assessment Report

| Report Date | 2011-05-06 07:09:46 |
| Page | 1 | of | 1 |

Module	Financial Governance		Organization			Perspective Hierarchy	
Perspective Value			Control			Control Status	
Control Stratification			Assessment in Scope			Assessment Type	
Assessment Status			Assessor			Assessment Start Date From	
Assessment Start Date To			Assessment Due Date From			Assessment Due Date To	
Assessment Result							

Organization	Perspective	Perspective Value	Control	Control Description	Control Status	Control Stratification	Control Method	Assessment Start Date	Assessment Due Date	Assessment Completion Date	Assessment Type	Assessment Status	Assessment Result	Open Control Issues	Assessor
			C1	12.Analize de la Cuenta de Cobranza (Caja Cuentas) diariamente compare los montos netos en armas de cuenta de cada cliente en Oracle con el estado de cuenta en Internet basado "Reporte Dia de Cobro". Caso necesaria del control el Anuldor de la Cuenta de Cobranza Sean en el Reporte Dia de Cobro.	In Use		Manual	2011-04-20	2011-05-31	2011-05-05 00:19:53.0	Assessment	In Review	Pass	1	Admin

The following reports are available out of the box in GRC Manager to track the audit activities.

Issues Management Report

This report is typically accessed by users with the Executive Manager, Audit Manager, and Internal Controls Manager roles. It answers the question, "What are the most critical outstanding issues or gap impacting the GRC program?" This is a key executive report. It provides the most critical outstanding issues or gap impacting the GRC program, and contains issue details and status including direct and indirect relationships to the hierarchy, and remediation details.

Controls Management Report

The following reports are available to manage controls in GRC Manager:

- **All Controls Validated by Organization**: This report is typically accessed by users with the Audit Manager and Internal Controls Manager roles. It answers the question, "What are my valid controls by organization?"

- **All Key Controls Certified by the Organization**: This report is typically accessed by users with the Audit Manager and Internal Controls Manager roles. It answers the question, "What are my key controls by organization?"

- **Control Assessment by Process**: This report displays the assessment status of controls that mitigate the risk within the process. For example, you can view this report to determine if all key controls that mitigate the risks in Financial Close process are operating effectively as assessed by management and internal audit.

- **Control Scope Report**: This report is typically accessed by users with the Audit Manager and Internal Controls Manager roles. It answers the question, "Which controls are in scope for financial compliance?"

Executive Reports

Oracle GRC Manager includes the following reports for the executive management:

- **Processes Sorted by Organization**: This report is typically accessed by users with the Audit Manager and Process Owner roles. It answers the question, "What are my current financial processes by organization and by major process area?"

- **Processes with Key Control**: This report is typically accessed by users with the Audit Manager, Internal Controls Manager, and Process Owner roles. It answers the question, "What are my financial processes with key controls, by organization and by SOX section?"

- **Risk Control Matrix**: This report is typically accessed by users with the Audit Manager and Internal Controls Manager roles. It answers the question, "What are my risks and controls by process area?"

- **Status of Compliance by Regulatory Requirements**: This report is typically accessed by users with the CXO, Audit Manager, and Internal Controls Manager roles. It answers the question, "Has every process owner certified their processes in preparation for 302 Certification?" This report provides associated processes, status of assessments, status of 302 assessment and survey completions, and the number of issues.
- **Summary of Aggregated Deficiencies**: This report provides details regarding the significance of internal control deficiencies and associated control information.

Summary

In this chapter, we have explained the **management of internal audit function** by describing key requirements, the InFission approach to internal audit, and automation of the internal audit function using Oracle GRC Manager as an audit management tool.

Internal audit function is essential to maintain effective risk management and controls within a significant business process. Internal audit function enables the organization to achieve its objectives while managing risks. The independent assessment of internal controls provides the independent assurance to the board of directors and stockholders that financial and operational information is reliable, operations are performed efficiently and achieve established objectives, assets are safeguarded, and actions and decisions of the organization are in compliance with laws, regulations, and contracts.

The Chief Audit Officer's role is very important to lead and manage the audit assessment program and ensure effective risk management and control assessment processes. Organization's line managers also have a critical role in supporting the assessment of the control processes in their respective areas.

9
IT Audit

IT Audit provides assurance over the effectiveness of information technology controls. IT controls mitigate the risk of computer generated data that can impact financial and operational results. In this chapter, we will:

- Describe IT Audit activities
- Provide an approach for managing the IT Audit program; and
- Review examples of automating Audit activities using Oracle GRC Controls applications — Access Controls Governor, Transaction Controls Governor, Change Controls Governor, and Preventive Controls Governor

As many organizations run their business on enterprise applications, such as Oracle E-Business Suite, PeopleSoft, JD Edward, the auditors must include IT controls within the scope of the overall audit program. Auditors should be familiar with how the IT controls work and also have the right approach and tools to assess the control over enterprise applications and computer systems that store, process, and report business information. Well designed IT controls can improve the audit effectiveness and accuracy while speeding by with the audit work plan. For example, auditors can test the segregation of duty controls in a purchasing application to ensure that access to enter a supplier is separated from the access to make a payment to the same supplier. Access controls testing tool can be of great value to the auditor in performing such an important task to ensure that the adequate controls exist. IT controls should be selected in a similar manner to business controls based on the risk assessed so as to reduce the impact of identified risks to acceptable levels.

IT Audit activities include planning, assessment, remediation, and monitoring of the computer system controls. These activities should enable the auditors and management to determine the design and operating effectiveness of computer system controls that maintain accuracy and completeness of information, safeguard assets, and mitigate the risks in achieving organizational objectives. An effective IT controls environment can also help the management improve business performance by monitoring controls within significant business processes such as Procure-to-Pay, Order to Cash, and Hire to Retire.

InFission IT Audit approach

The IT Audit Director (IAD) is responsible for the IT Audit plan at InFission. The IAD develops the IT Audit plan based on the overall audit objectives established by the Chief Audit Executive (CAE) and approved by the Audit Committee.

The goal of the IT Audit program at InFission is to provide reasonable assurance to management that the business objectives will be achieved with effective controls over information technology systems. IT controls are selected based on risk assessment, compliance requirements, and IT governance standards to enforce the policies and procedures to ensure effectiveness and efficiency of operations, reliability of financial reporting, and regulatory compliance.

IT Audit scope management

The scope of the InFission IT Audit plan includes assessment of controls that are classified into the following two categories:

- IT General Controls
- Application controls

The IT General controls provide overall assurance over the IT control environment, such as the IT organization structure and functions, IT policies and procedures for data center operations, software lifecycle management and maintenance, physical access to the data center, and availability to competent staff. IT general controls create the environment in which the systems and application controls operate. The InFission IT Audit plan for general controls includes the review of IT policies, standards, IT security and privacy guidelines, application lifecycle controls management, system continuity planning, and IT project and management. The auditors perform onsite testing at each data center in North America, EMEA, and APAC to ensure that the power supply, backup generators, cooling systems, and fire suppression systems are effective, and that the data center environment is clean and dust free with adequate protection from floods and water seepage. The auditors also review the physical access controls because there are certain operations and configurations that can be performed from the server console. For example, the physical access test ensures that all servers are physically secured within data center with locked doors that can only be accessed by authorized personnel using access swipe cards or biometric access devices. Auditors obtain the evidence of authorized physical access by reviewing data center's employee identification badges and all visitors' logs in the data center's access controls register.

The Application Controls provide assurance over critical business applications to ensure the proper authorization, completeness, accuracy, and validity of transactions for business processes supported by each application in scope of the Audit plan. InFission Audit plan includes Oracle E-Business Suite for Financial Management, Hyperion for consolidation and report, PeopleSoft for HRMS, and Seibel for CRM.

The InFission Application Audit scope includes four principal areas:

- Access Controls
- Transaction Controls
- Change Controls
- Preventive Controls

Access Controls include controls over segregation of duties, user provisioning, and access verification process. For example, an employee may violate an access control if she/he has access to create supplier and approve payment. The Access Controls audit includes assessment of the inherent design of application security roles that enable users to access the application functions as well as the risk of access granted to the users in each application function, menu, form, and module that support a business process.

Transaction Controls include controls that monitor the application data for exceptions and errors, for example, duplicate payments to a supplier. The IT Audit plan includes the assessment application controls over entering, correcting, posting, authorization, and reversing transaction. Transaction Controls assessment also includes verification of error-handling for transaction outside the normal course of business, tolerance levels, and business polices.

Change Controls include controls over the application configuration such as three-way match setting in Payables application and master data change, such as supplier bank accounts or address. Change Controls assessment requires the review of controls over application setups and master data changes as documented in user and system documentation for the application in scope. The auditor tests the application setups by independently reviewing the application or conducing application setup walk-through with the application controls owner.

Preventive Controls ensure compliance with business policies in the flow and accuracy in processing data within the selected application. For example, preventing setup of a supplier or processing transaction to a supplier that is on a Restricted Party Screening list issued by the United States or some other country for specific foreign entities (individuals, companies, and countries). The Preventive Controls assessment validates the input into the application to ensure data integrity and prevent errors. Flow controls prevent invalid numeric, character, and date fields against a range of valid value sets. Process controls embed application specific logic to prevent process flow control failures.

IT Audit plan management

The IT Audit plan is based on the audit objective to test the design and operating effectiveness of IT controls based on InFission IT controls framework. InFission IT organization has established an IT controls framework based on COBIT standard, which includes the following four domains:

- **Plan and Organize (PO)**: Provides direction to solution delivery (AI) and service delivery (DS)

- **Acquire and Implement (AI)**: Provides the solutions and passes them to be turned into services

- **Deliver and Support (DS)**: Receives the solutions and makes them usable for end users

- **Monitor and Evaluate (ME)**: Monitors all processes to ensure that the direction provided is being delivered to the organization

The IT Audit Director creates the annual IT Audit plan to assess the effectiveness of the IT controls that mitigate the risks to the four domains that we just discussed.

IT Audit team starts the audit by reviewing IT control documents, such as Annual IT Goals, Information System Architecture, Organization Structure, and Budgets.

IT controls are tested to identify all violations of IT policies and procedures. For example, IT management is notified of any non-compliance with IT development, change management, and maintenance procedures that have occurred as IT solutions are acquired and implemented.

IT auditors also review periodic end-users surveys to ensure that the IT services meet the delivery and support goals in line with business priorities. The survey results help determine if the IT costs are optimized, and if employees are able to use the IT systems productively and safely, with adequate confidentiality, integrity, and availability in place for information security.

Additionally, IT Audit plan includes the assessment of monitoring controls. IT controls managers continuously monitor and periodically evaluate certain IT controls to detect problems before it is too late. For example, the IT Security Manager monitors the user provisioning controls at the help-desk that mitigate the risk of unauthorized access to sensitive data and functions. The IT Director responsible for ERP Applications, monitors configuration controls changes to track who, when, what, and where a key setup control was changed.

All IT control documents, audit tests, user surveys, incidents, and remediation actions are managed in Oracle GRC Manager. In order to learn more about setting up an Audit plan, testing controls, tracking issues, and monitoring remediation actions in Oracle GRC Manager, refer to *Chapter 10, Cross Industry Cross Compliance*.

Automated application controls using Oracle GRC Controls Suite

Oracle GRC Controls Suite consists of the following four modules:

- Application Access Controls Governor (AACG)
- Transaction Controls Governor (TCG)
- Configuration Controls Governor (CCG)
- Preventive Controls Governor (PCG)

The following figure provides a view of the GRC Controls Suite:

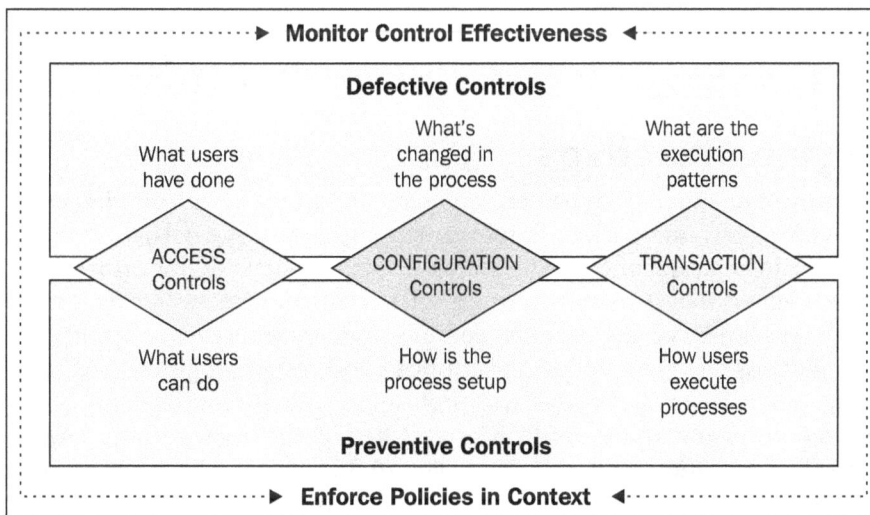

Oracle Application Access Controls Governor

Oracle Application Access Controls Governor (AACG) is a segregation of duties, control authoring, and handling solution that works within and across ERP systems, such as Oracle E-Business Suite and PeopleSoft—to detect and prevent incidents of user access control violations. It can also be extended to monitor user access incidents in other off-the-shelf, custom and legacy applications including J D Edwards, SAP, and Salesforce. Each AACG control specifies "entitlements" to a company's business-management applications that should not be assigned simultaneously to individual users. AACG then finds users whose access grants violate access controls.

The following figure shows the steps to set up and maintain application controls in Oracle AACG:

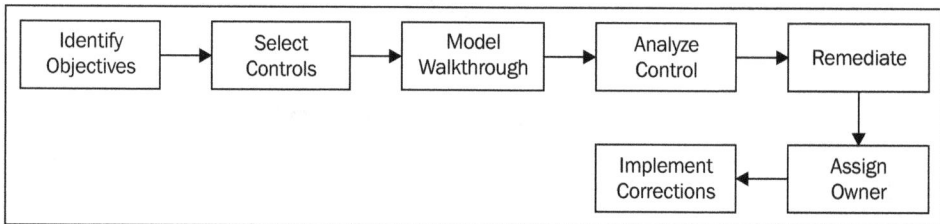

Identifying objectives

Access Control Objectives can be defined using an **Access Controls Matrix**, which provides the framework to implement access controls consistently within and across business applications. The Access controls matrix defines roles with access points across the rows and columns with confliction access levels identified in each cell. Application roles are designed to provide user access to application data and functions based on the job descriptions and responsibilities. AACG tool tests application roles to ensure that the application security model complies with segregation of duty and access controls established by the organization. The security model of each application may vary. However, AACG provides consistent results based on the access points defined in the Access controls matrix. The following screenshot gives an example of the Access Controls Matrix:

Microsoft Excel - EB_BV_Version_10_9_06_SOD_Risk_Program-10-04.xls

File Edit View Insert Format Tools Data Window Help GE Classification

D4 = HX

#	Task Group Description	Grp	1	2	3	4	5	6	7	8	9	10	11	12	13	14	14A	15	16	17	18	19	20	21	22	23	24	25	26	27	28	29	30	31
			AP Invoice Entry	AP Payments	AP Release Blocked Inv	AP Clear Vendor Acct.	Vendor Mast. Maint. FI	Vendor Mast. Maint. MM	Vendor Mast. Maint. CEN	Bank Reconciliation	AR Cash Application	AR Clear Customer Acct.	Material Master Maint.	Service Master Maint.	Requisitioning	Release Requisition	Process Requisition	Purchase Order Entry	Purchasing Agreements	Goods Receipt on PO	Service Receipts Entry	Physical Inventory	Sales Agrmts/Contracts	Customer Master Maint.	Customer Master (Credit)	Sales Invoicing	Sales Invoice Release	Sales Order Entry	Sales Order Release	Sales Pricing Maint.	Sales Rebates	Maintain Security	Post to Closed Periods	FI Close Coordinator
9	Vendor Mast. Maint. CEN	7	HX	HX					■									HX	X														HX	HX
10	Bank Reconciliation	8		HX						■	HX																					HX	HX	HX
11	AR Cash Application	9									■HX												X	X			X					X	HX	HX
12	AR Clear Customer Acct.	10										■											X					X				X	HX	HX
13	Material Master Maint.	11											■		X			X	X														HX	HX
14	Service Master Maint.	12												■	X			X	X														HX	HX
15	Requisitioning	13											X	X	■	X	X	X	X														HX	HX
16	Release Requisition	14													X	■	HX	X															HX	HX
17	Process Requisition	14A													X		■HX	X															HX	HX
18	Purchase Order Entry	15	X	HX	X	X	HX	HX	HX						X	X	X	■HX	HX	HX	HX												HX	HX
19	Purchasing Agreements	16	X	X	X		X	X	X						X	X	X	X	■HX	X													HX	HX
20	Goods Receipt on PO	17	HX		X														X	■HX		X											HX	HX
21	Service Receipts Entry	18	HX		X														HX	HX	■												HX	HX
22	Physical Inventory	19																				■X											HX	HX
23	Sales Agrmts/Contracts	20									X	X											■	X	X								HX	HX
24	Customer Master Maint.	21																						■	X								HX	HX
25	Customer Master (Credit)	22																						X	■	X							HX	HX
26	Sales Invoicing	23																								■	X			HX			HX	HX
27	Sales Invoice Release	24																								X	■						HX	HX
28	Sales Order Entry	25									X	X														X		■X	X	HX	X		HX	HX
29	Sales Order Release	26																										X	■				HX	HX
30	Sales Pricing Maint.	27																										HX		■HX			HX	HX
31	Sales Rebates	28													X	X															■X		HX	HX
32	Maintain Security	29	HX	HX	HX	HX	HX	HX	HX	HX	HX	HX	HX	HX	HX	HX	HX	HX	HX	HX	HX	HX	HX	HX	HX	HX	HX	HX	HX	HX	HX	■	HX	

| ◄ ► | Conflicting Functions / Groups & Trans \ Financial Rating of Conflicts / Sheet3 / |

Ready

In this example, the matrix provides a financial risk rating of access roles called "Responsibilities" in Oracle E-Business Suite that are assigned to a user. Each Responsibility should be designed to mitigate the access control violation risks. A responsibility design consists of menus, functions, and options a user can access to process a transaction, change a setup, or update a data object. The Oracle AACG software enables the IT auditor to test the security model design that controls the use access based on the risk level identified in the access controls matrix. The auditor can view the access points within the E-Business software and evaluate whether the design provides the level of control and granularity to selectively grant access as per the job requirements of all the users.

Once the role design is assessed, the auditor can also use the AACG software to verify whether all existing users have appropriate access as evidenced by their assigned Responsibilities and whether access to certain critical activities are allowed only to select **privileged** employees who are duly authorized. AACG software also helps review the necessary access to the administrator and **super user** rights, and how such rights are assigned and controlled. Ideally, no one in the IT group should have any access to the production data. All actions on the data by the super users should be logged and verified by the data owners regularly.

Selecting controls

The AACG software includes best-practice control libraries for PeopleSoft and E-Business Suite, called **models** that support the Segregation of Duties implementation for significant business processes, such as Order to Cash, Procure-to-Pay, Financials, and Human Resources.

Once the access controls objectives are defined, you can load the access controls from the best practices library provided with the AACG software. By doing so, you will have a number of entitlements and models to be reviewed with appropriate business owners, and compared against the company's goals for governance, risk, and compliance. It may be necessary to delete or edit models and entitlements, or add new ones.

Before selecting the access controls, you should review each loaded model and its entitlement to ensure that the control objectives of the company are being met.

In order to select controls from the model, log in to AACG and navigate to the **Manage Models** page, as shown in the following screenshot:

Model walk-through

The AACG software enables the control owners to walk-through the SOD control design by using the **Model Analysis** function, which provides the control owners an opportunity for reviewing and tweaking the definition of a potential control before actually creating permanent results. In fact, even some of the access control incidents and exceptions can be performed if the company does not require the history of the finding or how it was cleaned up. For instance, in some versions of Oracle EBS many conflict paths are generated because of the **AZN** menus. Implementers of AACG often have scripts to exclude these **AZN** menus in the business system. It may be acceptable and even desired by the company that these AZN menus are identified during model analysis. These should be cleaned up before a control is deployed and permanent incidents are generated.

In order to begin the model analysis process, log in to Oracle Application Access Controls Governor and review the **Access Control Model** under the **Manage Models** page:

View results online: Model results for Application Access Controls Governor include users whose access violates the model, the access paths by which they violate the model, the end access point involved in a conflict, and (if applicable) the entitlement involved in the conflict. The following screenshot gives an example of the online results:

Visualization: A graphical view of access paths causing conflicts is an easy way to grasp the hierarchy of an access path and the various paths a user has, which causes conflicts. The following screenshot gives an example of this visualization:

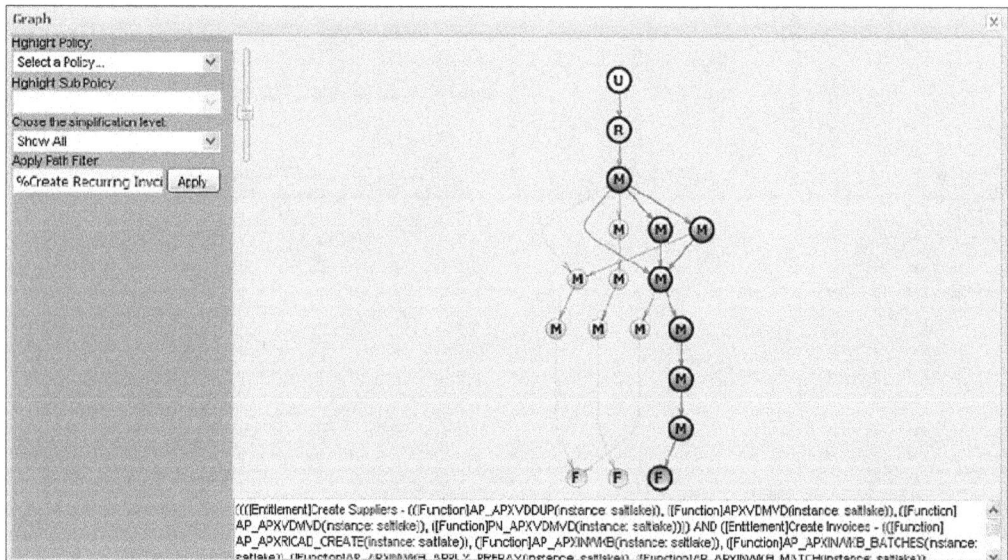

Extract to Excel: Results can be extracted to Excel for further analysis. The access path is broken out into individual columns that represent each access point in the path. These columns can be used to create pivots in Excel to easily view who has access to what and how. The following screenshot shows an example of this Excel analysis:

Remediation plan: Initial viewing of results from a model may result in immediate visibility to obvious areas that require remediation in the business system. You can determine if you require permanent incidents to be generated before any clean up in the business system happens, or you may choose to do some house cleaning before deploying your model as a control.

In addition, you may find it appropriate to add some global and path conditions to exclude obvious false positives noticed while viewing model results, or adjust the model logic as necessary before deployment as a control. Access model false positives are incidents that occur when the security configuration in the ERP system does not actually grant access to the access point in the model. For example, end dated users and responsibilities in Oracle EBS.

In order to remove false positives resulting from an end dated responsibility, you can set up a global condition to remove all incidents resulting from inactive Oracle EBS responsibilities, which have been end dated as follows:

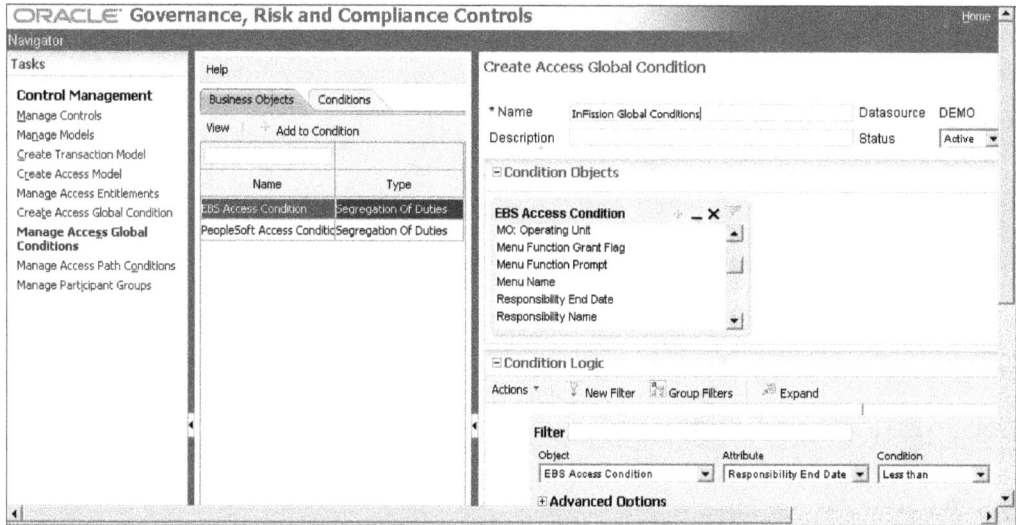

Deploy control: Once you are satisfied that the model identifies segregation of duties incidents as you intend, you are ready to track incidents and their status permanently, and deploy the model as a control.

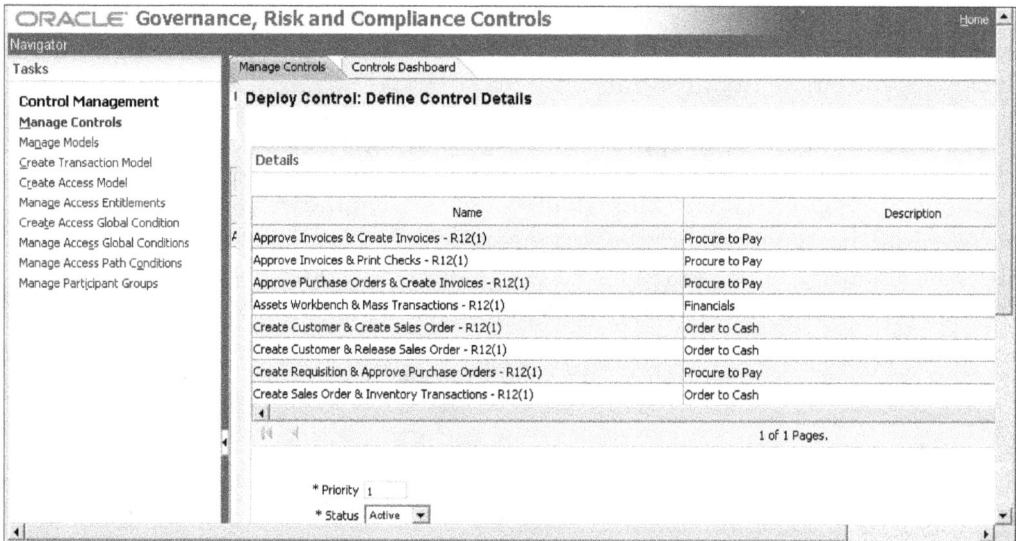

Analyzing controls

Incident analysis and remediation of control violations is an iterative process. This step requires participation of appropriate control owners and application administrators.

Once the initial walk-through using the model analysis described in the previous step is completed, you will have loaded the content as models and reviewed and updated the entitlement and model definitions to ensure they are applicable to your company, and you may have even done some initial clean up.

At this point, you should have deleted models that do not make sense for your company and promote those models that do make sense as controls.

When deploying the models as controls — based on the subject matter expert workshops and close interaction with the control participants who know and understand the control and risk — you should have been able to add a priority and any tags that will help you categorize and prioritize controls.

You are now ready to run control analysis. Your access control objectives will determine your next steps. If you already know, for instance, that the access controls in the Procure-to-Pay process are your highest priority, you may choose to run analysis only on controls with that tag. If you are not sure about where to focus your efforts first, you may want to run analysis for all controls to view the incidents by control. Next you can select the controls with the greatest number of incidents. This may help in giving you the direction that you need to select a focus area to begin remediation on.

Remediation

Depending on your company's access control objectives, determine focus areas to begin analyzing.

> A **focus area** is any category of information on which you want to base your remediation efforts — perhaps business process, or control, or any other category that produces a large number of incidents.

The **Controls by Type** and **Controls by Business Process** graphs provide an efficient way to see where the volume is the greatest:

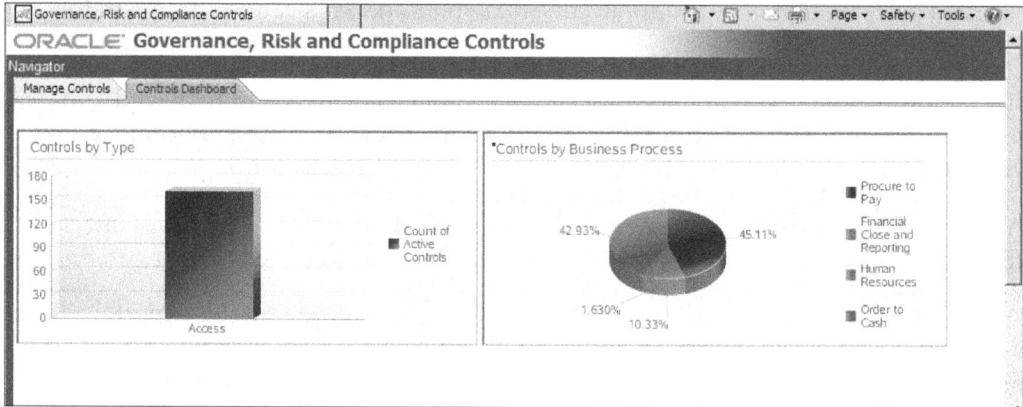

The **Pending Incidents by Priority** graph quickly brings focus to the distribution of incidents across your priority ranking:

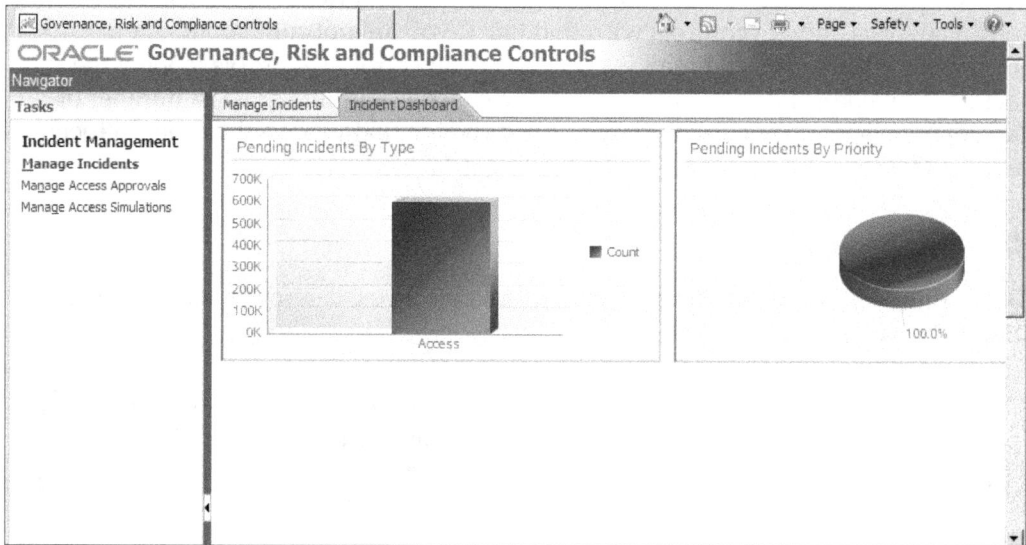

Use the Control Detail Listing Extract to create pivots, filter, and summarize data in a variety of ways to determine your focus area:

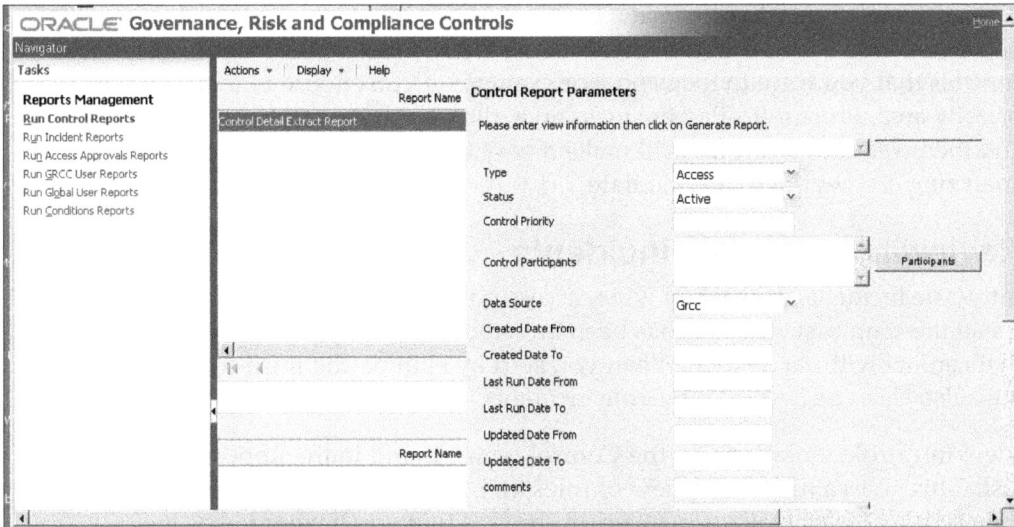

In addition to the graphs and extracts, visualization provides a visual hierarchy of the access paths causing conflicts to more easily analyze the sometimes long and hard to read conflict paths:

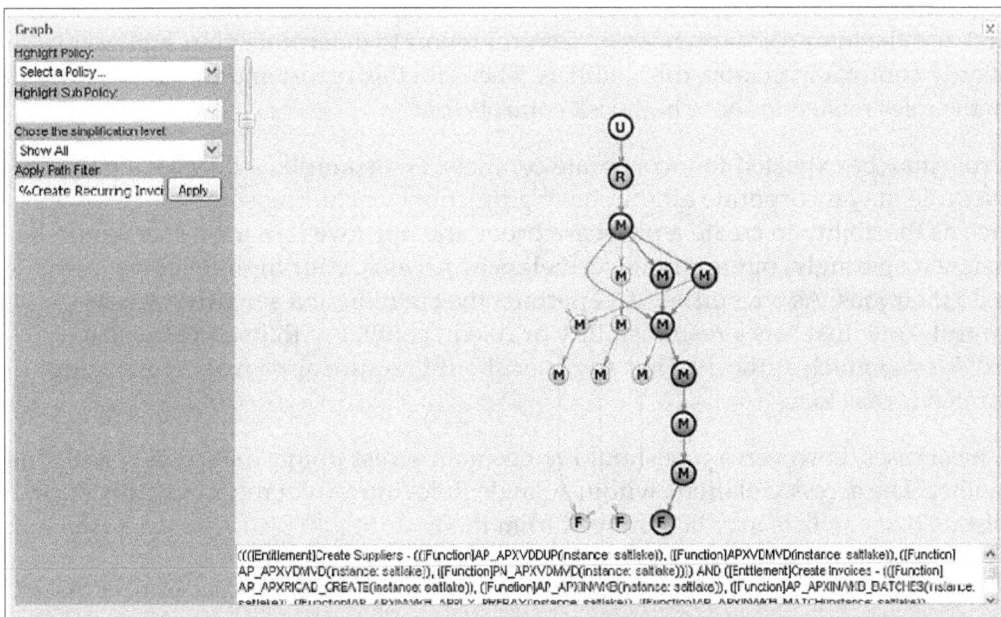

If an initial analysis run returned a high volume of incidents, you should not only decide on a focus area, but also create some filtered views that include only those controls that you want to focus on. For example, if you choose to focus on the priority area, Procure-to-Pay business area, filter on that priority and business area, and then create a view. This will make it easy to quickly select the records you are analyzing and working to remediate.

Reviewing intra-role incidents

Intra-role incidents are caused when access points within the same role conflict. Clean these up first. The role has been incorrectly set up if it contains access points that conflict with each other. When you start by eliminating intra-role incidents, you may also clean up several inter-role incidents.

View **intra-role violations** by the Control report found in the Report Management task. This gives a high-level view of roles that have conflicting access points within themselves. You may want to focus on controls that you have rated as the highest priority.

View **access violations** within a Single Role (intra-role) report. For a given role that has conflicting access points within itself, it shows the controls that are violated and their details—including the users and access points with incidents.

First, use the intra-role violations by Control report to determine your highest priority controls with intra-role conflicts. Then run this report and focus on cleaning up the roles related to those high-risk controls first.

A role may be expected to incorporate conflicts. For example, a Purchasing Super User role may incorporate all purchasing functions, including some that conflict, such as the ability to create a purchase order and approve it. Such a role would be assigned sparingly, but might nevertheless be necessary for high-level managers to do their jobs. As a result, AACG permits the creation of a **sensitive access control**—one that sets a responsibility or role in conflict with itself because it provides so much authority that any user should require approval before being granted access to it.

In most cases, however, a role should not contain access points that conflict with one another. The access violations within a Single Role (intra-role) report identify such roles so that conflicts may be removed from them.

Within the **Manage Incident** panel, analyze using visualization and various filters to determine when conflicting access points for one role have been violated. Carry out the following steps to remediate intra-role incidents:

- **Determine how to remediate**: These reports, along with online analysis, will help to give context to what access an individual role has, along with the users that have those roles. It is up to the business to decide how to remediate those incidents. Generally, the conflicting access points within an individual role should be separated out. One of the conflicting access points may already exist in another applicable role, or potentially a new role will need to be created so that the intra-role conflict can be cleaned up.

- **Simulate**: Before actually making any changes in your business system, you may want to simulate what would happen if you were to make the change. Navigate to **Simulation** and exclude an access point to see how your action would impact your conflicts, roles, controls, and users.

- **Remediate**: Following your company's change-tracking process, you can initiate a corrective action so that the change is made in your Business System Security model. For instance, if you decided to remove the Oracle Enter Journals function from the **GL_SU_JOURNAL** menu, you would need to follow your company process to request this change. Most likely the change would be made in a development instance, possibly then a test instance, and finally the production instance.

- **Repeat**: Remediation is an iterative process. Continue to focus on high priority, high risk, and high volume areas to clean up your business system.

Reviewing inter-role incidents

Inter-role incidents can be approached in a similar manner. Inter-role incidents occur when access points conflict with each other across roles for a single user:

- View users with Access Violations by Control report: This is a high-level listing of users that violate controls.

- View Access Violations by User report: This lists the top 10 users with incidents across roles, as well as details of every user who has violated a control, the roles and access points that cause the violation.

  First, use the Users with Access Violations by Control report to determine your highest priority controls with inter-role conflicts. Then run this report for those controls. By doing so, you will get a list of users who have violated those controls, and will be able to quickly see who has access to more than one role causing conflicts.

Within the **Manage Incident** panel, analyze using visualization and various filters to determine when one user has conflicting access points that span across roles. Carry out the following steps to remediate inter-role incidents:

- **Determine how to remediate**: These reports, along with online analysis will help to give context to what conflicting access an individual user has. It is up to the business to decide how to remediate those incidents. Generally, role access may need to be removed from a user or restructuring of a menu related to a role may need to be considered where there are conflicting access points.

- **Simulate**: Before actually making any changes in your business system, you may want to simulate what would happen if you were to make the change. Navigate to **Simulation** and exclude an access point to see how your action would impact your conflicts, roles, controls, and users.

- **Remediate**: Following your company change-tracking process, request that the change be made in your business system. For instance, if you decided to revoke a role assignment for a user, be sure to let that user know your plans and be sure this change actually makes it to the production system.

- **Repeat**: Remediation is an iterative process. Continue to focus on high-priority, high-risk, and high-volume areas to clean up your business system.

Additional reports to analyze incidents

Running a seeded report or extract is another way to analyze incidents and help with remediation. You can navigate to the **Reports Management** page to view additional reports, as shown in the following screenshot:

The following reports are the additional reports that are commonly used to help analyze incidents:

- **Incident by Control Summary Extract report**: Use this to get a summary of pending incidents for each control. See the last time the control was run, any comments associated and use as a general summary level report to help determine where to focus your remediation on.

- **Access Incident Details Extract report**: The ability to extract data from the **Manage Incidents** screen is for using pivots and filters to slice and dice data in a variety of ways. Generally, you start with graphs and other summary reports to understand where you should focus. Once you have determined the area on which you want to focus for remediation (that is controls, roles, risks, business areas, users, or a combination of these), go to the **Manage Incidents** screen and enter your filter to view the data to extract. Then select **Access Incident Details Extract Report** from the drop-down and click on **Extract**.

  Once you have the data in Excel or a similar application, slice and dice the data to view conflicts in a way that will help you with the remediation process. For instance, creating a quick pivot table in Excel is a great way to see where your conflicts are and what paths are causing the incidents.

- **Access Point report**: This report can be used to get conflict path information, which will help lead to access model hierarchies that need to be cleaned up in the system. For instance, if you find that the Access Violations within a Single Role report identifies the Vendors and Payment Actions functions as conflicting access points, you can use the Access Point report to find the access paths those functions are used in.

Assigning incidents to business owners

When a control is violated, all participants with assigned incident set to **Yes** are assigned to the incidents generated. It may be appropriate to reassign incidents to a business owner who is more directly interested in the incident. When that person logs on to the **Manage Incidents** screen, they will automatically be viewing all the incidents assigned to them.

Running simulation

In order to aid in cleanup, Application Access Controls Governor enables you to simulate graphically how incident generation would change if configuration of the business management application were altered, and to create remediation plans from the simulations. Each step in a simulation names an access point that might be excluded from another access point in Oracle EBS, for example, a function that might be excluded from a responsibility.

A simulation model enables you to select an access point and display its hierarchy — a diagram showing how the access point connects to all other access points that relate to it as **parents** and **children**. In the diagram, you select parent-child pairs of access points and then *remove* each child from its parent. As you do, the simulation feature builds a remediation plan, essentially listing, as steps, the child access points and the parents from which they would be removed. Once you are satisfied with your plan, you run statistics to determine how the removal of the child access points from their parents would impact your incidents, roles, controls, and users. You can print the remediation plan from your computer, in order to refer to it if you choose actually to implement the plan in your business-management system.

For example, to remove the Supplier maintenance function from Payables Manager, you can create the following simulation:

1. Analyze incidents in the **Manage Incidents** page, analyze the visualizations, and/or various reports.

2. Determine a child access point that you would like to remove from a parent access point.

3. Create a simulation to see how this would impact your incidents:
    ◦ Apply the child access point to a simulation model
    ◦ Filter by user and role to limit what is shown in the model to a readable amount of data
    ◦ Add a remediation step
    ◦ Run statistics
    ◦ Iterate through this process until you are satisfied with remediation steps

The following screenshot shows a simulation for the InFission Payables Manager Responsibility:

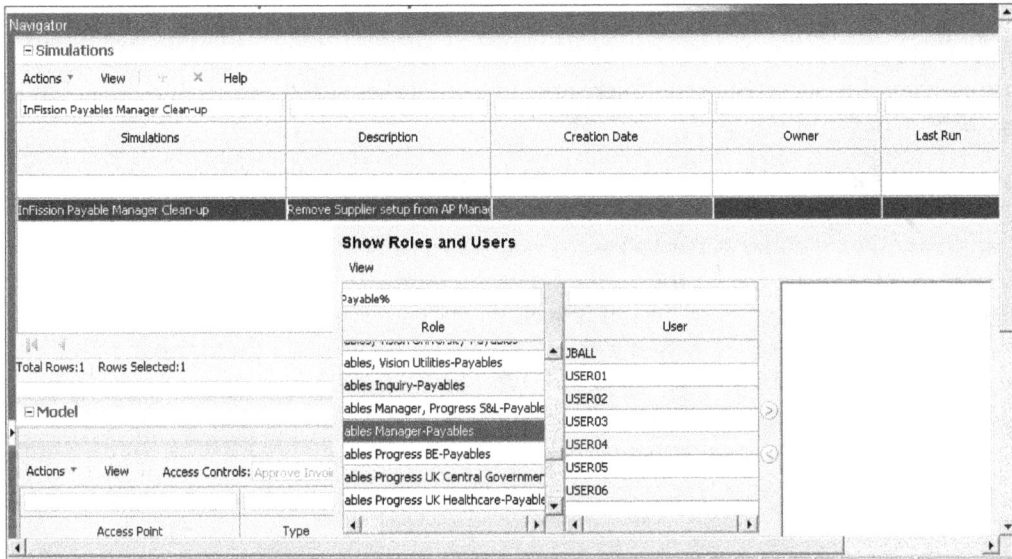

Keep in mind that the access point grid will show all access points involved in incidents of the selected controls. The model shows the entire access security hierarchy of the access point applied. In other words, the simulation model shows the data from the security model of the datasource, regardless of incidents.

The goal of using simulation is to get an idea of:

- What users and roles have access to my modeled access point?
- What access paths is my modeled access point involved in?
- What conflict paths would I clean up if I remove access point A from access point B?
    - ○ What user incidents would that impact?
    - ○ What role incidents would that impact?
    - ○ What controls would that impact?
    - ○ What conflict paths would remain that I still need to work on cleaning up?
    - ○ What other users and roles would I affect, regardless of incidents?
- What is the remediation plan I am comfortable with so I can send it to the person in charge of the business system security model to make the changes?

During simulation, as you view the model hierarchy and add remediation steps, you will find yourself asking the above questions mentioned earlier for various access points. You can continue to apply different access points to the model, in essence *redrawing* the model with the newly applied access point while leaving the remediation steps you have added. The model is a *means to an end*. It is used to simply view the security model hierarchy in various ways to help analyze who has access to what, and how.

Access paths are visually represented in the model. When a child is removed from a parent, access paths that are no longer accessible will be grayed out. Keep in mind that there may be many paths to get to an access point. The access paths are only gray if *all* ways of accessing the access point are eliminated with the remediation steps. Be sure to also consider what is seen on the screen may not be a complete picture of the access security hierarchy. Look for the arrows on the right and left of each level that allow you to scroll through to see additional access points in the hierarchy. Also keep in mind if you have filtered your model, not all access points may be displayed on the screen.

In some cases the links that show as *gray* can be misleading. For instance, if not all of the access points are displayed on the screen (you must scroll to them), it is possible that access points *off the screen* would be remediated and therefore cause their children to be remediated, and would still show links as accessible (not gray). In order to ensure links are appropriately grayed, consider filtering results in the model to show specific users and roles. In the end, the model is just a visual representation of the hierarchy. The statistics will show the accurate results based on the remediation steps.

- **Implement corrective actions**: Remediation will involve making changes in the system that is being analyzed. For instance, in Oracle E-Business Suite, a menu structure or responsibility may need to be changed. These changes will generally first need to happen in a development instance, then most likely in a test instance, and finally in a production instance. It is important you have a change-tracking process to ensure the changes are made from system to system.

- **Make changes in the underlying system**: The act of remediation is to make actual changes in the underlying system in which incidents exist. Options for remediation may be different depending on the business system. Some common changes that may need to be made in the business system include inactivating users, revoking role assignments, and changing menu structures.

Generally it is a system administrator type person who will be making the security model change in the business system. We assume this person is familiar with the best way to implement the remediation steps. For instance, in Oracle EBS, if we have a remediation step that removes function one from menu one, the system administrator type person has a few ways to do this:

- Function exclusion on responsibility form
- Uncheck grant flag on menu for that function
- Remove **prompt** for that function in that menu
- Remove entire line for that function in that menu

Remember conditions set up in AACG are considered for exclusions in results (in the Oracle EBS example, prompt, grant flag).

A specific Oracle EBS example to keep in mind is the concept of **same level menu/functions**. Oracle EBS uses this to grant access to functionality through a form menu, for instance. In order for a user to get to the function, he or she must go through another function (form). It is up to the system administrator to decide the best route to remove the desired conflicting access. For instance, instead of removing each function in a same-level **sub function** type menu, it might make more sense to just remove the same level menu from the parent menu. Analysis and simulation are just ways to analyze conflicting user access; it is ultimately up to the system administrator and business owner to come to an acceptable solution for remediating the incident.

Revaluate

A common approach to remediation is to analyze incidents, prioritize, add focus with conditions, clean up, and revaluate. It is an iterative process. Initial remediation may require new analysis runs to be executed several times in a day or — depending on how long it takes to run through the previous steps — a longer period. Perhaps remediation can be done throughout the week, with a new analysis run at the end of each week to provide a fresh look at where incidents stand. Analysis and remediation are slightly different for every company. This document was intended to provide guidelines and example approaches based on best practices.

Managing access approval

Once most of the remediation has taken place, and the control owners have mitigated the access risks to an acceptable level, the AACG Manage Access Approvals feature is enabled. This feature implements preventive SOD controls — it applies access controls to users as they are being assigned duties in the **Oracle FND Users** form or the **PeopleSoft User Profile** page. It rejects role assignments that violate a preventive control, and accepts assignments that violate a monitor control (or no control). If an assignment violates an approval required control, AACG suspends the assignment and displays an entry for it in a **Manage Access Approvals** panel, for review by the participants designated by the control. If a reviewer approves, the assignment is allowed; if he rejects, it is disallowed.

In order to enable **Access Approvals**, you must not only turn it on, but also create at least one GRCC role that incorporates the **Manage Access Approvals** permission, assign that role to users, and for those users (or participant groups to which they belong) set the **Assign Incidents** to **Yes** in **Controls**.

In order to turn **Manage Access Approvals** off in Oracle:

1. Log in to Oracle E-Business Suite.
2. Select **GRC Controls** in your list of **Responsibilities**. (First, ensure that the GRC Controls responsibility is available to you).
3. Under the heading **Preventive Controls Governor**, click on the **Form Rules** link.
4. A **GRC Controls** (Oracle rules) form appears. It provides access to three Preventive Controls Governor applications. Make sure the **Form Rules** tab is selected.
5. In the **Rule Name** field, query for a rule named **User Responsibility Assignment Rules**. (Press the *F11* key, type the rule name in the **Rule Name** field, and then press *Ctrl + F11*).
6. With the rule loaded in the **Form Rules** form, clear its **Active** checkbox. (Clear the one that applies to the entire rule, nearest to the top of the form. Ignore **Active** checkboxes in the **Rule Elements** section of the form).
7. Save the rule. Click on **File** in the menu bar, and then on **Save** in the **File** menu.
8. The following screenshot shows the **Oracle EBS User security** form with the **Actions** menu to activate a requested responsibility after the preventive control is enabled:

Oracle Transaction Controls Governor

Oracle Transaction Controls Governor (**TCG**) evaluates transaction risk in Oracle E-Business Suite and PeopleSoft. It may also be configured to work with other business-management applications as well. TCG implements **models** and **controls** that specify circumstances under which individual transactions display evidence of error, fraud, or other risk.

The following figure shows the steps to set up and maintain transaction controls in Oracle TCG:

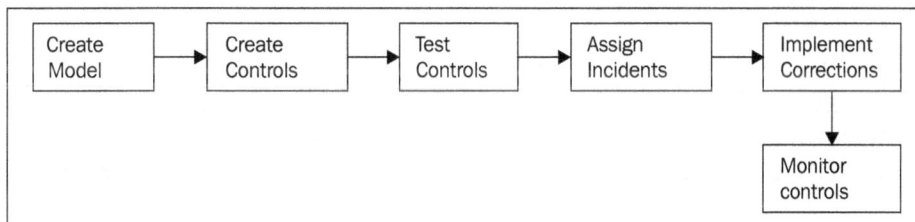

Create model

The first step in setting up a new Transaction control is to create a *model*. A TCG model returns **temporary** results — a snapshot of risk that is replaced each time the model is evaluated. Once a model design is reviewed and approved, you can convert it into a control. A control returns **permanent** results — records of violations that remain available to be resolved no matter how often the control is run.

You cannot create a control directly in TCG. A model and the control into which it is converted are structurally alike (the principal difference between them being the temporary or permanent nature of the results each generates). Although the creation of a model is a preliminary step in the creation of a control, models may be created to run on their own, so that users, such as auditors can assess the risk inherent in a system at a given moment.

A TCG model or control specifies circumstances under which transactions entail risk and so require a review. A model or a control into which the model is converted, consists of one or more elements such as filter, function, or pattern. Each, in a distinct way, defines an aspect of the risk a transaction may present and captures records of transactions that meet its definition.

Each of these elements cites a business object and an attribute of that object, which supply transaction data for analysis. They identify tables and columns in the business management application database. At the same time, they represent components of the user interface for that application:

- A **business object** corresponds to one or more database tables, but is given a business language name that evokes the user screen those tables support

- An **attribute** corresponds to a database column in a business object's tables, but is given a business language name that evokes the UI field that column supports

There are two types of TCG controls or models:

- A **Defined** control or model contains filters or functions. These elements enable the user creating a model to define circumstances under which transactions are considered to pose a risk. A model or control can incorporate any number of filters or functions (and so any number of business objects and attributes from which they are derived).

  For example, the following screenshot shows a model, which includes two filters, both based on a Payables Standard Invoice business object. One filter would select transactions for which an Invoice Canceled Date attribute is not blank.

From the transactions captured by the first filter, the second filter would select those invoices for which an Amount Paid attribute is not equal to zero. The model would therefore identify invoices on which payments had been made even though the invoices had been canceled:

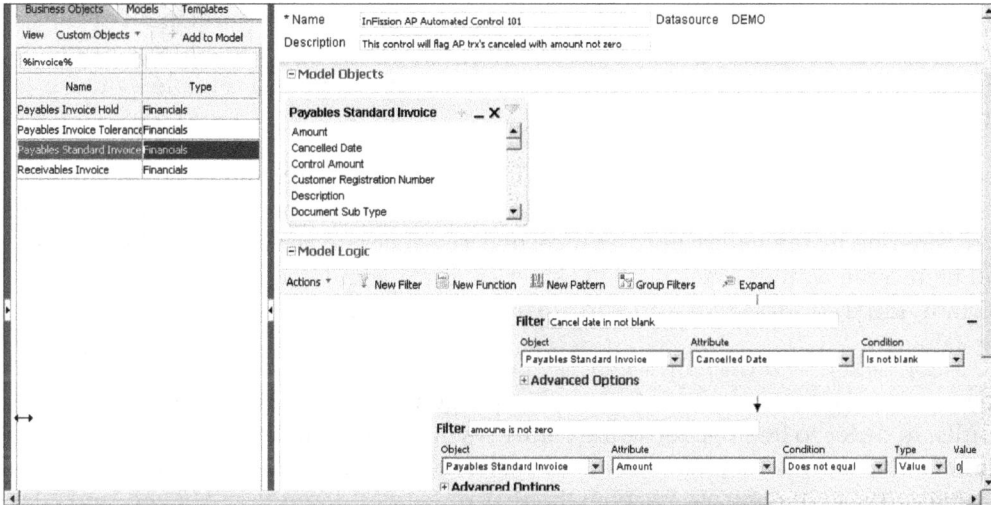

- A **Pattern** control or model contains a pattern—an Oracle-supplied statistical function that identifies a baseline set of transactions then uncovers outliers to the baseline, as a way of discovering unknown risk. A control or model can use only one pattern (which can be combined with any number of filters or functions). The following screenshot shows a standard deviation pattern filter for Payables Standard Invoice business object to identify invoices with less than or greater than 20 percent deviation:

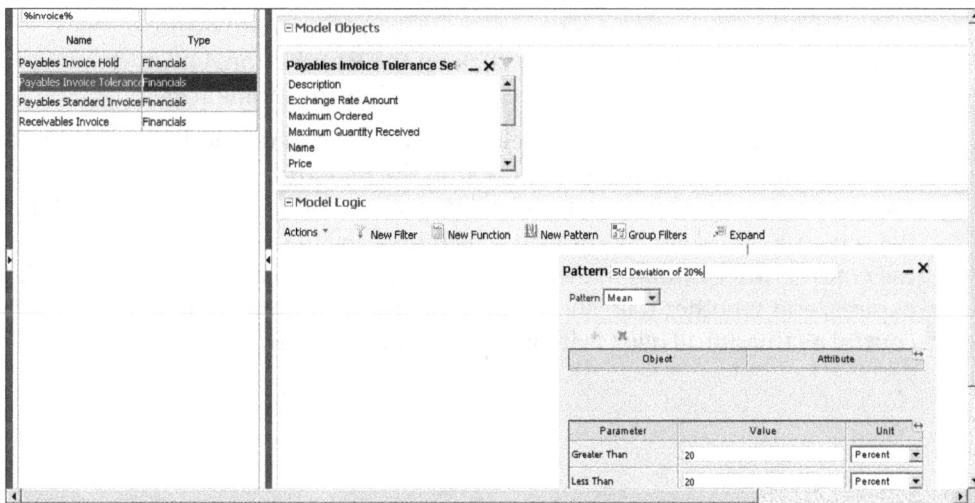

Testing the controls

Once you define the TCG models and controls, you can view the violations of controls which are called **incidents**. So that incidents may be resolved, each control must name one or more **participants**. Participants are those GRCC users who are associated with controls either as individuals or as members of participant groups. At least one participant (either individual or group) is assigned to address incidents generated by the control. Other participants observe the decisions made by those who are entitled to act.

If you have defined tags to categorize a TCG model or control, and then assign tag values to controls, then you will be able to sort displays of controls and the incidents they generate by tag value. For instance, one might create an Economic Region tag, and then create values for it, such as America, European Union, Asia Pacific, and so on. Individual controls that apply to a particular region would then be given its tag value.

You can select one or more controls in TCG to generate the incidents and analyze results. In order to begin, choose the controls you want to analyze from the list on the **Manage Controls** homepage. In order to select one, click on its row. In order to select a continuous set of controls, click on the first row, hold down the *Shift* key, and click on the last. In order to select a discontinuous set, hold down the *Ctrl* key as you click on controls.

Then, do either of the following:

1. Evaluate the selected controls once, immediately. Before doing so, you may consider synchronizing data from the datasources against which the controls will run. This would ensure that transaction data is up to date. (You can synchronize data from the **Manage Application Data** page, which is opened from the **Administration Management** tasks.) In order to evaluate the controls, select **Actions | Run**, or click on the **Run** button. GRCC displays status of the run at the base of the **Manage Controls** home page.

2. Create a schedule on which the selected controls run regularly. In order to do so, select **Actions | Schedule**, or click on the **Schedule** button. A **Schedule Parameter** dialog will open. In this dialog, enter values that set a name for the schedule, the date and time at which it starts, the regularity with which the controls are evaluated, the date and time (if any) on which the schedule expires, and whether data should be synchronized immediately before each control evaluation. Then click on the **Schedule** button.

While a control is being evaluated, you can stop the evaluation. In order to do so, select **Actions | Cancel Analysis**, or click on the **Cancel Analysis** button. Assigning incidents owners (participants).

You can assign the incidents generated by the evaluation of TCG controls to business process owners and control owners using the participant assignment function. The participants are responsible for accepting the risk or implementing corrective actions for each incident generated from the evaluation of transaction controls where the record of a transaction exceeds the risk defined by a control.

A participant with access to GRCC can view assigned incidents by navigating to **Manage Incidents** home page which presents incidents belonging to the person who is currently logged on to GRCC. Incidents will belong to a user that generated the incident until the incidents are assigned to the participant. From the **Manage Incidents** home page, you can navigate to other pages, which show an **Incidents** dashboard or detailed records of individual incidents.

The GRCC **Manage Incidents** pages enable you to review incident details, and to set the status of incidents to reflect whether anything should be, or has been, done about them.

Initially, incidents appear in the **Manage Incidents** homepage at an **Assigned** status, which means that you (potentially along with others) have been designated to address them. You can update an **Assigned** incident to any of the following statuses:

- **Accepted**: It means you have determined that nothing needs be done to resolve the incident
- **Remediate**: It means you have decided that some action must be taken in the business management application to resolve the incident
- **Resolved**: It means you have confirmed that the remedial action has been carried out in the business management application

Implementing corrections

The participant responsible for the incident will implement the corrective action, as required, outside of TCG. For example, you may determine that a purchase order should be canceled if a transaction control shows that it is suspect; that action would be completed in the business management application to which it applies.

As you implement correction, you can monitor the progress within TCG for following the steps in order to manage incidents:

1. In order to review, edit, or assign status to incidents, open the **Manage Incidents** homepage. Select **Manage Incidents** under **Incident Management** in the **Tasks** panel. You can set the **Manage Incidents** page to display either a list of controls that have generated incidents, or a list of incidents generated by those controls. In the control list, each control links to a list of the incidents only it has generated. From any list of incidents, you can open pages that provide details of individual incidents.

2. For a list of controls, select **Control Summary** in the **View By** listbox.

3. For each active control, the **Manage Incidents** page displays the name, type (access or transaction), priority, the dates on which the control was most recently updated and evaluated, tag values (user-defined classifications), control participants (users or groups of users selected when the control was created to resolve the incidents it generates), the datasource to which the control applies, and comments appended to it by participants. The listing for each control also shows the number of pending incidents it has generated. (An incident is considered to be pending if it is at the **Assigned** or **Remediate** status.)

4. For a general list of incidents, select **Incident** in the **View By** listbox. For a list of incidents generated by a specific control, double-click on its pending incidents value in the **Control Summary** list. In either case, the **Manage Incidents** page displays the following values for each pending incident:

    ° ID value generated by TCG

    ° Name of the control that generated it

    ° Status

    ° Type (access or transaction)

    ° Priority

    ° Datasource in which it exists

    ° Dates on which it was created, most recently updated, and closed, and on which its control was last run

    ° Participants to whom it is assigned and who most recently updated its status

    ° Comments configured for it

Each record contains **Grouping** and **Grouping Value** fields. For transaction incidents, the contents of these fields vary as follows:

- If a transaction control uses a filter to find transactions with similar values for a specified attribute, the **Grouping** field displays the word **Similar** and the specified attribute, and the **Grouping Value** field displays the value of that attribute for a given incident.

- If a transaction control uses a function to calculate a value for a specified attribute across a group of transactions, the **Grouping** field identifies the calculation (count, sum, or average) and the specified attribute, and the **Grouping Value** field displays the calculated value for a given incident.

- If a transaction control uses a pattern to create a baseline value, the **Grouping** field displays the pattern type and the attribute upon which the pattern is based, and the **Grouping Value** field displays the baseline value.

- Finally, each record provides an **Incident Information** value. For a transaction incident, this is the value of the first attribute among those selected (for the control that generated the incident) to characterize the suspect transaction.

Monitoring controls

You can monitor controls in TCG by tracking incident status using summary graphs and detail reports. By default, the **Manage Incidents** page shows only pending incidents. You can, however, create views to display lists of incidents at any status. In the listbox above the **Status** column, select the status for which you want to generate a list of incidents. Then click on the **View** button. In order to restore the list of pending incidents, click on the **Clear View** button and then click on the **View** button.

A list of controls or incidents may have more entries than can be displayed at once. If so, the list is divided into pages. Click on a right-pointing triangle to advance from one page to the next, or a left-pointing triangle to move back one page at a time. Click on an icon that looks like a triangle pointing rightward at a vertical line to move to the last page, or a triangle pointing leftward at a vertical line to move to the first page. In order to open incidents, set status, assign participants to incidents, or add comments, you will need to select one or more controls or incidents. However, you can select from only one page at a time. If you wish to select multiple controls or incidents, you can define a view so that those of you who want to select appear in one page.

Users can run summary and detail reports concerning TCG about transaction controls and about the incidents they identify.

All these reports can be run (or be scheduled to run) from GRCC **Reports Management** pages. The control and incident reports can also be run contextually, from the GRCC pages in which controls are managed and incidents are resolved. Some of these reports may produce either output formatted to be printed or read on-screen, or text files suitable for export to another program, such as a spreadsheet, for further analysis. Others, known as extract reports, produce only the latter.

Oracle also provides **Report Templates**, which enable users not only to generate reports about activity in GRCC, but also to modify the layouts of those reports. Although the templates display information about the use of GRCC, they run separately, using functionality provided by an instance of Oracle Business Intelligence Publisher (BIP).

Reviewing summary graphs to monitor incidents

TCG incidents can be viewed graphically using two different graphs that display summary information about pending incidents, which is described as follows.

In order to view them, click on the **Incident Dashboard** tab in the **Manage Incidents** page:

- A **bar graph** depicts counts of pending incidents sorted by the type of control that generated them. One bar represents access incidents, and the other transaction incidents. The height of each is proportional to the number of incidents generated by controls of the type it represents. Hold the cursor over a bar, and a pop up message displays its control type and number of incidents.

- A **pie graph** depicts counts of pending incidents sorted by severity. Each pie slice represents a priority assigned to controls that have generated incidents. The area of each slice is proportional to the number of incidents generated at its priority. Hold the cursor over a pie slice, and a pop up message displays the priority value and the number of incidents at that priority.

In order to return to the **Manage Incidents** home page, click on the **Manage Incidents** tab.

Generating reports to monitor control status

You can monitor control status using the detail reports described as follows:

A **Control Detail Extract** report provides information about controls configured in GRCC. For each control, the data includes name, description and comments, type (Access or Transaction), priority, the users who created and most recently updated the control, the dates on which they did so, and status (active or inactive), as well as the number of pending incidents it has generated. The report also lists tag values assigned to the control, its participants, and related controls. Finally, it displays the processing logic of the control and, for an access control, any conditions defined for it and entitlements that belong to it.

The **Incident Summary Extract** report lists incidents generated by access and transaction controls. For each incident, the report provides the name of the control that generated it, its status, its type (access or transaction), its priority, the datasource in which it exists, values of tags associated with it, dates on which it was created and most recently updated, and on which its control was last run, the users to whom it is assigned and who most recently updated its status, and comments configured for it. The report also provides an **Incident** attribute among those selected (during configuration of the control that generated the incident) to characterize the suspect transaction.

The **Incident by Control Summary Extract** report lists access and transaction controls that have generated pending incidents—those at the **Assigned** or **Remediate** status. For each control, the report shows the control name, type (access or transaction), and priority, the datasource to which it applies, values of tags associated with it, dates on which it was most recently run and most recently updated, participants assigned to it, comments configured for it, and the number of pending incidents it has generated.

The **Transaction Incident Details Extract** report lists incidents generated by transaction controls. For each incident, it provides not only the information that would be included in the Incident Summary Extract report, but also the values for all attributes selected to characterize suspect transactions. Because these attributes are chosen during configuration of the control, they vary from one control to another, so each run of the report must focus on a single control. You can select this control as you run the report.

000000000000000000

Configuration Controls Governor

Oracle Configuration Controls Governor (CCG) provides internal control of your ERP application setups, which enables you to take snapshots to document ERP application setups and create comparisons of snapshots, to show how ERP application setups have changed across time, operating units or organizations, sets of books, ERP instance versions, and ERP instances. In addition, CCG can also provide continuous monitoring of ERP application changes by tracking all changes to the application objects. The following steps are needed to set up ERP controls using CCG and monitor changes:

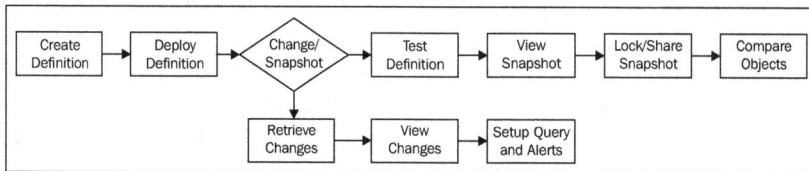

Creating definitions

You can begin using CCG by creating the following definitions:

- Snapshot definitions record setup data for a specified ERP application on a specified ERP instance
- Change tracking definitions setup ongoing monitoring of specified ERP applications and instances.

Creating a snapshot definition

Perform the following steps in order to create a snapshot definition:

1. Select **Workbench | Apps** from the menu bar. A list of application definitions will appear:

2. Click on the **Add** definition screen and enter the following information:
   - ° **Name**: A short name that will identify this definition.
   - ° **Instance**: ERP instance that contains the application setup data to snapshot, migrate or track.
   - ° **Type**: There are three choices in type. **Snapshot** — to report on ERP application setup data, **Migration** — to migrate setup data, and **Change Tracking** — to monitor changes to setup data. For this procedure, choose **Snapshot**.
   - ° **Application**: ERP application to snapshot or track.

3. Click on **Save**. The page is refreshed, displaying the objects, Global Conditions, Sharing, and Programs sections.

4. Click on **Add object** and the **Objects** page will appear.

   The page contains the following fields:
   - ° **Object**: Group of setup data to be recorded. Clicking will list objects that belong to the ERP applications. Configuration controls include a wide range of objects, and you can use **MetaBuilder** to add custom objects.
   - ° **Enabled**: When checked, the object's setup data will be recorded whenever the definition is executed.

5. **Operator** and **Value**: CCG uses values are entered here to filter the data to be recorded. The fields displayed depend on the object chosen, until you choose an object, no fields are displayed. For example, for the AP Terms Object in the following screenshot you see Name, Description, Cutoff Day, and so on:

6. In order to filter setup data, set the **Operator** and **Value** of one or more fields.

7. Click on **Save**. The page refreshes, displaying a summary of the object.

8. In order to include another object in the reporting, repeat steps 4 to 6. You may add as many objects as you wish.

9. Click on **Back**. The definition page will reappear.

10. Check **Include** in **Schedulable items list** checkbox.

11. In order to add global conditions to the definition, enter the following information for Oracle E-Business Suite:

    ° **Organization**: ERP organization should be included in the snapshot.

    ° **Set of Books**: ERP set of books should be included in the snapshot. For PeopleSoft Enterprise, enter **SetID**. This gathers values, such as vendors, ChartFields, or customers into groups. It may be used by any number of business units.

12. Click on **Save**.

Testing a snapshot definition

Once the definition is complete, test it. First, schedule the definition to run once:

1. Click on **Schedule a Job**. The **Schedule a Job** page will appear, as shown in the following screenshot:

2. Click on **Schedule** to start the job immediately. The **View Current Jobs** page appears. Click on **Refresh** to see your job (in this example, **5444**):

3. In order to add global conditions to the definition, enter the following information for Oracle E-Business Suite:

    ° **Organization**: ERP organization to include in snapshot.

    ° **Set of Books**: ERP set of books to include in snapshot. For PeopleSoft Enterprise, enter SetID. This gathers values such as vendors, ChartFields, or customers into groups. It may be used by any number of business units.

4. Click on **Save**:

5. Next, view the resulting snapshot reports:

    ° Monitor the job until it is completed.

    ° Click on **Details** to the right of **Generate Occurrence**. The **Apps Occurrence Objects** page appears. Expand the row for any object to view its conditions.

6. Begin to generate a snapshot report. Do either of the following:

    ° Include multiple objects in the report. Click on **Export all** to include all objects, or click on the checkboxes to the left of objects you want to include and click on **Export** selected.

    ° Include one object in the report, and select values for it. Click on the **Values** link for an individual object to view its primary records. (In order to filter the values, click on **Revise Search**.):

ORACLE® Configuration Controls Governor   Welcome ADMINISTRATOR Logout

Home   Workbench   Administrator   Jobs   Help

CCG Occurrence Object Values   Current Location: Workbench > CCG

24 Jul 11 Definition: InFission_AP_Snapshot_001 Instance: DEMO Type: Snapshot Application: AP 12.0.4 Object: AP Payment Terms

Revise Search

Results Per Page [10 ▼]   Results 1 - 10 Of 43   First | <Prev | Next> | Last

☐   **Name| Language**

☐   1/10 NET 30|US

☐   10 Net (terms date + 10)|US

☐   1000 Immediate, Balance 60 days|US

☐   15 Net (terms date + 15)|US

☐   2/10 NET 30|US

☐   2/10 Net 45|US

☐   2N30 - FulcrumWay GRC Chnage|US

☐   30 Days Net, 14 Days -2%|US

☐   30 Net (terms date + 30)|US

☐   30EM /3% 30NET|US

Results Per Page [10 ▼]   Results 1 - 10 Of 43   First | <Prev | Next> | Last

Revise Search

Locking the definition

Once the definition passes its test, lock it and perform the following steps:

1. Select **Workbench | Apps** from the menu bar. You are returned to the **Apps Definitions** page.

2. Click on **Edit** to the right of the definition's name.

3. Click on **Lock definition**. A confirmation message will appear.

4. Click on **OK** to continue, or click on **Cancel** to return to testing the existing definition.

Sharing the definition

Once you have locked the definition's conditions, you may make it visible to other users. If those users have been assigned the necessary roles, they can view existing occurrences (Apps User) and schedule the definition (Apps Snapshot Scheduler).

1. Select **Workbench | Apps** from the menu bar.

2 Click on **Edit** to the right of the definition's name.

3. Click on **Share**. The **Share** page will appear.

4. Select the **Apps** users to share with, and click on **Share**.

5. Click on **Save**.

Comparing snapshots

CCG lets you find the differences between ERP application setups by comparing snapshot occurrences. You can compare occurrences from different points in time and different ERP instances. In order to summarize, you will have to perform the following steps:

1. Search for the occurrences to compare.
2. Run the comparison.
3. View the reports.

The following are the detailed instructions. First, search for the occurrences to compare:

1. Select **Workbench | Apps** from the menu bar. A list of definitions will appear.
2. Find the definition that generated one of the occurrences you want to compare.
3. Click on **Occurrences** to the right of the definition name. A list of occurrences will appear.
4. Find the first occurrence that you want to compare.
5. Click on **Compare**. A page will be displayed with the first occurrence and a search form.
6. If the second occurrence was generated by the same definition as the first, click on **Search** to find the second occurrence. Once you have located the second occurrence, click on **Compare**. If you want to generate the second occurrence now, click on **Schedule**.

The **Comparison Options** page will appear:

ORACLE᾿ Configuration Controls Governor   Welcome ADMINISTRATOR Logout

Home   Workbench   Administrator   Jobs   Help

CCG Occurrences   Current Location: **Workbench > CCG**

Compare Occurrences

Occurrence 1:

Start Date/Time	Status	Instance	Definition	Type	Application	Scheduled by
⊞ 24 JUL 11 13:16:34	Complete	DEMO	InFission_AP_Snapshot_001	Snapshot	AP 12.0.4	AMADMIN

Revise Search

Results Per Page 10 ▾   Results 1 - 10 Of 25   First | <Prev | Next> | Last

Occurrence 2:

Start Date/Time	Status	Instance	Definition	Type	Application	Scheduled by	
⊞ 18 MAR 10 02:07:54	Complete	DEMO	Demo_Design_AP_snap_1	Snapshot	AP 12.0.4	AMADMIN	Compare
⊞ 18 MAR 10 02:21:45	Complete	DEMO	Demo_Design_AP_snap_2	Snapshot	AP 12.0.4	AMADMIN	Compare
⊞ 18 MAR 10 02:29:57	Complete	DEMO	Demo_Design_AP_snap_1	Snapshot	AP 12.0.4	AMADMIN	Compare
⊞ 18 MAR 10 02:36:45	Complete	DEMO	Demo_Design_AP_snap_2	Snapshot	AP 12.0.4	AMADMIN	Compare
⊞ 18 MAR 10 02:39:37	Complete	DEMO	Demo_Design_AP_snap_2	Snapshot	AP 12.0.4	AMADMIN	Compare
⊞ 18 MAR 10 05:52:13	Complete	DEMO	DBD_AP_Snapshot	Snapshot	AP 12.0.4	TRAIN06	Compare

7. If the second occurrence was generated by the same definition as the first, click on **Search** to find the second occurrence. Once you have located the second occurrence, click on **Compare**. If you want to generate the second occurrence now, click on **Schedule**. The **Comparison Options** page will appear:

ORACLE᾿ Configuration Controls Governor   Welcome ADMINISTRATOR Logout

Home   Workbench   Administrator   Jobs   Help

Comparison Options   Current Location: **Workbench > CCG**

for Definition: **InFission_AP_Snapshot_001** 24 JUL 11 17:22:26 Compare To: **InFission_AP_Snapshot_001** 24 JUL 11 13:16:34 Version: **12.0.4** ScheduledBy: **AMADMIN**

Method

○ Compare same records
○ Compare two organizations/sets of books
○ Force comparison and map Values

Schedule   Back

The following options are available:

- ° **Compare Same Records**: Matches primary records in two snapshot occurrences, and then identifies the differences in their fields' values.
- ° **Compare Two Organizations/Sets of Books**: Matches primary records in snapshots of two different organizations and/or sets of books, and then identifies the differences in their fields' values. Both snapshots must cover the same instance, product family version, and objects. It must have at least one global condition and must have global conditions on the same parameters (both must have global conditions for **Organization**, for **Set of Books**, or for both **Organization** and **Set of Books**).
- ° **Force Comparison/Map Values**: Matches primary records according to your specifications, and then identifies the differences in their fields' values.

Defining change tracker

Change Tracker monitors changes to ERP application setup data.

Before you can use the Change Tracker, you must run one or more Change Tracking definitions, which specify the objects to monitor and the level of detail to record.

Each time you configure Oracle CCG for an ERP instance, it automatically generates Change Tracking definitions for the ERP applications that you have licensed.

You can save a considerable amount of time by using these definitions instead of building your own from scratch.

In order to summarize, you will have to:

1. Search for an autogenerated change tracking definition.
2. Edit the definition to specify what to track.
3. Run the definition to deploy Change Tracking functionality to the ERP instance.
4. View the **Change Tracker**.
5. Optionally, specify **Change Tracker** queries and alerts.
6. Log in to **Oracle CCG** as the Baseline Definition Owner that was specified when the ERP Instance was configured.
7. Select **Workbench | Apps** from the menu bar. A list of **Apps** definitions will appear.
8. Find the **Change Tracking** definition named for the ERP application and instance to monitor appears.

Once you have located the definition, edit it:

1. Click on **Edit** to the right of the definition name. The definition page will appear (the objects listed depend on the application).

2. Check the **Include in Schedulable Items list** checkbox.

3. Set the following checkboxes for each object to be tracked:

   ○ **All**: Capture all the changes listed below

   ○ **Insert**: Capture inserts and new records

   ○ **Update**: Capture updates to existing records

   ○ **Delete**: Capture deletions of existing records

4. Finally, click on **Save**:

Deploying change tracker

In order to deploy **Change Tracking** to the ERP instance:

1. Click on **Schedule**. The **Schedule a Job** page will appear.

2. Click on **Schedule** to start the job immediately. The **View Current Jobs** page will appear.

3. Click on **Refresh** to see your job.

Viewing change tracker results

In order to view the Change Tracker:

1. Select **Workbench | Apps** from the menu bar.

2. Click on the **Change Tracker** button. The **Change Tracker** will appear and it will display the information.

3. In order to view an instance's applications, click on any button in the **Instance** row and select the instance.

   Note that if no applications are visible even after you choose an instance, select **Jobs | View Current Jobs**. Verify that the **Change Tracking Transfer** program has run at least once. (This program transfers change tracking data from the ERP instances to Oracle CCG). If it has not, select **Jobs | View Future Jobs** and see whether it is scheduled to run. If it is not, contact your CCG Administrator.

4. If the information shown seems out of date, perhaps the Change Tracking Transfer program has not run recently. Select **Jobs | View Future Jobs** and determine when it last ran.

5. In order to view details about an instance's changes, click on any **Changes** link.

6. Next, to view information about specific applications' changes on an instance, click any of the checkboxes on the left, and then click on **Changes** to view the Object values.

The following screenshot shows an example of General Ledger Open and
Close Period changes in the Demo instance:

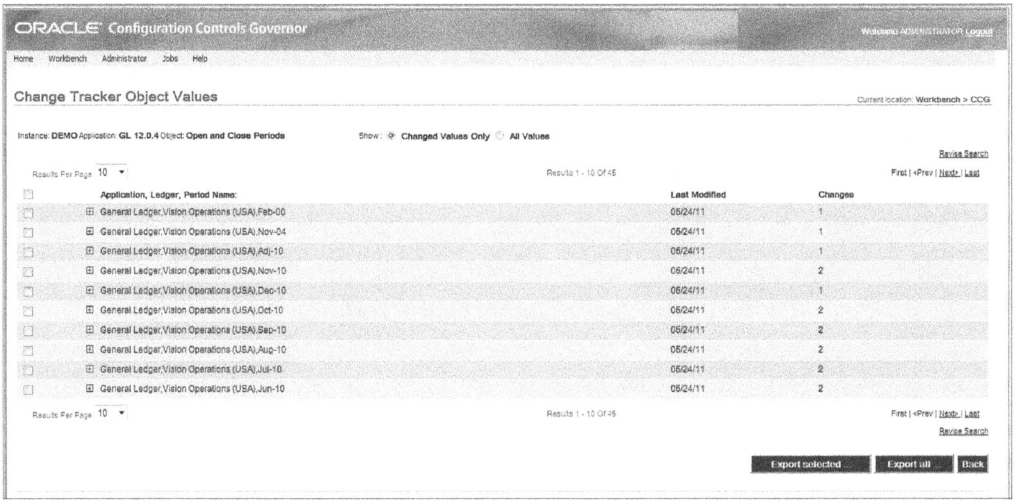

Setting up queries and alerts

Optionally, you can set up queries and alerts. A query stores a set of criteria for
filtering the data shown in the Change Tracker. The Change Tracker automatically
loads the last query used.

An alert is an e-mail message that lists new changes. Alerts are generated when the
Change Tracking program runs. Alert recipients are specified in queries, so each alert
message contains only the changes filtered by the query.

In order to set up a query:

1. While viewing the Change Tracker, click on **Query**. The **Change Tracker
    Queries** page will appear (a few sample Queries are shown in the
    following screenshot).

2. You can add, edit, and delete queries using the links and buttons on
    this page.

3. Click on **Add query....** and the **Add query** page will appear.

4. Enter a name, check the **Enabled** checkbox, and click on **Save**. The page will be refreshed, displaying the **Dates**, **Change Method**, **Types**, **Instances**, **Applications**, **Objects**, **Responsibilities**, **Users**, and **Alerts** sections, as shown in the following screenshot:

5. In order to find all changes for all instances, leave the rest of the query blank. In order to narrow the query's results, set one or more items.

   ° **Dates**: Enter both values to specify a date range. Enter only **From** to specify changes since a date. Enter only **To** in order to specify changes until a date or leave blank for all dates.

   ° **Change Method**: Specifies the origin of the change (only application user's changes and SQL/nonstandard changes).

   ° **Types**: Check any/all, or leave all blank for all types.

   ° **Instances**: Specify one or more instances, or leave blank for all instances.

- ° **Applications**: Specify one or more applications, or leave blank for all applications.

- ° **Objects**: Specify one or more objects, or leave blank for all objects.

- ° **Responsibilities**: Specify one or more responsibilities, or leave blank for all responsibilities.

- ° **Users**: Specify one or more users, or leave blank for all users.

- ° **Alerts**: Specify one or more e-mail addresses to send an alert message each time the Change Tracking Transfer program discovers new changes.

6. Click on **Save**. The list of queries will reappear, as shown in the following screenshot:

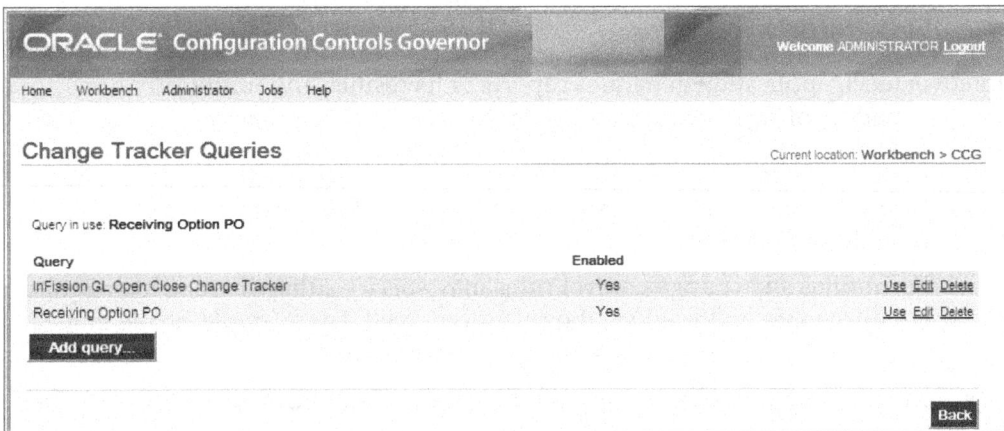

7. Clicking on **Use** to the right of any query displays the **Change Tracker** with only the changes found by the query. Each time you visit the **Change Tracker**, it automatically loads the last query used.

8. In order to set up an alert:

    i. Add or edit a query

    ii. In the **Alerts** section, click on **Add Alert....** Enter an alert recipient's e-mail address

    iii. Add as many recipients as you like

    iv. Set the rest of the query's options to select only the changes to be reported in the alert

    v. Click on the **Save** button

Preventive Controls Governor

Preventive Controls Governor (PCG) is a set of applications that run within Oracle.

E-Business Suite as a component of the Governance, Risk, and Compliance Controls Suite. Preventive Controls Governor applications include:

- **Form Rules**, which modifies the security, navigation, field, and data properties of Oracle EBS forms
- **Flow Rules**, which defines and implements business processes
- **Audit Rules**, which tracks changes to the values of fields in database tables that underlie Oracle EBS
- **Change Control**, which regulates changes to the values of fields in Oracle EBS forms. It can monitor change, require a reason for a change, or require approval for a change

Moreover, each application generates reports of its results, and utility programs provide a variety of supporting features, including the following:

- Form Rules includes a **Form Extensions** tool, which enables users to create forms that open from (and so extend the capabilities of) existing Oracle E-Business Suite forms.
- Form rules and change-control rules may specify **subscribers**, which define circumstances under which the rule is enforced. For example, a rule may apply to a specified set of users or responsibilities.
- Rules of any type may be migrated from one Oracle EBS instance to another.
- Form rules and flow rules may be gathered into **libraries**, which may be migrated from one Oracle EBS instance to another.

Creating rules

In this chapter, we provide instructions to create Form Rules, which enable users to write rules that modify the security, navigation, field, and data properties of Oracle E-Business Suite forms.

In order to use the Form Rules application, ensure that its **Oracle Rules Form** tab is selected in the GRC Controls. Each Form Rule consists of subordinate rules, called **rule elements**. Each element targets a form, a block within a form, or a field within a block. Each form also specifies an **event** that triggers processing, for example, the act of opening a target form or navigating to a target block or field. Finally, each element defines customizations to the target form, or to its blocks, fields, tabs, or other components. Rule elements can do the following:

- Set security attributes. These can mandate that data entry be required; that updates, insertions, or deletions be prevented; or that items be hidden from view.

- Establish navigation paths from a target form to other Oracle EBS forms, or to forms created through use of a tool called Form Extensions.

- Display the messages.

- Define default values for fields, compile lists of values to be selected from fields, or set other field attributes.

- Run structured query language (SQL) statements.

- Execute processes defined in the Flow Rules application.

Each Form Rule may specify **subscribers**, which designate users, responsibilities, or other entities to which the rule applies. If no subscriber is defined for a rule, it applies universally. Form Rules also provides a tool for migrating rules from one Oracle E-Business Suite instance to another.

In order to work with Form Rules, begin by naming a rule and providing basic information for one or more elements—for each, a target and an event that initiates processing.

As the target for an element, select, at minimum, an Oracle E- Business Suite form.

Depending on the event you intend to call, you may also specify a block or a field on the form. If, for example, you choose a **When New Form** event (which triggers the rule element to run when a user opens a specified form), you designate only the form as a target. If, among several other events, you choose **When New Item** (which triggers the rule element to run each time a user navigates to a field), you typically designate a form, a block within the form, and finally a target field within the block.

In order to select a block or a field, you may first use a specialized event—the **Event Tracker**—to *capture* the blocks and fields that belong to a form.

The following figure shows the steps required to set up Form Rules:

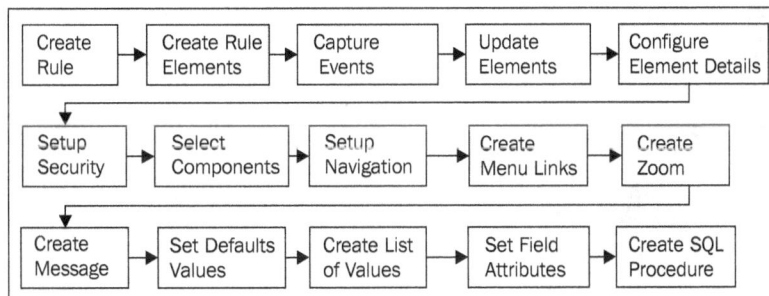

Creating a Form Rule

When Form Rules starts, the following form opens. Use it to create or review form rules:

In order to create a new rule:

1. Type a name for the rule in the **Rule Name** field.

2. In the **Description** field, briefly explain the purpose of the rule.

3. Select the **Debug** textbox to cause Form Rules to display messages as the rule is being run. Otherwise, clear the textbox to prevent the display of such messages.

4. Select the **Active** checkbox to make the rule active, or clear the textbox to hold the rule in reserve.

5. The **Subscribers Exist** checkbox is read-only. It will be selected if you have defined at least one subscriber for the rule (or any of its elements), or cleared if you have not.

Creating a Rule Element

Once the rule itself is named and described, you can create rule elements, one per row in the **Rule Elements** grid:

1. In the **Seq** field, type a number.

2. In the **Element Name** field, type a name for the element.

3. Specify the form that either is itself the target of the element, or contains a block or field that is to be the target. Do this in either of the following two ways:

   ° In the **Form Name** field, select the internal name for the form. Form Rules then supplies a corresponding value in the **User Form Name** field.

   ° In the **User Form Name** field, select a user-friendly display name for the form. Form Rules then supplies a corresponding value in the **Form Name** field.

Form Rules does not recognize blocks, fields, or other items on a form until you run the Event Tracker. If the target of an element is to be a block or field, or if you expect to cite specific items as you define how an element modifies its target, use the fragment of the element that you have created so far, as a vehicle to run the **Event Tracker**.

Capturing Events with Event Tracker

Use the Event Tracker to capture blocks and fields for either of the two purposes: for selection in the **Block Name** and **Field Name** fields of the home **Form Rules** form as you set the target of a rule element, or for selection later as you define how the element modifies a target form or items on it. Moreover, as you run the Event Tracker, you can set some security attributes for the target form.

Capturing Items from a Form

In order to capture blocks, fields, or other form items, complete these steps:

1. Fill in the **Seq**, **Element Name**, and **Form Name** fields in a row of the **Rule Elements** grid.

2. In the **Event** list of values, select the value **Event Tracker**.

3. Save the rule. Click on **File** in the menu bar, then on **Save** in the file menu.

4. Respond to two messages that appear as a result of selecting the
   Event Tracker:

   i. The first provides brief instructions on the use of the Event Tracker.
       After reading the message, click on the **OK** button to close it.

   ii. In the second, click on the **Append** button to add items to an existing
       collection of **metadata** (items already captured) for the form that you
       have chosen. Otherwise select the **Replace** button to discard older
       metadata and begin a new collection.

5. Open the Oracle EBS application that contains the form you have chosen.

Navigate to the form and in it, navigate to each block and field that you may want
to select as you work with Form Rules rule elements. Create or update a record and
save your work.

By doing so, you capture a reference to each item you navigate with the cursor, and
you also capture the **undocumented** events associated with the form. The items you
capture become available in Form Rules in any rule element that targets the form, not
only in the element from which you launched the Event Tracker.

Using the Event Tracker to set security

When you open an Oracle EBS form for which you are running the Event Tracker, an
Oracle Rules Actions menu provides options for setting security properties on the
form. In order to use the menu, carry out the following steps:

1. Create a rule element, select the **Event Tracker**, and open the Oracle EBS
   form that is the target of the element. The **Oracle Rules Actions** menu
   appears with the Oracle EBS form only if it is the target of a rule element for
   which the **Event Tracker** has been selected.

2. Click on a field for which you want to set security or one that exists in a block
   or tab for which you want to set security.

3. Click on **Oracle Rules Actions** in the menu bar, and then on any of the
   following options.

   ° **Prevent Update to Block**: Prevent an existing value from being
     changed for any field in the block where the cursor is located.

   ° **Prevent Insert to Block**: Prevent an original value from being entered
     for any empty field in the block where the cursor is located.

   ° **Prevent Update to Field**: Prevent an existing value from being
     changed for the selected field.

   ° **Hide Field**: Remove the selected field from the form.

- ° **Make This Field Required**: Prevent a user from selecting a new record or closing a form if no value has been saved in the selected field.

- ° **Enforce Uppercase on This Field**: Requires that data entered in the selected field should be all in upper case.

- ° **Hide This Tab**: Remove the tab that contains the selected field, and all the fields associated with it, from the form.

- ° **Get Field Properties**: Capture the properties of the selected field. (This is essentially the same as simply navigating to the field with the Event Tracker running.)

4. A message informs you that a rule is created. Click on the **OK** button to close the message.

The security attributes you configure through use of the Event Tracker take effect when you complete the definition of the Rule Element from which you are running the Event Tracker.

Updating Element definition

In order to complete the rule element, open **Form Rules** (if you have closed it to apply the Event Tracker to an Oracle EBS form) and select the rule with which you want to work. If you have created a fragmentary element for the purpose of running the Event Tracker, select that element. If you are creating a new element from scratch, perform step 1 to step 3 of the previous section and then carry out the following steps:

1. In the **Event** field, select (or replace the value **Event Tracker** with) an event that determines the circumstances under which the rule element is to be evaluated.

2. Choose among the following options:

   - ° **When New Form**: The element fires when a user opens its target form. If you select this event, you cannot enter values in the **Block Name** and **Field Name** fields.

   - ° **When New Block**: The element fires when a user navigates from one block to another in the target form. Else, if you select a value in the **Block Name** field (which is recommended), the element fires when a user navigates to the specified block.

- ○ **When New Item**: The element fires when a user navigates from one field to another in the target form. Else, if you select a value in each of the **Block Name** and **Field Name** fields (which is recommended), the element fires when a user navigates to the specified field.

- ○ **When New Record**: The element fires when a user navigates from one record (new or existing) to another. You may select a block name if you want to restrict the firing to the selection of a record within the specified block.

- ○ **When Validate Record**: The element fires whenever a user saves a record. You may select a block name if you want to restrict the firing to the saving of a record while the cursor is located in the specified block.

- ○ **Zoom Special**: This special event makes a zoom regardless of subscribers. It ignores the subscribers until the moment the zoom action is selected on the Oracle Form. So it enables conditional use of the zoom to navigate to different entities. In essence, the zoom shows up regardless of the subscribers, but does not function when a user tries to zoom and the subscriber evaluates as false.

- ○ **Undocumented events**: Undocumented events associated with the target form appear in the **Event** list of values if they have been captured by the Event Tracker. You can also capture undocumented events manually. No matter how such events are captured. However, Oracle does not support them and the installation of a patch may cause them to disappear.

- ○ **Audit**: The Audit event is no longer supported. Do not select it.

3. If you want the element to target a block or a field, and you have selected an event that allows it to do so, select the block in the **Block Name** field, which offers a selection of values captured by the Event Tracker.

4. If you want the element to target a field, and you have selected an event that allows it to do so, select the field in the **Field Name** field, which offers a selection of values that have been captured by the Event Tracker and that exist in the block you selected in step 2.

5. Select the **Debug** textbox to cause Form Rules to display messages as the rule element is being run. Else, clear the textbox to prevent the display of such messages.

6. Select the **Active** checkbox to make the element active or clear the textbox to hold the element in reserve.

7. Save the rule. Click on **File** in the menu bar, then on **Save** in the **File** menu.

Configuring element details

When you have created a rule element—selected its target form, block, or field, and chosen the event that triggers its use—you need to configure element details.

In order to do so, click on the element in the **Rule Elements** grid of the home **Form Rules** form, and then click on the **Details** button. A **Business Rule Details** form then appears. Click on its tabs to expose panels in which you can assign security attributes, set navigation paths, create messages, define default values, lists of values, or other field attributes, run SQL statements, and run processes defined in the Flow Rules application.

However, note that certain fields are already completed. The values on display reflect the selections you made for the rule element in the home **Form Rules** form.

These include the **Form Name**, **Element Description**, **Event**, **Block Name**, and **Field**.

Name fields near the top of the form. You can alter these values only indirectly, by changing rule-element values in the home **Form Rules** form.

Setting up security

You can assign security attributes to forms, blocks, tabs, fields, and descriptive flexfields (DFF). Attributes are available to each of these components in varying combinations. You can restrict the ability to update, insert, or delete data; require that data to be entered or those text entries to be in upper or lower case; or hide screen items. In order to set these security attributes, use the **Security** panel, which is selected by default when you open the **Business Rule Details** form.

If you navigate to another panel in the **Business Rule Details** form, you can return to the **Security** panel by clicking on the **Security** tab.

If you have used the Event Tracker to set security attributes, each setting occupies a row in the **Security** panel. In order to set security attributes for field instances, use the **Field Attributes** panel, not the **Security** panel.

Selecting Components

In each row of the security grid, select a component whose attributes you want to set:

1. In the **Type** listbox, choose whether you want to set security attributes for the target form, or for a block, tab, field, or DFF on the form.

2. In the **Block/Tab** and **Field Name** fields, select the component whose type you identified in the previous step:

   ° If you selected the **Form** type, leave both fields blank

       °   If you selected the **Block, Tab**, or **DFF** type, choose a value in the **Block/Tab** field and leave the **Field Name** field blank

       °   If you selected the **Field** type, choose values in both the fields

If you intend to set security for a number of fields, you can select them all at once:

1. Click on **Tools** in the menu bar, and then on **Oracle Rules Form Elements** in the **Tools** menu. The following **Form Elements** form will appear:

This form displays a selection of fields that depends on the choices you made as you created the Rule Element in the home **Form Rules** form:

       °   If you left the **Block Name** and **Field Name** fields blank as you created the rule element in the home **Form Rules** form, the **Form Elements** form shows all fields captured by the Event Tracker, from all blocks on the target form

       °   If you selected a **Block Name** but not a **Field Name** as you created the rule element in the home **Form Rules** form, the **Form Elements** form shows all the fields from the selected block that were captured by the Event Tracker

       °   If you selected a **Block Name** and a **Field Name** as you created the Rule Element in the home **Form Rules** form, the **Form Elements** form shows only the selected field

2. For each field you want, click on the **Include Flag** checkbox. Else, to select all fields, click on the **Select All** button. (The **De-Select All** button removes check marks from all checkboxes).

3. When you are satisfied with your selection, click on the **Accept** button. The **Form Elements** form closes, and the fields you chose appear in the **Security** grid of the **Business Rule Details** form. (You can click on the **Close** button to close the **Form Elements** form without accepting any selected fields).

Setting up navigation paths

You can create entries in the **Tools**, **Actions**, or **Reports** menu of a target form, each of which, when clicked, opens another form (or, in a special case, executes a Form Rules rule element). You can also create **zooms** – similar links that are activated when a user clicks on the **Zoom** button in the toolbar.

Typically, such a link becomes active when a form is first opened, and so you would create such links for rule elements that use the **When New Form** event. Moreover, a navigational link works only if the source and destination forms are both available within a single responsibility. If a user does not have access to a form, a navigational link created in Form Rules will not take him there.

In order to create navigation links, click on the **Navigation** tab in the **Business Rule Details** form:

Creating menu links

In order to add a navigation link to a menu in the target form, complete a row in the **Menus** section:

1. In the **Sequence** field, select a sequence number prefixed by the name of the menu to which you want to add the link. (The higher the number you select, the more remote is the possibility of overwriting an existing menu option).

2. In the **Label** field, type a name for the link. This name will appear as an option in the menu you selected in the previous step.

3. In the **To Function** list of values, select the user function name that corresponds to the form to which you are creating a link. In order to ascertain the user function name:

    i. Determine the internal name for the form to which you are creating a link.

    ii. Switch to the Application Developer responsibility and select **Application | Form** option. Using the form name you determined in the previous step, query on the **Form** field and note the corresponding value in the **User Form Name** field. (In order to query, press the *F11* key. Type the value for which you are querying in the appropriate field, and then press *Ctrl + F11*).

    iii. Still in the Application Developer responsibility, select **Application | Function** option. In the **Form** field of its **Form** tab, query on the user form name value that you determined in the previous step. Then click on the **Description** tab and make a note of the value in the **User Function Name** field.

4. If your function takes parameters, the **Parameters** field displays a template indicating what those parameters are. Replace the placeholders (the text surrounded by angle brackets) with actual values. If the **Parameters** field remains blank after you select a function, you need not supply parameters. However, you can, enter **QUERY_ONLY="YES"** to make the destination form open in query-only mode.

5. In the **Icon Name** field, accept the default value.

6. Ensure that the **Active** checkbox is selected.

Creating zooms

A zoom enables a user to move from a block to another form by clicking on the **Zoom** button in the Oracle EBS toolbar. You can create only one zoom per block.

In order to do so, use the **Zooms** section of the **Navigation** panel:

1. In the **From Block** list of values, select the block from which you want to enable the zoom. The list of values (LOVs) presents all of the blocks for the target form that you have captured through the use of the Event Tracker.

2. In the **To Function** list of values, select the user function name that corresponds to the form for which you are creating a link.

3. If the function takes parameters, the **Parameters** field displays a template indicating what those parameters are. If so, replace the placeholders (text surrounded by angle brackets) with actual values. If the **Parameters** field remains blank after you select a function, you need not supply parameters. However, you can enter **QUERY_ONLY="YES"** to make the destination form open in query-only mode.

4. Ensure that the **Active** checkbox is selected.

Creating messages

You can write messages that appear when a user performs an action corresponding to the event you have chosen for a rule element—for example, opening a form, navigating to a field, or saving a record. Click on the **Messages** tab in the **Business Rule Details** form.

In order to create a message:

1. In the **Sequence** field, enter a number that reflects the order in which you want this message to appear in relation to other messages you may create in other rows.

2. In the **Description** field, briefly explain the purpose of the message.

3. In the **Message Type** listbox, select one of the following:

   ° **Note**: The message appears, but the user is able to continue working

   ° **Error**: The message appears, and the user is prevented from saving a record

4. As a result, select this type for messages associated with rule elements that use the When Validate Record event.

5. Write the message in the **Message** textbox. A message can contain not only text, but also field names. Use the following syntax: **#:BLOCK. FIELD_NAME#**. At run time, the field names are replaced by values associated with the currently selected record.

6. A message can be made to appear only when certain data conditions are met, for example, a promotional message may appear when a user enters a certain item on an order. In order to make this happen:

   i. Create the message for a rule element based on the **When New Item** event.

   ii. Create an element subscriber with a **Data filter** type so that the message appears only when the correct data is entered.

Setting default values

You can set the default values of fields in the form that is the target of a rule element. In order to do so, click on the **Default Values** tab in the **Business Rule Details** form:

Regardless of the event you select to trigger the rule element, you can set values for any number of fields in any number of blocks on the form (provided that the fields and blocks have been captured through use of the Event Tracker). Devote one row in the grid to each field:

1. In the **Block** list of values, select the block that contains the field for which you want to set a default value.

2. In the **Field** list of values, select the field for which you want to set a default value.

3. In the **Default Type** listbox, select one of these values:

   ° **Static**: The default value is a constant

   ° **Form**: The default value is a copy of the value entered for another field on the form

   ° **SQL**: The default is a value returned by a SQL statement

4. In the **Default Value** field, type an entry appropriate for the selection that you made in the **Default Type** listbox:

    °   If you select **Static**, type the value that serves as the default.

    °   If you select **Form**, identify the field that returns a default value. Use the format **BLOCK_NAME.FIELD_NAME** — the internal names for the block that contains the field and the field itself.

    °   If you select **SQL**, type a SQL statement that returns values for use as defaults.

5. Ensure that the **Active** checkbox is selected.

Creating and modifying lists of values

You can both alter existing lists of values or create new LOVs. Before you do so, you must run the Event Tracker on fields for which you want to create or modify LOVs.

Altering an existing LOV

In order to alter an existing List of Value (LOV) select the field and then modify the SQL statement that compiles the values displayed in the field. However, you cannot modify the SELECT portion of the SQL statement, which identifies the database columns that return values to the LOV.

You can alter only the where and sort by portions of the statement, which specify the conditions under which records are selected to be returned, and the order in which they are arranged.

1. In Form Rules, ensure that you have created a rule and rule element that you want to use to modify the LOV. The element must select, as a target, the form on which the LOV exists. (It is often the case that this element would use When New Form as an event. If so, the form is all you need to select as a target. If you choose an event that requires you to do so, also choose a block and/or a field).

2. Navigate to the form that contains the LOV you want to change, and click in the LOV.

3. Run a trace file:

    i.   Click on **Help** in the menu bar, then **Diagnostics** in the **Help** menu, and then click on **Trace** in the **Diagnostics** submenu. Select the **Regular Trace** radio button. If you have not already used a **Diagnostics** option, an **Enable Diagnostics** dialog prompts you for your Oracle password. Enter it and click on the **OK** button to clear the dialog. A note informs you that tracing is activated and provides the path and name of a trace file. Click on the **OK** button to clear the note.

    ii.   In the LOV that you want to change, select any value.

    iii. Click on **Help** in the menu bar, then **Diagnostics** in the **Help** menu, and then click on **Trace** in the **Diagnostics** submenu. Select the **No Trace** radio button. (Another message informs you that tracing is deactivated and provides the path and name of a trace file. Click on the **OK** button to clear the note.)

    iv. Open Form Rules and use a utility called **TKProf** to examine your trace file.

    v.   Click on **GRC Controls Utilities** in the menu bar, and then on **Oracle Rules TKProf Utility** in the **GRC Controls Utilities** menu.

    vi. A concurrent request runs, and a message informs you of its identification number. Make a note of the number and click on the **OK** button to close the message.

    vii. Click on **View** in the menu bar, and then on **Requests** in the **View** menu.

    viii.A **Find Requests** form will open. Click on the **Specific Requests** radio button and, in the **Request ID** field, enter the ID number for your request. Click on the **Find** button.

    ix. A **Requests** form will appear. Its grid contains an entry for your request. When its status is set to **Completed** (you may need to click on the **Refresh Data** button), click on the **View Log** button.

    x.   In the log file, search for the SQL statement that generates values for the LOV. (Typically, it begins as `select displayed_ field,description,lookup_code_from`.) Leave the log file open.

4. In Form Rules, select the rule and element you want to use to modify the LOV.

5. Click on the **Details** button and in the **Business Rule Details** form, click on the **List of Values** tab:

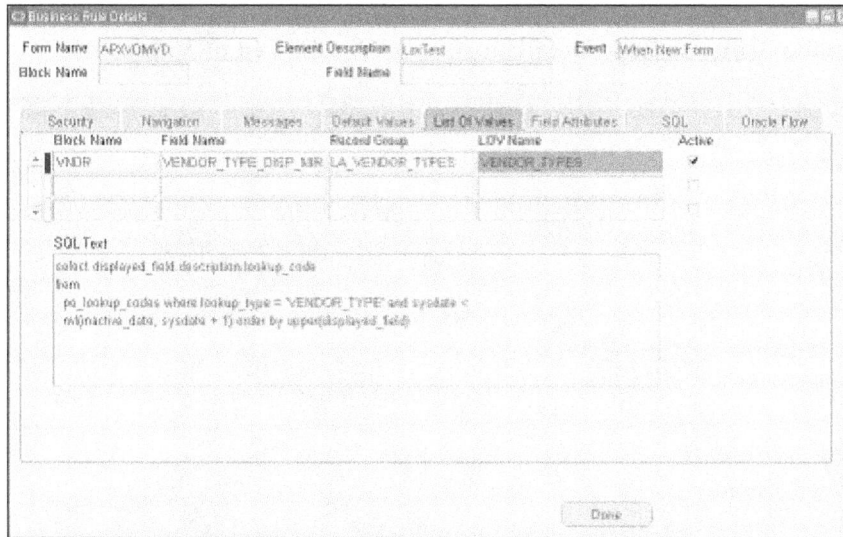

6. In the **Block Name** field, select the block where the LOV exists. In the **Field Name** field, select the field where the LOV exists. Accept the default values in the **Record Group** and **LOV Name** fields, and be sure the **Active** checkbox is selected.

7. In the log file, copy the SQL statement for your LOV (highlight it and press *Ctrl + C*). In the **Form Rules Business Rule Details** form, click on the **SQL Text** area of the **List of Values** panel. Press *Ctrl + V* to paste the SQL statement there.

8. Close the log file (click on the × symbol in its upper-right corner). In the **Form Rules List of Values** panel, edit the SQL statement as you desire. Remember that you can modify only the `where` and `sort by` clauses. If any bind variables exist in the statement (they may appear as `:1` or `:5`), you may have to open the form to identify the actual SQL that is being executed.

Creating a new List of Value

In order to create a new List of Value (LOV) you will need to convert an existing text-entry field for use as a list of values. The process involves identifying the field (after first having used the Event Tracker to capture it) and creating a SQL statement that compiles values that the field is to display. Carry out the following steps to create a new list of values:

1. Ensure that you have created a Form Rules rule and Rule Element that you want to use to create the LOV. The rule element must specify, as a target, the field you intend to make into a list of values (and therefore, of course, the block and form that contain the field), and it must use the When New Item event.

2. In Form Rules, select the rule and element, click on the **Details** button and in the **Business Rule Details** form, click on the **List of Values** tab:

3. In the **Block** field, select the block where the LOV exists. In the **Field Name** field, select the field where the LOV exists. The **Record Group** field defaults to a value that begins with **LA_** and the **LOV Name** field defaults to **APPCORE_ZOOM**. Now, accept these values. Be sure the **Active** checkbox is selected.

4. The **SQL Text** field displays a **stub** SQL statement. You may edit it or replace it entirely, in order to create either a static list or one that returns values determined at runtime. Keep the following points in mind:

   ○ The SQL statement can specify only two return columns, with the aliases NAME and VALUE

   ○ The template constitutes one line of a SQL statement that returns one value

In order to create multiple values in a static LOV, use the UNION statement. For example, the following SQL statement returns the values High, Medium, and Low:

- SELECT 'High' NAME, 'High' VALUE FROM DUAL
- UNION
- SELECT 'Medium' NAME, 'Medium' VALUE FROM DUAL
- UNION
- SELECT 'Low' NAME, 'Low' VALUE FROM DUAL

In the template, the value DUAL is a placeholder for a table name. In order to create a static list of values, leave it as is. In order to create a list of values determined at runtime, replace it with the name of the table that supplies values.

Setting field attributes

You can designate the display properties of blocks and fields, such as the positioning, color, size, and weight of items. You can also set security properties for field instances. In order to do so, click on the **Field Attributes** tab in the **Business Rule Details** form:

Set an attribute for one block, field, or field instance in each row of the grid:

1. In the **Seq** field, type a number that reflects the order in which you want this attribute to be set with respect to other attributes listed in the grid.

2. In the **Type** listbox, choose whether you want to set an attribute for a block, field, or field instance.

3. Select the component whose type you identified in the previous step. If you have selected the **Block** type, choose a value in the **Block Name** list of values and leave the **Field Name** list of values blank. If you have selected the **Field** or **Field Instance** type, choose values in both the **Block Name** and **Field Name** LOVs. (The LOVs display blocks and fields that you have captured through the use of the Event Tracker.)

A **field** is a set of similar values, while a **field instance** is an individual value for a field. For example, when a form presents a grid, a field is an entire column in the grid, and a field instance is an individual cell in the column.

Field attributes apply no matter what the value of a field is. If you create field instance attributes, you need to define the instances to which the attributes apply. In order to do this, create a data subscriber that targets the field that you selected in step 3. The attributes that you create would take effect when the subscriber definition evaluates to true.

Take care that field instance security attributes defined here do not conflict with field security attributes defined in the **Security** panel.

1. In the **Property** listbox, select an attribute that you want to set for the component you have identified. Attributes vary by component type. For descriptions, see the lists following step 6 of this procedure.

2. In the **Value** field, type or select the value that sets the attribute. For example, if you selected **Background Color** in the **Property** field, you would select a specific color, for example red, in the value field.

3. Select the **Enabled Flag** checkbox to activate the attribute or clear the checkbox to deactivate the attribute.

Blocking Attributes

You can set the following block attributes:

*   **Blockscrollbar X Pos**: Sets the horizontal starting point for the scroll bar from the left of the block. Just type in the required number of pixels.

*   **Blockscrollbar Y Pos**: Sets the vertical starting point for the scroll bar, from the top of the block. Type a number of pixels.

*   **Current Row Background Color**: For the row on which the cursor is focused, it sets the color of the space surrounding field entries. Select from six colors.

*   **Current Row Font Size**: Sets the type size for entries in the row on which the cursor is focused. Select a number from 1 to 18 points.

*   **Current Row Font Weight**: Sets the thickness of type for entries in the row on which the cursor is focused. Select from nine weights.

*   **Current Row Foreground Color**: For the row on which the cursor is focused, it sets the color of field entries. Select from six colors.

*   **Next Navigation Block**: Sets the block to which the cursor moves if a user presses the *Tab* key from the last field in the current block. Type a block name.

- **Previous Navigation Block**: Sets the block to which the cursor moves if a user presses *Shift + Tab* from the first field in the current block. Type a block name.

- **Query Allowed**: Determines whether a user can query fields in the block—search for records with a field set to a value that matches a search value. Select **TRUE** or **FALSE**.

- **Query Data Source Name**: Sets the database table or view searched for records in response to a query. Type the name of a database table or view.

Field attributes

You can set the following field attributes:

- **Background Color**: Sets the color of space surrounding field entries. (For a field instance in a selected row, the **Current Row Background Color** setting for the block takes precedence.) Select from six colors.

- **Conceal Data**: Presents asterisks rather than actual entries for a field. Enter the value as **TRUE** and in order to set the value to **FALSE**, do not select this attribute.

- **Font Size**: Sets the type size for field entries. (For a field instance in a selected row, the **Current Row Font Size** setting for the block takes precedence). Select a number from 1 to 18 points.

- **Font Weight**: Sets the thickness of type for field entries. (For a field instance in a selected row, the **Current Row Font Weight** setting for the block takes precedence.) Select from nine weights.

- **Foreground Color**: Sets the color of field entries. For a field instance in a selected row, the **Current Row Foreground Color** setting for the block takes precedence.) Select from six colors.

- **Format Mask**: Imposes formatting on numeric or date fields:
    - **999"-"99"-"999**: Social Security Number
    - **$999,999,999.99**: Monetary value, US currency up to $1 billion
    - **999,999,999.9999**: Numeric with thousand separators, up to four decimals
    - **999,999,999.99**: Numeric with thousand separators, up to two decimals
    - **L99G999D99**: Local currency with thousand separators, up to two decimals

- ○ **0999**: Number, up to four digits, with leading zeros
- ○ **DD-MONTH-YYYY**: Date, with month spelt out
- ○ **DD-MON-YYYY HH24:MI:SS**: Date and time, with month abbreviated

- **Height**: Sets the vertical dimension of the field. Type a number of pixels.
- **Hint Text**: Creates a message that provides information about the field in a status bar at the bottom of the screen. Type the message of up to 30 characters.
- **Next Navigation Item**: Sets the field to which the cursor moves if the user presses the *Tab* key. Select from a list of field names.
- **Previous Navigation Item**: Sets the field to which the cursor moves if the user presses *Shift + Tab*. Select from a list of field names.
- **Prompt Text**: Creates a display name that identifies the field on screen. Type the label of up to 30 characters.
- **Width**: Sets the horizontal dimension of the field. Type a number of pixels.
- **X Pos**: Sets the horizontal starting point for the field from the left of its block. Type a number of pixels.
- **Y Pos**: Sets the vertical starting point for the field from the top of its block. Type a number of pixels.

Field instance attributes

You can set the following field instance attributes:

- **Insert Allowed**: Determines whether a user may enter data if the field instance is blank. Select **TRUE** or **FALSE**.
- **Navigable**: Determines whether a user may select the field instance. Select **TRUE** or **FALSE**.
- **Required**: Determines whether a user must enter data in a field instance. Select **TRUE** or **FALSE**.
- **Update Allowed**: Determines whether a user may alter existing data in a field instance. Select **TRUE** or **FALSE**.

Creating SQL procedures

You can create SQL statements that are executed when a user performs an action corresponding to the event you have chosen for a rule element.

1. In order to do so, click on the **SQL** tab in the **Business Rule Details** form. Create any number of statements, one per row in the grid:

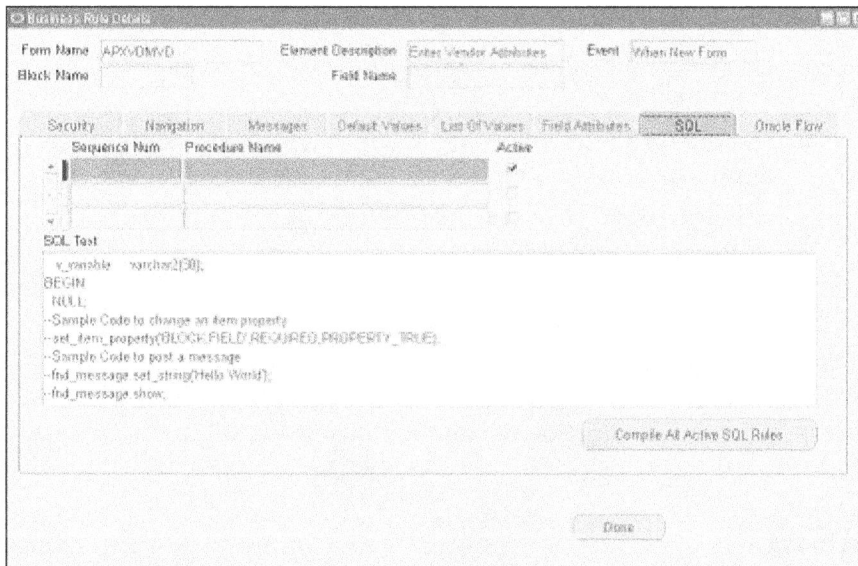

2. In the **Sequence Num** field, type a number that reflects the order in which you want this SQL statement to be executed in relation to other statements that you may create in other rows.

3. In the **Procedure Name** field, type a name for the SQL statement.

4. Ensure that the **Active** checkbox is selected to use the statement, or clear the checkbox to hold the statement in reserve.

5. The **SQL Text** field displays a template. Substitute actual values for placeholder values in the template, or replace the template entirely with a statement of your own.

    °   You may not reference the Form Bind variables directly

    °   In order to reference a field, you must use the name_in function

    °   Declare variables before **BEGIN** keyword. Do not use the word **Declare** in the SQL text

6. Click on the **Compile All Active SQL Rules** button. (Else, as an alternative, click on **Tools** in the menu bar and then on **Oracle Rules Compile All Active SQL Rules** in the **Tools** menu.) This has the following two effects:

    °   A concurrent request runs to compile the code. A message informs you of its identification number. Make a note of the number and click on the **OK** button to close the message.

    °   A validation procedure determines whether the SQL is syntactically correct.

7. Review the concurrent program log for errors:

    i. Click on **View** in the menu bar, and then on **Requests** in the **View** menu.

    ii. A **Find Requests** form opens. Click on the **Specific Requests** radio button and, in the **Request ID** field, enter the ID number for your request. Click on the **Find** button.

    iii. A **Requests** form will appear. Its grid contains an entry for your request. When its status is set to **Completed** (you may need to click on the **Refresh Data** button), click on the **View Log** button.

8. If successful, exit Oracle EBS and log in. SQL rules are implemented via the custom library, which may be cached when you log in. In order to test recently compiled rules, log out and log in to the application.

Summary

In this chapter, you learned to establish an IT Audit management program to mitigate information technology risks. The scope of an IT Audit plan includes testing general computer controls, as well as application controls. IT Audit approach requires an assessment of the controls framework adopted by the IT organization. In addition, we have provided instruction to set up IT and Application controls using Oracle GRC Control Suite, which can be deployed to improve your overall control environment.

IT Audit plan starts by reviewing the control documentation that defines the IT standards, organization structure, budgets, policies, and procedures. IT auditors evaluate controls in many different ways, including manual control testing, assessment of periodic end-user surveys, and effectiveness of monitoring controls. Oracle GRC Manager can be used to manage the IT Audit plan.

Organization can improve the overall control environment by automating IT general controls and application controls using the Oracle GRC Controls Suite, which includes Access Controls Governor, Transaction Controls Governor, Configurations Controls Governor, and Preventive Controls Governor. Access Controls Governor can help reduce the **segregation of duties** risk by detecting incidents where the ERP security configuration has inherent conflicts or users have been granted access to roles and responsibility that create a conflict. Transaction Controls Governor can indentify if the user with access to ERP system has created transactions that violate a business policy, or control. Auditors can use this application to improve the testing effectiveness by continuously monitoring selected controls. Configuration Controls Governor enables IT organization to reduce the cost and risk of maintaining, upgrading, and implementing ERP systems by tracking configuration changes in the ERP system and comparing results across various ERP instances as required to manage the application lifecycle. Business Process Owners can set up fine-grain controls using the Preventive Controls Governor to optimize the application flow and stop errors and frauds before it is too late.

10

Cross Industry Cross Compliance

In this chapter, we change our focus to look more closely at compliance aspects. This is a discussion of the laws, regulations, and frameworks that an enterprise is subject to. We will present the law, regulation, or framework and then underline both the practices and technologies that best help you meet it and confirm that it has been met. There are different degrees of rigor in different areas of compliance in varying industries and countries that we will focus on in subsequent chapters. This topic should begin with a discussion involving both the head of internal audit and chief legal counsel.

Sarbanes-Oxley

First among equals in the cross industry regulations is Sarbanes-Oxley. The regulation resulted in real focus on risk management and controls verification. Section 404 requires the management to state that they confirm the effectiveness of internal controls, and for auditors to attest that the management's assertion is well founded. Here we will run through a few key sections of Sarbanes and point out what area of the technology and applications are most helpful in meeting the requirement. While the act is clearly passed in the United States, it applies to any entity that is raising money in the U.S., not just U.S. companies. As such, a very large portion of the companies in the world are subject to the regulations under Sarbanes-Oxley.

Important sections of the act and the technologies that apply

The famous sections of Sarbanes-Oxley are explained in *Chapter 5, Risk Assessment and Control Verification*, *Chapter 6, Documenting Your Controls*, and *Chapter 7, Managing Your Testing Phase: Management Testing and Certifying Controls*. What we explain here are some sections that are also very important, that were not so much of a gold rush for the auditing profession, but nonetheless, have some significant technology impacts.

Title 1: Establishment and Operation of the Public Company Accounting Oversight Board

Sections 101 through 109 establish the composition of the Board of Directors and the requirement for Public Accounting firms to register with the **Public Company Accounting Oversight Board (PCAOB)**.

Section 103 is probably the only section where technology may assist. It is again more targeted at the public accounting firm than the company being audited, but it is a great statement of best practice. It requires the accounting firm to hold working papers that back an audit opinion for seven years. This should probably be reflected in the document management system of the audited company and the records retention policies for those record types. (Refer to the *Managing Records Retention Policies with Content Management Server* section in *Chapter 2, Corporate Governance*.)

Title 2: Auditor Independence

Sections 201 through 209 are all about **auditor independence**.

Sections 201 and 202 are all about services that an auditor cannot provide to the clients that they are auditing to ensure that any audit opinion is not colored by the prospect of other business with that client. To this end you should implement **Holds** with the Accounts Payable system to ensure that invoices are vetted by the audit committee to ensure that the services rendered are actually audit services. This is the thrust of section 202 to get pre-approval of any non-audit services. In order to set up the Audit firm as a supplier and ensure purchase orders and payments are subject to holds and approvals, log in using the Payables Management responsibility and navigate to **Supplier Inquiry**. Inquire on a supplier and click on the **Edit** icon, as shown in the following screenshot:

In order to release holds from an invoice, find the invoice from which you want to release holds and click on the **Holds** button to navigate to the **Invoice Holds** window. Release a hold by selecting a **Release Name**. You can select from all the **Invoice Approvals** defined with the type **Invoice Release Reason**.

Title 4: Financial Disclosures

Title 4 is all about **financial disclosures** and contains the famous Section 404. Section 409 is all about **real time disclosures**. It requires disclosure to the public on a rapid and current basis on such additional information concerning material changes in the financial condition or operations in plain English, which may include trend and qualitative information and graphic presentations. Refer to the section on Monitoring execution with Oracle Business Intelligence in *Chapter 2, Corporate Governance*, for how to provide insight and early warning on the financial condition of the company. For example, Infission might be able to see the disruption to its supply chain for its disk drive component from the floods in Thailand.

Title 8: Legal Ramifications for Corporate Fraud

Title 8 is all about accountability for altering documents. Section 802 imposes penalties for destroying or altering documents with intent to destroy them, and also establishes a minimum records retention period for Audit Working papers and other correspondence regarding the audit. (Refer to the *Managing Records Retention Policies with Content Management Server* section in *Chapter 2, Corporate Governance*.)

ISO 27001 – Information Security Management System (ISMS)

The following diagram shows the key objectives for an Information Security System:

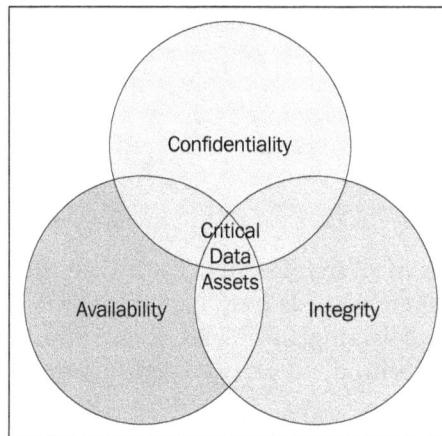

The ISMS must protect **information assets** from any threats to their availability, integrity, and confidentiality. The ISMS includes Organizational structures, policies, planning activities, practices, procedures, processes, and resources. It is set up to ensure that processes, technology, and user behavior all align to this goal.

ISO 27001 provides a specification against which a deployment and ISMS can be verified by an accredited certification body, such as the UK Accreditation Service. Such organizations are permitted to grant a formal certificate.

The components of an Information Security Management System

While the ISMS specification has other components, six of them are crucial.

- A defined scope
- An information security policy
- A risk assessment
- A risk treatment plan
- For each risk treatment, state the control objectives and controls to be implemented
- A Statement of Applicability for the controls listed in ISO 27001 annex A

The risk assessment process

The following is a diagram of the information risk assessment process:

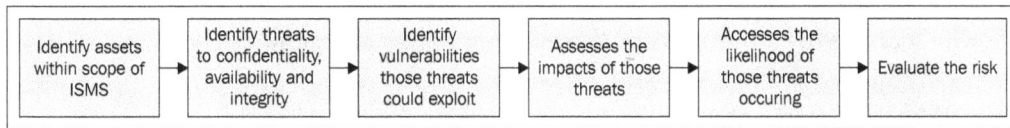

Identify assets within scope of ISMS	Identify threats to confidentiality, availability and integrity	Identify vulnerabilities those threats could exploit	Assesses the impacts of those threats	Accesses the likelihood of those threats occuring	Evaluate the risk

Identify the systems and information assets that are critical to the achievement of the organization's tasks and objectives, as well as the people who are responsible for the protection of those assets.

Then identify what can go wrong or what can attack those assets. Next, determine if the information assets are actually open to exploitation by the threats. If an information asset is exploited by threat, the impact must be assessed. This is generally done in qualitative terms, but can be monetized by evaluating the loss to the enterprise of the information not being available. For example, if the customer master is unavailable and orders cannot be entered for three days. The likelihood from almost certain to highly unlikely must also be assessed before the risk level can finally be calculated and added to the risk register.

The Risk Treatment Plan

For each risk in the risk registry, the enterprise needs to develop a risk treatment plan. The enterprise may choose to pass the risk to another party through insurance or other contractual means. The enterprise may choose to apply controls that will reduce the likelihood and/or impact to acceptable levels. The management must positively accept the residual risks they are accepting. The risk treatment plan should also include a plan to address security incidents if a control should fail.

The Statement of Applicability

Appendix A of the ISO 27000 standard contains a set of controls arranged in control areas and applicable control objectives. These are very generic controls that have wide applicability and part of the process is to explain their application with the ISMS, or explain why they were felt to not be applicable. The groupings are as follows:

* Clause A5 Security Policy
* Clause A6 Organizing Information Security

- Clause A7 Asset Management
- Clause A8 Human Resources Security
- Clause A9 Physical and Environmental Security
- Clause A10 Communications and operations management
- Clause A11 Access Control
- Clause A12 Information System acquisition, development and maintenance
- Clause A13 Information security incident management
- Clause A14 Business continuity management
- Clause A15 Compliance

While listing all of the controls would change the nature and utility of this book, we have given you a sample here so that you can see how they fit into the GRC Applications.

Clause	Control Description
A5	Information Security Policy
A6	Organization of Information Security
A6.1	Internal Organization: To provide management direction and support for information security in accordance with business requirements and relevant laws and regulations
A6.1.1	Management commitment to Information Security
A6.1.2	Information Security coordination
A6.1.3	Allocation of Information Security Responsibilities
A6.1.4	Authorization process for information processing facilities
A6.1.5	Confidentiality Agreements
A6.1.6	Contact with Authorities
A6.1.7	Contact with Special Interest Groups
A6.1.8	Independent review of Information Security
A6.2	External Parties: To maintain the security of organizational information processing facilities and information assets accessed, processed, communicated to, or managed by external parties.
A6.2.1	Assessment of risks related to external parties
A6.2.2	Addressing security when dealing with customers
A6.2.3	Addressing security in third-party agreements
A7	Asset management
A7.1	Responsibility for Assets: To achieve and maintain appropriate protection of organizational assets

Clause	Control Description
A7.2	Information classification: To ensure that information assets receive an appropriate level of protection
A8	Human Resources Security
A8.1	Before Employment: To ensure that all employees, contractors, and third-party users understand their responsibilities and are suitable for the roles they are considered for, and to reduce the risk of theft, fraud, or misuse of the facilities
A8.2	During employment to ensure that all users are aware of information security threats and concerns, their responsibilities and liabilities, are equipped to support organizational security policy, and to reduce the risk of human error
A8.3	Termination or change of employment: To ensure that all users exit an organization or change employment in an orderly manner
A8.3.1	Termination responsibilities
A8.3.2	Return of Assets
A8..3.3	Removal of Access Rights
A9	Physical and Environmental Security
A9.1	Secure Areas: To prevent unauthorized physical access, damage, and interference to the organization's premises and information
A9.2	Equipment security: To prevent loss, damage, theft, or compromise of assets and interruption to the organization's activities
A10	Communications and operations management
A10.1	Operational procedures and responsibilities: To ensure the correct and secure operation of information processing facilities
A10.2	Third-party service delivery management
A10.3	System planning and acceptance: To minimize risks of system failures
A10.4	Protection against malicious and mobile code
A10.5	Back up
A10.6	Network security management
A10.7	Media Handling: To prevent the unauthorized disclosure, modification, removal, or destruction of assets, and interruption to business activities
A11	Access control
A11.1	Business requirement for access control: To control access to information
A11.2	User Access Management: To ensure authorized users' access and to prevent unauthorized access to information systems
A11.3	User responsibilities: To prevent unauthorized user access and compromise or theft of information
A11.4	Network Access Control: To protect networked services from unauthorized access

Clause	Control Description
A11.5	Operating System Access Control: To prevent unauthorized access to information systems
A11.6	Application and Information access control: To prevent unauthorized access to information held in information systems
A11.7	Mobile computing and telenetworking: To ensure information security when using mobile computing and telenetworking facilities
A12	Information Systems acquisition, development, and maintenance
A12.1	Security requirements of Information Systems: To ensure that security is an integral part of information systems
A12.2	Correct processing in applications to prevent errors, loss, unauthorized modification, or misuse of information or applications
A12.3	Cryptographic controls: To ensure confidentiality, authenticity, or integrity of information by cryptographic means
A12.4	Security of system files: To ensure the security of system files
A12.5	Security in development and support processes: To maintain the security of application system software and information
A12.6	Technical Vulnerability Management: To prevent the damage resulting from exploitation of published vulnerabilities
A13	Information Security Incident Management
A13.1	Reporting information security events and weaknesses: To ensure timely, corrective action is taken
A13.2	Management of information security incidents and improvements: To ensure a consistent and effective approach is applied to the management of information security incidents
A14	Business Continuity Management
A14.1	Information Security aspects of Business Continuity Management: To counteract interruptions to business activities, to protect critical business processes from the effects of major failures or disasters, and to ensure timely resumptions
A15	Compliance
A15.1	Compliance with legal requirements
A15.2	Compliance with security policies and standards
A15.3	Information Systems Audit

Oracle's products and ISO 27000

The first component of the ISMS that we need to identify is where the list of critical information assets can be seen. Those information assets that are subject to data security through **FND Grants** are exposed as **FND_OBJECTS** in the Grants User interface. The following is a screenshot of the Grants user interface:

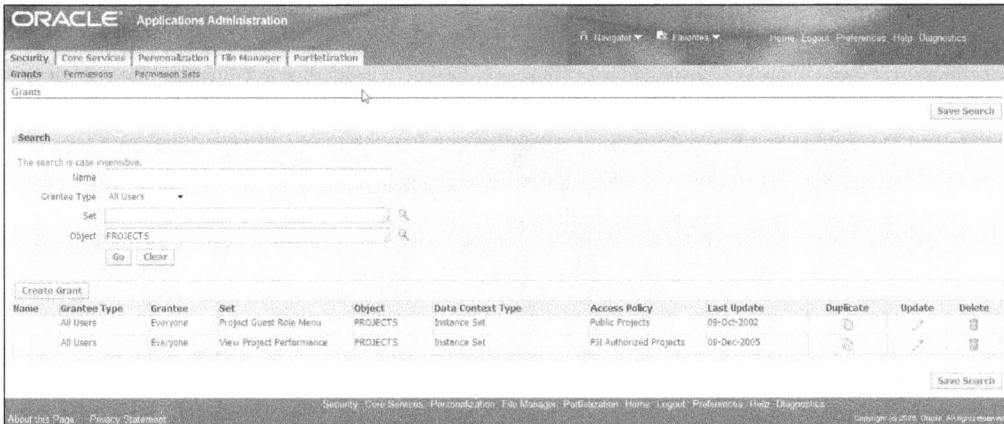

You can navigate to the **Grants** user interface from the Functional Administrator responsibility, by selecting the **Security** tab.

You can also see the list of database resources in **Authorization Policy Manager** (**APM**). APM is the successor to the E-Business Suite security model from Fusion Middleware. When you open the Authorization Policy Manager, you can either choose the **Search Database Resources** in the main area or choose **Database Resource** in the **Search** drop-down in the left-hand search panel:

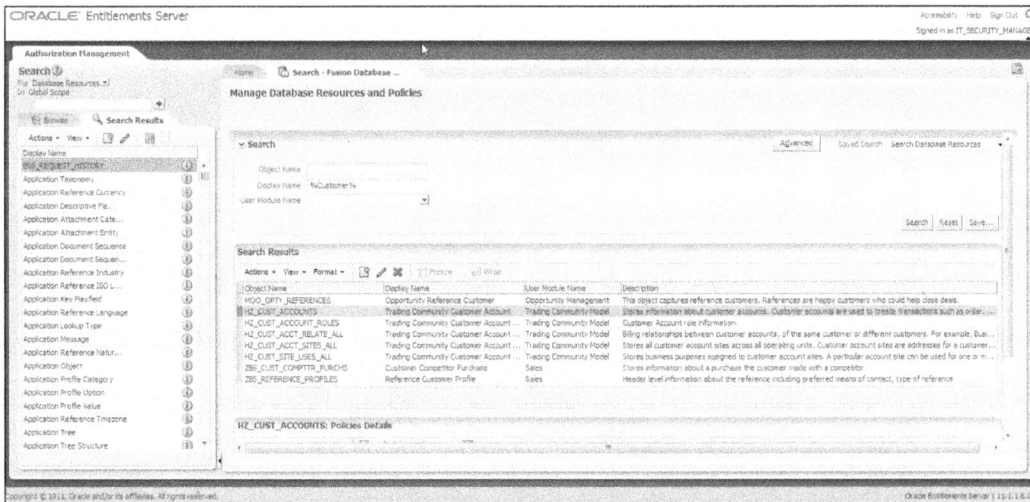

In Oracle, the risk library would be stored in the **eGRCM Risk Registry**. I have generally found standards' bodies reluctant to give a standard list of risks, although they do give a standard set of control objectives. To my eye the list of control objectives is a rewording of the risks. A risk is something that can go wrong and the control objective is to prevent it from going wrong. In this example, we have taken some of the higher-level control objectives in the appendix and translated them into risks for illustrative purposes. The following is a screenshot from the eGRCM Risk Registry:

Manage Risk

Search: Risk — Advanced

Match: All / Any
Name: A
Description:
Status:

Search | Reset

Search Results: Risk

Actions ▾ View ▾ | Detach | Add to Favorites

Name	Description	Status	State
A6.1R	Lack of management direction and support for information security in accordance with business requirements and relevant laws and regulations.	Active	In Review
A6.2R	The loss of confidentiality or availability of organizational information processing facilities and information assets accessed, processed, communicated to or managed by exter	Active	In Review
A8.1R	Rrisk of theft, fraud or misuse of the facilities.	Active	In Review
A8.2 R	Failure of employees to be are aware of information security threats and concerns, their responsibilities and liabilities. Failure ofemployees to support organizational security	Active	In Review

The controls from Appendix A of ISO 27000 would be stored in the eGRCM Controls Registry. The statement of applicability can be derived from whether the control is deemed to be applicable to any risk:

Manage Controls

Search Controls — Advanced

Match: All / Any
Name: A   Status:
Description: Type:
State: Enforcement Type:

Search | Reset

Search Results: Controls

Actions ▾ View ▾ | Detach | Add To Favorites

Name	Description	Status	State	Method
A6.1.2	Information Security Coordination	Active	In Review	Manual
A6.1.4	Authorization process for information processing facilities	Active	In Review	Manual
A6.2.2	Addressing security when dealing with customers	Active	In Review	Manual
A6.1	Internal Organization: to provide management direction and support for information security in accc	Active	In Review	Manual
A6.1.5	Confidentiality Agreements	Active	In Review	Manual
A6.1.1	Management Commitment to Information Security	Active	New	Manual
A6.1.3	Allocation of Information Security Responsibilities	Active	In Review	Manual
A6.2	External Parties: To maintain the security of organizational information processing facilities and infor	Active	In Review	Manual
A6.2.1	Assessment of risks related to external parties	Active	In Review	Manual

Control Objectives for IT (COBIT)

COBIT provided by ISACA provides control objectives for IT processes. While COSO gives a general framework, COBIT provides control objectives for each IT process. We will demonstrate where those processes are likely to be running in the Oracle solution and show the settings and configurations that may best meet those control objectives.

Managing IT processes in Oracle GRC applications to support COBIT Framework

InFission IT Audit team has implemented IT controls by following the COBIT standard that is supported by Oracle GRC applications. The COBIT framework is supported as follows:

COBIT Objective	Control description	InFission IT Control management system
Plan and Organize (PO)	Provides direction to solution delivery (AI) and service delivery (DS)	IT plans, policies, and budgets are maintained in Oracle GRC Manager
Acquire and Implement (AI)	Provides the solutions and passes them to be turned into services	IT project policies and procedures documents are maintained in Oracle GRC Manager
Deliver and Support (DS)	Receives the solutions and makes them usable for end users	Oracle GRC Controls
Monitor and Evaluate (ME)	Monitors all processes to ensure that the direction provided is followed	Oracle GRC Controls

InFission COBIT Framework setup in Oracle GRC Manager

InFission IT audit team has implemented the COBIT Framework using the Oracle GRC Manager Perspectives to support hierarchical structure to meet COBIT objectives. This approach enables the audit team to reuse components that support other GRC initiatives such as Sarbanes-Oxley (SOX). The common components include risk, controls, and process documents. In addition, this approach also enables the IT audit team to share information with other auditors and managers.

The InFission COBIT Perspective is set up as follows:

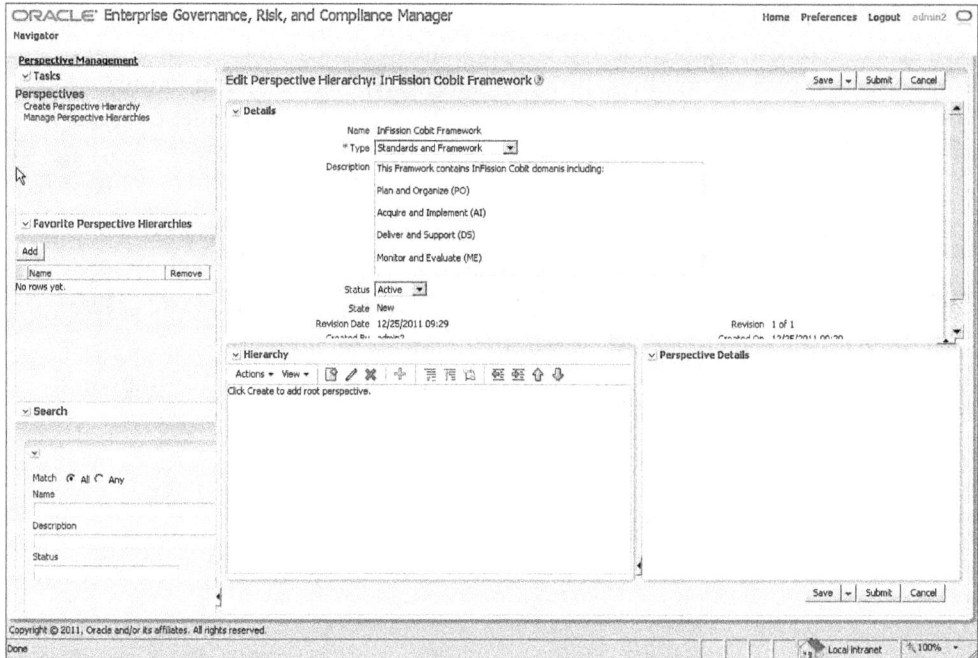

The perspective hierarchy and the structure of the perspective items, is set up as follows:

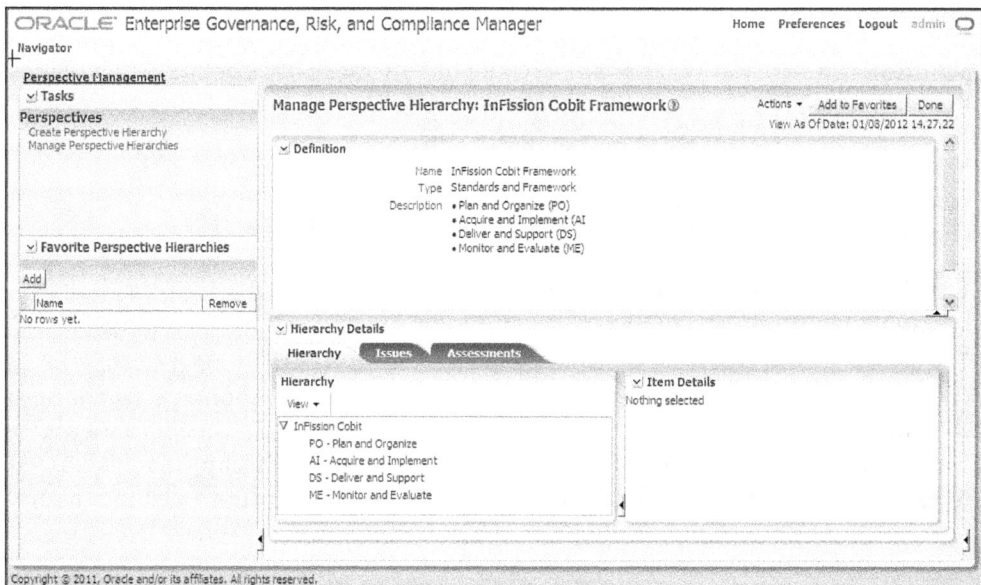

InFission IT Controls Management Approach

InFission's approach to managing IT Controls consists of managing the COBIT domains as explained in the following sections.

Plan and Organize (PO)

InFission IT management is responsible for strategy and tactics to develop the annual IT plan and origination structure that can best contribute to the achievement of the business objectives. The CIO is responsible for the strategic vision that is planned, communicated, and managed for different perspectives. An effective organization structure and technological infrastructure is put in place to ensure successful execution of the plan.

The InFission IT plan consists of the following planning documents that are maintained in Oracle GRC Manager and Process elements:

- Annual IT Goals
- Information system architecture
- Technological direction statement
- IT organization structure
- IT Budget
- Annual IT Management Letter
- Compliance Requirements
- IT Risks
- Project Plans
- Quality Plans

The following screenshot shows the Annual IT Goals process in Oracle GRC Manager:

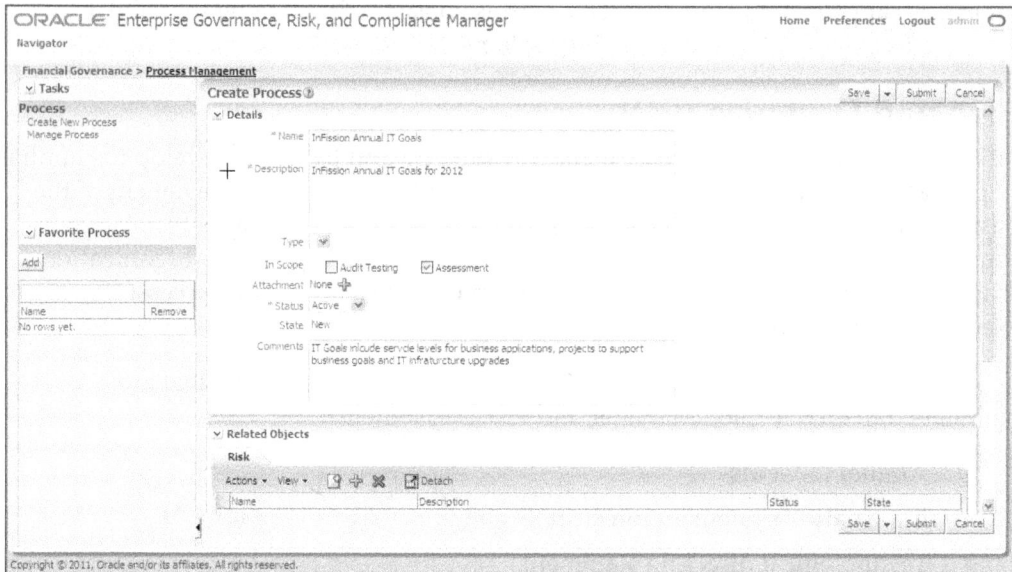

Once the plan and the organization structure are approved by the board, the IT Audit Director is responsible for assessing the controls to address the following management questions:

- Are the IT and business strategies aligned?
- Is the enterprise achieving optimum use of its resources?
- Does everyone in the organization understand the IT objectives?
- Are IT risks understood and managed?
- Is the quality of IT systems appropriate for business needs?

Acquire and Implement (AI)

InFission IT management implements the annual plan to meet its strategic objectives by indentifying the IT solutions needed to support business processes. Once the IT needs are approved, the solutions are developed or acquired, as well as implemented and integrated into the business process.

In addition, IT management manages the changes in and maintenance of existing systems by using the COBIT AI domain to make sure the solutions continue to meet business objectives.

InFission uses Oracle GRC Manager to acquire and implement IT services. The IT acquisition and implementation process consists of the following elements:

- Documentation for all automated solutions
- Policies to acquire and procedures to maintain application software
- Policies to acquire and procedures to maintain technology infrastructure
- General IT development and maintaining procedures
- Methodology to install and validate systems
- Procedure to manage changes

The InFission Change Management process is set up in Oracle GRC Manager as follows:

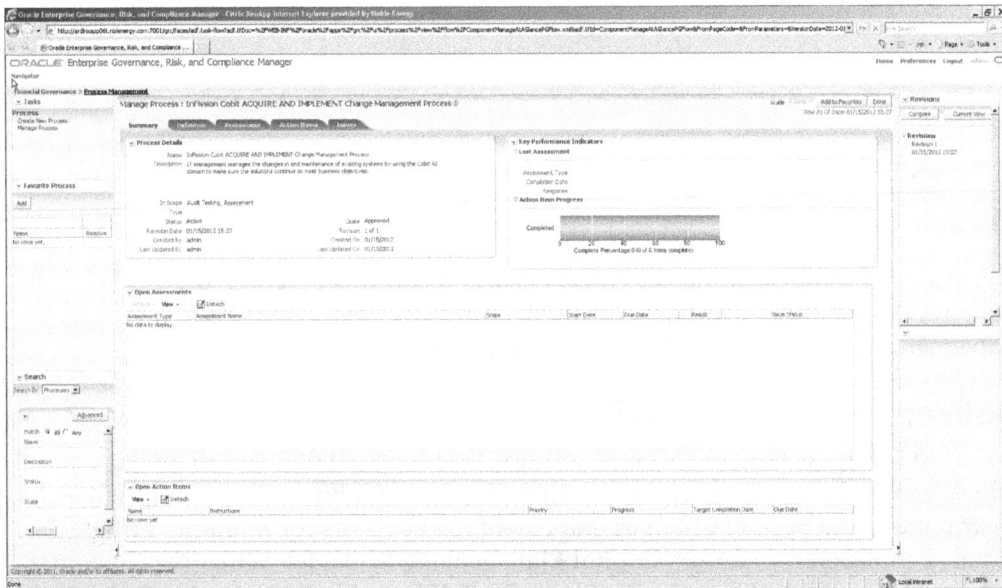

The IT Audit assesses the effectiveness of IT controls related to this COBIT domain by asking the following management questions through a survey in Oracle GRC Manager:

- Are new projects likely to deliver solutions that meet business needs?
- Are new projects likely to be delivered on time and within the budget?
- Will the new systems work properly when implemented?
- Will changes be made without upsetting current business operations?

The following screenshot shows the assessment setup in Oracle GRC Manager to answer these questions for the Oracle E-Business Suite Upgrade project:

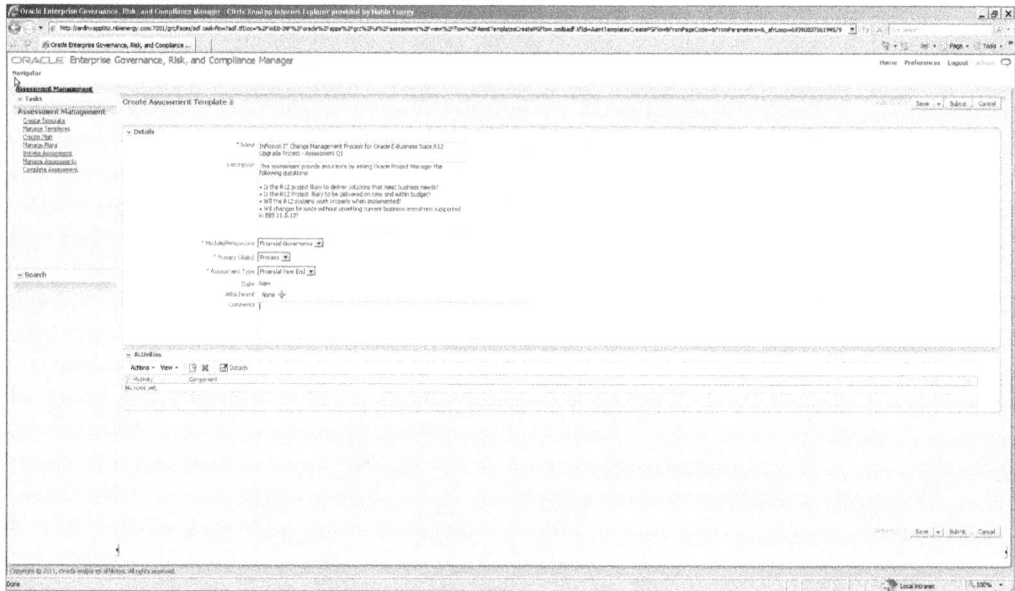

The assessment may include activities, risks, and controls based on the COBIT framework to select IT solutions, develop, or acquire these solutions and implement/integrate them into the current business process.

Deliver and Support (DS)

InFission IT support organization is responsible for actual delivery of all mission-critical enterprise applications, which includes Oracle E-Business Suite for Financial, Distribution, and Supply Chain Management, JD Edwards for Manufacturing Plants, PeopleSoft for Human Capital Management, Seibel for managing Customer Relationship, and Hyperion for Financial Consolidation and Disclosure. Oracle GRC Controls suite (Application Access Controls Governor, Transaction Controls Governor, Configuration Controls Governor, and Preventive Controls Governor) is deployed to maintain effective IT controls over the Delivery and Support process. Application Access Controls Governor (AACG) and Transaction Controls Governor (TCG) maintain security and transaction controls within and across all the mission-critical applications. Preventive Controls Governor (PCG) provides the fine-grain controls embedded within Oracle E-Business Suite to prevent Financial Misstatement Risks in the Financial Close Process, as well as Fraud Risks (FCPA) in the Procure to Pay process. The Change Controls Governor controls configuration changes in PeopleSoft and Oracle E-Business Suite.

These control modules provide assurance over the Delivery and Support process by enabling IT management to address the following questions:

- Are IT services being delivered in line with business priorities?
- Are IT costs optimized?
- Is the workforce able to use the IT systems productively and safely?
- Are adequate confidentiality, integrity, and availability in place for information security?

The reports provided to IT management with the GRC Controls Suite, deliver visibility to the following aspects:

- Manage third-party services
- Manage performance and capacity
- Ensure continuous service
- Ensure systems security
- Identify and allocate costs
- Educate and train users
- Assist and advise customers
- Manage the configuration
- Manage problems and incidents
- Manage data
- Manage facilities
- Manage operations

The following example shows how InFission has implemented a PCG control on the **Sales Order** form to require Sales Channel information.

The seeded **Oracle Order** form, shown in the following screenshot shows that **Sales Channel** is not mandatory:

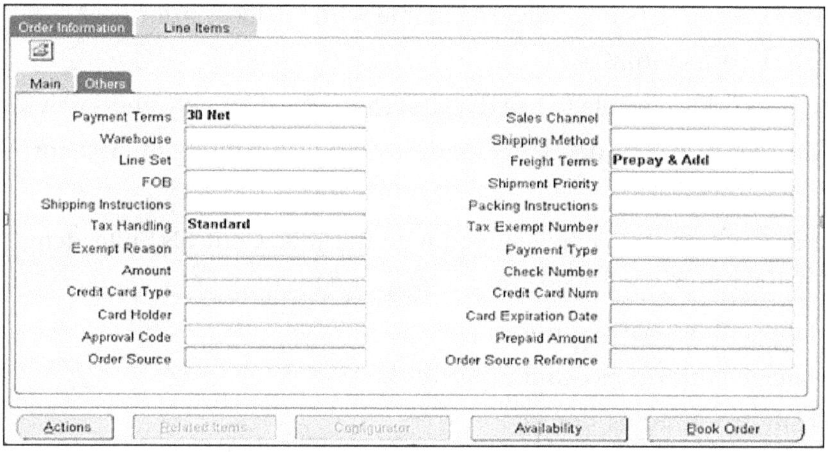

Using the PCG Event Tracker for Form Rules, the PCG controls administrator can make the **Sales Channel** field mandatory by selecting the **OracleFormsRules Actions** menu:

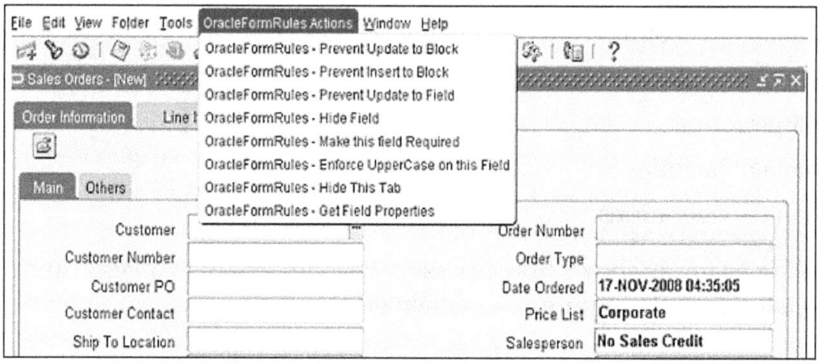

Next, select the option **Make this Field Required** from the **Oracle Form Action** menu, as shown in the following screenshot:

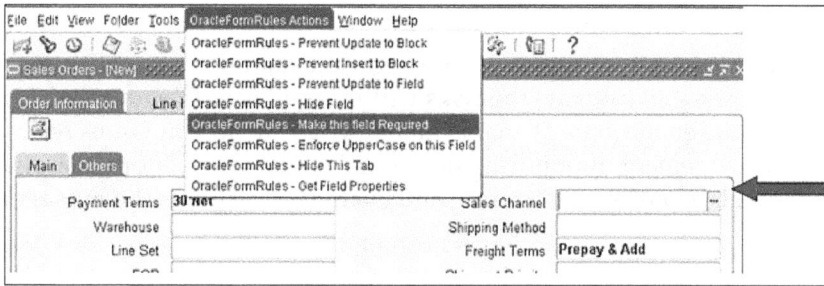

The PCG administrator can add other fine-grain controls at the field, block, or form level available under the **Form Rules** tabs:

Once the control is implemented, **Sales Channel** is now a mandatory field:

Monitor and Evaluate (ME)

InFission IT management is responsible for regular evaluation of quality and compliance controls that mitigate the risks within significant IT processes. The Oracle GRC Controls suite enables the IT management to take action on issues related to performance management, monitoring of internal control, regulatory compliance, and governance. IT Controls monitoring and evaluation requires the management to:

- Monitor the processes
- Assess internal control adequacy
- Obtain independent assurance
- Provide for independent audit

With the Oracle GRC Controls tools, IT managers can address the following questions:

- Is IT's performance measured to detect problems before it is too late?
- Does management ensure that internal controls are effective and efficient?
- Can IT performance be linked back to business goals?
- Are adequate confidentiality, integrity, and availability controls in place for information security?

For example, IT managers responsible for Oracle E-Business configuration controls review the **Change Tracker Alerts** to see **Who**, **When**, **What**, and **Where** a setup control was changed:

Additionally, the CCG Snapshot Comparison Reports ensure that Application Setup controls are monitored:

California Breach Law

The California Breach Law imposes duties on any company that employs or sells to people in California. It imposes a duty of care not to disclose personally identifiable information to other parties and to take reasonable steps to protect the information from purposes other than those for which it was released. Any person or business that conducts business in California, which owns or licenses computerized data that includes personal information, must disclose any breach of the security to any resident of California whose unencrypted personal information was acquired by an unauthorized person.

Personal information means an individual's first name or first initial and last name in combination with any one or more of the following data elements, when either the name or the data elements are not encrypted:

- Social security number
- Driver's license number or Identification Card number
- Account number
- Credit or debit card number, in combination with any required security code, access code, or password that would permit access to an individual's financial account

The following tables show some examples of data, which might be considered as **Personally Identifiable Information (PII)**.

PII Columns: Trading Community Architecture

The following are the columns holding Personally Identifiable Information (PII) in the Trading Community Architecture tables:

PII Attributes	Table	Column
Person name	HZ_PERSON_PROFILES	PERSON_FIRST_NAME, PERSON_LAST_NAME, PERSON_LAST_NAME_PREFIX, PERSON_MIDDLE_NAME, PERSON_NAME, PERSON_NAME_SUFFIX, PERSON_PREVIOUS_LAST_NAME, PERSON_PRE_NAME_ADJUNCT, PERSON_SECOND_LAST_NAME, PERSON_TITLE, PERSON_ACADEMIC_TITLE, PERSON_INITIALS

PII Attributes	Table	Column
	`HZ_PARTIES`	`PARTY_NAME PERSON_FIRST_NAME, PERSON_LAST_NAME, PERSON_LAST_NAME_PREFIX, PERSON_MIDDLE_NAME, PERSON_TITLEPERSON_ACADEMIC_TITLE, PERSON_NAME_SUFFIX, PERSON_PRE_NAME_ADJUNCT, PERSON_SECOND_LAST_NAME, PREFERRED_NAME, SALUTATION`
	`HZ_ADDTNL_PARTY_NAMES`	`PERSON_FIRST_NAME PERSON_LAST_NAME, PERSON_LAST_NAME_PREFIX, PERSON_MIDDLE_NAME, PERSON_NAME_SUFFIX, PERSON_PREVIOUS_LAST_NAME, PERSON_PRE_NAME_ADJUNCT, PERSON_SECOND_LAST_NAME, PERSON_TITLE`
Maiden name	`HZ_PARTIES`	`PERSON_PREVIOUS_LAST_NAME`
	`HZ_ADDTNL_PARTY_NAMES`	`PARTY_NAME`
Business address	`HZ_PARTIES`	`COUNTRY, ADDRESS1, ADDRESS2, ADDRESS3, ADDRESS4, CITY, STATE, POSTAL_CODE, PROVINCE, COUNTY, HOME_COUNTRY`
	`HZ_ADDTNL_PARTY_IDS`	`COUNTRY, STATE_PROVINCE`
	`HZ_LOCATIONS`	`ADDRESS1, ADDRESS2, ADDRESS3, ADDRESS4, COUNTRY, CITY, POSTAL_CODE, ADDRESS_LINES_PHONETIC, POSTAL_PLUS4_CODE, SALES_TAX_GEOCODE, GEOMETRY`
	`HZ_LOCATION_PROFILES`	`ADDRESS1, ADDRESS2, ADDRESS3, ADDRESS4, CITY, POSTAL_CODE, COUNTY, COUNTRY, STATE, PROVINCE`
Business telephone number	`HZ_PARTIES`	`PRIMARY_PHONE_COUNTRY_CODE PRIMARY_PHONE_AREA_CODE PRIMARY_PHONE_NUMBER, PRIMARY_PHONE_EXTENSION`

PII Attributes	Table	Column
	HZ_CONTACT_POINTS	PHONE_AREA_CODE, PHONE_COUNTRY_CODE, PHONE_EXTENSION, PHONE_NUMBER, RAW_PHONE_NUMBER, TRANSPOSED_PHONE_NUMBER, TELEX_NUMBER
Business e-mail address	HZ_PARTIES	EMAIL_ADDRESS
	HZ_CONTACT_POINTS	EMAIL_ADDRESS
	JTF_RS_SALESREPS	EMAIL_ADDRESS
User Global Identifier	HZ_PARTIES	USER_GUID
Account name	HZ_CUST_ACCOUNTS	ACCOUNT_NAME
Mail stop	HZ_PARTY_SITES	MAILSTOP
GPS location	HZ_PERSON_PROFILES	LAST_KNOWN_GPS
Student examination hall ticket number	HZ_ADDTNL_PARTY_IDS	Row
Club Membership ID	HZ_ADDTNL_PARTY_IDS	Row
Instant Messaging address	HZ_CONTACT_POINTS	INSTANT_MESSAGING_ADDRESS
Personal phone number	HZ_CONTACT_POINTS	N/A – Row
	HZ_PARTIES	PRIMARY_PHONE_CONTACT_PT_ID, PRIMARY_PHONE_PURPOSE, PRIMARY_PHONE_LINE_TYPE, PRIMARY_PHONE_COUNTRY_CODE, PRIMARY_PHONE_AREA_CODE, PRIMARY_PHONE_NUMBER, PRIMARY_PHONE_EXTENSION
Personal e-mail	HZ_CONTACT_POINTS	N/A – Row
	HZ_PARTIES	EMAIL_ADDRESS
Personal address	HZ_PARTY_SITES	N/A – Row
	HZ_PARTIES	COUNTRY, ADDRESS_1, ADDRESS_2, ADDRESS_3, ADDRESS_4, CITY, POSTAL_CODE, STATE, PROVINCE, COUNTY
	HZ_LOCATIONS	N/A – Row

PII Attributes	Table	Column
National Identifier, Passport number, Drivers License number, Residency number (19 attributes)	HZ_ADDTNL_PARTY_IDS	N/A – Row
Tax Registration number	HZ_PERSON_PROFILES	TAX_REFERENCE
Tax Payer ID	HZ_PERSON_PROFILES	JGZZ_FISCAL_CODE
Tax Payer ID	HZ_PARTIES	JGZZ_FISCAL_CODE
Person Identification number	HZ_CONTACT_POINTS	PAGER_PIN
Citizenship number	HZ_CITIZENSHIP	DOCUMENT_REFERENCE

PII Columns: Procurement

The following are the columns holding Personally Identifiable Information (PII) in the Procurement tables:

PII Attributes	Table	Column
Business address	POZ_SUPPLIER_REGISTRATIONS	ADDRESS_LINE1, ADDRESS_LINE2, ADDRESS_LINE3, ADDRESS_LINE4
Business telephone number	PO_REQUISITION_LINES_ALL	REQUESTER_PHONE SUGGESTED_VENDOR_PHONE
	POZ_CONTACT_REQUESTS	PHONE_AREA_CODE, PHONE_EXTENSION, PHONE_NUMBER
	POZ_SUPPLIER_SITES_ALL_M	PHONE
	POZ_ADDRESS_REQUESTS	PHONE_AREA_CODE, PHONE_EXTENSION, PHONE_NUMBER
Business e-mail address	POR_CAT_FAV_LIST_LINES_TLP	SUGGESTED_VENDOR_CONTACT_EMAIL
	POR_NONCAT_TEMPLATES_ALL_B	SUPPLIER_CONTACT_EMAIL
	PO_REQUISITION_LINES_ALL	REQUESTER_EMAIL
	PO_REQUISITION_LINES_ALL	SUGGESTED_VENDOR_CONTACT_EMAIL

PII Attributes	Table	Column
Business telephone number	PO_REQUISITION_LINES_ALL	REQUESTER_PHONE SUGGESTED_VENDOR_PHONE
	PO_HEADERS_ALL	EMAIL_ADDRESS
	PO_HEADERS_ARCHIVE_ALL	EMAIL_ADDRESS
	PO_HEADERS_DRAFT_ALL	EMAIL_ADDRESS
	POZ_ADDRESS_REQUESTS	EMAIL_ADDRESS
	POZ_CONTACT_REQUESTS	EMAIL_ADDRESS
	POZ_OSN_REQUESTS	EMAIL_ADDRESS
	POZ_SUPPLIER_SITES_ALL_M	EMAIL_ADDRESS
Tax Payer ID	POZ_SUPPLIERS	INDIVIDUAL_1099
Tax Registration number	POZ_SUPPLIER_REGISTRATIONS	TAX_REGISTRATION_NUMBER
Tax Payer ID	POZ_SUPPLIER_REGISTRATIONS	TAXPAYER_ID

PII Columns: Financials

The following are the columns holding Personally Identifiable Information (PII) in the Financials tables:

PII Attributes	Table	Column
Business e-mail address	IBY_TRXN_CORE	INSTR_OWNER_EMAIL
	IBY_PAYMENTS_ALL	REMIT_ADVICE_EMAIL
	IBY_TRXN_SUMMARIES_ALL	DEBIT_ADVICE_EMAIL
	IBY_EXTERNAL_PAYEES_ALL	REMIT_ADVICE_EMAIL
	IBY_EXTERNAL_PAYEES_ALL	DEBIT_ADVICE_EMAIL
National Identifier	EXM_CARD_HOLDER_DETAILS	NATIONAL_IDENTIFIER
Tax Registration number	ZX_LINES	TAX_REGISTRATION_NUMBER
	ZX_REGISTRATIONS	REGISTRATION_NUMBER

PII Attributes	Table	Column
	`ZX_PARTY_TAX_PROFILE`	`TAX_REGISTRATION_` `NUMBER`
	`EXM_EXPENSES`	`MERCHANT_TAX_REG_NUMBER`
	`EXM_CREDIT_CARD_TRXNS`	`MERCHANT_TAX_REG_NUMBER`
National Taxpayer Identifier	`JE_ES_MODELO_190_ALL`	`VENDOR_NIF`
	`EXM_EXPENSES`	`MERCHANT_TAXPAYER_ID`
	`EXM_CREDIT_CARD_TRXNS`	`MERCHANT_TAX_ID`

It is important to note that California Breach is the law that actually states that the breach must be notified to consumers if the information was not encrypted. Notice may be provided in writing, or electronically if the electronic notice is consistent with federal law regarding electronic records and signatures.

Gartner Research estimates that organizations are being required to spend at least $90 for each personal electronic record affected by a data security breach. The Ponemon Institute claims the cost is even higher, reporting that organizations spend as much as $140 per lost customer record.

Oracle's products and California Breach Law

There are some key technologies to be examined that protect data through encryption. First among equals is transparent data encryption.

Transparent data encryption

Transparent data encryption enables simple and easy encryption for sensitive data without requiring users or applications to manage the encryption key. This freedom can be extremely important when addressing, for example, regulatory compliance issues. No need to use views to decrypt data, because the data is transparently decrypted once a user has passed necessary access control checks. Security administrators have the assurance that the data on disk is encrypted, yet handling encrypted data becomes transparent to applications. The following diagram shows the flow from unencrypted to cipher text and back:

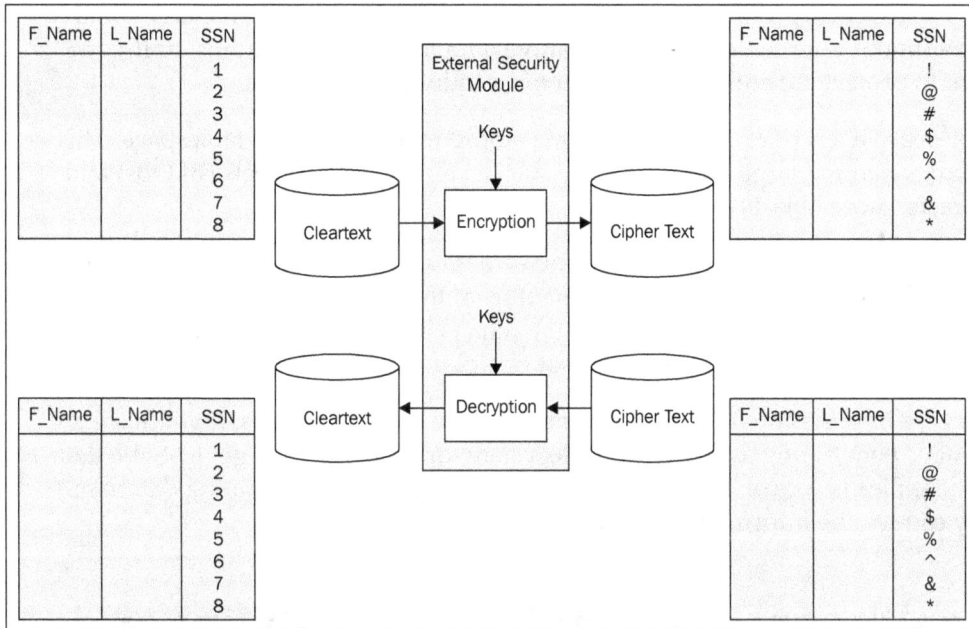

E-Business Suite with transparent data encryption

Oracle Advanced Security is an optional licensed Oracle 11g Database add-on. Oracle Advanced Security Transparent Data Encryption (TDE) offers two different features **Column encryption** and **Tablespace encryption**. 11.2.0.1 TDE Column encryption was certified with E-Business Suite 12 as part of our overall 11.2.0.1 database certification. As of today, 11.2.0.1 TDE Tablespace encryption is now certified with Oracle E-Business Suite Release 12.

You can find more information from support note 828229.1, Using TDE Tablespace Encryption with Oracle E-Business Suite Release 12 or Steven Chan's blog at `https://blogs.oracle.com/stevenChan/entry/tde_tablespace_encryption_11_2`. Tablespace encryption enables you to encrypt an entire tablespace. All objects created in the encrypted tablespace are automatically encrypted. Tablespace encryption is useful if you want to secure sensitive data in tables. You do not need to perform a granular analysis of each table column to determine the columns that need encryption.

Tablespace encryption is a good alternative to column-based transparent data encryption if your tables contain sensitive data in multiple columns, or if you want to protect the entire table and not just individual columns.

Tablespace encryption encrypts all data stored in an encrypted tablespace. This includes internal large objects (LOBs) such as binary large objects (BLOBs) and character large objects (CLOBs).

Transparent Data Encryption encrypts the data as it is written to disk. Data is transparently decrypted as it is retrieved from the disk for an authorized user. The user is not aware of the fact that the data is being encrypted and decrypted. However, if the backup media gets lost or stolen, the data is not compromised.

It is very important to note that this protects the data in the files. If you have an intruder penetrating as far as your filesystem, or your backups get lost, the data in those files is secure. However, if someone gets access to a running database, they can see the information in the clear.

Healthcare Information Portability and Protection Act (HIPPA)

Title II of HIPPA, known as the Administrative Simplification (AS) provisions, requires the establishment of national standards for electronic health care transactions and national identifiers for providers, health insurance plans, and employers. This is intended to help people keep their information private.

We will take you through the duties imposed by HIPPA. We will also help you identify information that is subject to HIPPA and explain some of the protections afforded by the applications and technologies to protect this data.

In order to quote a little from the legislation, a paraphrasing from section 1173 is as follows:

"Each person who maintains or transmits health information shall maintain reasonable and appropriate administrative, technical, and physical safeguards:

- to ensure the integrity and confidentiality of the information
- to protect against any reasonably anticipated
    - threats or hazards to the security or integrity of the information
    - unauthorized uses or disclosures of the information
- otherwise to ensure compliance with this part by the officers and employees of such a person."

Further, the health care transactions are as follows:

- Health claims or equivalent encounter information.
- Health claims attachments.
- Enrollment and disenrollment in a health plan.
- Eligibility for a health plan.
- Health care payment and remittance advice.
- Health plan premium payments.
- First report of injury.
- Health claim status.
- Referral certification and authorization.

Oracle's products and HIPPA

From the preceding information you can see that the information that needs protection is concentrated in the benefits and payroll modules of E-Business Suite. That having been said, it will be quite pervasive.

Scrambling and data masking

One needed technology to ensure that the information is not available to developers is **masking**, or the practice of **safe cloning**.

Many copies of production environments are created, also known as cloning, for various purposes. These copies are typically used for performance tests by DBAs or developers or to test upgrade/patching of the production database. Cloning of the production environment to the test area introduces several risks to an organization. Oracle provides a rapid clone utility to clone Oracle applications environment.

Following are some of the key steps that need to be considered:

- Change all the passwords in the cloned environment
- Scramble sensitive and critical data including social security number, credit card information, salary, and so on
- Update DB links information in the cloned environment to point to the corresponding development environment

The OEM Data Masking is a part of Database Management Pack, whereas OEM Data Scrambling is a part of Application Management Pack for EBS.

Enterprise Manager 10g Grid Control allows you to manage all of your Oracle E-Business Suite systems from a single console. The Application Management Pack (AMP) for Oracle E-Business Suite, Release 2.0.0 and 2.0.1 extends EM 10g Grid Control to manage Oracle Applications systems.

One of the key features of the Applications Management Pack is the ability to clone an Oracle E-Business Suite system automatically. While cloning environments, administrators can modify the standard cloning process to include some custom actions. One such custom action is **data scrambling**.

Data scrambling is the process of obfuscating or removing sensitive data, and can be used by functional administrators and database administrators when cloning an environment that contains sensitive information:

Name	Health_Claim	Health_Claim_Date
Bob Smith	Back Pain	1/1/2010
John Doe	Stress	6/28/2004
Fred Bloggs	Eye Strain	4/19/2007

Name	Health_Claim	Health_Claim_Date
gjhgjhgd	Back Pain	1/1/2010
jhgjhgkkj	Stress	6/28/2004
kjhkkssff	Eye Strain	4/19/2007

The scrambling process is irreversible, so the original data cannot be derived from the scrambled data.

The scrambling process is repeatable (with the same parameters) and can be used for multiple cloning processes.

The Applications Management Pack has predefined masking for EBS.

In order to configure data scrambling, use Oracle Applications Manager, and navigate to **Sitemap | Maintenance | Cloning Data Scrambling Configuration**.

Data scrambling is configured through the Oracle Applications Manager. In order to enable data scrambling, set the site-level profile option **OAM: Data Scrambling Enabled** to **Yes**.

Functional administrators define the attributes and map them to database columns. They then collect attributes together to define policies and policy sets. The following diagram shows the flow of instance creation from production through to test environments:

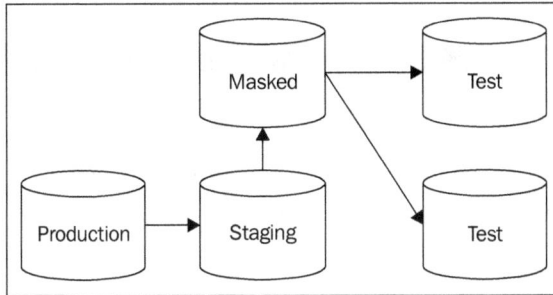

The configuration defined in Oracle Applications Manager for data scrambling can be utilized within the Apps Management Pack during the cloning process.

The Database Administrator specifies the policy sets to scramble the source data, initiates, and then monitors the data scrambling process. The source data from the original instance is then sent through the data scrambling engine. Test Instances are then cloned from the scrambled instance:

You can also use the data masking pack from within Enterprise Manager if you particularly wanted to define your own masking formats or wanted to have a consistent approach to both E-Business Suite and other applications in your portfolio. The following is a screenshot of the Enterprise Manager Column Masking Definition:

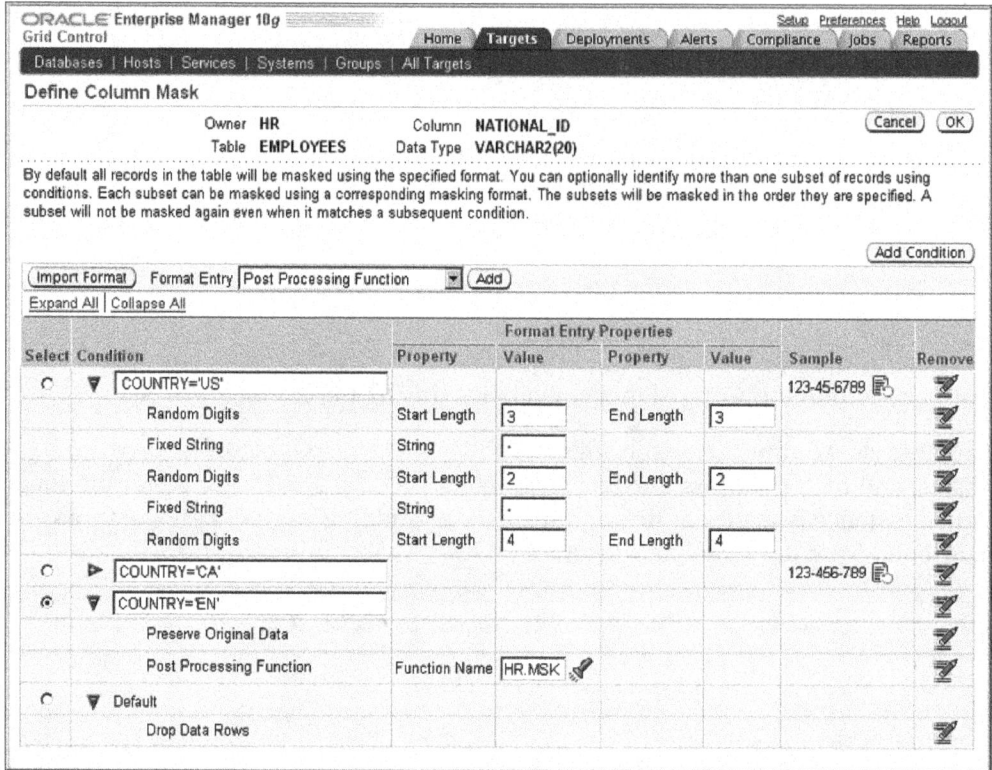

Data vault

Another important technology that ensures that access to data at the database level can be limited appropriately to the authorized individuals is **data vault**. Data vault restricts the access of DBAs to appropriate realms. A **realm** is a collection of schemas within the database. The following diagram shows realms protecting against highly privileged users:

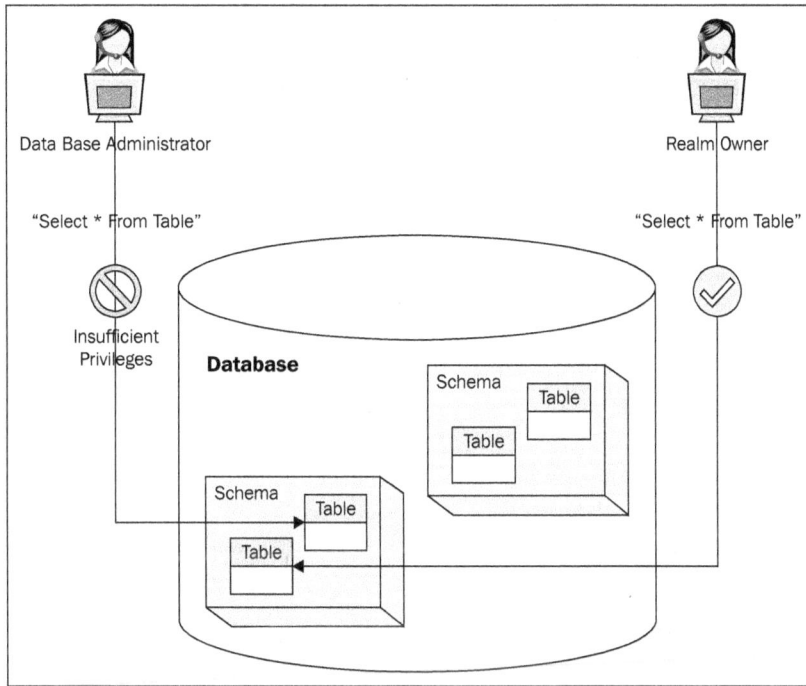

Oracle Database Vault restricts access to specific areas in an Oracle database from any user, including users who have administrative access. For example, you can restrict administrative access to employee salaries, customer medical records, or other sensitive information. The following diagram shows administering the data vault from within Oracle Enterprise Manager:

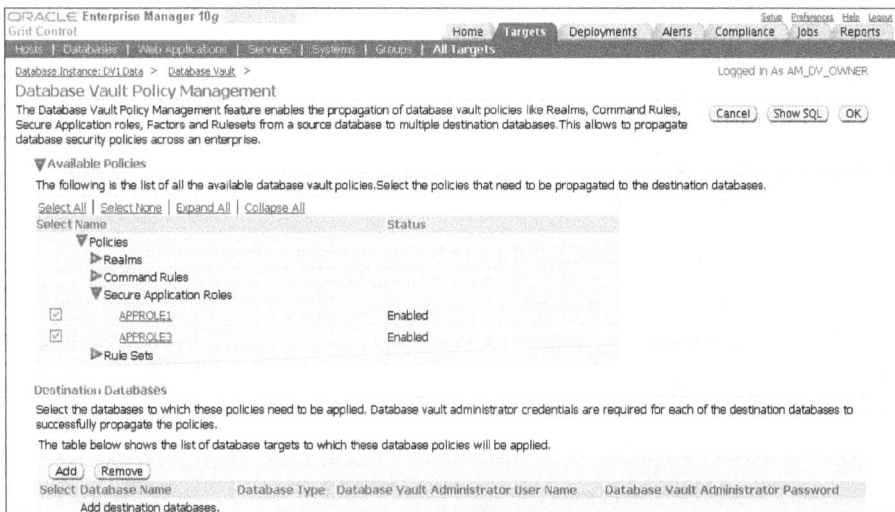

Database vault allows you to configure separate realms for different security classifications. You can also restrict the privileges of administrators within their realm. Backup and recovery, performance turning, and high availability are all part of the job description of a DBA. However, the ability to view sensitive application data is beyond what is needed for that job. Database vault splits up the duties into three:

Role	Privileges
Account Management	Create, drop, or modify database users
Security Administrator	Set up database vault realms, command rules, and authorizing authorize accounts to them
Resource Administration	Normal backup and maintenance activities

Oracle Database Vault prevents the DBA from accessing the schemas that are protected by the realm. Although the DBA is the most powerful and trusted user, he/she does not need access to application data residing within the database.

Protecting database objects with realms and rules

Oracle Database Vault uses realms to set up boundaries around a set of objects in specific schemas; specific conditions must be met to access data protected by those boundaries. Realms specify a set of conditions that must be met before a given command can be executed on a set of database objects.

This provides very granular control over what can be done to certain objects, and by whom. You can define rules to restrict access based on business-specific factors such as data access connections from a particular database, from a particular machine, and from specific IP addresses. You can also specify the time of day or authentication modes for data access.

Preseeded realms for the E-Business Suite

Oracle delivers a set of preseeded Database Vault Realms for your E-Business Suite Release 11*i* environment via the following patch:

Oracle E-Business Suite Release 11*i* Realm Creation Patch (Patch 5999012).

This patch contains the master `fnddvebs.sql` script. The `fnddbvebs.sql` script creates realms around Oracle E-Business Suite 11*i* product schemas and gives authorization only to those users required to allow the Oracle E-Business Suite to function normally.

The `fnddvebs.sql` script creates six realms. Each realm protects different product schemas and has its own set of user authorizations.

Realm	What is Protected
E-Business Suite Realm	All tables in Oracle E-Business Suite 11*i* Product Schemas
EBS Realm – Applsys Schema	Most tables in the APPLSYS Schema
EBS Realm – Applsyspub Schema	Objects required for E-Business Suite authorization
EBS Realm – Apps Schema	All objects in the APPS Schema (except the views)
EBS Realm – MSC Schema	Tables in the MSC Schema (except those that require partitions to be exchanged)
CTXSYS Data Dictionary	Objects in the CTXSYS (Oracle text) Schema

The following screenshot is the realms definition within Oracle Data Vault:

Pre-seeded Realm Authorizations

Within the realm creation patch the realms are authorized to a set of users.

Realm	Who is authorized
E-Business Suite Realm	All Oracle E-Business Suite 11*i* Product Schemas, and APPS, APPLSYS, SYSTEM, CTXSYS
EBS Realm – Applsys Schema	APPS, APPLSYS, SYSTEM, and CTXSYS
EBS Realm – Applsyspub Schema	APPS, APPLSYS, SYSTEM, APPLSYSPUB, and CTXSYS
EBS Realm – Apps Schema	APPS, APPLSYS, SYSTEM, CTXSYS, and all product schemas
EBS Realm – MSC Schema	APPS, APPLSYS, SYSTEM, CTXSYS, and MSC
CTXSYS Data Dictionary	All Oracle E-Business Suite 11*i* Product Schemas and APPS, APPLSYS, and SYSTEM

> Note that Apps is a schema that does not contain any tables. It contains synonyms of all the tables in Oracle Apps. However, it also contains packages, functions, and procedures.
>
> Applsys schema contains all the tables required for administrative purpose. All the technical products' database objects are consolidated into this schema. Applsyspub schema is responsible for checking passwords.

Payment Card Industry (PCI)

The **Payment Card Industry Data Security Standard (PCI DSS)** is a worldwide information security standard defined by the Payment Card Industry Security Standards Council. The standard was created to help organizations that process card payments, prevent credit card fraud through increased controls around data, and its exposure to compromise. The standard applies to all organizations, which hold, process, or exchange cardholder information from any card branded with the logo of one of the card brands. The main requirements are as follows:

- Install and maintain a firewall configuration to protect cardholder data
- Do not use vendor-supplied defaults for system passwords
- Protect stored cardholder data
- Encrypt transmission of cardholder data across open, public networks
- Use and regularly update anti-virus software
- Develop and maintain secure systems and applications
- Restrict access to cardholder data by business need-to-know
- Assign a unique ID to each person with computer access
- Restrict physical access to cardholder data
- Track and monitor all access to network resources and cardholder data
- Regularly test security systems and processes
- Maintain a policy that addresses information security

Oracle's products and PCI

Oracle Payments serves as a payment data repository on top of the **Trading Community Architecture (TCA)** data model. The TCA model holds the party's information. Oracle Payments stores all of the party's payment information and its payment instruments, such as credit cards and bank accounts. This common repository for payment data provides data security by allowing central encryption management and masking control of payment instrument information.

Oracle Payments

Oracle Payments integrates with other Oracle applications, such as Oracle Receivable, iStore, and Order Management. You can access this credit card security feature setup by selecting the **Payment Administrator** responsibility in **Oracle Payments** and then clicking the **System Security Management** link.

The following screenshot shows the **Oracle Payments Setup** screen:

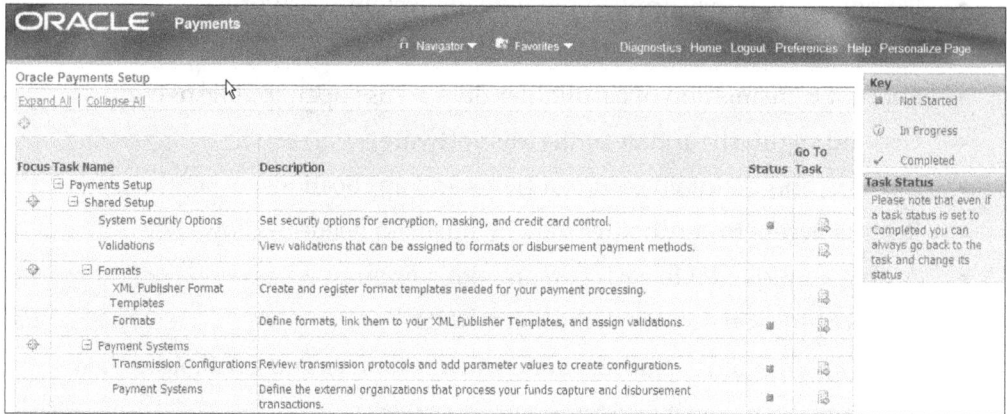

In the **System Security Options** task, you set up the masking and verification options. The following image is a screenshot of the **System Security Options** page:

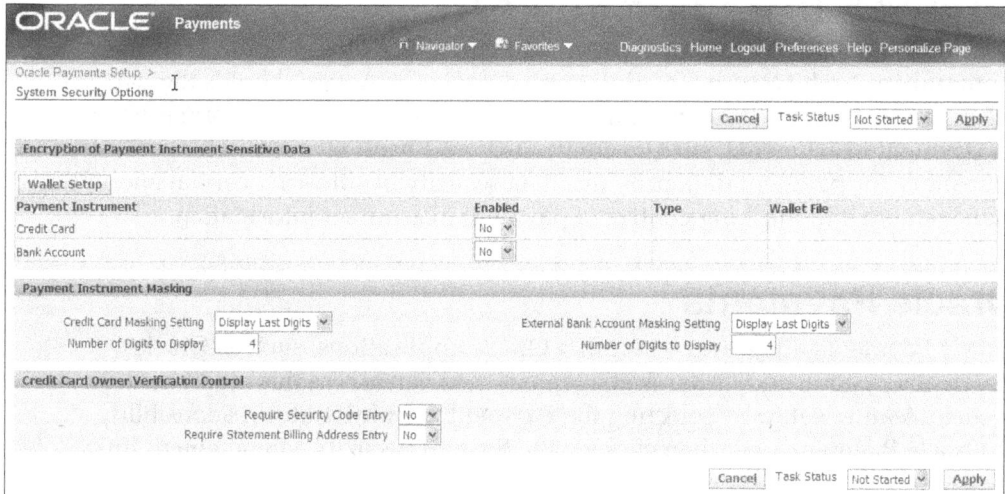

The following is a diagram of the key entities in the encryption process, which shows how the entities are related in **Crows foot notation**:

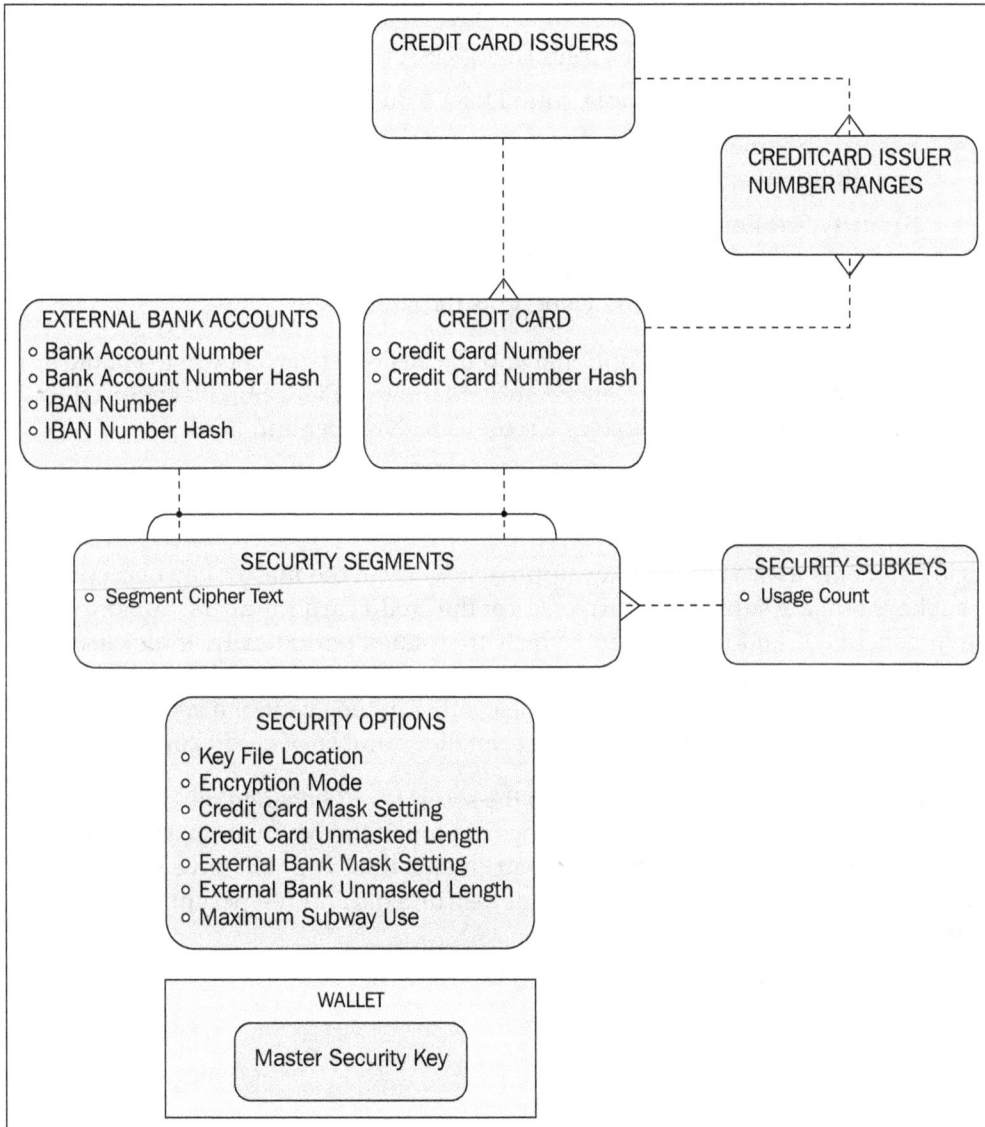

```
┌─────────────────────────────────────────────────────────────────────────────┐
│                        ╭─────────────────────────╮                           │
│                        │   CREDIT CARD ISSUERS    │                           │
│                        │                          │                           │
│                        ╰─────────────────────────╯                           │
│                                                        ╭──────────────────╮  │
│                                                        │ CREDITCARD ISSUER │  │
│                                                        │  NUMBER RANGES    │  │
│                                                        │                   │  │
│                                                        ╰──────────────────╯  │
│                                                                               │
│   ╭──────────────────────────╮   ╭──────────────────────╮                    │
│   │ EXTERNAL BANK ACCOUNTS    │   │     CREDIT CARD       │                    │
│   │ ○ Bank Account Number     │   │ ○ Credit Card Number  │                    │
│   │ ○ Bank Account Number Hash│   │ ○ Credit Card Number  │                    │
│   │ ○ IBAN Number             │   │   Hash                │                    │
│   │ ○ IBAN Number Hash        │   │                       │                    │
│   ╰──────────────────────────╯   ╰──────────────────────╯                    │
│                                                                               │
│       ╭──────────────────────────────────────────╮  ╭────────────────────╮  │
│       │           SECURITY SEGMENTS               │  │  SECURITY SUBKEYS   │  │
│       │ ○ Segment Cipher Text                     │  │ ○ Usage Count       │  │
│       │                                           │  │                     │  │
│       ╰──────────────────────────────────────────╯  ╰────────────────────╯  │
│                                                                               │
│       ╭──────────────────────────────────────╮                               │
│       │           SECURITY OPTIONS            │                               │
│       │ ○ Key File Location                   │                               │
│       │ ○ Encryption Mode                     │                               │
│       │ ○ Credit Card Mask Setting            │                               │
│       │ ○ Credit Card Unmasked Length         │                               │
│       │ ○ External Bank Mask Setting          │                               │
│       │ ○ External Bank Unmasked Length       │                               │
│       │ ○ Maximum Subway Use                  │                               │
│       ╰──────────────────────────────────────╯                               │
│                                                                               │
│       ┌──────────────────────────────────────┐                               │
│       │              WALLET                   │                               │
│       │   ╭──────────────────────────────╮   │                               │
│       │   │     Master Security Key       │   │                               │
│       │   ╰──────────────────────────────╯   │                               │
│       └──────────────────────────────────────┘                               │
└─────────────────────────────────────────────────────────────────────────────┘
```

The following bullets explain the entities and give examples of the data that would be held in them:

- **Credit Card Issuers**: For example, VISA, Mastercard
- **Credit Card**: For example, John Doe's VISA Card
- **Bank Account**: For example, John Doe's bank account
- **Security Segments**: This holds the encrypted credit card or bank account numbers
- **Security Subkey**: A random number that is used as a key to encrypt a subset of the bank accounts and credit cards
- **Master Key**: The master key encrypts the subkeys

In R12 Payments, encryption is optional and the customer can choose to enable it. As per Payment Card Industry Data Security Standard (PCI DSS), it's required to encrypt payment instruments such as Credit Card Number and Bank Account numbers.

Key management

Oracle Payments uses a chained key approach wherein the master key encrypts the subkeys and the subkeys in turn encrypt the credit card numbers. Subkeys are system-generated random numbers, which are rotated periodically. If the current subkey has exceeded its usual count, then a new one is generated automatically using a random number function. This means that in the event of a single key being compromised, the exposure is limited to a smaller number of credit card numbers.

In order to rotate the keys, you can go to the setup UI and change the master key. That only re-encrypts the subkeys but does not touch the payment instrument data. If you want to re-encrypt the payment instruments then you will have to decrypt both the encryption keys and the payment instruments and re-encrypt with a new master key and subkeys.

The following diagram shows the encryption and decryption hierarchy:

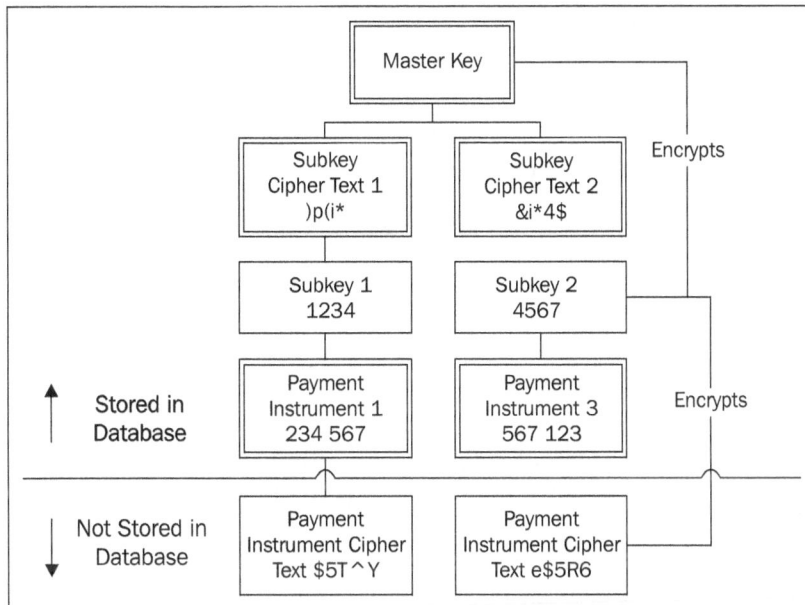

```
                          ┌──────────────────┐
                          │   Master Key     │
                          └──────────────────┘
                 ┌────────────────┬─────────────┐        Encrypts
         ┌───────────────┐  ┌───────────────┐
         │    Subkey     │  │    Subkey     │
         │ Cipher Text 1 │  │ Cipher Text 2 │
         │     )p(i*     │  │     &i*4$     │
         └───────────────┘  └───────────────┘
         ┌───────────────┐  ┌───────────────┐
         │   Subkey 1    │  │   Subkey 2    │
         │     1234      │  │     4567      │
         └───────────────┘  └───────────────┘
                    ┌───────────────┐  ┌───────────────┐
  Stored in         │   Payment     │  │   Payment     │     Encrypts
  Database          │ Instrument 1  │  │ Instrument 3  │
                    │   234 567     │  │   567 123     │
                    └───────────────┘  └───────────────┘
─────────────────────────────────────────────────────────────
  Not Stored in     ┌───────────────┐  ┌───────────────┐
  Database          │   Payment     │  │   Payment     │
                    │Instrument Cipher│ │Instrument Cipher│
                    │  Text $5T^Y   │  │  Text e$5R6   │
                    └───────────────┘  └───────────────┘
```

Federal Sentencing Guidelines

On May 1, 1991, as an extension of the Sentencing Reform Act, the United States Sentencing Commission submitted the **Federal Sentencing Guidelines for Organizations (FSGO)** to the Congress. It is a set of standards that govern the sentences the federal judges impose on organizations convicted of federal crimes. Enacted on November 1, 1991, core to the guidelines was the Commission's intent to "prevent and deter organizational wrongdoing" through its design of the organizational sentencing guidelines. These guidelines describe the elements of an organization's compliance and ethics program that are required to be considered for eligibility for a reduced sentence if convicted. Revisions to the Federal Sentencing Guidelines for Organizations that took effect in November 2004 contain requirements for companies to heighten their efforts to detect and prevent violations of law, and to implement efforts to establish an ethical culture.

The amended guidelines stated the need for directors and executives to take an active role in the management of its compliance and ethics program and the importance of promoting an organizational culture that is compliant with the law and demonstrates ethical culture. The amended guidelines outline minimum requirements for an effective compliance and ethics program and the amended FSGO has become synonymous with an effective compliance program.

Under the Federal Sentencing Guidelines, an effective compliance and ethics program is one that is intended "to achieve reasonable prevention and detection of criminal conduct". Maintaining an effective program can help a company to:

- Avoid prosecution
- Advocate for a nonprosecution or deferred prosecution agreement
- Mitigate the penalty imposed

It also has benefits in civil and administrative litigation.

Standards for an effective compliance and ethics program

In order to be effective, the program must be both documented and demonstrably pervasive inside the corporation. Under the guidelines, in order to have an effective program, the company must, at a minimum, adhere to the following:

- Establish standards and procedures to prevent and detect criminal conduct
- Ensure that the governing authority (most often, the Board of Directors) and all high-level personnel exercise oversight with respect to the implementation and effectiveness of the program
- Exclude from positions of substantial authority any individual that the company knows, or should know, is engaged in illegal or unethical activities
- Conduct training on and disseminate information about the program's standards and procedures
- Monitor, audit, and evaluate the program, as well as provide a mechanism for anonymous or confidential reporting
- Promote and enforce the program through appropriate incentives and disciplinary measures
- Respond appropriately to criminal conduct that is detected and act to prevent further similar conduct

The recent amendments stress that **responding appropriately** includes taking steps to provide restitution or remediate harm if there is an identifiable victim or victims, as well as self-reporting, cooperating with authorities, or undertaking other remediation. These are important steps in the civil arena as well. The amendments also add that to prevent further criminal conduct after learning of misconduct, the company should take steps to assess risk and enhance the compliance and ethics program.

The head of compliance, most likely the chief audit executive must be able to talk directly to the board or the audit committee if a breach of ethics is discovered.

Oracle's products and Federal Sentencing Guidelines

We will show how Oracle's learning tools address some of the most important requirements under the Federal Sentencing Guidelines.

Creating the ethics program in iLearning

You will remember the *Communicating and confirming Corporate Strategy with iLearning* section on iLearning from *Chapter 2, Corporate Governance*. In that chapter we described how Infission created the learning content. At that time, we were mostly concerned with the governance imperative of communicating corporate strategy, but from this chapter we can see the compliance imperative and risk management imperative from the Federal Sentencing Guidelines.

The example that we used for course content in *Chapter 2, Corporate Governance*, is instructive for the Federal Sentencing Guideline:

- **Course Category**: Governance and Compliance courses
- **Course**: Business Ethics for Salespeople
- **Class**: Foreign Corrupt Practices Act training on July 15th 2010
- **Enrollment**: John Doe enrolled in California Breach Laws training on July 15th 2010
- **Learner**: John Doe
- **Offering**: California Breach Laws web-based training
- **Learning Materials**: Data Privacy Awareness training courseware
- **Test Bank**: questions on California Breach Law

The following screenshot shows the course catalog in Oracle iLearning:

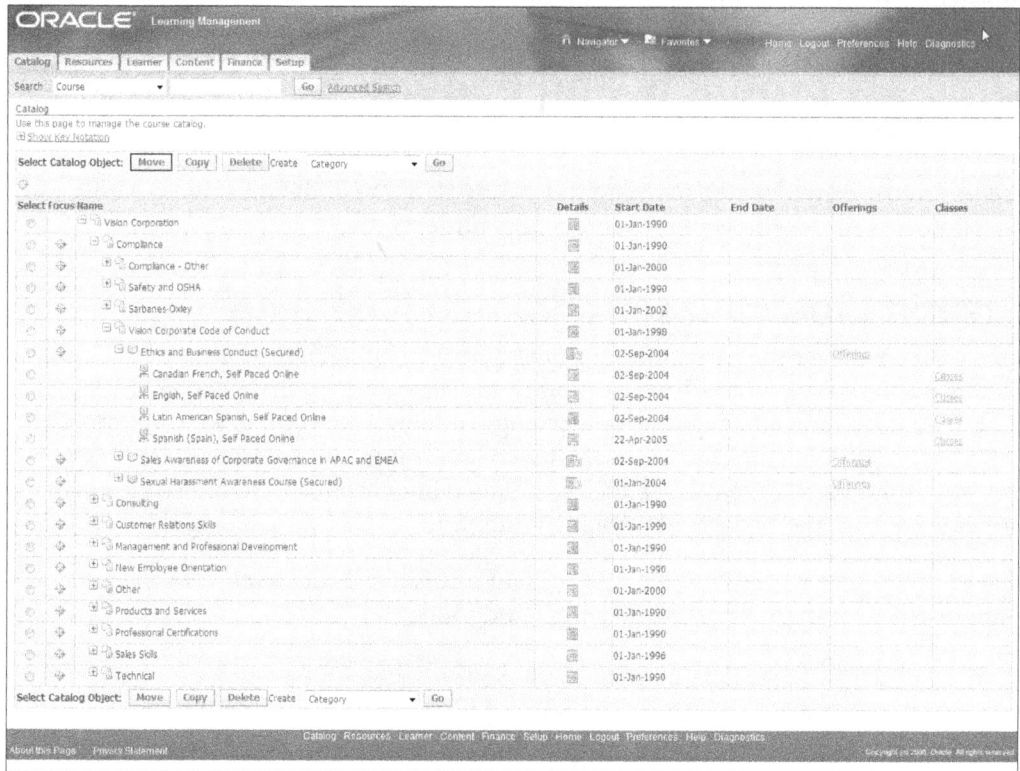

Monitoring the ethics program in iLearning

You can see how your learners have done on a class or set of classes by navigating to the Learning Management Administrator responsibility and clicking on the **Learner** tab to review the enrollment and subscriptions, as shown in the following screenshot:

You can orient your search by class to check, for example, how employees are doing in absorbing the data privacy laws and regulations as part of your security awareness program. You can orient your search by learner to confirm that the business ethics course has been taken and successfully completed by a new Sales Manager.

There are also a number of reports to help you track the absorption of compliance or strategic concepts. An example is the Evaluation Master Report that will show evaluations for a course and class name with a summary of the questions.

Summary

This is the first chapter where we started to look at compliance. In this chapter we looked at compliance issues that will be faced by companies in almost any industry. We started off looking at Sarbanes-Oxley and moved on to ISO 27000 that defines the Security Management System Requirements, and then on to COBIT that defines control objectives for Information Technology. Aspects of all three of these regulations fit very well as a perspective in the eGRCM application. Next, we looked at the California Breach Law, HIPPA, and Payment Card Industry regulations. These have the common theme of privacy and we showed Oracle capabilities for hiding, encrypting, and masking values. We rounded out our examination of cross industry compliance by looking at federal sentencing guidelines and showed how a learning management solution provides a defensible position and demonstrates due diligence.

11
Industry-focused Compliance

In this chapter we shift our focus to look at compliance in particular industries. There are different sets of regulations that apply to different industries. Not only will these conversations involve the Head of Internal Audit and the Chief Legal Counsel, but they will also bring in the Chief Operating Officer. In this chapter, we also leave our friends at Infission and talk to some colleagues at a pharmaceutical company and at a bank to get a feel of the regulations they are subject to. Of course with Infission being a high-tech manufacturer, this is where we will start.

Hi-tech manufacturing

We are going to look at a couple of regulations in the hi-tech manufacturing arena. They are standards put forward by the **International Organization for Standardization (ISO)**.

ISO 9000

Next, we will sit with the VP of operations to discuss quality processes and audits. **ISO 9000** is a quality standard that originated in the manufacturing world, although it has now spread to non-manufacturing industries as well. The quality system goes through formal verification by an outside auditor. The standard is very process and procedure manual centered.

The ISO 9000 family of standards represents an international consensus on good quality management practices. It consists of standards and guidelines relating to quality management systems and related supporting standards.

ISO 9001:2008 is the standard that provides a set of standardized requirements for a quality management system, regardless of what the user organization does, its size, or whether it is in the private or public sector. It is the only standard in the family against which organizations can be certified, although certification is not a compulsory requirement of the standard. ISO 9000 requires that you fully document your business processes that ensure high quality product and service. You must then prove that you do what you have documented.

The following diagram shows an overview of the ISO 9000 process:

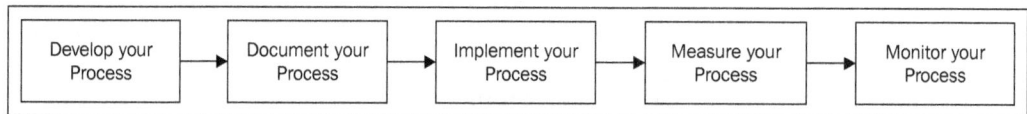

Develop your Process	→	Document your Process	→	Implement your Process	→	Measure your Process	→	Monitor your Process

We will now take a look at the components of the Oracle solution that best address this standard, namely Oracle Tutor and Oracle Quality.

Oracle Tutor

Oracle Tutor is both a set of template procedure manuals and an authoring tool to modify or create procedure manuals from scratch. While we have written about Oracle Tutor in the ISO 9000 compliance area, those of us who were active in the compliance space when Sarbanes first became a business issue, saw a great deal of time and money was spent establishing procedure manuals.

Oracle Tutor is broken down into:

- A library of about 400 model procedure documents
- A specialized **authoring tool** running in Microsoft Word
- A **publication tool** that automatically builds the role index
- A methodology for generating procedure manuals

Your end product is a set of desk manuals that are published to a website and are organized by the role that uses them:

ORACLE Tutor

Process Flows   Document   Impact Analysis   Sample UPK   Sample UPK
                 Register   Reports   Player   Topics

Desk Manual Index

Accountant   Human Resources Manager
Accounting Clerk   Human Resources Representative
Accounts Payable Clerk   Human Resources Specialist
Accounts Payable Supervisor   Information Services Manager
Accounts Receivable Clerk   Inventory Control Manager
Accounts Receivable Supervisor Legal Affairs Representative
Administrative Assistant   Manager
Assembler   Manager's Manager
Auditor   Manufacturing Clerk
Benefits Analyst   Manufacturing Engineer

Oracle Tutor's appeal is that it is very simple. The Tutor's **Author** component runs inside Word, and hence becomes familiar immediately. You can start from a model document with standard sections and modify the content to tune it to your precise process. The following is a screenshot of the Tutor running inside Word:

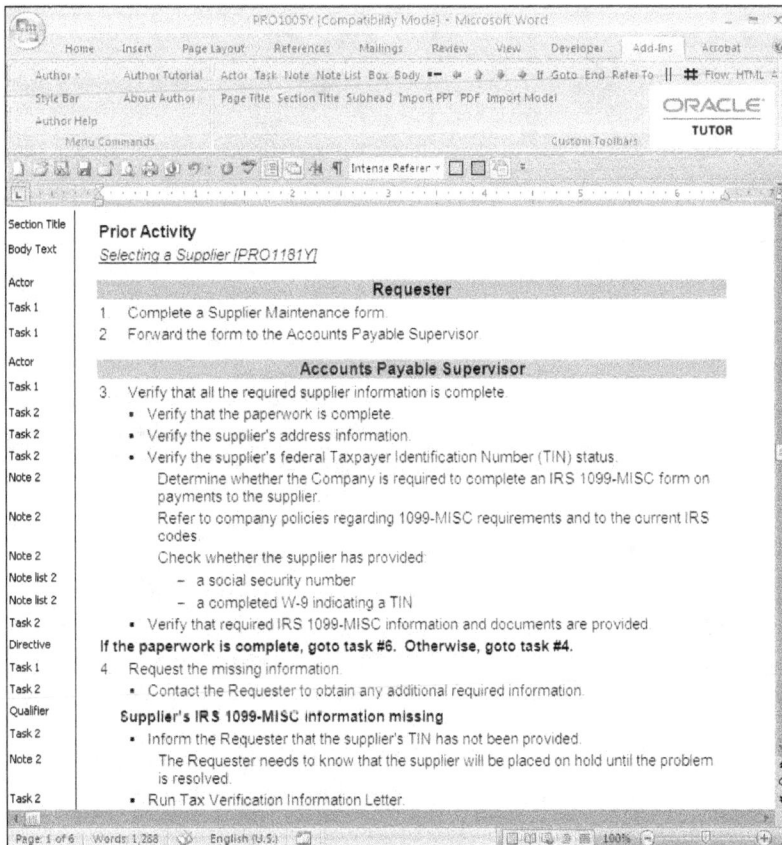

PRO1005Y [Compatibility Mode] - Microsoft Word

Home   Insert   Page Layout   References   Mailings   Review   View   Developer   Add-Ins   Acrobat

Author ·   Author Tutorial   Actor Task Note Note List Box Body ■▬ ⊕ ⊕ ⊕ ⊕ If Goto End Refer To || ⊞ Flow HTML ^
Style Bar   About Author   Page Title Section Title Subhead Import PPT PDF Import Model
Author Help
Menu Commands   Custom Toolbars

ORACLE
TUTOR

Intense Referer ·

Section Title	**Prior Activity**
Body Text	*Selecting a Supplier [PRO1181Y]*
Actor	**Requester**
Task 1	1. Complete a Supplier Maintenance form.
Task 1	2 Forward the form to the Accounts Payable Supervisor.
Actor	**Accounts Payable Supervisor**
Task 1	3. Verify that all the required supplier information is complete.
Task 2	• Verify that the paperwork is complete.
Task 2	• Verify the supplier's address information.
Task 2	• Verify the supplier's federal Taxpayer Identification Number (TIN) status.
Note 2	Determine whether the Company is required to complete an IRS 1099-MISC form on payments to the supplier.
Note 2	Refer to company policies regarding 1099-MISC requirements and to the current IRS codes.
Note 2	Check whether the supplier has provided:
Note list 2	– a social security number
Note list 2	– a completed W-9 indicating a TIN
Task 2	• Verify that required IRS 1099-MISC information and documents are provided.
Directive	**If the paperwork is complete, goto task #6. Otherwise, goto task #4.**
Task 1	4. Request the missing information.
Task 2	• Contact the Requester to obtain any additional required information.
Qualifier	**Supplier's IRS 1099-MISC information missing**
Task 2	• Inform the Requester that the supplier's TIN has not been provided.
Note 2	The Requester needs to know that the supplier will be placed on hold until the problem is resolved.
Task 2	• Run Tax Verification Information Letter.

Page: 1 of 6   Words: 1,288   English (U.S.)   100%

One of the biggest headaches of the procedure manual is that the procedure is probably developed as text but can be very easily followed if we represent it in the form of a diagram. Keeping the diagram and the text in sync is painful. However, Tutor builds the process diagram from the paragraph headings automatically. The newest release of Tutor also allows you to import the paragraph headings from Visio as well as interoperate between different process modeling tools. The following screenshot shows an example of a flow diagram in a Tutor document:

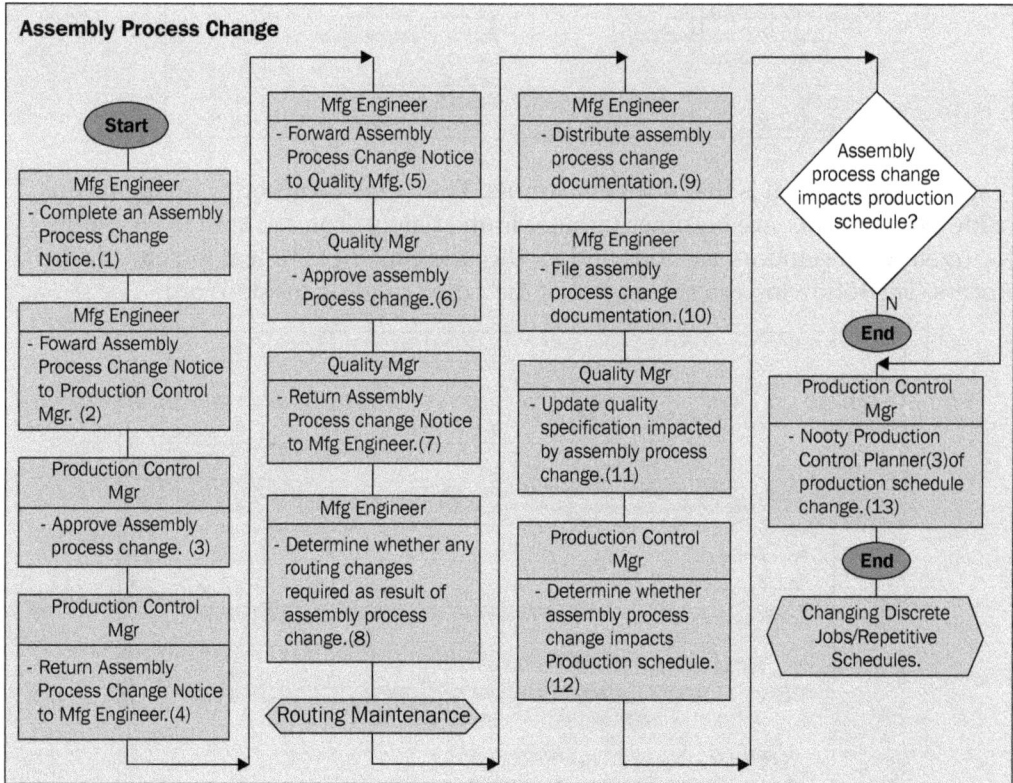

Assembly Process Change

```
Start

Mfg Engineer
- Complete an Assembly
  Process Change
  Notice.(1)

Mfg Engineer
- Foward Assembly
  Process Change Notice
  to Production Control
  Mgr. (2)

Production Control
Mgr
- Approve Assembly
  process change. (3)

Production Control
Mgr
- Return Assembly
  Process Change Notice
  to Mfg Engineer.(4)

Mfg Engineer
- Forward Assembly
  Process Change Notice
  to Quality Mfg.(5)

Quality Mgr
- Approve assembly
  Process change.(6)

Quality Mgr
- Return Assembly
  Process change Notice
  to Mfg Engineer.(7)

Mfg Engineer
- Determine whether any
  routing changes
  required as result of
  assembly process
  change.(8)

Routing Maintenance

Mfg Engineer
- Distribute assembly
  process change
  documentation.(9)

Mfg Engineer
- File assembly
  process change
  documentation.(10)

Quality Mgr
- Update quality
  specification impacted
  by assembly process
  change.(11)

Production Control
Mgr
- Determine whether
  assembly process
  change impacts
  Production schedule.
  (12)

Assembly
process change
impacts production
schedule?   N

End

Production Control
Mgr
- Nooty Production
  Control Planner(3)of
  production schedule
  change.(13)

End

Changing Discrete
Jobs/Repetitive
Schedules.
```

Oracle Quality

The next piece of the ISO 9000 process is to define the measurements and tolerances for the process. **Oracle Quality** is integrated with the Oracle Applications product suite to provide unified quality data definition and data collection throughout the enterprise and across your supply and distribution networks. Once you have the procedures in place, it is the function of Oracle Quality to measure that process and confirm that it is improving. Much of the quality management theory is setting targets, tolerances around those targets, and measuring the proportion of transactions that fall outside of those tolerances.

Oracle Quality components and how they are related

The following diagram shows the main components of the Oracle Quality system and how they are related to each other in **Crow's foot notation**:

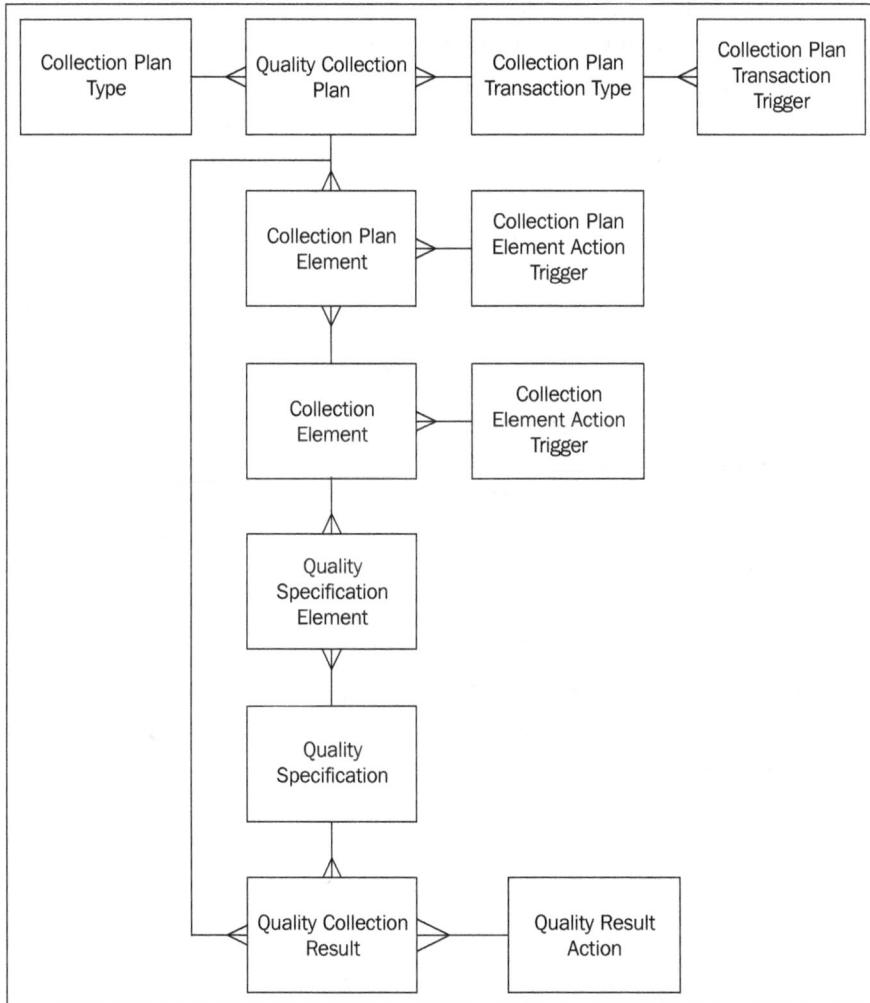

Each component can be described as follows:

- **Quality Collection Plan**: The collection plan is a set of collection elements and their tolerances. For example, Infission purchases the chassis for its computers. These chassis are stamped, drilled, folded, and black powder coated. All folds must be between 89.850 and 90.150. The surface must have powder coating to a depth of between 0.2 and 0.3 of a millimeter. The surface must be flat within a range of 0.005 and 0.007 millimeters.

- **Collection Plan Transaction Type**: The Collection Plan Transaction Type is the transaction that causes the data collection to occur. For example, a receipt from production to finished goods may cause an inspection and data collection to occur.

- **Collection Element**: A collection element is any fact or measurement that could be collected by the inspection. For example, the depth of the powder coat on the surface of the aluminum.

- **Collection Plan Element**: A Collection Plan Element is the collection elements under the plan. For example, flatness.

- **Quality Specification Element**: A Quality Specification Element is the limits for a given collection plan element. For example, a surface is expected to be flat to within 0.005 and 0.007 millimeters.

- **Quality Specification**: A Quality Specification is the assignment of a specification to a customer, supplier, or item.

- **Quality Collection Result**: A Quality Collection Result is the collection of observations.

- **Quality Result Action**: The results may be out of tolerance requiring corrective actions, such as returning product to a vendor or creating a rework job in manufacturing.

The following diagram shows collection plan results flowing through the quality system:

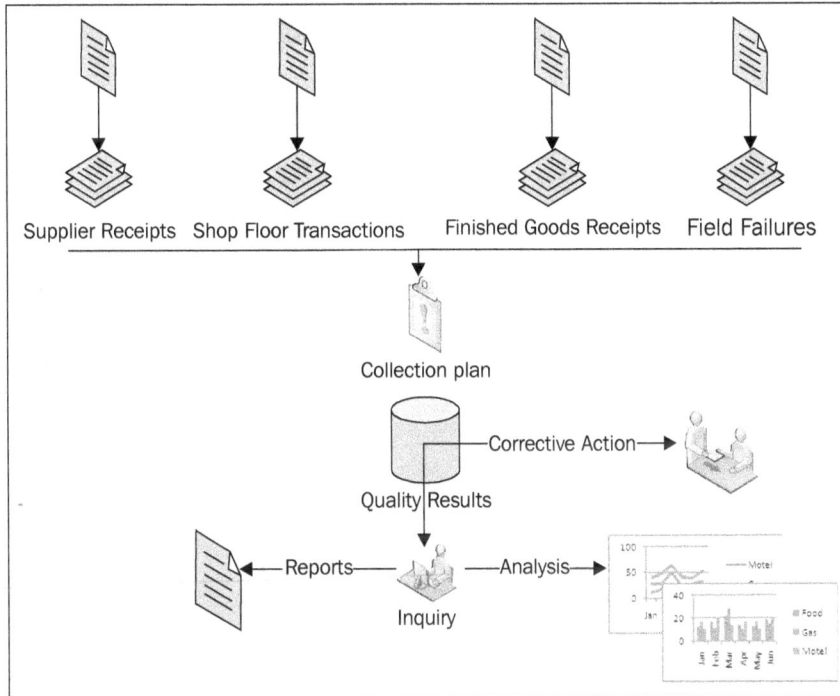

Collections can be triggered by a transaction type such as a supplier receipt. Quality results are recorded according to the defined collection plan. The collection plan results are compared against the specification limits and if necessary corrective actions are taken. The results are pooled to allow inquiry, analysis, and reporting.

Responsibilities for accessing Oracle Quality

You can access Oracle Quality from the Manufacturing and Distribution Manager responsibility. The Quality Workbench is also available as a separate responsibility, which is limited to recording and reviewing collection results.

Creating a collection plan

The following screenshot shows the **Collection Plans** definition:

In order to create a collection plan, choose the **Manufacturing and Distribution Manager** responsibility and choose the **Set Up** menu. From the **Set Up** menu, choose **Collection Plan**.

The collection plan allows you to specify the collection elements that you will record on each transaction listed in the collection plan transactions. In order to associate a collection plan to a type of transaction, click on the **Transaction** button:

In order to set up collection elements, choose the **Manufacturing and Distribution Manager** responsibility and choose the **Set Up** menu. Now, choose the **Collection Elements** tab.

> Note that access to the Collection Plan Element UI should be closely controlled as being able to introduce raw SQL into the application opens the application to SQL Injection attacks.

For each collection element, you can state the data type, valid values, and validation as well as the tolerances around the **Target Value**, as shown in the following screenshot:

In order to set specification limits for a specification element, click on the **Spec Limits** button from the **Collection Elements** UI. This is a very important UI because a lot of the quality management theory is all about bringing a process under control. This generally means reducing variability in the process. Once variability has been reduced, the process can be reliably brought into specification. As shown in the following screenshot, you are setting control limits around the specification:

You can optionally create a specification that is specific to a supplier, customer, or an item. For example, you may have a specification imposed on you from a customer to test the color match of your PC's casing because they are using them onboard with their own test and measurement equipment, such as a chromatograph.

In order to create a specification, you are again in the Manufacturing and Distribution Manager responsibility in the **Set Up** menu, this time in the **Specification** tab:

For each element in the specification, you can set the target value and tolerances within the specification.

Entering collection results

Now that the **Collection Plan** is set up, when a triggering event occurs, the quality results will have to be entered:

In order to enter results, navigate to the **Results** menu under the **Manufacturing and distribution manager** or navigate to **Collection Results** under the **Workbench** menu. You can enter results against a collection plan. Corrective actions may result. Results can be collated for reporting. For example, control charts or pereto charts can be generated from the quality results data:

Auditing ISO 9000

The ISO 9001:2008 standard requires that every element of the quality system should be internally audited every year. The development of an internal audit system includes the selection and training of auditors, maintaining an internal audit schedule, and using a standard operating procedure for management of your internal audits.

Of course the audit procedure and internal audit schedule should be represented in the GRC Manager.

There are great examples and resources available from ISO 9000 Resources (http://www.iso9000resources.com/).

Section 4 is a great place to start an internal audit because it addresses the "big picture" items. If there are any non-conformances from a Section 4 audit, fix the problems before auditing Sections 5 through 8. This will save a lot of effort documenting the same problem over and over.

Questions

---

1. General quality system requirements

Has the organization established, documented, implemented, and maintained a quality management system in accordance with the ISO 9001 Requirements?

Is the Quality Management System (QMS) continually improving?

Has the organization:

1) Identified the process needed for the QMS throughout ISO 9001 organization?

2) Determined the proper interaction between the process ISO 9001. Is there a flow chart that shows the process flow for the entire organization?

3) Determined and documented criteria and methods to ensure that the ISO 9001 operations and process control are effective?

4) Got resources and information necessary to support ISO 9001 operations and maintenance of their process?

5) Got resources to measure, monitor, and analyze their processes?

6) Implement corrective and preventive actions needed to achieve the planned results as documented in the quality plans?

7) Does the company have documentation to show continuous improvement in their process?

Does the organization have documentation in accordance with the requirements of the ISO 9001 Standard?

How does the company control quality processes that are performed outside of the ISO approved facility?

2. Documentation requirements

2.1 General

Does the QMS documentation system include:

1) Quality Manual?

2) Documented company quality policy and quality objectives?

3) Documented level 1 and level 2 procedures as required by ISO 9001?

4) Documentation on how the company can effectively plan, operate, and control its processes?

5) Creation and management of records that demonstrate compliance with the ISO standard?

Questions

2.2 Quality manual

Has a quality manual been created and maintained that includes:

1) The scope of the quality management system and any justification for exclusion to the standard (such as obsolete product lines)?

2) Description of the interaction between the process of the quality management system (usually in the form of a flow chart showing product flow from design and order to delivery and service)?

3) The procedures required by the ISO standard or references to the required procedure control numbers.

2.3 Control of documentation

Are all QMS documents (manuals, procedures, data sheets, work instructions, records, and procedures) controlled (including revision control, controlled access to originals, and control of distributed copies)?

Does the company have a document control procedure that includes:

1) Notification of the ISO approval body prior to implementation of any change to an agency controlled document?

2) Approval, update, and distribution processes for changes to all quality documents.

3) Ensures that the current revision documents (with no confusion about the current revision) are available at the point of use?

4) Ensures that the documents remain legible and easily identifiable?

5) A process for controlling documents of external origin.

6) Control of obsolete documents to ensure they are not used in current production.

2.4 Control of records

Does the company create and maintain records?

Does the company have records to provide evidence that the QMS is effective (examples include management review records, corrective and preventive actions logs, customer survey, or feedback records)?

Has a documented procedure been written to define the following record control mechanisms:

1) Identification and retrieval?

2) Storage and protection?

3) Retention time and disposition?

Environmental compliance and ISO 14000

We continue our conversation with the VP of Operations and the Manufacturing Manager by discussing the environmental management aspects that should conform to ISO 14000. We look at how environmental audit procedures fit into GRC Manager.

Requirements of ISO 14001

ISO 14001 is a voluntary international standard developed by the International Organization for Standardization (ISO), based in Geneva, Switzerland. At its core, it sets the requirements for establishment of an **Environmental Management System**. The following diagram shows the environmental impacts and sphere of the environmental management system:

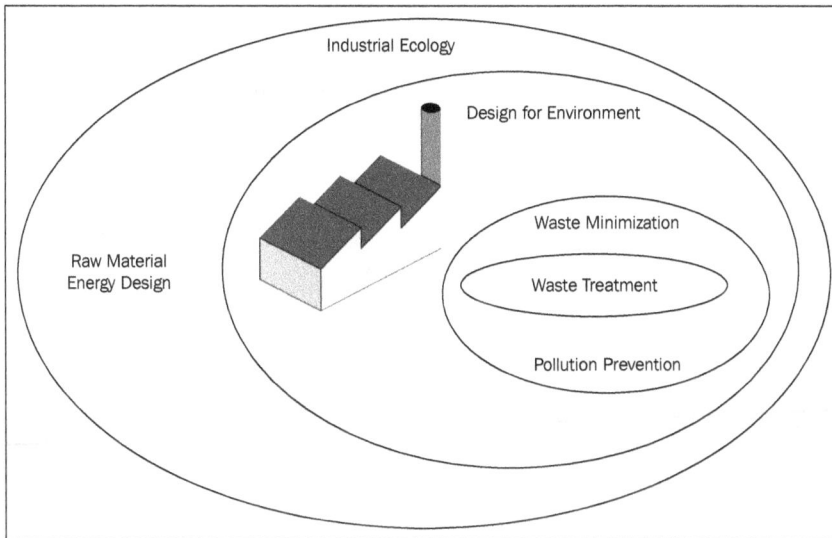

The implementation of ISO 14001 is a cyclic process requiring the development of a comprehensive environmental policy statement, a planning process to operationalize the policy, its implementation and operation, checking and implementing corrective action if needed, and management review, which feeds back to rewriting the environmental policy statement. The following diagram is a pictorial representation of that process:

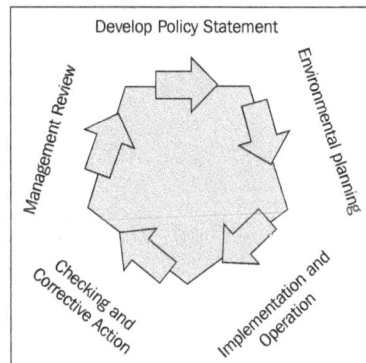

Some of the procedures required in order to obtain ISO 14001 Certification include:

- Identification of significant environmental aspects
- Identification of legal and other requirements
- Internal and external communication and awareness building
- Information collation and analysis
- Operational control
- Emergency preparedness and response
- Monitoring and measurement of resource consumption
- Equipment calibration
- Evaluating legal and regulatory compliance
- Maintaining records
- Audit and management review

ISO 14000 compliance auditing

ISO 14001 specifies the need to conduct periodic environmental management system audits. Basic level internal industrial environmental audits have several purposes, such as to assure the investors through the board of directors of compliance status and to assist manufacturing sites in their environmental efforts. The environmental audit will cover: environmental labeling, environmental performance evaluation, and manufacturing lifecycle assessments. Internal environmental audits are generally carried out by the internal audit staff and follow the same structures as the financial and operational audits, such as planning, scoping, gathering findings, and recording issues and recommendations. You will notice that other aspects of the ISO 14000 compliance problem also fit into components of the Oracle solution, which we have mentioned earlier, for example:

- Section 4.2.3 of ISO 14001 deals with objectives and targets as we have reviewed in balanced scorecard
- Section 4.3.2 of ISO 14001 deals with training and education as we have reviewed in iLearning

- Section 4.3.4 of ISO 14001 deals with document control as we have reviewed in Universal Content Manager
- Section 4.4.4 of ISO 14001 deals with EMS Audits as we have reviewed in GRC Manager

Organization certification

While ISO 14000 is a voluntary standard, an organization can have its Environmental Management System certified by an external accredited registrar. The external auditor will typically review:

- The EMS Manual
- Analysis of environmental impacts
- Regulatory requirements
- Audit reports
- Improvement plans

How ISO 14000 fits into GRC Manager

Mostly, GRC manager addresses the audit and management review aspects of the Environment Management System (EMS). However, the risk assessment and risk management protocols within GRC Manager provide a great framework for the EMS.

The first thing to note about GRC Manager is that the risk and controls can be looked at from many perspectives. Environmental compliance is just another perspective. In order to set up perspectives, you can click on the navigator and navigate to **Setup and Administration**. Expand **Object Type maintenance** from the table and click on **Manage Perspectives**:

Name	Description
Corporate Risk	Corporate level Risks
Financial Governance Risk	Financial Governance Risk UDT
IT Risk	IT Risk
Risk	Risk Object

You would set up environmental checklists in the **Survey Section** of GRC Manager. In order to navigate to the **Set up surveys**, choose **GRC Tools** from the navigator, and then choose **Manage Survey Templates** from the **Tasks** pane:

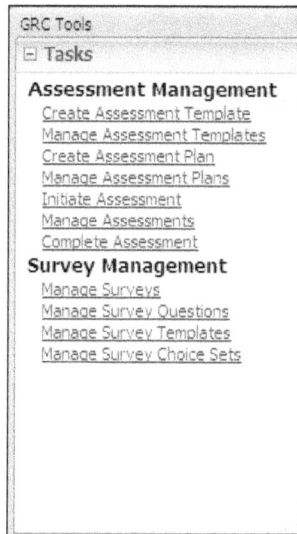

```
GRC Tools
⊟ Tasks

Assessment Management
  Create Assessment Template
  Manage Assessment Templates
  Create Assessment Plan
  Manage Assessment Plans
  Initiate Assessment
  Manage Assessments
  Complete Assessment
Survey Management
  Manage Surveys
  Manage Survey Questions
  Manage Survey Templates
  Manage Survey Choice Sets
```

The following is a **General information data sheet**. This is a standard part of constructing the information that you need for an environmental audit:

General information data sheet
Plant name:
Address:
Contact person:
Date:
Major products:
10 most used raw materials:
Recent changes in products or manufacturing processes:
Is the property owned or leased:
When was the property first acquired:
Provide the history of the land use of the property:
Describe the other industries (light, heavy industrial, refineries, steel mills, and so on):

The general information data sheet fits into the GRC Manager's survey capability. In order to create a survey in Enterprise GRC Manager, you will need to have the GRC Administrator job role. In order to create a survey, select the **New** icon from the **Manage Survey** screen and then select the template on which you wish to base the survey:

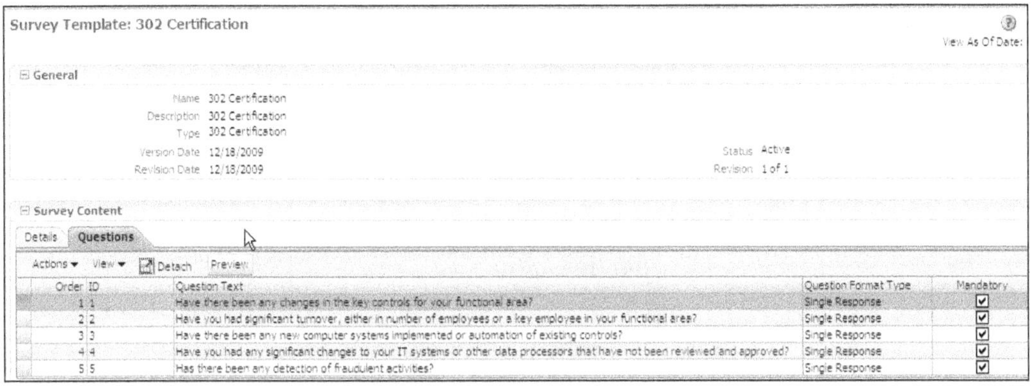

You can also expand your information on environmental risks and controls. The following is an **Air emissions data sheet**. It would also fit well into the survey capability. You can also see that we will discover both the risks that will need to go in the risk register as well as the controls that will need to go in the controls register as a result of this survey.

Air emissions data sheet

Plant name:

Address:

Contact person:

Date:

Number of stacks

Sources being vented by stacks:

1) Heat (y/n)

2) Manufacturing (y/n)

3) Other (y/n)

   Nature of emissions:

      Toxic gases and vapors

      Aerosols

Air emissions data sheet
Irritant gases
Asphyxiants
Dust and ash
Air Permits:
Name
Permit number
Regulated and permitted emissions:
Volatile organic compounds
Carbon monoxide
Nitrogen oxides
Sulfur dioxide
Lead
Control equipment:
Filters
Scrubbers
Backwashes
Baghouse
Incinerator

Example environmental risk portfolio

An emissions data sheet could be represented in either a survey or in the risk library. We are going to show it in the Risk Library. Navigate to **Risk Management capabilities**, choose **GRC Tools** from the navigator, and select **Risk Management**:

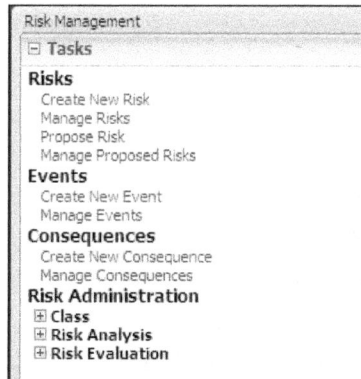

The list of environmental risks would be represented in the Risk Library, as shown in the following screenshot:

Name	Description
Accuracy of automated posting	Accuracy of automated posting were generated
Atriance and Neutropenia	Signal of neutropenia occurrence in patients taking Atriance
Authorized purchases - PO not obtained.	Authorized purchases - PO/EMR not obtained.
Back dated entries passed in previous y...	Back dated entries passed in previous year for fraudulent reasons
Back dating entries to previous year (e...	Back dating entries to previous year (even after books closed for the year) to manipulate data
Breach of limit and approved counterpa...	Breach of limit and approved counterparties list (intentionally)
Cash misappropriated - intentionally	Cash misappropriated - intentionally
Change to requirements projects	Adding or changing requirements without consideration for the IT project's overall objectives or the associated increases in time, costs or resources.
Contractual terms and conditions impac...	Contractual terms and conditions impacting revenue recognition are not reviewed and transactions are accounted for inaccurately
Credit/Debit memos and adjustments ar...	Credit/Debit memos and adjustments are inaccurate or unauthorized
Customer set-up in the system is unaut...	Customer set-up in the system is unauthorized or inaccurate
Doubtful accounts are not accurately st...	AR and doubtful accounts are not accurately stated
Duplicate invoices paid on the same inv...	Duplicate invoices paid on the same invoice
Duplicate payment for expense report.	Provide validation to ensure we don't make two payment for an expense report.
Embezzlement of cheques	Embezzlement of cheques
Employee earnings are mis-reported	Employee earnings are mis-reported

The best way to show the controls in place to mitigate for those risks is by documenting the relationship between risks, such as **Toxic Gases and Vapors** being released into the environment, and mitigating controls, such as **Filters and Scrubbers** in the **Related Controls** tab of the **Risk**. Click on a risk and you can view and manage the related controls of that risk:

Beyond the risks, GRC Manager also maintains a registry of consequences. A consequence is the outcome when and if a risk event happens. For example, consequences of a failure in the control of heavy metals disposal may include factory shutdown, environmental cleanup and restoration, employee health costs, and workers compensation.

RoHS WEEE

RoHS stands for **Restriction of Hazardous Substances** and is a directive, which came into effect on 1st July, 2006.

WEEE stands for the **Waste Electrical and Electronic Equipment Directive**. In this section, we expand our environmental conversation with the Manufacturing Manager to include how he manages heavy metal content in his electronics. We will show how Oracle has expanded the governance and compliance theme into the Product Lifecycle Management (PLM) applications.

RoHS WEEE and hazardous substance compliance

The RoHS regulations implement the provisions of the European Parliament and Council Directive on the Restrictions of the Use of Certain Hazardous Substances in Electrical and Electronic Equipment (2002/95/EC).

This directive was established to:

- Protect human health and the environment
- Complement the Waste of Electrical and Electronic Equipment (WEEE) directive (2002/96/EC)

Who needs to comply?

The RoHS directive places the responsibility for electrical or electronic equipment compliance on the producer of the electrical or electronic equipment. It is the producer who must determine whether his/her product is electrical or electronic equipment under the directives, and if so, then ensure its compliance.

Oracle Agile Product Governance and Compliance

This product by Oracle best addresses the hazardous substance compliance regulations such as RoHS and WEEE. It is a part of the **Agile Product Lifecycle Management Suite, Product Governance and Compliance (PG&C)**. The following diagram depicts the process flow through the Product Governance and Compliance process:

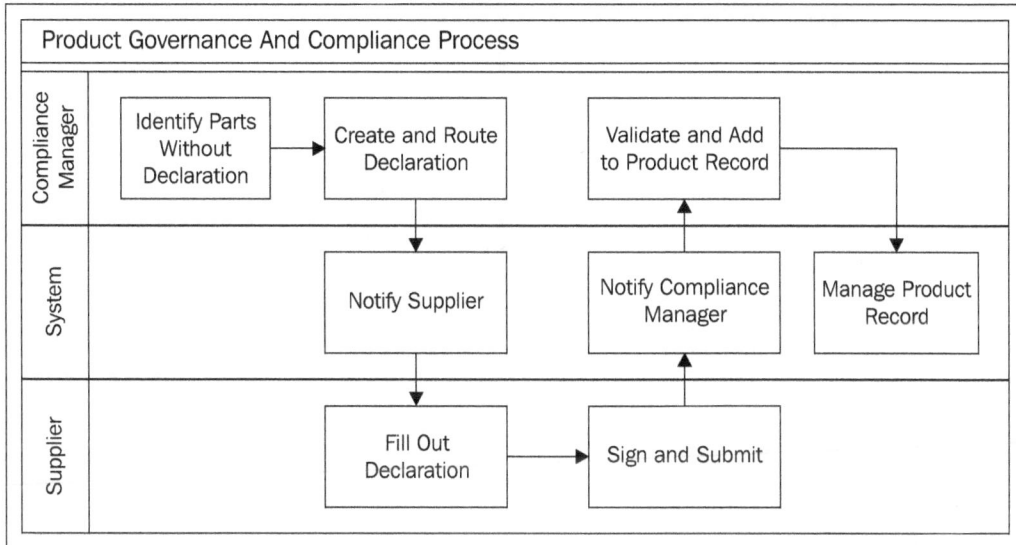

In the product governance and compliance process, the **Original Equipment Manufacturer (OEM)** sends parts composition requests to a supplier. The supplier makes a declaration of composition and returns it back to the originator. The originator then goes through a roll-up to work out the **Bill of Substances** of the OEM's parts.

Major components of PG&C and how they relate to each other

The following diagram shows the major components of the PG&C system and how they relate to each other in Crow's foot notation:

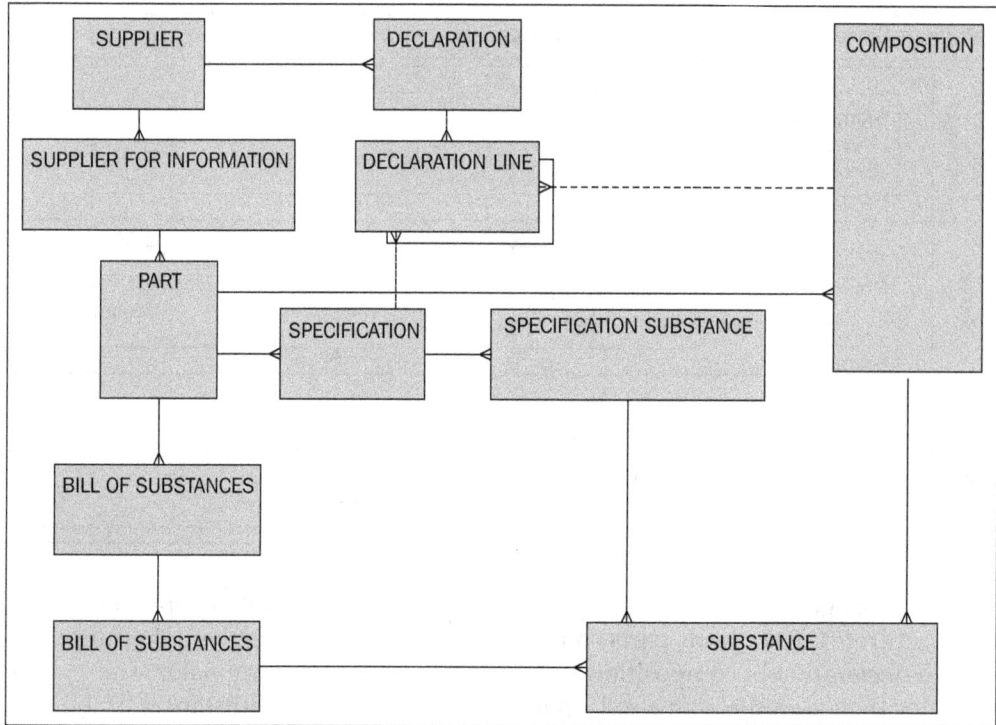

The major components of the PG&C system are as follows:

- **Substance**: The substance that is subject to reporting, certification, and waste management responsibilities.

- **Part**: The part within which the substance is incorporated and for which quantities of the substance be accounted.

- **Specification**: The weight and parts per million limits to which the substances must comply for a part.

- **Bill of Substances**: The bill of substances is a hierarchical list of substances contained in parts that require compliance.

- **Supplier**: In PG&C, it is the supplier of the declaration of composition.

- **Request for Information**: The supplier is sent a request for information for the composition of parts.

- **Declaration**: Declaration is a response to a request for information. A declaration can confirm that a part or parts are within the specification.

- **Composition**: The composition shows the weights of substances within a part.

Defining specifications

PG&C introduces the notion of specifications, which define what a substance that is subject to product governance needs to be compliant with. The actual specifications are likely to be unstructured data held in the attachments associated to the specification. In order to create a specification in PG&C, click on the **Create New** drop-down button to activate the menu and click on the **Specifications** link:

Specifications have their own attributes, attachments, and change history. They also define at which level of a product hierarchy to validate for compliance and which potential exemptions are allowed. Specifications can optionally contain substances including threshold based constraints or constraints based on **intentional adding**. The following screenshot shows the **Substances** within a specification:

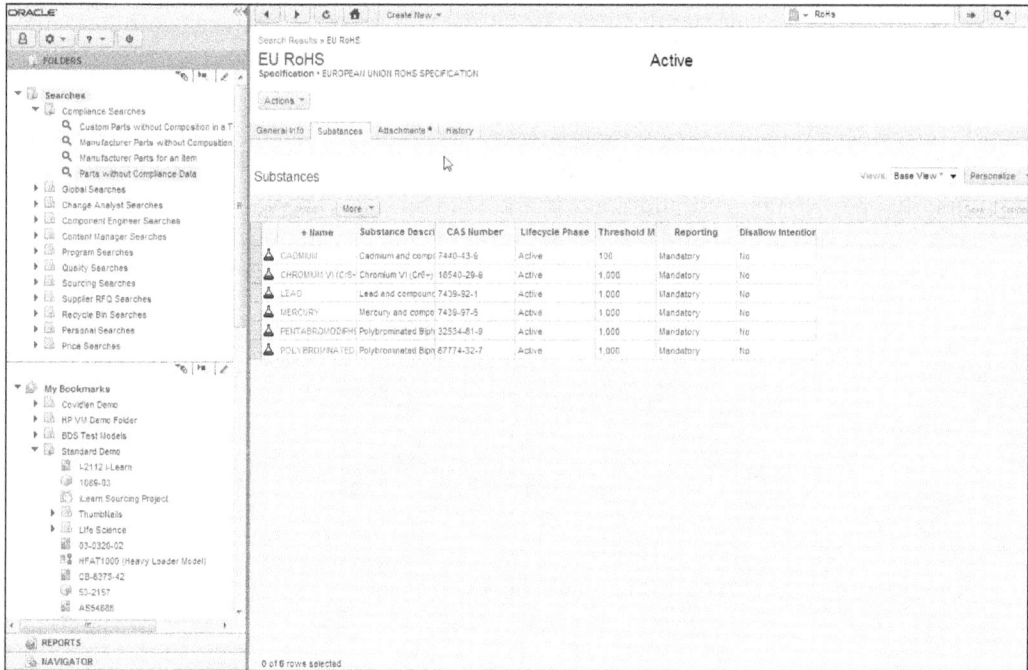

Non-substance based specifications are handled as well. For example, to allow for disassembly and recovery of materials it may be specified that components may not be glued.

Defining substances

It is possible in PG&C to keep track of thousands of substances, including very detailed information per substance such as trade names, where a given substance is used, other common names for the substance, and the CAS number. A **Chemical Abstract Service (CAS)** is a service of the **American Chemical Society** that issues unique and authoritative numbers identifying tens of millions of substances.

Using the aliasing feature, import will automatically convert incoming data into the official substance name used within Agile PG&C.

Besides substances, PG&C has support for substance groups and materials as well. The following screenshot shows the **Search Results for** screen for searching a substance:

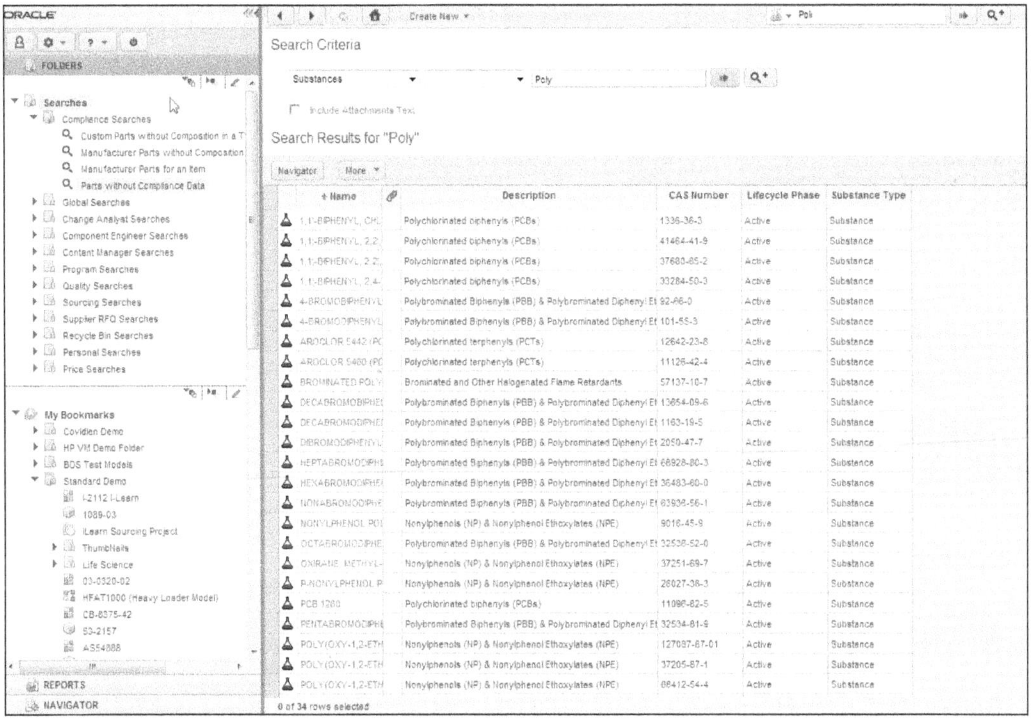

From here you can edit a substance by clicking on the **Create New** button to create a new substance. The following is a screenshot of the **Define Substance** page:

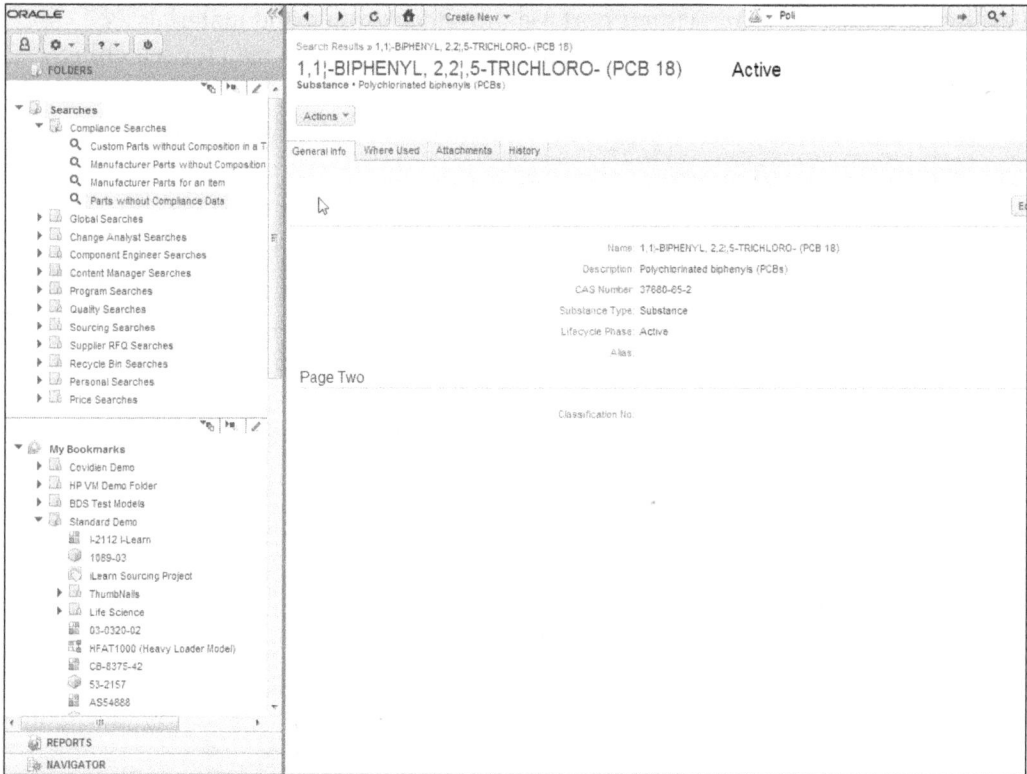

Defining declarations and compositions

For each **Internal Part Number (IPN)**, **Manufacturers Part Number (MPN)**, and assembly, PG&C allows us to track down the specifications. Specifications are pushed down as bills of materials to notify each assembly level and component within the Bill of Material (BOM) about what it has to be compliant with across the **Approved Manufacturer Lists (AML)** and **Approved Vendor Lists (AVL)**.

Compliance data collections happen through a declaration process. Declarations are used to gather data at different levels of granularity from a simple part level "yes or no" type declaration to full disclosures at the homogeneous material level. A homogeneous material might be a metal or plastic. A non-homogeneous material might be a wire that has copper wire, sheathing, and plastic coating. All kinds of partner, part, and/or substance related information can be requested from a supply chain. The following screenshot shows the declarations and compositions associated to a specification:

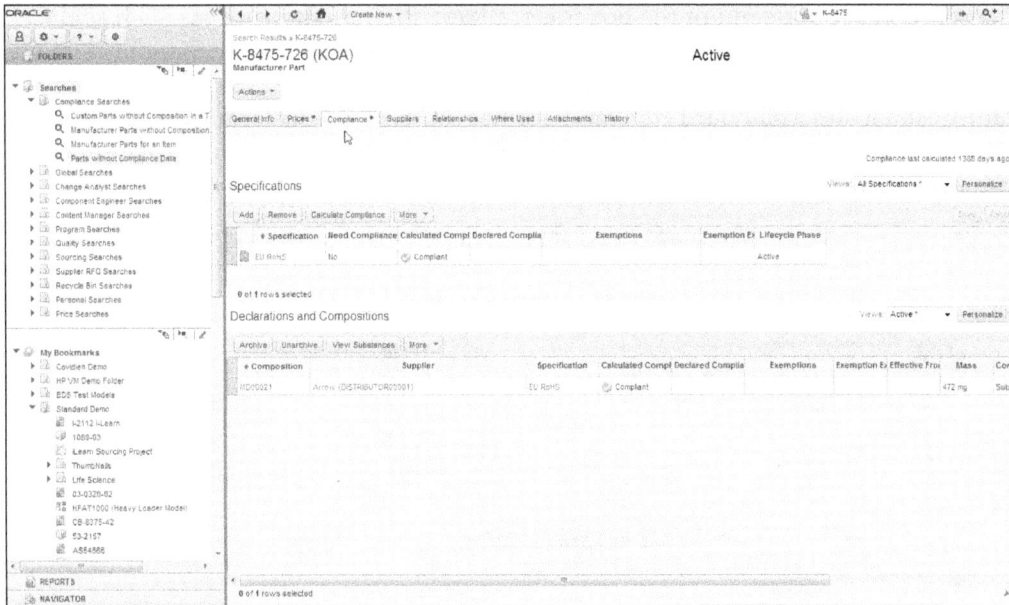

The declaration process with suppliers and content providers can be managed electronically online through a configurable workflow process, including the ability for electronic sign-offs. The following screenshot shows the declaration workflow for the collection of product data. You can see the status of each action in the workflow in the lower section of the screen:

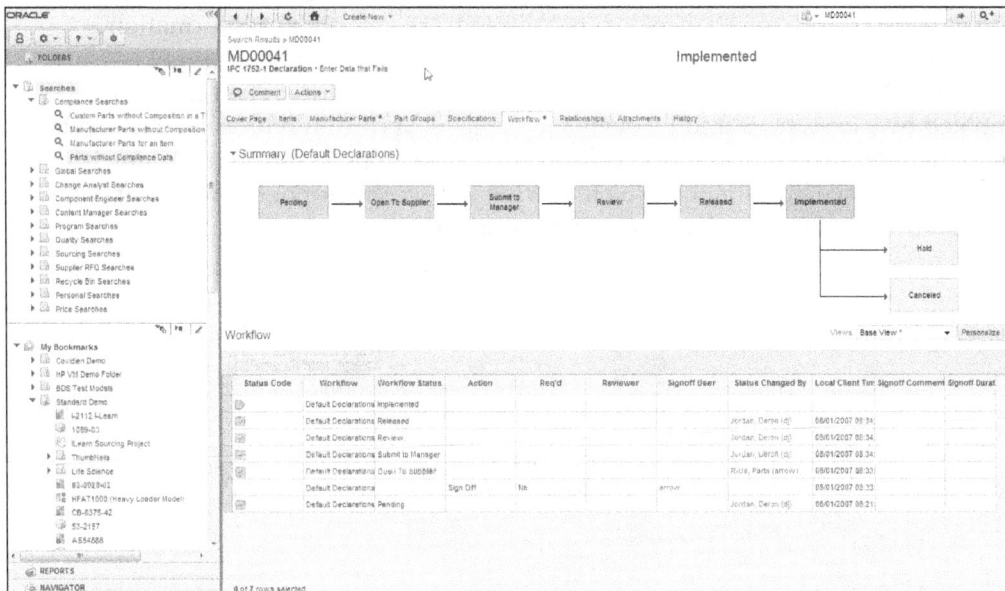

The solution supports out of the box integration with industry formats such as IPC 1752-1 and 1752-2 XML as well as Japan Green Procurement Survey Standardization Initiative format for collecting data from supply chain partners. IPC-175x standards family establishes a standard reporting format for material declaration data exchange between supply chain participants. PG&C also supports integration of custom excel formats. The following screenshot shows a printed declaration from PG&C:

MD00071 Implemented Print Cancel

Substance Declaration • ACME ROHS DECLARATION FOR P00112 PDA CASING ASSEMBLY

Cover Page

Name: MD00071
Description: ACME ROHS DECLARATION FOR P00112 PDA CASING ASSEMBLY
Date Sent To Supplier: 09/16/2008 11:53:15 AM PDT
Compliance Manager: Shane Moorhead (shanem)
Compliance Manager Phone: 408-555-1212
Date Released: 09/16/2008 11:53:07 AM PDT
Supplier: ACME Inc. (CTRMR00023)
Status: Implemented
Date Submitted By Supplier: 09/16/2008 11:51:57 AM PDT
Supplier Contact Phone: 408-555-1212
Supplier Contact Fax: 408-555-1215
Originator: Shane Moorhead (shanem)
Has Invalid Substance: No

Declaration Type: Substance Declaration
Workflow: Default Declarations
Due Date: 09/17/2008 12:00:00 AM PDT
Compliance Manager Title: Compliance Manager
Compliance Manager Email: demo@demo.oracle.com
Compliance Manager Fax:
Final Complete Date: 09/16/2008 11:53:15 AM PDT
Supplier DUNS Number: 2546-9854
Supplier Contact Title: Customer Engineer
Supplier Contact Email: demo@demo.oracle.com
Supplier Address: 123 ACME DRIVE
Supplier Contact Name: Andy Acme (acme)
Need Rollup: No

Items

Item Number	Item Rev	Item Description	Item Lifecycle Phase	Specification	Calculated Compliance	Declared Compliance	Exemptions	Exemption Expiration Date	Effective From Date	Mass	Mass Disclosure
P00112	B	PDA CASING ASSEMBLY	Production	EU RoHS	Compliant					0.65 Pound	Partially Disclosed

Substances for Item

Substance Name	CAS Number	Threshold Mass PPM	Mass	Result Mass	Result PPM	Calculated PPM	Calculated Compliance	Declared PPM	Declared Compliance	Exemptions	Exemption Expiration Date	Reporting	Conversion Factor	Ca
CADMIUM	7440-43-9	100	2.5E-4 Ounce	0.00708738078125 Gram	24.038461538462	24.038461538462	Compliant					Mandatory		
CHROMIUM VI (Cr6+)	18540-29-9	1,000	0.0 Gram	0.0 Gram	0	0	Compliant					Mandatory		
LEAD	7439-92-1	1,000	7.5E-4 Ounce	0.021262142343750002 Gram	72.115384615385	72.115384615385	Compliant					Mandatory		
MERCURY	7439-97-6	1,000	0.0 Gram	0.0 Gram	0	0	Compliant					Mandatory		

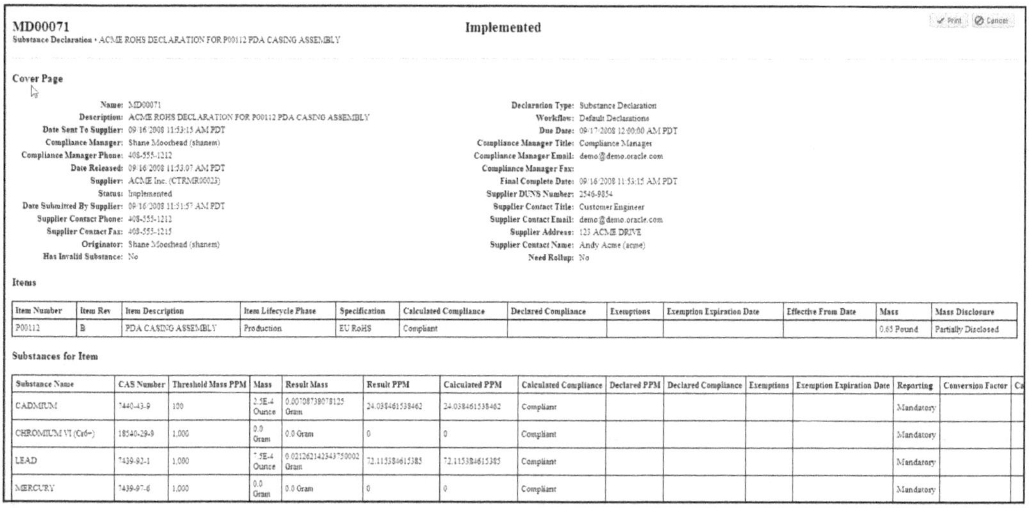

Reviewing compliance data for assemblies

For any given component in the bill of material, there may be many manufacturers and vendors. Once compliance data is collected, the compliance information is rolled up by **Rev** throughout the BOM across Approved Manufacturers Lists and Approved Vendors Lists using a best or worst case algorithm. The roll-ups can be initiated by a user, triggered by events in Agile PLM (through process extensions), and scheduler driven to automatically synchronize all BOMs in the system with the latest compliance information. The following is a screenshot of the **BOM** tab where you can review the compliance status of the assembly:

You can use the screens, compliance reports, or searches to identify suspect parts.
The following screenshot shows one such report:

You can instigate an engineering change or corrective action request to manage the compliance risk with the Approved Manufacturer List on this part. Alternatively, every time you create a new pending **Rev**, the system will calculate the compliance impact of the change.

Life sciences and medical instrument manufacturing

Next, we will leave the Infission corporation to talk to some colleagues who manage manufacturing at a medical instruments company — **Lilean Brosh**. We will interview them on what they consider to be their most urgent compliance issue. We will dive into the details of **CFR 21**, and show how the audit procedures of this standard fit into GRC Manager. We will also show how some of the records management requirement of **CFR 21 Part 11** are managed through digital signature aspects of Oracle Workflow.

Title 21: Code of Federal Regulations

This regulation relates to the Food and Drug Administration's primary jurisdiction for the premarket review and regulation of products that comprises any combination of a drug and a device; a device and a biological product; a biological product and a drug; or a drug, a device, and a biological product. An example of a biological product is a vaccine.

The thrust of CFR 21 is good manufacturing practices to protect human health. It requires product sampling and testing, which proves that the manufacturing practice is sufficiently good, and an electronic records protocol that brings about personal accountability for signing those records.

There are many aspects of good manufacturing practices that support food and drug manufacturers in Oracle E-Business Suite Process Manufacturing. They are as follows:

- **Stability studies management**: These studies characterize the effects of aging on the quality and shelf life of a material
- **Receiving holds**: They help companies validate the quality of expired or expiring material
- **Quality controlled batch processing**: This gives you a view of the grade and quality of your on-hand materials before you begin production

In this book, our focus is on audit and compliance activities, so we will not expand the manufacturing pieces. The main compliance issue is that if you are manufacturing food, pharmaceuticals, or medical devices, you must keep records according to the standards in CFR 21 Part 11. Electronic record keeping is available on critical business events including:

- Approval of specifications
- Creation and approval of manufacturing samples
- Entry and evaluation of results
- Approval of stability study stages

The penalties under CFR 21 are substantial, such as $1,000,000 for any 30-day period, where the amount doubles for every 30-day period of continued violation after the first 30-day period. The respondent must prove any affirmative defenses and any mitigating factors by a preponderance of the evidence.

The requirements of electronic records

We need to point out that CFR 21 Part 11 is a pretty broad set of requirements, and many of its requirements are also part of the overall ERP system itself. For example, Sec. 11.300 Controls for identification codes/passwords quotes, " Maintaining the uniqueness of each combined identification code and password, such that no two individuals have the same combination of identification code and password."

You can review the entire document at `http://www.accessdata.fda.gov/scripts/cdrh/cfdocs/cfCFR/CFRSearch.cfm`.

As such, we are going to concentrate on the requirements that are uniquely met by the E-records management solution. These requirements are as follows:

- Electronic records, electronic signatures, and handwritten signatures executed to electronic records must be trustworthy, reliable, and generally equivalent to paper records and handwritten signatures executed on paper.
- Electronic records shall contain information associated with the signing that clearly indicates all of the following:
    - The printed name of the signer
    - The date and time when the signature was executed
    - The meaning (such as review, approval, responsibility, or authorship) associated with the signature
    - In a human readable form of the electronic record
- This last point is more complex than it might at first seem, because the electronic record has to be readable at some arbitrary point in the future when the application that created it may no longer be available.

Oracle's E-records Management Solution

Oracle delivers an E-records management capability as part of its manufacturing execution system, where the framework is configured to capture signatures at many events. You must follow the steps listed in the **Implementing E-records** section of the Oracle E-Records Implementation Guide. If you do not follow these steps, then these E-records or E-signatures will not be required at all. You must set up the profile option **EDR: E-records and E-signatures**:

E-Records can be enabled in the following applications:

- Oracle Engineering
- Oracle Inventory
- Oracle Bills of Material
- Oracle Work in Process
- Oracle Quality
- Oracle Shipping
- Oracle Purchasing

The best way to explain how it works might be through a transaction flow such as a new product introduction.

The following diagram shows the procedure for the online flow using Item Creation:

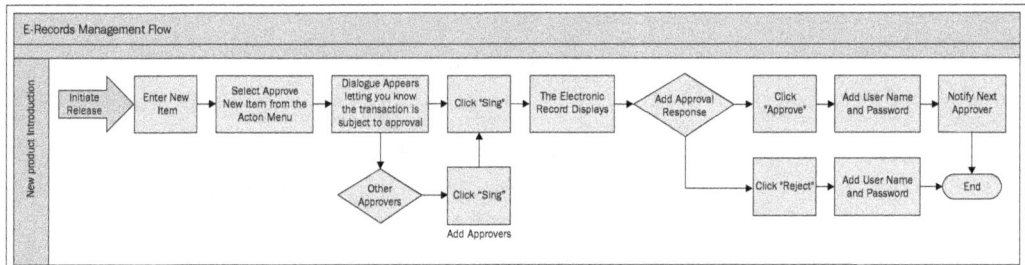

E-records management features

The following are the features of the E-records management system:

- **E-signatures**: When providing an approval response for any transaction for which electronic signatures have been configured, you must provide your login credentials.

- **Electronic records**: Records are extracted into an applications agnostic (XML) format and stored in an evidence store. The records are presented to the signer to ensure that the user signs what he/she sees at the time when they give their approval response.

E-records management components

The following are the components of the E-records management system:

- **Workflow business events**: The E-records framework makes use of Business Events that are subscribed to by approval workflows.
- **XML gateway**: The XML gateway extracts records from the application's tables into XML format to populate the evidence store.
- **Workflow Notification system**: The workflow notification system prompts the users to provide their approval response.
- **XML publisher**: XML publisher formats the XML extracts from the evidence store to ensure that the user signs what he/she sees.
- **Evidence store**: The evidence store is an XML repository, which is extracted from the tables that store the transactions that are signed in E-records. As they are not the raw application's tables and the fact that they are in XML, there is some chance that they remain human readable, even when the applications are upgraded and the tables become obsolete.

Responsibilities in E-records management

The following are the responsibilities seeded with, and used to access the E-records functionality:

- **ERES Administrator**: This person has the responsibility for overall administration of the Oracle E-records application. Only a small number of people should be assigned this responsibility.
- **ERES User**: This person can access the Oracle E-records application for user tasks such as querying the evidence store. No administration-related functions are exposed to this responsibility.
- **iSignatures Administrator**: This person is the administrator for the iSignature process. This person can do all the functions of a user, in addition to updating and deleting other users' files.
- **iSignatures User**: This person can upload files and send them for approval. However, they can only update or delete their own files.

Functions in the E-records process

The following are the functions in the E-records process. The details of setting up for E-records management are beyond the scope of this book and are very well explained in Oracle Manufacturing Implementing Oracle E-records in the Discrete Manufacturing Guide. In short you enable a business event that is seeded by Oracle for a transaction that you wish to capture E-records for and set up the approval rules and routing rules to route notifications to approvers. The style sheet that determines the format of the E-record and whether an E-signature is required is set in the configuration option. When a transaction that is set up for e-records occurs, it is extracted into the evidence store and the approver(s) is/are notified. Once approved in E-records, the original transaction is marked as approved.

Upload and approve files

The first step is to upload a file. Remember that this process is triggered from a business event and it is automatically extracted. As shown in the following screenshot, in this example, the E-record that is extracted is a quality test assay:

You can select the file and click on the **Send for Approval** button to send it for approval, as shown in the previous screenshot.

Signers can modify the approvers list by clicking on the **Update Signers** button. Click on the sign icon to authenticate.

> Note that the user must set up an ad hoc signer capability configuration variable to enable this feature. This feature was available in the 11*i*.10 release.

Notify approvers

In order to set up E-records, a notification workflow subscription for the appropriate business event is created and approvers are notified. In the following screenshot, we will see the notification details, which indicate that the users need to sign-in:

In the paper world, if you are a signer of a document, you can easily see who signed it before you, and any other comments that they may have included with their signatures. Extending this concept to the electronic recordkeeping world, Oracle E-records gives the signers of electronic records an ability to view previous signers' comments during their signing process.

This improves the usability and aids in collaboration, so that signers can see if any prior signers had rejected the record, and for what reason. They can also see who else had approved the record before them.

You can click on the **Attachments** link to view the E-record. The signer enters his/her **Signature Type**, **Signer Reason**, and **Signer Comment** for approval, and then clicks on **Approve**, **Reject**, **Cancel** or **Reassign** to take action:

Searching the evidence store

If at a later stage you wish to review the evidence store to verify whether a given transaction was approved and who reviewed it, the E-records functionality allows you to search the evidence store as part of the administrative tasks.

Once you have located the E-record, you can click on it to open it, see the attachments, which are the transactions that were approved, and also the list of signatories who signed the transaction.

The **E-record details** page has the following details:

- **E-record number**
- **Signature details** includes signer, date signed, reason, comments
- **Acknowledgement details** includes whether the transaction was a success/failure, who acknowledged it, and the date
- **Additional Information** includes print history
- **Related E-records** includes all e-records for related events

Banking and financial services

Infission has a plan for expansion. These plans are more than can be financed out of profits, so the treasurer, being the guy who is responsible for the corporate finance, is off to talk to some old colleagues who now find themselves in the financial sector. While we are there, we will talk to them about the major compliance issues in the banking and finance sector.

Basel

The first compliance issue that they tell us about is the Basel accords. The purpose of **Basel II**, which was initially published in June 2004, is to create an international standard that banking regulators can use when creating regulations about how much capital banks need to put aside to guard against the types of financial and operational risks that the banks face. While not a law, in and of itself, the signatories of the G10 are requested to advise their banking supervisory organizations to implement its directives. Advocates of Basel II believe that such an international standard can help in protecting the international financial system from the types of problems that might arise should a major bank or a series of banks collapse. In practice, Basel II attempts to accomplish this by setting up rigorous risk and capital management requirements designed to ensure that a bank holds capital reserves appropriate to the risk the bank exposes itself to through its lending and investment practices. It needs to ensure that the accord is implemented uniformly else a short term advantage accrues to the country with lower capital adequacy requirements, and that country becomes a point of weakness in the global system.

Requirements of Basel

The requirements of the Basel accord are grouped under three pillars which aim to have a holistic approach to managing risks.

The three pillars

The first pillar — **Minimum Capital** — focuses on capital requirements to better reflect the true nature of risks. The second pillar — **Supervisory Review** — aims at a more involved supervisory and regulatory system. The last pillar — **Market Disclosure** — will potentially result in greater discipline imposed by the market.

The first pillar—Minimum capital requirements

In the first pillar of the accord, the calculation of the total minimum capital requirements for credit, market, and operational risks is explained. The capital ratio is calculated using the definition of regulatory capital and risk-weighted assets. It boils down to having enough money in reserve to cope with the vagaries of being in business. There are a number of methods discussed in the accord. The objective here is simply to give you a sense of what the methodologies are for assessing risk and valuing it:

- **Credit risk** is the risk of not being paid by a borrower.

- **Market risk** is the risk that the value of a marketable asset decreases. The risk factors include stock prices, interest rates, exchange rates, and commodity prices.

- **Operational Risk** is the risk inherent in participating in a given industry or market. It includes the risk of human and procedural failures and errors.

Credit risk

In order to assess the capital requirements to cover the credit risk, the institution is required to have classified their marketable assets for their risk weighting. The risk weighting is a multiplier that is applied to a class of assets in order to arrive at a "value" for the exposure. Very risky assets have a high multiplier. Very safe assets have a low multiplier. An institution is required to have qualifying capital reserves that cover a percentage of that exposure.

Market risk

Market risks are broken down into:

- **Interest rate risk**: The way that the interest risk is valued is based on the net balance of what is owed and owing within maturity bands. For example, if a bond is expected to mature within the next year, it represents less of a risk than the one that will mature after 20 years, because the amount by which prevailing interest rates can change is commensurably less. The way you turn that into a value for the risk is that each maturity band is given a risk weighting to factor it up or down.

- **Currency risk**: You can calculate the net present value of the projected cash flows in each currency and convert it back to the reporting currency at the current spot rate. The standard assumption is that you should provide eight percent of the exposure to foreign exchange rate variation.

- **Commodity risk**: The first thing the bank must do is express its commodity holdings in a standard unit of measure and value them at the current spot rate in the national currency. Then it has to value the commodities that it currently owns separately from the commodities that it has agreed to buy or sell in the future. It must apply a spread rate to the net of what it has agreed to buy and sell, to account for any movement in prices in the future.

Operational risk

Operational risk can be quantified using very simplified assumptions. The standardized approach uses revenue as a proxy for both scale of operations and their complexity and a percentage of that revenue is added to the "exposed" value. The different lines of business have different factors to account for their risks.

Business line	Required capital as a percentage of sales
Corporate finance	18 percent
Trading and sales	18 percent
Retail banking	12 percent
Commercial banking	15 percent
Payment and settlement	18 percent
Agency services	15 percent
Asset management	12 percent
Retail brokerage	12 percent

According to the accord as part of the bank's internal operational risk assessment system, the bank must systematically track relevant operational risk data, including material losses by the business line. Its operational risk assessment system must be closely integrated into the risk management processes of the bank. For instance, this information must play a prominent role in risk reporting, management reporting, and risk analysis. The bank must have techniques for creating incentives to improve the management of operational risks throughout the firm. There must be regular reporting of operational risk exposures, including material operational losses, to business unit management, senior management, and to the board of directors. The bank must have procedures for taking appropriate action according to the information within the management reports.

The second pillar—Supervisory review process

In the language of the accord, the four key principles of supervisory review are:

- Banks should have a process for assessing their overall capital adequacy in relation to their risk profile and a strategy for maintaining their capital levels.

- Supervisors should review and evaluate the banks' internal capital adequacy assessments and strategies, as well as their ability to monitor and ensure their compliance with regulatory capital ratios. Supervisors should take appropriate supervisory action if they are not satisfied with the result of this process.

- Supervisors should expect banks to operate above the minimum regulatory capital ratios.

- Supervisors should seek to intervene at an early stage to prevent capital from falling below the minimum levels required to support the risk characteristics of a particular bank and should require rapid remedial action if capital is not maintained or restored.

The third pillar—Market discipline

The committee aims to encourage market discipline by developing a set of disclosure requirements, which will allow market participants to assess key pieces of information on the scope of application, capital, risk exposures, risk assessment processes, and hence the capital adequacy of the institution. The committee believes that such disclosures have particular relevance under the framework, where reliance on internal methodologies gives the banks more discretion in assessing capital requirements.

Oracle's solutions in the banking sector

Oracle Reveleus delivers a suite of analytical applications for multi-jurisdictional Basel II compliance and risk management. The following diagram shows the **Oracle Financial Services Data Warehouse** architecture:

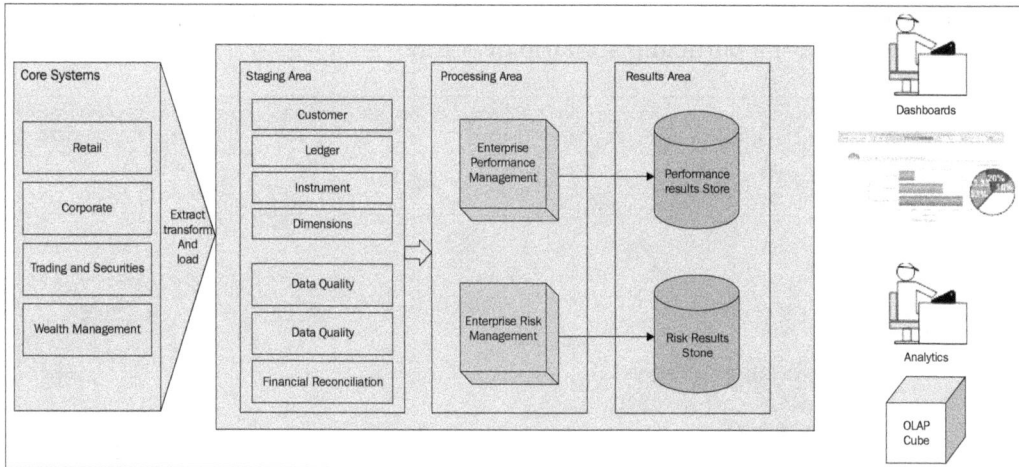

Comply with pillar one—Capital adequacy

Oracle Reveleus embeds a process called **Internal Capital Adequacy Assessment Process (ICAAP)**, which models a firm's internal assessment of capital that it considers adequate to cover all material risks to which it is exposed.

The objective of ICAAP is to ensure that a bank understands its risk profile and has systems in place to assess, quantify, and monitor risks. While **regulatory capital** is the capital that the regulator requires a bank to maintain, **economic capital** is the capital that a bank needs to maintain and is in general, estimated using internal risk models.

Theoretically, a bank could suffer losses causing a complete erosion of its asset value. It is reasonable to look at the erosion, which would almost never happen. We need to consider losses so big that there is a very high probability that they will never occur and then see what would be the erosion in equity in that scenario(s). This forms the basis of economic capital measurement. The following Reveleus UI shows some good examples of scenarios that have been considered during a stress testing exercise:

Stress Scenario	Brief Particulars of Stress Scenario
Asian Crisis	Mild Recession
Asian Crisis-Management Action 1	Asian Crisis-Management Action 1
Black Monday	Medium Recession
Black Monday-Management Action 1	Black Monday-Management Action 1
Depreciation of USD	
General Liquidty Crisis	Severe Recession
General Liquidty Crisis-Management Action 1	General Liquidty Crisis-Management Action 1

Stress Scenarios employed under ICAAP

The following Reveleus report shows the liquidity gap for a set of stress testing scenarios and also for a particular scenario over time:

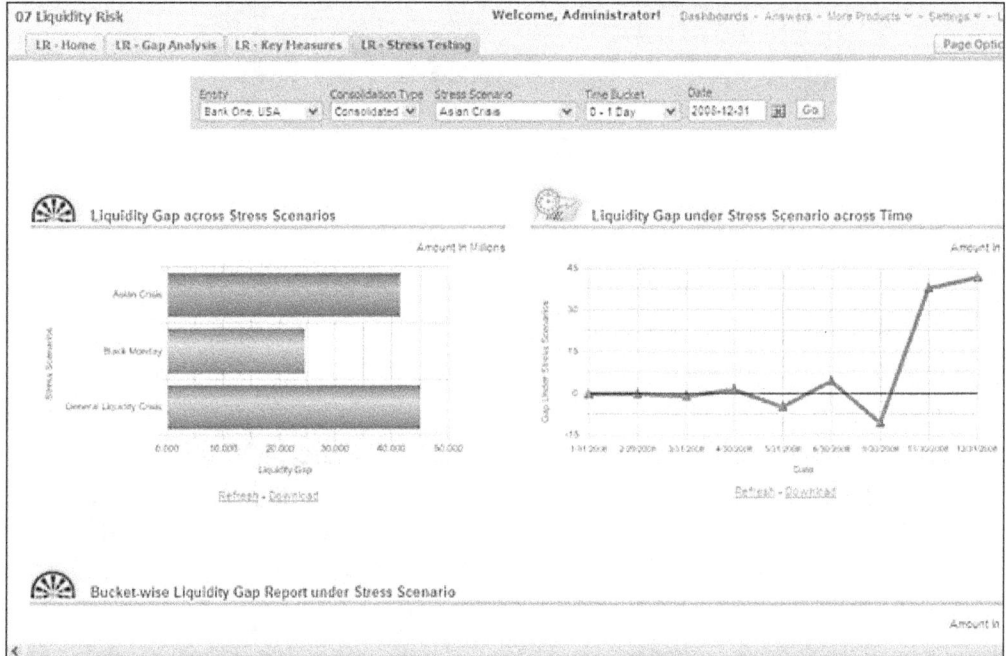

Comply with pillar two—Management review

The Basel II Accord has mandated the need for financial institutions to develop suitable internal procedures and systems in order to improve risk management practices. The following screenshot shows a sample risk registry for a bank:

Bank's Risk Identification, Materiality and Assessment Methodology - An Example				
Risk Category	Risk Sub-Category	Risk Materiality	Justification (if immaterial)	Risk assessment methodology used
Credit Risk	Credit Risk	Very High		Internal EC Model
	Counterparty Credit Risk	High		Internal Model
	Equity Risk in Banking Book	Immaterial	Equity Assets as share of total assets < 1%	Simple Risk Weight Approach
	Country / Transfer Risk	Medium		Strict Limitation (Structural Limit)
	Securitisation Risk	Immaterial	No involvement in securitisation as originator or investor	Not considered
	Concentration Risk	High		Factored in to EC Model
	Residual Risk from CRM	Medium		Factored in to EC Model
Market Risk	Interest Rate Risk	Low		Standard supervisory methods
	Equity Risk in Banking Book	High		VaR Model
	Commodities Risk	Immaterial	No dealing in commodities	Not considered
	Foreign Exchange Risk	Low		Shortcut Method
Operational Risk		Low		Basic Indicator Approach
Interest Rate Risk in Banking Book		High		VaR Model
Other Risks	Liquidity Risk	Low		Qualitative Measure
	Strategic Risk	Medium		Factored in to Business Risk
	Reputational Risk	Low		Factored in to Business Risk
	Pension Risk	Immaterial	Bank does not have pension liabilities	Not considered
	Business Risk	Medium		Earning-at-risk Modelling

Oracle Reveleus Basel II Analytics provides a host of powerful dashboards and reports to help strengthen the senior management's ability to manage risk such as the following heat map:

This heat map shows the degree of risk that remains in each operational risk category across each line of business.

Comply with pillar three—Disclosure

Oracle Reveleus Basel II Analytics provides pre-configured reports covering all market disclosure requirements of Basell II related to capital, credit risk, market risk, and interest rate risk.

Patriot Act

The following are the requirements under the **Patriot Act** on financial institutions:

- To strengthen U.S. measures to prevent, detect, and prosecute international money laundering and financing of terrorism

- To subject to special scrutiny foreign jurisdictions, foreign financial institutions, and classes of international transactions or types of accounts that are susceptible to criminal abuse

- To require all appropriate elements of the financial services industry to report potential money laundering

- To strengthen measures to prevent the use of the U.S. financial system for personal gain by corrupt foreign officials and facilitate repatriation of stolen assets to the citizens of countries to whom such assets belong

Oracle's solution for Patriot Act – Oracle Mantas

The **Oracle Mantas Behavior Detection Platform** is the industry's most comprehensive solution for anti-money laundering, and detecting risks in both client and broker activities. The following flow diagram shows the Mantas information flow:

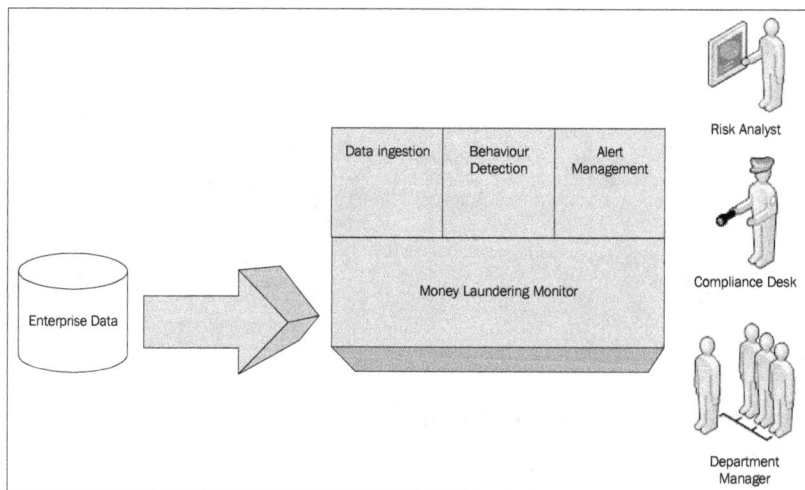

The following are the examples of behavior that could be indicative of money laundering:

- Transactions to or from high risk geographies or entities
- Structuring/avoidance of reporting thresholds
- Change in behavior (activity, income, or source)
- Account activity (ATM, escalation, or control changes)

Transactions that conform to the identified patterns are reported and alerted to risk analysts and auditors through Mantas's alerting capability.

Major components of Mantas

- **Data Ingestion Engine**: The data ingestion engine manages the extraction, transformation, and load of data into the normative Financial Services data model
- **Detection and Correlation Engine**: The detection and correlation engine discovers patterns and anomalies in the ingested data

The following screenshot shows the correlated events in Oracle Mantas:

In order to review correlation details, navigate to **Investigations | Search | Lists | Alert**. From the **Alert** section click on **Alert Associations**.

The detection and correlation engine monitors transactions for suspicious activities. The detection engine may note a precipitous drop in a position in an account. This drop may not be outside the normal boundaries of the account holder's trading pattern.

- **Scenario modeling**: Oracle has developed the sequence matcher, link analysis, outlier detection, and rule matcher. For instance, Oracle scenario allows a firm to configure sixty different parameters to look at the rapid movement of funds through wires. The parameters can be set separately based on whether the account is new or seasoned, based on risk levels associated with the account, and with the other parties on the wire.

- **Case management**: Oracle Mantas Case Management is a comprehensive, enterprise-wide investigations platform. Oracle houses the workflow and document management needs of investigating a prima facie case of malfeasance. Alerts track suspicious activity and an alert can be promoted to a case if deemed worthy of further investigation. The following is a screenshot from the **Case Management** capability in Mantas:

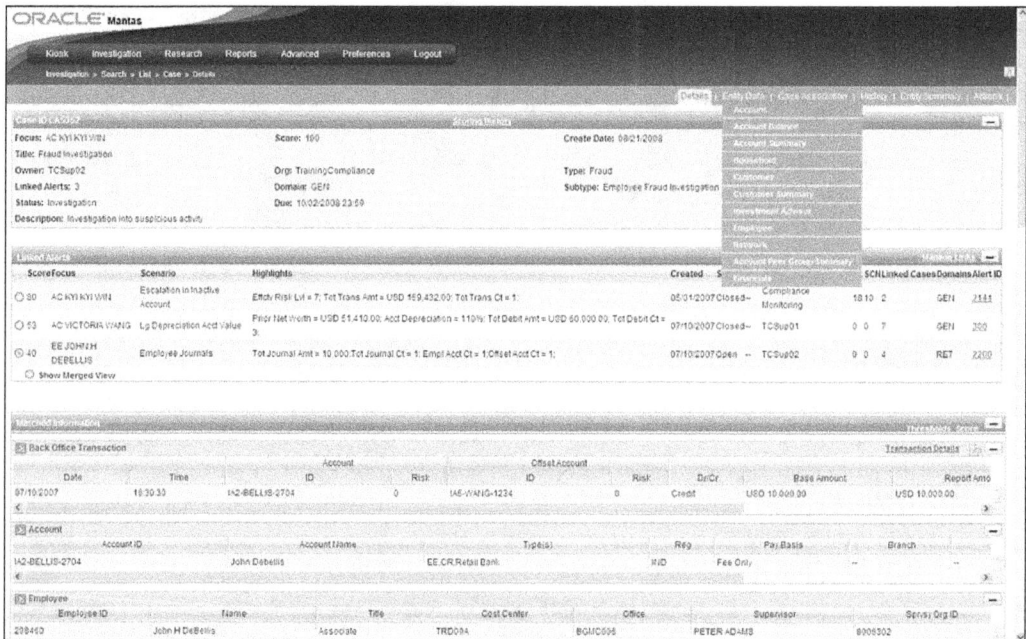

In order to manage cases click on **Investigation** and then search for **Search List of Cases**:

- **Analytic reporting**: The fraud analytics and business intelligence capabilities of Oracle Mantas provide comprehensive reporting and dash boarding for financial crime and compliance management. The following screenshot shows the compliance dashboard:

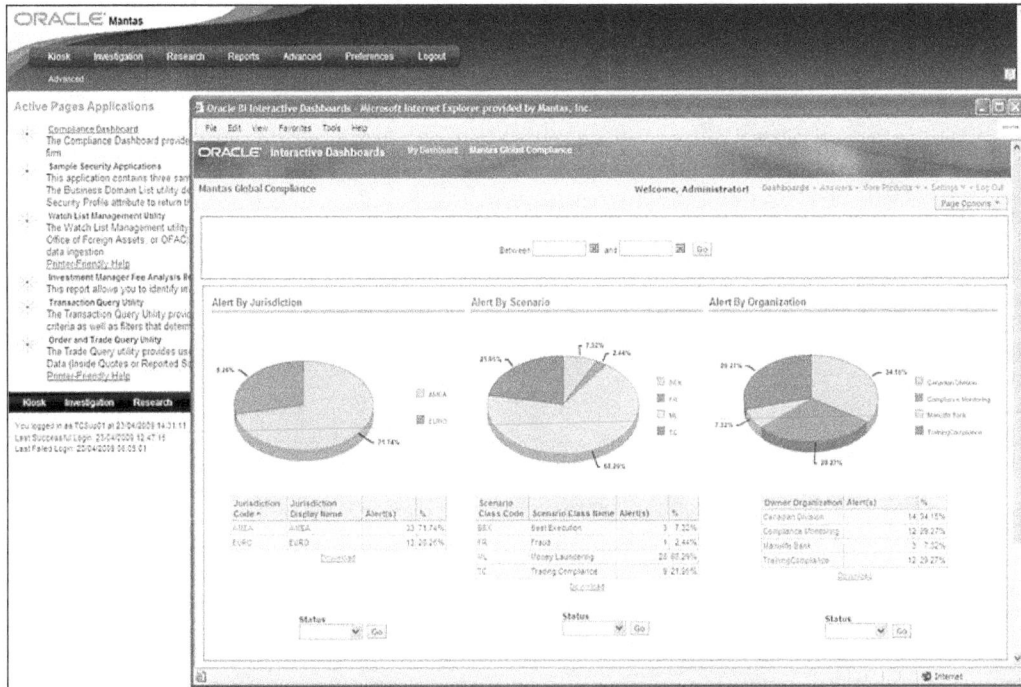

In order to navigate to **Fraud Analytics**, click on **Advanced** from the main menu and then click on **Compliance Dashboard**.

- **Regulatory reporting and filing**: Filing of regulatory reports with regulators and law enforcement officials continues to be an integral part of the war on financial crimes such as fraud, money laundering, terrorist financing, and drug trafficking. **Oracle Mantas Regulatory Reporting Electronic Filing**, assists financial institutions in gathering investigation information, generating regulatory reports, and filing for submissions with regulatory bodies. It provides a global coverage of regulatory reporting requirements and supports report management and report workflow capabilities.

Summary

In this chapter, we looked at regulations that apply to particular industries. We showed the major compliance issues in high-tech manufacturing, pharmaceutical and life sciences, and banking industries. These compliance issues will generally still involve audit staff, but will require specializations of audit procedures and will definitely involve other departments such as Chief Operating Officer, QA Managers, Manufacturing Managers, and Compliance Officers. We also showed the more specialized tools that are available for each of these compliance issues.

12
Regional-focused Compliance

In this chapter, we will discuss how organizations can build and manage an integrated compliance platform to address regional regulations in major economic zones around the world. Many of the successful organizations must operate in a global economy to meet market demands, optimize supply chain, employ skilled workers, and acquire assets. As a result, such organizations are impacted by regional regulations that vary by country. The cost of compliance is growing for organizations that operate in multiple economic regions with the rise in the penalties imposed for non-compliance by the regional regulators. According to the Competitive Enterprise Institute report on U.S. federal regulatory compliance, the cost for compliance had reached an estimated $1.157 trillion in 2007.

Many organizations that manage compliance in silos are seeking ways to take a more holistic approach to implement an integrated framework for coordinating and monitoring compliance activities. The increased risk exposure in complex and global business processes requires that compliance management be part of an integrated framework. Redundant and disparate compliance activities create barriers for regional process owners.

In this chapter we will cover the following topics:

- Provide an approach to establish a common framework for assessment and monitoring of regional controls.

- Share how InFission has set up an integrated financial governance framework using Oracle GRC Manager to replace regional compliance silos, which are reactive, unreliable, inefficient, and inconsistent. You will learn how this Financial Governance framework has lowered the barrier to do business across the borders. For example, this framework enables the compliance team to use different perspectives in Oracle GRC Manager to comply with data privacy and bribery laws in the United States, the United Kingdom, and the European Union, which are markedly different. These benefits achieved by InFission should help you identify sources of value to create a business case for a similar framework in your organization. You will also be able to use the InFission benchmark to control the cost of compliance, which is growing for most organizations.

- We will discuss how you can manage regional compliance programs including the United States' Sarbanes-Oxley, Canada's Bill 198, the United Kingdom's Corporate Governance Code, the European Union's 8th Directive, Japan's Financial Instruments and Exchange Law, and Australia's Corporate Law Economic Reform Program (CLERP) in Oracle GRC Manager Financial Governance module.

- Describe a holistic view of compliance InFission Financial Governance framework that has streamlined regional compliance process and provided the management with full visibility into the risks across its local entities and global processes that are distributed across the USA, Canada, the UK, Germany, Australia, and Japan. We provide examples of managing different regional compliance activities within the Oracle GRC Manager platform. We will also discuss how InFission is using this platform to manage compliance activities with overlapping control objectives to comply with regional regulations and how this platform can efficiently address the requirements under various local regulations.

Regulatory compliance in major economic regions

In this section, we will provide a brief overview of regional regulations that impact InFission financial reporting and disclosure compliance activities:

The Sarbanes-Oxley Act of 2002 (USA)

The Sarbanes-Oxley Act of 2002, enacted July 30, 2002, also known as Sarbox or SOX, is a United States federal law enacted on July 30, 2002, which set new or enhanced standards for all U.S. public company boards, management, and public accounting firms. It is named after sponsors U.S. Senator Paul Sarbanes (D-MD) and U.S. Representative Michael G. Oxley (R-OH).

The bill was enacted as a reaction to a number of major corporate and accounting scandals including those affecting Enron, Tyco International, Adelphia, and WorldCom. These scandals, which cost investors billions of dollars when the share prices of affected companies collapsed, shook public confidence in the nation's securities markets.

It does not apply to privately held companies. The act contains 11 titles or sections, ranging from additional corporate board responsibilities to criminal penalties. It requires the Securities and Exchange Commission (SEC) to implement rulings on requirements to comply with the new law. Harvey Pitt, the 26th chairman of the SEC, led the SEC in the adoption of dozens of rules to implement the Sarbanes-Oxley Act. It created a new, quasi-public agency, the Public Company Accounting Oversight Board (PCAOB) charged with overseeing, regulating, inspecting, and disciplining accounting firms in their roles as auditors of public companies. The act contains 11 titles that describe specific mandates and requirements for financial reporting. Each title consists of several sections, which are summarized as follows:

Public Company Accounting Oversight Board (PCAOB)

Title I consists of nine sections and establishes the Public Company Accounting Oversight Board, to provide independent oversight of public accounting firms providing audit services (auditors). It also creates a central oversight board tasked with registering auditors, defining the specific processes and procedures for compliance audits, inspecting and policing conduct and quality control, and enforcing compliance with the specific mandates of SOX.

Auditor Independence

Title II consists of nine sections and establishes standards for external auditor independence, to limit conflicts of interest. It also addresses new auditor approval requirements, audit partner rotation, and auditor reporting requirements. It restricts auditing companies from providing non-audit services (for example, consulting) for the same clients.

Corporate Responsibility

Title III consists of eight sections and mandates that senior executives take individual responsibility for the accuracy and completeness of corporate financial reports. It defines the interaction of external auditors and corporate audit committees, and specifies the responsibility of corporate officers for the accuracy and validity of corporate financial reports. It enumerates specific limits on the behavior of corporate officers and describes specific forfeitures of benefits and civil penalties for non-compliance. For example, Section 302 requires that the company's *principal officers* (typically the Chief Executive Officer and Chief Financial Officer) certify and approve the integrity of their company's financial reports quarterly.

Enhanced Financial Disclosures

Title IV consists of nine sections. It describes enhanced reporting requirements for financial transactions, including off-balance-sheet transactions, pro forma figures, and stock transactions of corporate officers. It requires internal controls for assuring the accuracy of financial reports and disclosures, and mandates both audits and reports on those controls. It also requires timely reporting of material changes in financial conditions and specific enhanced reviews by the SEC or its agents of corporate reports.

Analyst Conflicts of Interest

Title V consists of only one section, which includes measures designed to help restore investor confidence in the reporting of securities analysts. It defines the codes of conduct for securities analysts and requires disclosure of knowable conflicts of interest.

Commission Resources and Authority

Title VI consists of four sections and defines practices to restore investor confidence in securities analysts. It also defines the SEC's authority to censure or bar securities professionals from practice and defines conditions under which a person can be barred from practicing as a broker, advisor, or dealer.

Studies and Reports

Title VII consists of five sections and requires the Comptroller General and the SEC to perform various studies and report their findings. Studies and reports include the effects of consolidation of public accounting firms, the role of credit rating agencies in the operation of securities markets, securities violations and enforcement actions, and whether investment banks assisted Enron, Global Crossing, and others to manipulate earnings and obfuscate true financial conditions.

Corporate and Criminal Fraud Accountability

Title VIII consists of seven sections and is also referred to as the **Corporate and Criminal Fraud Accountability Act of 2002**. It describes specific criminal penalties for manipulation, destruction, or alteration of financial records or other interference with investigations, while providing certain protections for whistleblowers.

White Collar Crime Penalty Enhancement

Title IX consists of six sections. This section is also called the **White Collar Crime Penalty Enhancement Act of 2002**. This section increases the criminal penalties associated with white-collar crimes and conspiracies. It recommends stronger sentencing guidelines and specifically adds failure to certify corporate financial reports as a criminal offense.

Corporate Tax Returns

Title X consists of one section. Section 1001 states that the Chief Executive Officer should sign the company's tax returns.

Corporate Fraud Accountability

Title XI consists of seven sections. Section 1101 recommends a name for this title as **Corporate Fraud Accountability Act of 2002**. It identifies corporate fraud and records tampering as criminal offenses and joins those offenses to specific penalties. It also revises sentencing guidelines and strengthens their penalties. This enables the SEC to resort to temporarily freezing transactions or payments that have been deemed *large* or *unusual*.

Canada Bill 198 (Canadian Sarbanes-Oxley)

In Canada, **Bill 198** is an Ontario legislative bill effective April 7, 2003, which provides for regulation of securities issued in the province of Ontario. The legislation encompasses many areas. It is perhaps best known for clauses that provide equivalent legislation to the U.S. Sarbanes-Oxley Act to protect investors by improving the accuracy and reliability of corporate disclosures. Thus, it is also known as the **Canadian Sarbanes-Oxley Act** or C-SOX (pronounced as *see-socks*).

In October 2002, the Provincial Government of Ontario, Canada introduced an omnibus bill in the legislature entitled **Keeping the Promise for a Strong Economy Act (Budget Measures), 2002**, now simply referred to as Bill 198. It was enacted as Chapter 22 of the Statutes of Ontario, 2002. Bill 198 received Royal Assent on December 9, 2002 and the amendments to the securities provisions were proclaimed in force on April 7, 2003. Bill 198 amends Part XXIII.1 of the **Ontario Securities Act**.

As a budgetary legislation, it touched on many different aspects of government operation. Provisions included measures about corporate disclosure, auto insurance, and tax. Thus, only a small portion of Bill 198 was relevant to Sarbanes-Oxley issues.

In June 2003, all Canadian securities commissions (except the British Columbia Securities Commission) issued three regulations for public comment designed to build on Bill 198:

- Multilateral Instrument (MI) 52-108, which would require issuers of securities to employ only those auditors participating in an independent oversight program established by the Canadian Public Accountability Board.

- MI 52-109, which would require chief executive officers and chief financial officers to personally certify that their company's annual and interim filings do not contain any misrepresentations and that such filings fairly present the corporation's financial condition. MI 52-109 has been agreed to by the Canadian Securities Administrators (CSA), and covers additional Sarbanes-Oxley issues.

- MI 52-110, which regulates the role and composition of the audit committees of any company issuing securities.

UK Corporate Governance Code 2010

The UK Corporate Governance Code 2010 (from here on referred to as **the Code**) is a set of principles of good corporate governance aimed at companies listed on the London Stock Exchange. It is overseen by the Financial Reporting Council and its importance derives from the Financial Services Authority's Listing Rules. The Listing Rules themselves are given statutory authority under the Financial Services and Markets Act 2000 and require that public listed companies disclose how they have complied with the code, and explain where they have not applied the code – in what the code refers to as *comply* or *explain*. Private companies are also encouraged to conform; however, there is no requirement for disclosure of compliance in private company accounts. The Code adopts a principles-based approach in the sense that it provides general guidelines of best practice. This contrasts with a rules-based approach, which rigidly defines exact provisions that must be adhered to.

European Union's 8th Directive

The 8th EU Directive, also known as the audit directive or Euro SOX, regulates the auditing of financial statements in the European Union (EU). Its aim is to ensure that investors and other interested parties can rely fully on the accuracy of audited financial statements, thereby helping to prevent corporate scandals in the EU. Its similarity to the Sarbanes-Oxley Act (SOX) in the U.S. explains why the directive is often referred to as Euro SOX. EU member states were required to translate it into national law by June 29, 2008.

The 8th EU Directive sets out the duties of auditors and defines certain professional principles to ensure their impartiality and independence. It calls for external quality control, robust public scrutiny of the auditing profession, and improved cooperation between the responsible EU entities. In addition, international accounting standards must be applied to all audits conducted within the EU, thus laying the foundation for balanced effective international cooperation with regulatory authorities of non-EU countries, such as the US-based Public Company Accounting Oversight Board (PCAOB).

Where public interest entities are concerned, only article 41 (para. 2) of the directive is directly relevant, under which the audit committee is obliged to:

"(a) monitor the financial reporting process;

(b) monitor the effectiveness of the internal control system (ICS), internal audit system where applicable, and risk management system;

(c) monitor the statutory audit of the annual and consolidated accounts."

The Directive requires the use of international accounting standards (IAS, IFRS, SIC/IFRIC). There is no prescribed procedure similar to that defined in section 404 of the Sarbanes-Oxley Act.

Financial Instruments and Exchange Law (Japan SOX)

The internal control portions of the FIEL were largely enacted in response to corporate scandals such as the Kanebo, Livedoor, and Murakami Fund episodes.

The Internal Control Committee of the Business Accounting Council of the Japanese Financial Services Agency provided final Implementation Guidance for Management Assessment and Audit of Internal Controls over Financial Reporting (ICFR) in February 2007. The Implementation Guidance provides details to Japanese companies on how to implement a Management Assessment of Internal Control over Financial Reporting as required under the Financial Instruments and Exchange Law.

Corporate Law Economic Reform Program (CLERP – Australia)

Commonly called CLERP 9, it is the most recent reform to the Corporations Act 2001 (Commonwealth), which governs corporate law in Australia. It was enacted in July 2004.

It is based on the reform proposals contained in the CLERP 9 discussion paper, *Corporation disclosure: strengthening the financial reporting framework*, which was released by the Australian government in September 2002. The CLERP Act also contains a number of reforms flowing from the recommendations contained in the report of the HIH Insurance Royal Commission released in April 2003.

The CLERP Act proposes three bodies to represent a range of interests:

1. The Financial Reporting Council to oversee standard setting for audit and accounting

2. The Australian Securities Exchange's Corporate Governance Council to oversee the development of best practice guidelines for corporate governance within listed companies

3. The Shareholders and Investors Advisory Council to provide a forum for the consideration of retail investors' concerns

CPA Australia suggested that the legislation should build a framework that also identifies the conduct and practices of board of directors, staff who prepare financial reports, and internal and external audit functions. It also suggested including the roles of institutional investors, credit rating agencies, financial analysts, and investment banks.

InFission approach to Regional Compliance

At InFission, the Director of Compliance is responsible for the regional compliance program. The Director of Compliance manages the enterprise compliance program based on the regional requirements and oversight from the Chief Audit Executive (CAE). The enterprise compliance program is based on an integrated framework, which includes regional compliance requirements. Regional Compliance Managers are responsible for compliance within their respective regions. The following figure shows the InFission Compliance PMO structure:

```
                    ┌─────────────────┐
                    │    InFission     │
                    │ Compliance PMO   │
                    └─────────────────┘
```

United States Sarbanes-Oxley	Canada Bill 198	United Kingdom Code 2010	European Union Eighth Directive	Japan Financial Instruments Law	Australia CLERP

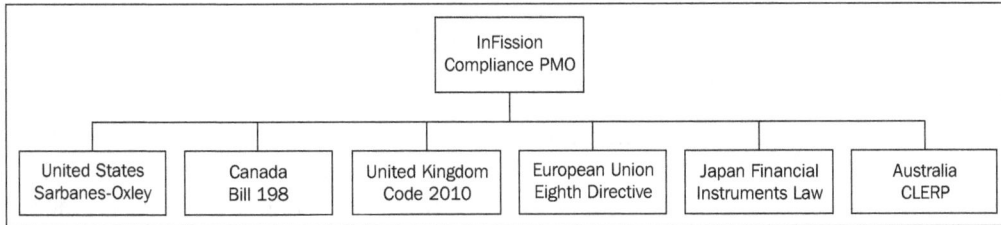

The InFission regulatory compliance program is designed to maintain oversight and control over business processes, transactions, and information systems, which are in scope for each regional regulation. Regional Compliance Managers determine scope of the compliance program by identifying the compliance requirements, changes to the local regulations and impact of these regulations on the organization. The impact assessment is based on the risk of non-compliance, appropriate level of response to mitigate the risks and budgeted cost of compliance management. Regional Compliance Managers are also responsible for communicating and training regional business process owners that are responsible for monitoring the controls to provide assurance as to the effectiveness of compliance.

Each regional compliance program follows a company's standard approach for compliance program management, which includes:

- Document controls such as objectives, policies, procedures, control classification, control owner information, and control automation details
- Walk-through significant business processes to ensure that all the managers responsible for controls within the business processes have the knowledge and training to ensure that the controls are operating effectively for compliance with the regional regulation
- Test and monitor business activities for ongoing control assessment, and reporting across standardized compliance framework
- Manage incidents of compliance gaps reported by management and auditors
- Mitigate compliance risks through the measurement of loss events and root cause analysis of control failure

This standard approach to regional compliance management helps InFission identify and prioritize major risks resulting from regulatory mandates, as well as maintain oversight and control over business processes to mitigate these risks.

Managing regional compliance using Oracle GRC Manager

The InFission Compliance department has built an integrated compliance platform using Oracle GRC Manager. This platform enables the firm to support all regional compliance requirements, provide central reporting and management, and replace error-prone spreadsheets that cannot provide a global view of compliance risks the company faces in each region.

Oracle GRC Manager provides reports and management dashboards on consolidated compliance data across all regional operations with the ability to drill down into each region. Managers are able to track critical issues in real time and make decisions based on complete, consistent, and current information. This **integrated controls monitoring** capability helps InFission reduce compliance risks by shortening the cycle time between the occurrence of an issue (control failure, fraud incident, and so on) and its remediation actions. It allows issues to be detected quickly and dealt with in a timely manner, and provides better visibility on compliance risks across different mandates and methods of mitigation. Failures can be treated individually, as well as aggregated to track areas of weakness and to implement remediation more efficiently.

Setting up Financial Governance module

InFission has configured the Financial Governance module in Oracle GRC Manager to comply with all regional regulations for financial reporting. The following figure identifies the steps that InFission has followed to enable GRC Manager to support regional compliance needs:

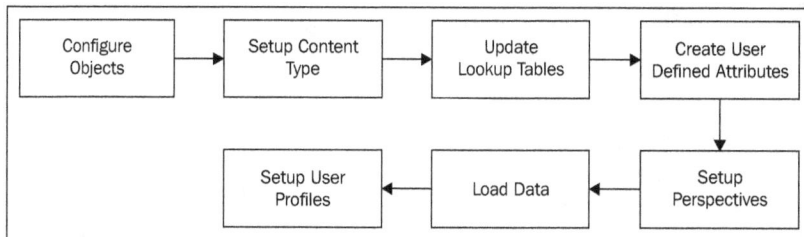

The Financial Governance module includes the following objects:

- Process
- Risk
- Event
- Consequence

- Control
- Issue
- Perspective

These objects are related together in the Financial Governance module, as shown in the following figure:

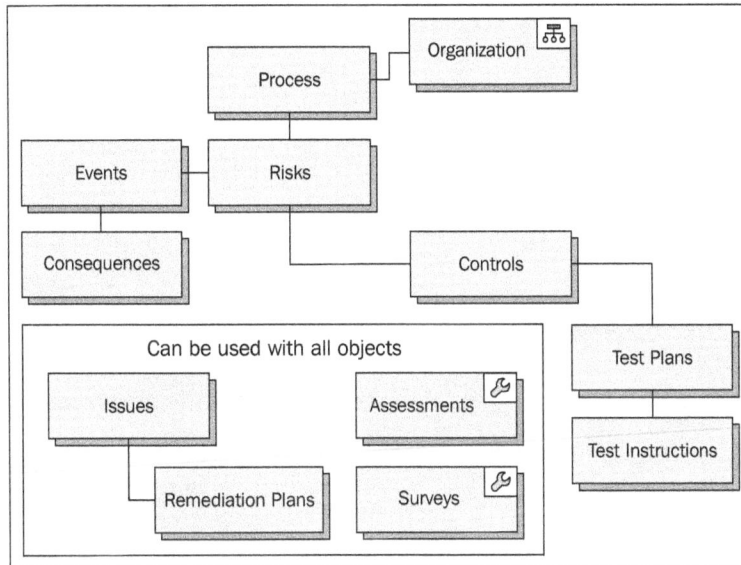

Regionalizing your Financial Governance Framework

Within the Financial Governance module, InFission has configured the objects that support all the regional compliance requirements. Objects are reusable, and are the fundamental building blocks that describe common core objects such as risks or controls. There are also base objects, which are general-purpose objects that are used as defined in the module template. For example, in the Financial Governance module template, a base object is defined as a **process**. When included in a business model, objects support specific GRC initiatives, such as regional compliance requirements.

The type and number of objects that you can use are defined by the template used when you create a module. User-defined attributes can extend objects.

In order to configure an object:

1. From the **Navigator**, choose **Setup and Administration**.

2. In the **Module Management** task list, choose **Configure Module Objects**, as shown in the following screenshot:

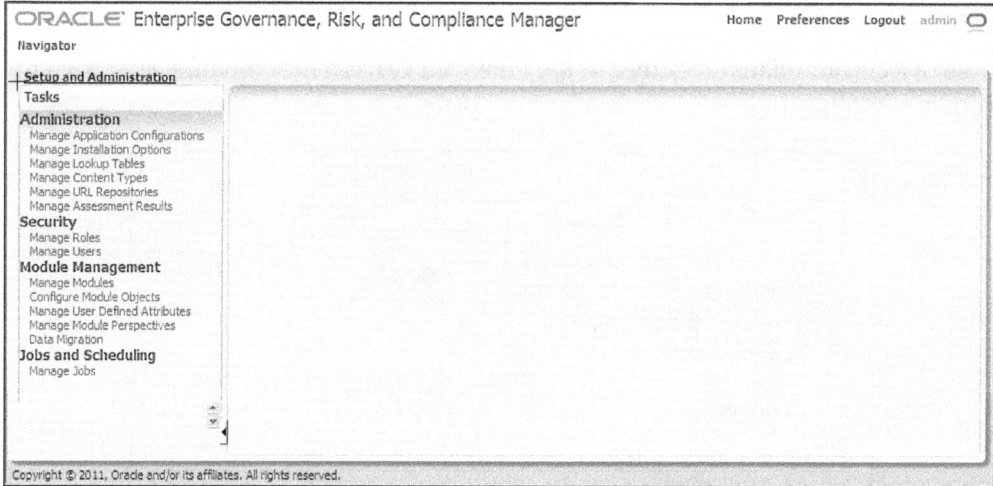

3. Select an object in the **Financial Governance** module, for example, **Risk**:

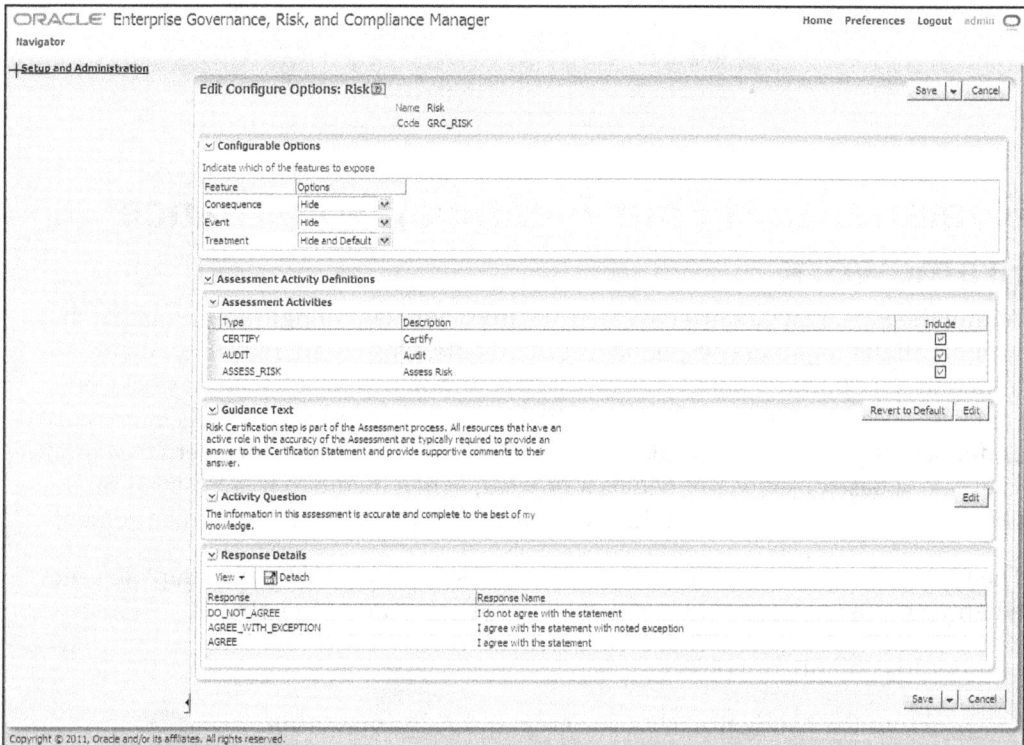

For each object, within the **Financial Governance** module, the configuration options can be set to meet the regional compliance requirements.

For example, the Compliance PMO has configured risk objects to show events and consequences based on the regional regulatory events and consequences. Each Regional Compliance Manager is responsible for identifying events by monitoring the circumstances that can place InFission's regional business at the defined risk. For each event, the Compliance Manager also determines the consequence by projecting the outcome or impact of an event. This approach ensures that enterprise risk response is *regionalized* based on regional compliance risk analysis.

Once the risk analysis is approved by the Compliance PMO, the Regional Compliance Manager determines the risk treatment to mitigate the risks that fall outside a tolerance level defined by the Compliance PMO. The Regional Compliance Manager reviews the risk treatment options with the regional process owners to leverage the internal controls that mitigate the risks. In GRC Manager, mitigating controls are associated with risks under a **Related Controls** tab within **Manage Risk** pages to capture the outcome of the regional risk treatment discussions.

In certain locations, where regulatory compliance laws do not apply, the Compliance PMO can disable the compliance risk analysis by simply disabling risk events, consequences, and treatments so they are unavailable to users.

Assessment Activity Definition option is configured to select only those activities that apply to the InFission regions. The Regional Compliance Managers have the option to select from multiple assessment activities including **Design Review**, **Operational Assessment**, **Audit**, **Documentation Update**, and **Certification**.

For each activity you select, use a **Guidance Text** option to configure a description of how to complete the activity, and an **Activity Question** option to create the question that the users are required to answer while performing assessments.

Setting up Content Type for Regulatory Documentation

Regional Compliance Managers are required to collect the necessary documentation from the Business Managers to ensure that the compliance evidence is available to regulatory auditors and management. Compliance Managers set up **Content Type** in GRC Manager to identify regulatory documentations attached to objects such as risks, controls, and issues. When a manager uploads the documentation to an object, she or he must specify a Content Type.

In order to create a Content Type:

1. From the **Navigator**, choose **Setup and Administration**.

2. In the **Administration** task list, choose **Manage Content Types**.

3. Add, edit, or delete Content Types on the screen, as shown in the following screenshot:

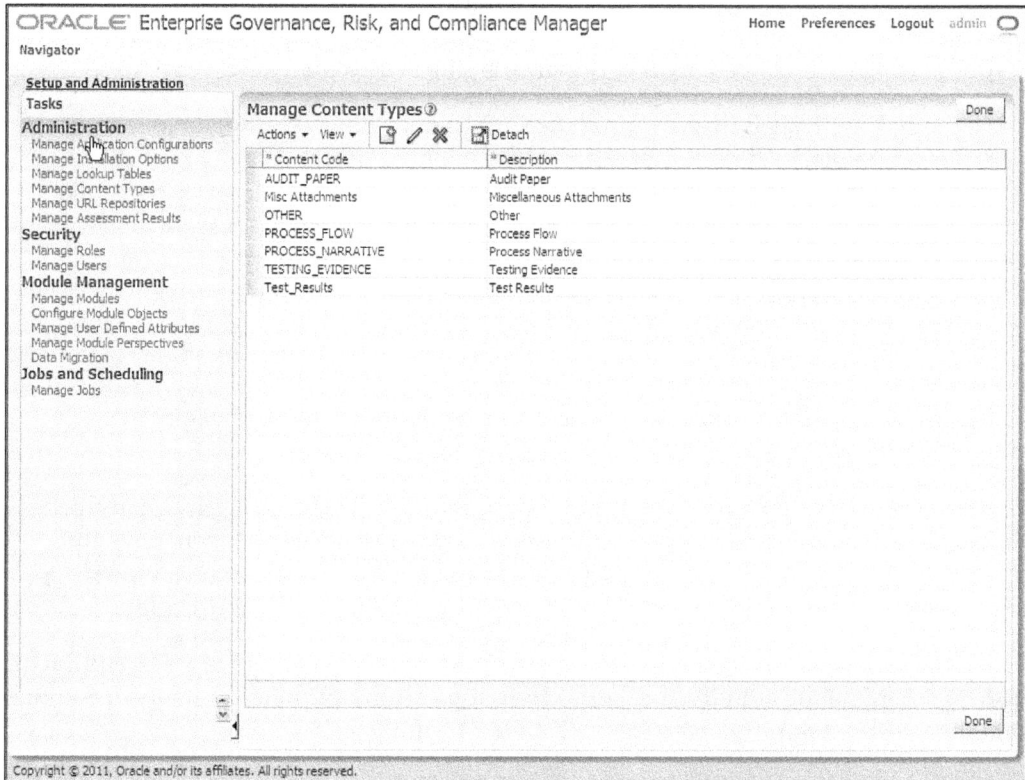

When creating a new Content Type, specify:

- **Content Code**: This is an internal identifier and must be unique
- **Description**: This appears on the menu where users select the attachment Content Type

Attachments are supporting documents that are associated with objects. You can attach documents in many formats, including URL references, documents produced from many popular software applications, or other formats available to an organization. Examples of an attachment include business process narratives, business process flow charts, control test instructions, and supporting issue remediation documentation.

When you specify an attachment, you must choose the following:

- The type of attachment, either a **desktop file** (a file located on your PC) or a URL (a link to a website)
- A filename or URL. If you enter a URL, it must be fully qualified, for example, `http://www.riskslibrary.com`

Updating Lookup tables

Each Regional Compliance Manager has the ability to update lookup types in the user-defined attributes specific to that region. A lookup table provides a list of values for a specific type of lookup. Lookup tables are associated with various attributes across the eGRCM business components. For example, InFission's Compliance PMO can monitor regional compliance activities by assigning assessment types and survey types for each regional compliance framework.

In order to update Lookup tables:

1. From the **Navigator**, choose **Setup and Administration**.
2. In the **Administration** task list, choose **Manage Lookup Tables**.

3. Add, edit, or delete Lookups on the screen, as shown in the following screenshot:

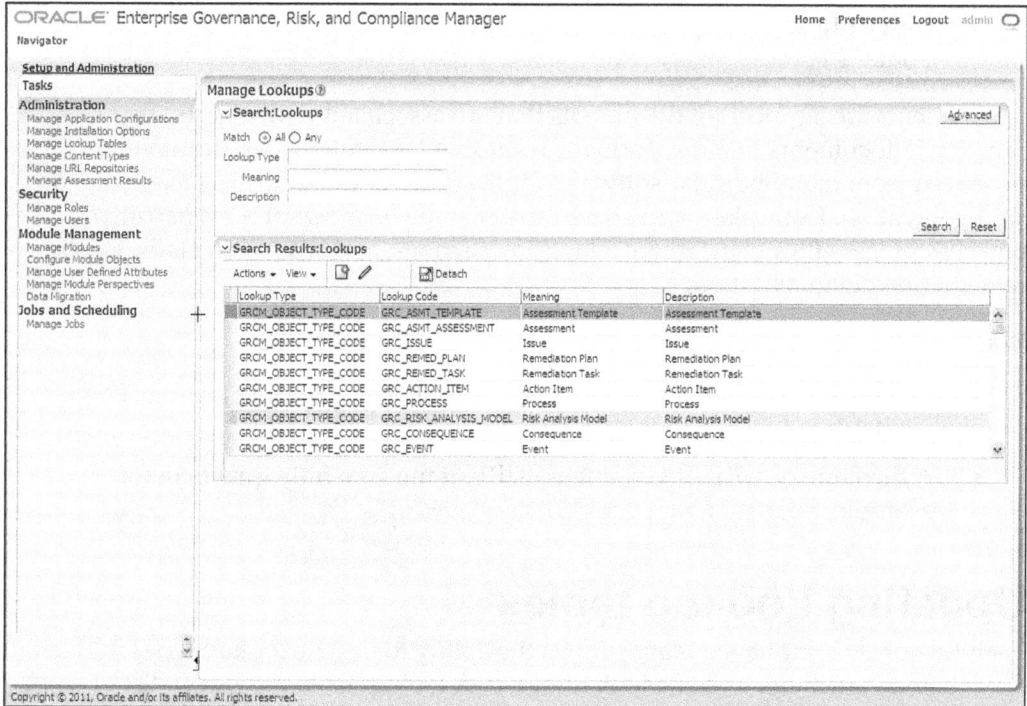

Consider the following choices when you create Lookup codes:

- What will be the code for the lookup value? This is the identifier for the lookup value. For example, if a lookup is to be a range, the codes in the lookup might be integers from 1 to 5.

- What is the meaning for the lookup code? This is the descriptive term used for the code and is the value that the user selects from a list of values. For example, the meaning of the code 1, on a scale of 1 to 5, might be lowest.

- What is the description for this lookup value?

- Select the **Used for User Defined Attribute** checkbox for each value that is to be used with a UDA.

For example, say you have created a new UDA called Risk Level, and you need to create a Lookup table that contains the list of values for it. You might define the first Lookup as follows:

- **Type**: GRC_VALUESET_RISK_LEVEL
- **Code**: 1
- **Meaning**: Low
- **Description**: Low risk level
- **Used for User Defined Attribute**: Selected

Creating user-defined attributes (UDA) for regional compliance

UDAs are additional metadata associated with records to capture specific business information details to meet the guidelines for regional regulations. These details can vary across regions, and the ability to configure them accommodates that variation. UDAs can be added to objects such as risks, controls, process, perspectives, issues, assessments, and survey templates in the Financial Governance module. These attributes appear automatically in the **Additional Information** region of the object **Create**, **Edit**, and **Manage** pages. When creating a user-defined attribute (UDA), you can select properties, such as data type. You can create unlimited UDAs for an object.

InFission uses UDAs to specify additional information for an object, meet regional compliance requirements, and to track compliance activities within a region.

For example, a control object that exists in Financial Governance module has been configured to mitigate the regulatory compliance risks specific to each region, as shown in the following figure:

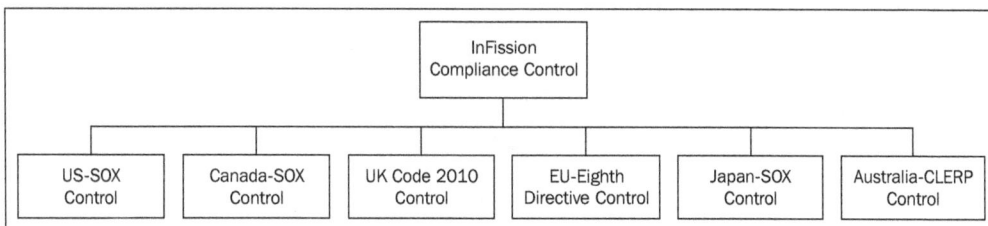

In order to create a user-defined attribute:

1. From the **Navigator**, choose **Setup and Administration**.

2. In the **Administration** task list, choose **Manage User Defined Attributes**.

3. Edit a **User Defined Attribute** for the **Object Types**:

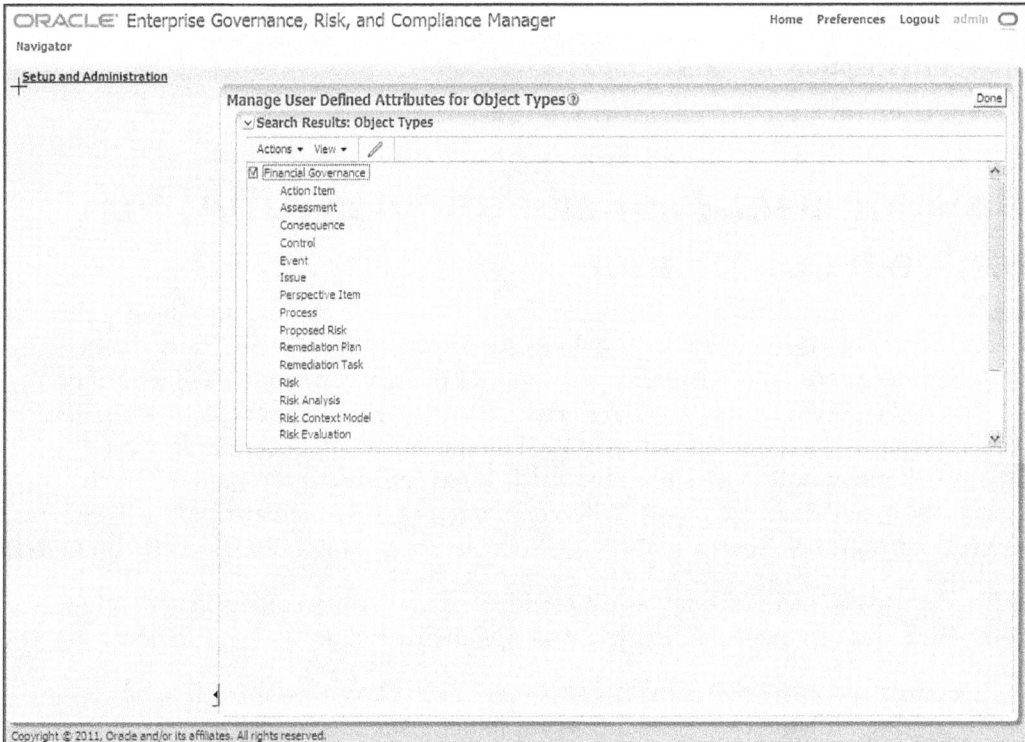

4. For example, to add an InFission Compliance Coordinator to the Control Object, edit the Control Object on the **Control** page, as shown in the following screenshot:

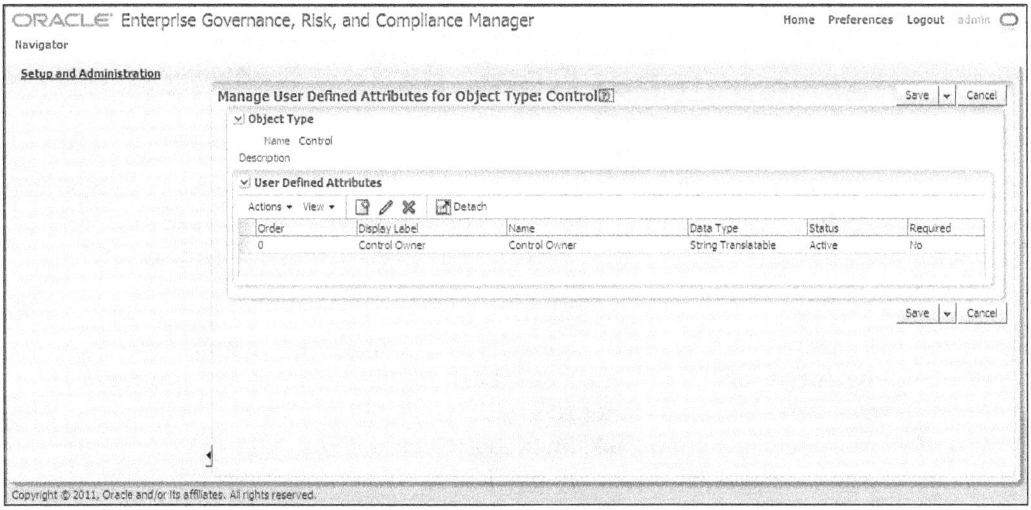

5. Next, add the **Compliance Coordinator** UDA:

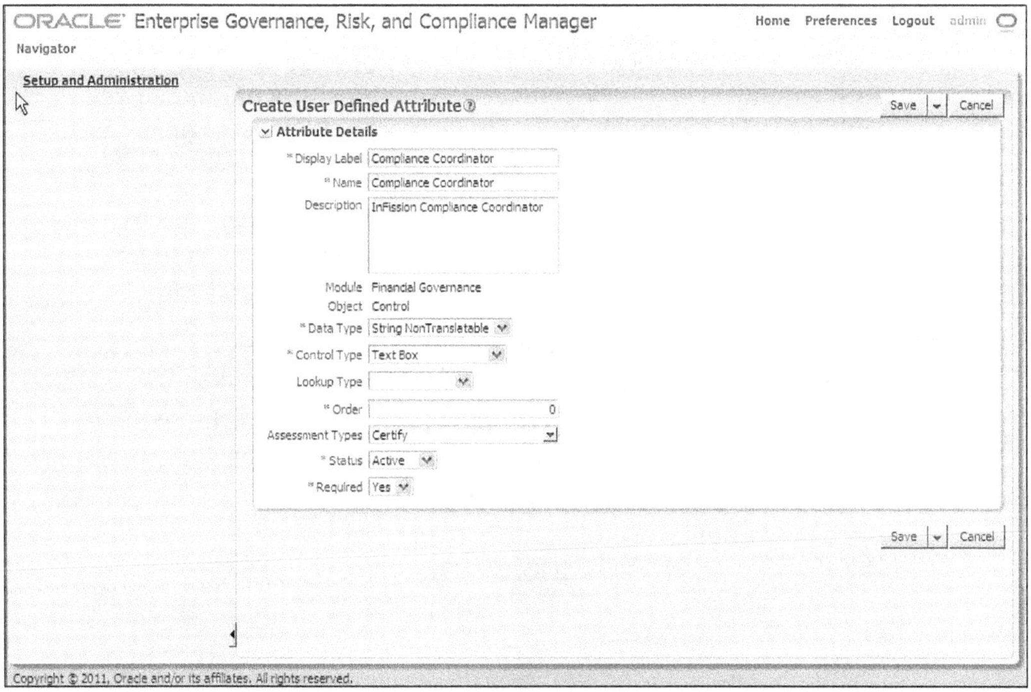

UDAs support multiple datatypes, such as String non-translatable, String translatable, Date, and Number. If you want to use a lookup value set with the UDA, it should be defined as String non-translatable. Use the String translatable datatype when the display type is free-form text or multiple-line text.

Setting up Regional Compliance Framework using perspectives

Perspectives provide hierarchical shape, structure, and organization for core business components such as risks, controls, and GRC components. They also support key user activities such as analytics and reporting. Perspective management provides a centralized interface for users to define different views into the GRC data.

InFission uses perspectives to relate regulation mandates to key compliance risks, while assessing and prioritizing these risks. Each regulation implies a number of risks, which can sometime span other regulations. The Compliance PMO has a central view of these compliance risks, which are evaluated to identify the most critical areas and priorities for action. In particular, this is important for InFission because it follows a compliance management approach based on risk and materiality (scoping) to determine key controls and to optimize their compliance practice.

By using a compliance perspective, InFission is able to implement controls that ensure compliance to multiple regulations to reduce risks. By centralizing the controls in a unified environment and moving away from fragmentation across various systems, redundancies can be removed. Additionally, a number of key controls that fulfill similar requirements originating from different regulations are maintained and tested at the same place.

Before creating a new perspective hierarchy, consider the class of perspective that you need to create. In addition to any perspective classes created by your GRC Administrator, there are the following five pre-seeded perspective classes:

- **Organization** describes the internal structure of a business. It is empty by default, and you must populate it to describe your organization.
- **Financial Governance Accounts** is a delivered perspective, but it does not contain any values. You can add accounts to fit your business needs.
- The **Major Process** perspective hierarchy does not contain any values as that depends on how your company is structured.

- A **Laws and Regulations** perspective describes Sarbanes-Oxley regulations. You can create other law and regulation perspectives when needed.
- A **Standard and Framework** perspective describes the COSO Internal Control Framework. You can create others when needed.

InFission has implemented the following perspective hierarchy using the seeded perspective classes:

InFission Organization Structure perspective

The following figure shows the InFission corporate structure hierarchy:

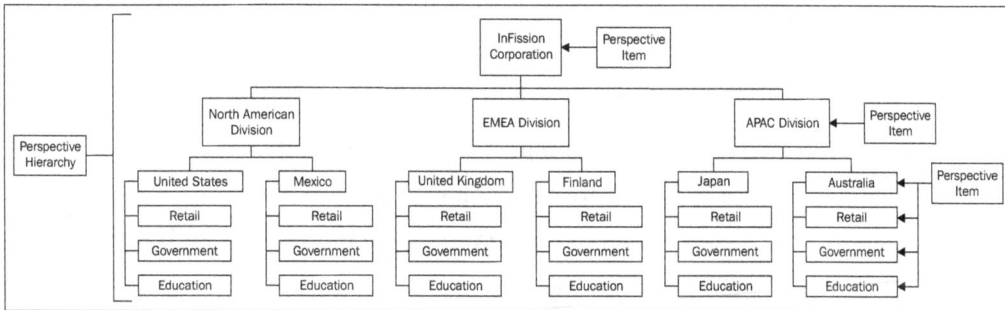

InFission Regulatory Compliance perspective

The following figure shows the InFission perspective hierarchy for U.S. Sarbanes-Oxley:

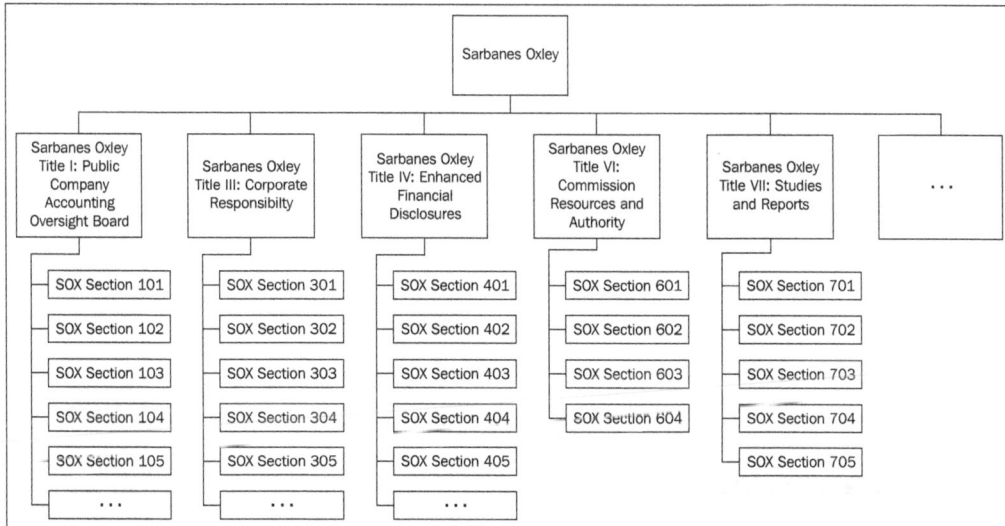

InFission Standard and Framework perspective

The following figure shows the InFission perspective hierarchy for regional compliance framework:

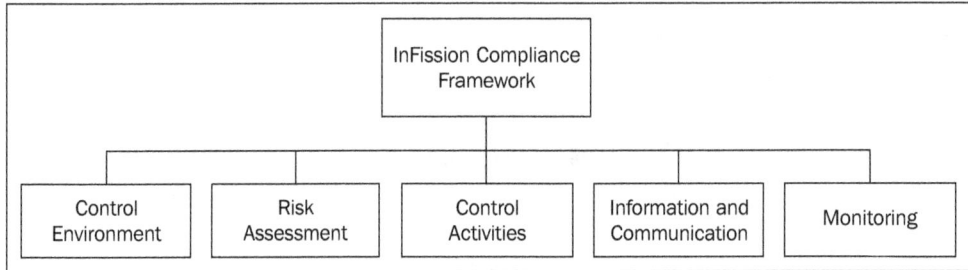

The perspective hierarchy can be created and managed as follows:

1. From the **Navigator**, choose **Perspective Management**.

2. In the **Perspective** task list, choose **Manage Perspective Hierarchies**.

3. Add, edit, or delete **Perspective Hierarchies** on the screen, as shown in the following screenshot:

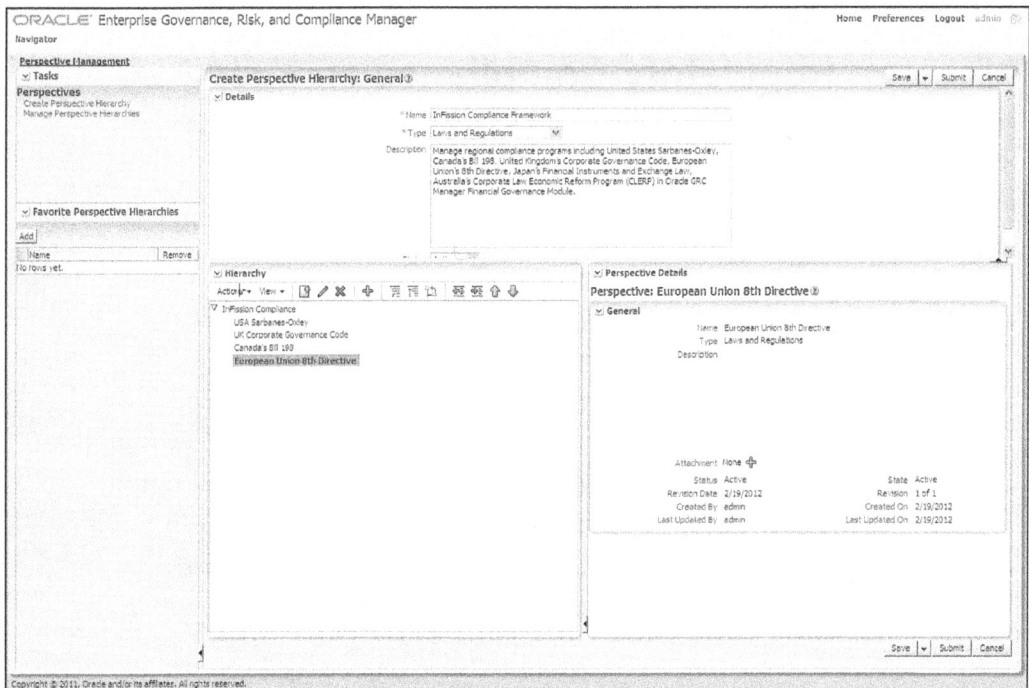

You can manage perspectives for compliance in the Financial Governance module to add or delete associations with perspectives, and specify whether they are required.

In order to associate a perspective with an object:

1. From the **Navigator**, choose **Setup and Administration**.

2. In the **Module Management** task list, choose **Manage Module Perspectives**.

3. Select the module for which you want to associate perspectives with objects.

4. Choose **Create** from the **Actions** menu or select the **Create** icon, as shown in the following screenshot:

5. Enter the following required values:

   ○ **Name**: Choose the name of the perspective.

   ○ **Associated Object**: Select the object that you want to associate with the perspective.

   ○ **Required**: Specify if the user must always choose this perspective for the object. For example, you might require that a user always selects the **Organization** perspective when he/she creates a new process object for the Financial Governance module. You can modify this setting later.

   ○ **Status**: Specify if this association is active or inactive. You can modify this setting later.

The following screenshot shows the dialog box to add the InFission compliance perspective to the Financial Governance module:

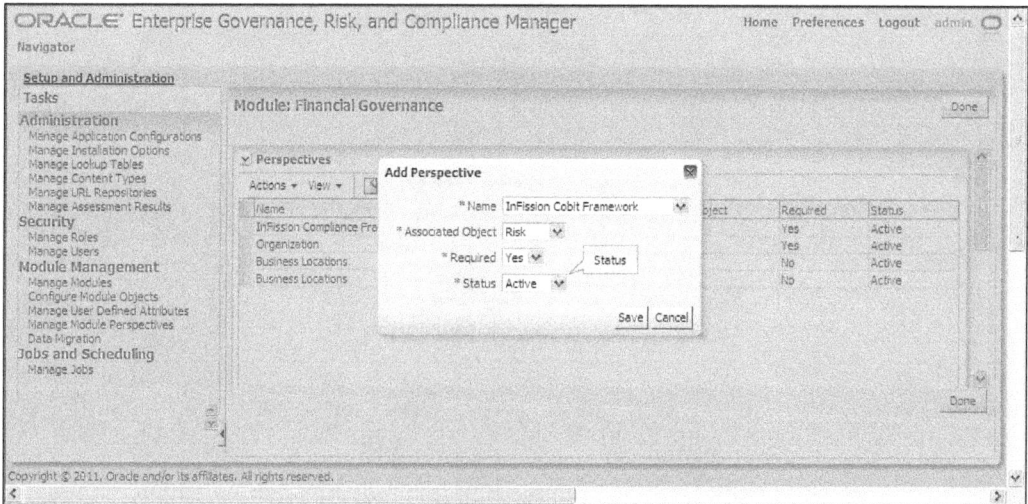

Once the InFission Compliance Perspective is successfully added to the Financial Governance module, you can maintain it as shown in the following screenshot:

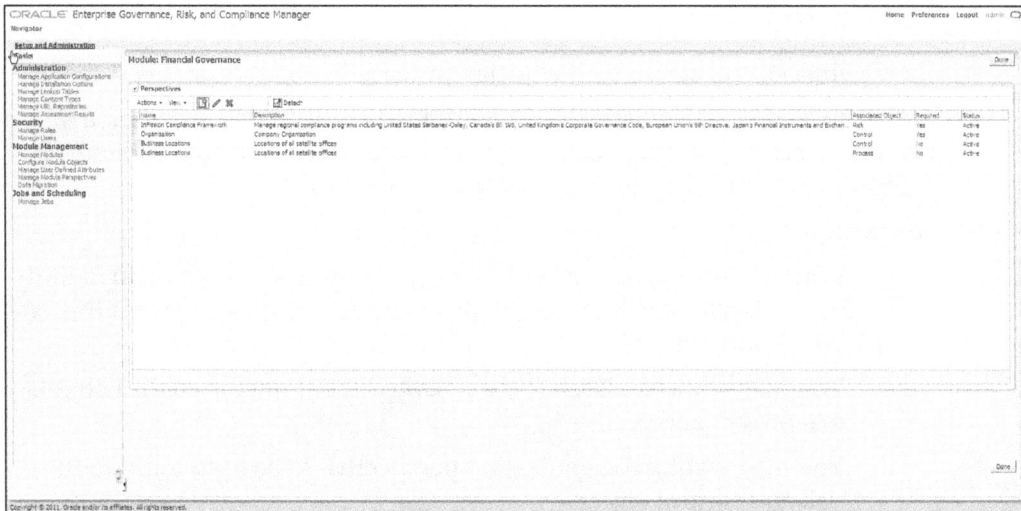

Users can associate perspective hierarchies to objects within a module and specify UDAs for a perspective hierarchy. When a perspective hierarchy is associated with a given object, it appears in records for that object under a special perspectives section. If the perspective hierarchy is marked as required, this information must be provided for records when they are created or edited.

A perspective associates a record with a specific piece of information, and that information can serve as a filtering value as users search through large sets of data or run reports. It can also serve to allow or deny access to a record, based on how data roles are constructed.

Specific perspective hierarchies may be associated with specific objects within specific modules. This gives a lot of flexibility in how you set up your perspectives within the modules. Start with a few simplistic perspectives until you understand better how you may want to use them in future.

Perspective hierarchies provide structure to the objects being managed in the application by grouping objects together with a common category, which can then be used for sorting, filtering, and reporting. Perspectives are also the drivers for data-level security.

Once the perspective is created within a module, you can maintain it as follows:

- View perspectives, define their association with the module, and edit the list.
- Associate a perspective with objects within the module, and specify if a perspective is required for each object. This allows the same or different perspectives to be associated to objects within modules.
- For example:
  - You may want to put perspective values on control objects to identify the region to which each belongs, whereas you may not want this on your corporate risk
  - You may want to associate the risk object, but not the control object, to a project perspective
  - You may want the organization perspective to be used for both the risk and control objects

You cannot delete a perspective if data is associated with it. The **Delete** icon and button are inactive for rows representing these perspectives in the perspective grid. But the perspective can be disabled through use of the status flag, which can be set to **Inactive**. The version history is updated for this change as well.

If the perspective is changed from not required to required, nothing happens to the data. This indicates only that the perspective value is required when a save action is initiated on an object.

Loading data

eGRCM provides the ability to upload the initial set of operational data by using seeded import templates. Two templates are provided for this purpose:

- **Financial Governance Import Template**: Use this template (`FinancialGovernanceImportTemplate.xml`) to load data into the Financial Governance module
- **New Module Import Template**: Use this template (`NewModuleTemplate.xml`) to load data into a custom eGRCM module

The import templates support the following objects and associations:

- Processes (base object).
- Risks.
- Controls.

- Perspectives.

- Associations between risk and control that is identifying which risks are associated with which controls.

- Associations between process (base object) and risk that is identifying which processes are associated with which risks.

- Perspective associations for objects.

- Perspective hierarchies.

- Additional details for objects such as user-defined attributes.

- Loading in a library from a provider. In order to load data, the user must map it to the import template. The data can be incorporated with the initial import.

In order to load data into the Financial Governance module:

1. From the **Navigator**, choose **Setup and Administration**.

2. In the **Module Management** task list, choose **Data Migration**.

3. Select the module for which you want to import the data file:

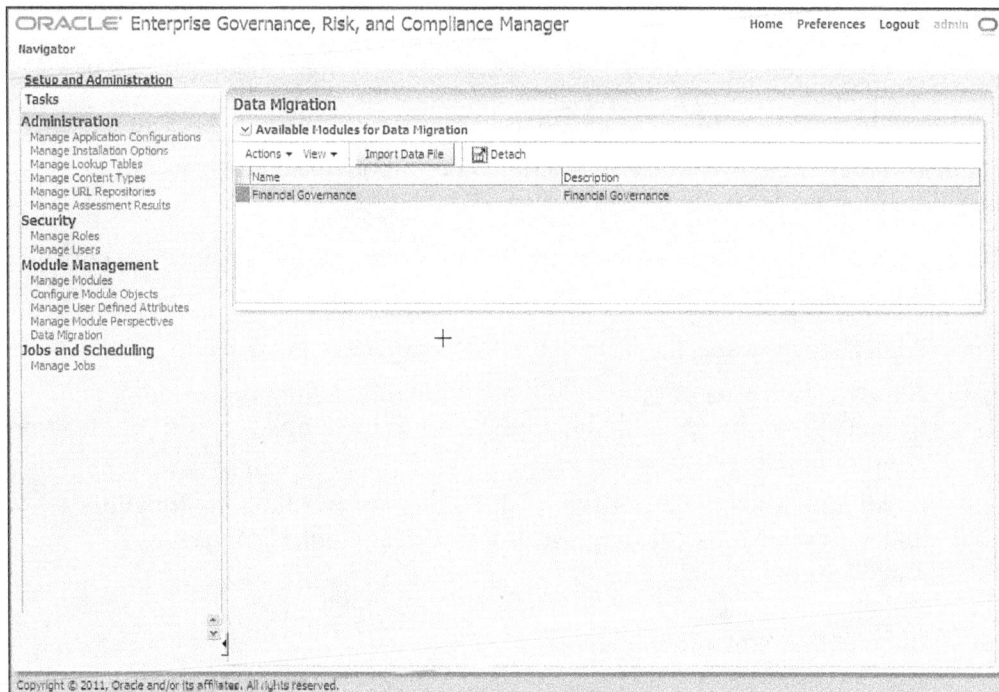

Note the following points:

- The data migration process supports only an initial load, and it is a one-time process. Data load cannot be run iteratively.
- Imported data will not go through the review and approval process.
- Imported records appear immediately in the application. Their state is defined in the import template.
- The imported data log is associated with the username of the user who ran the report.

Setting up user profile for regional roles

eGRCM GRC security employs a standard **Role-based Access Control (RBAC)** model. You can combine security components—privileges, data roles, duty roles, and job roles—to define who can do what on which set of data. Within the job role, two types of duty role, (which ultimately invoke sets of privileges) determine *what* set of data, and data roles determine *which* set of data.

This structure supports reusability. In order to define new job roles, you can use a given functional-access definition (set of duty roles) over and over again with varying data-access definitions (sets of data roles). Likewise, you can use a given data definition with any number of functional definitions. Keep the concept of reusability in mind as you build out duty and data roles.

GRC assigns individual users distinct combinations of rights to data and functionality. In order to define access to functionality, it uses the following components:

- A **privilege** is a specific feature that GRC can make available to users.
- A **duty role** is a set of privileges. Each duty role defines one or more tasks that a user can complete in the application. For example, creating controls or approving changes to them.
- A **job duty role** is a set of duty roles. It encompasses the functionality that a user needs to do a large-scale job such as Control Manager or Risk Manager.

In order to define access to data, GRC uses the following components:

- A **primary data role** defines a set of data that satisfies (in most cases) three conditions:
    - ° The data belongs to a specified module
    - ° The data exists in one or more specified states, such as **New**, **In Edit**, or **Awaiting Approval**
    - ° The data is subject to a particular action, for example, **Create** or **Delete**
- A primary data role that supports assessment activities additionally grants access only to data associated with a specified value for a seeded perspective called **Activity Type**.
- A **composite data role** is a set of primary data roles. It defines the data to which a user can apply the functionality granted in a job duty role. Users may create **custom perspective data roles**, each of which combines a composite data role with a filter that allows access only to data associated with a specified perspective value.

In order to combine functionality and data access, GRC uses the following components:

- A **job role** comprises a job duty role and a composite data role (or custom perspective data role)
- Each eGRCM user is assigned one or more job roles

The following figure illustrates the relationships among these components:

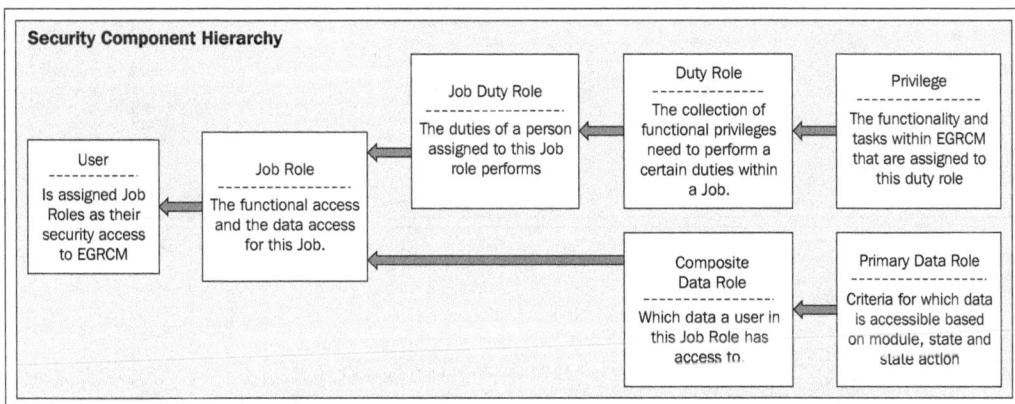

Security Component Hierarchy

		Job Duty Role	Duty Role	Privilege
User	Job Role	The duties of a person assigned to this Job role performs	The collection of functional privileges need to perform a certain duties within a Job.	The functionality and tasks within EGRCM that are assigned to this duty role
Is assigned Job Roles as their security access to EGRCM	The functional access and the data access for this Job.		Composite Data Role	Primary Data Role
			Which data a user in this Job Role has access to.	Criteria for which data is accessible based on module, state and state action

A privilege is the most granular aspect of the functional access within the application. The privilege is a reference to a specific application resource and is the means to grant functional access to the user. Each privilege has a name that describes the functionality it grants, a navigator entry that identifies the navigator component within which it is included, and an activity that identifies the type of activity within the application it is part of. A privilege grants the user access to a page, but it also enables navigation links as well as page and table actions.

The following figure illustrates elements of the user interface that can be enabled by a privilege:

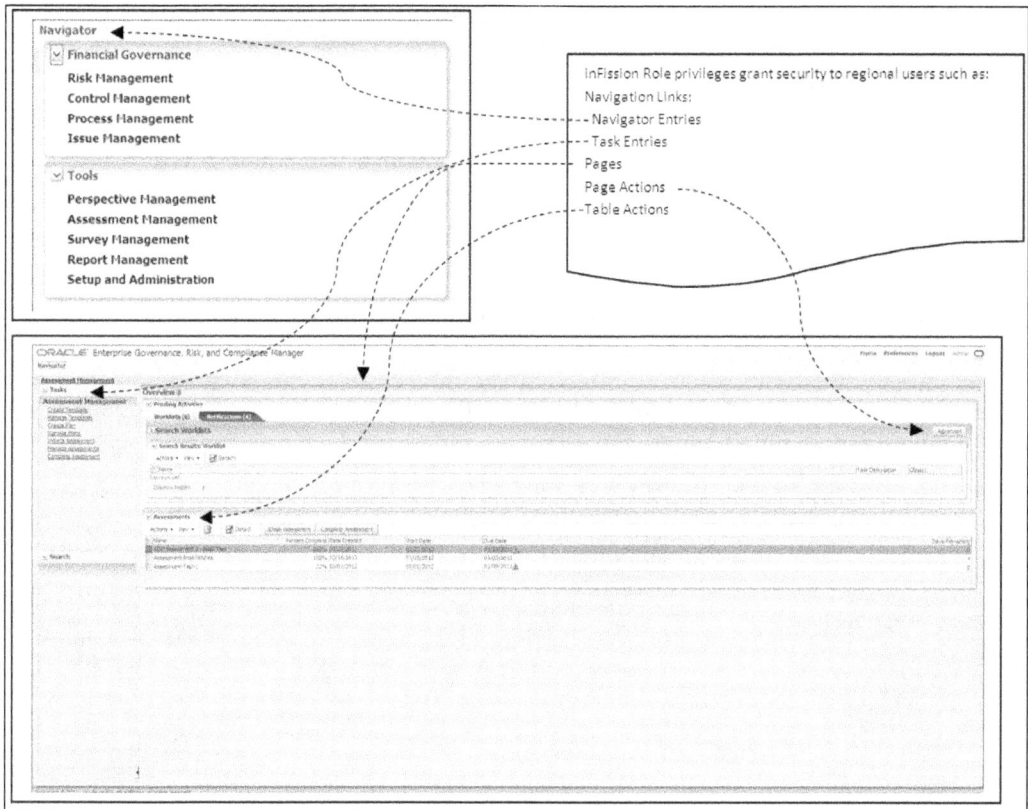

Assessing Regional Compliance using Oracle GRC Manager

InFission Compliance PMO initiates quarterly assessment of regional compliance risks and controls to ensure that the appropriate levels of documentation and control are in place. This process utilizes the GRC Assessment tool, where an evaluation is made about the validity and effectiveness of controls, risks, perspectives, and other regional components.

The following flowchart shows the risk and controls assessment flow in eGRCM:

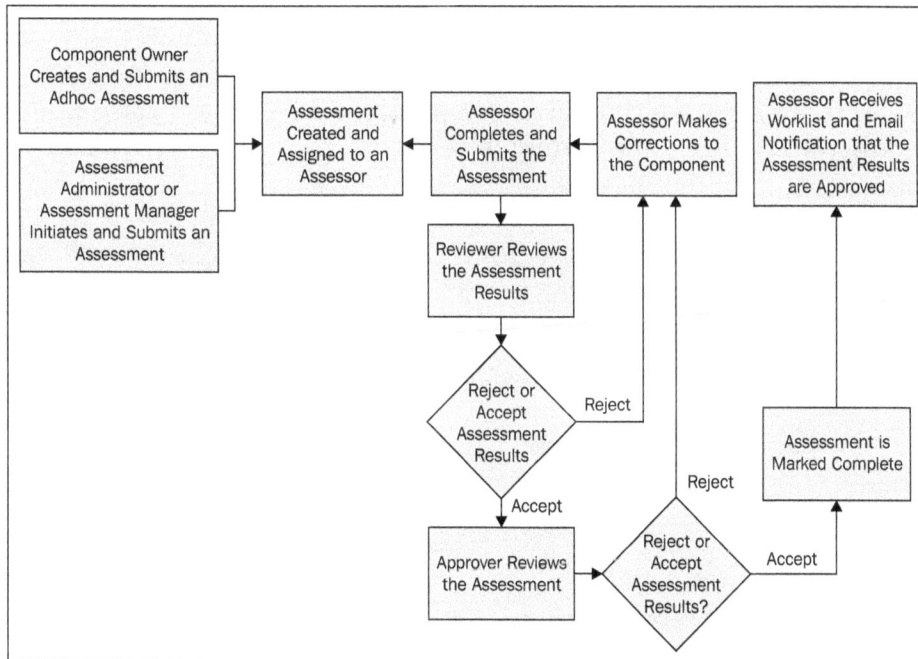

When a perspective assessment is initiated, the assessor delegate for each perspective item receives a worklist item to complete the assessment. Note that the assessment must be completed hierarchically, from the lowest level up.

The certification process of a perspective is performed from the bottom of the perspective hierarchy to the top node. A parent node cannot be certified until all its subordinates have been certified. The certification process is as follows:

1. A user (usually the perspective hierarchy owner) creates an assessment to certify the perspective hierarchy.

2. Worklist entries are created for the delegates who are assigned the assessor responsibility for the perspective items within the hierarchy.

3. A worklist entry is sent to the delegates assigned to perform the certification activity for the lowest level within the hierarchy. The certification process controls when it is appropriate for the assessors at each level to complete the certification.

   The following screenshot shows the InFission Compliance PMO view of the certification, which includes perspectives for the United States, United Kingdom, Canada, and European Union:

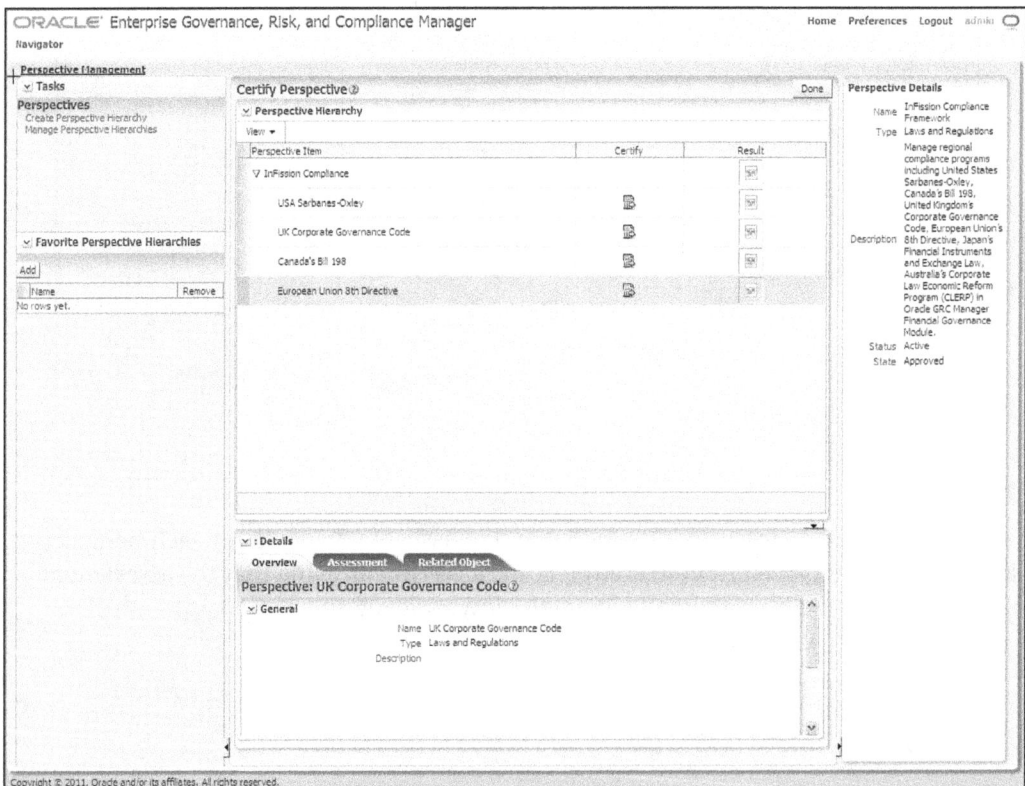

The **Certify Perspective** page only shows that they certify actions for the items that the manager with a region owns and the subordinate items that have already been certified. All subordinate perspective items must have the certification completed before moving up to the next level within the perspective hierarchy.

4. All the subcertifications within a regional perspective must be certified at the lowest level before the process moves up to the next level within the certification hierarchy. The assessors responsible for those items can then perform the certification activity.

5. The process continues until the principal officer for the region certifies at the top level. The certification at the top level ensures that all subcertifications within the hierarchy are completed. The certification is complete when the top level (root node) is certified.

Unlike other object assessments, perspective assessments do not go through review and approval cycles. Once the root node is certified, the assessment is complete and can be closed.

Monitoring Regional Compliance in Oracle GRC Intelligence

InFission Corporate Compliance team monitors all the regional compliance activities using **Oracle Fusion GRC Intelligence (GRCI)**, which provides dashboards and reports that present summary and detailed views of regional compliance data generated in Oracle Enterprise Governance, Risk and Compliance Manager (eGRCM).

Managers responsible for compliance with a region use the GRCI dashboards embedded within eGRCM. The dashboard contains the three tabs Certifications, Issues, and Analysis in which reports display graphic and tabular views of eGRCM data, highlighting potential trouble areas such as ineffective controls, processes with issues, and unmitigated risks. The GRC dashboard includes a set of reports that display broad views of data; from each of them, you can *drill-down* to other reports that provide more detailed and focused views.

Regional Compliance Dashboards

eGRCM InFission Compliance Managers can access GRCI dashboard from eGRCM by selecting the **Analytics** tab. Each of the primary GRCI reports provides a graph, as well as a table that displays values depicted in the graph.

Within a graph, you can position the mouse cursor over a bar to reveal a display of the data that the bar represents. In the following illustration, for example, the cursor is positioned over the **InFission Procurement Process** bar, and a pop-up window reveals that the bar represents an issue as shown in the following screenshot:

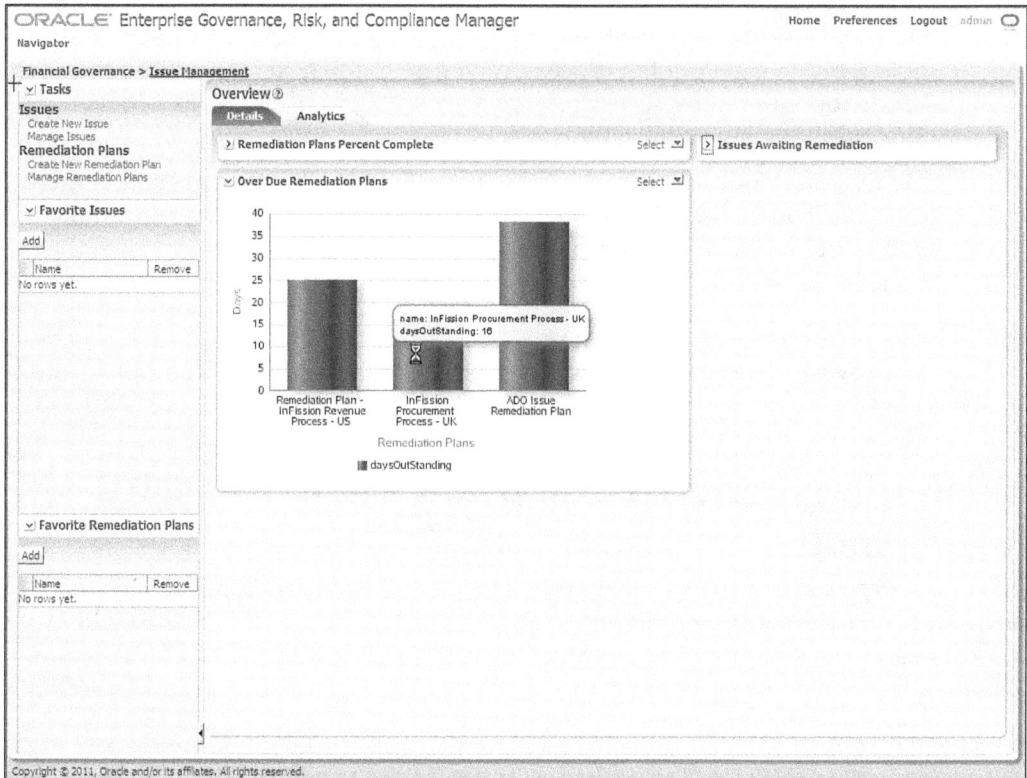

Moreover, you can select a bar within a graph to open a subsidiary report that provides details about the item that you have selected. For example, from the issue graph, which is shown in the previous screenshot, you can select a bar representing an issue that has been open past the due date to open an **Issue Detail** report. The subsidiary report would present information about the bar that you select, for example, issue details for the InFission Procurement Process – UK perspective.

Regional Compliance reports

In this section, we will provide information on reports that are frequently utilized within the three dashboard tabs that are available to Compliance Managers:

Certification reports

Click on the **Certifications** tab to view the following Compliance Status report:

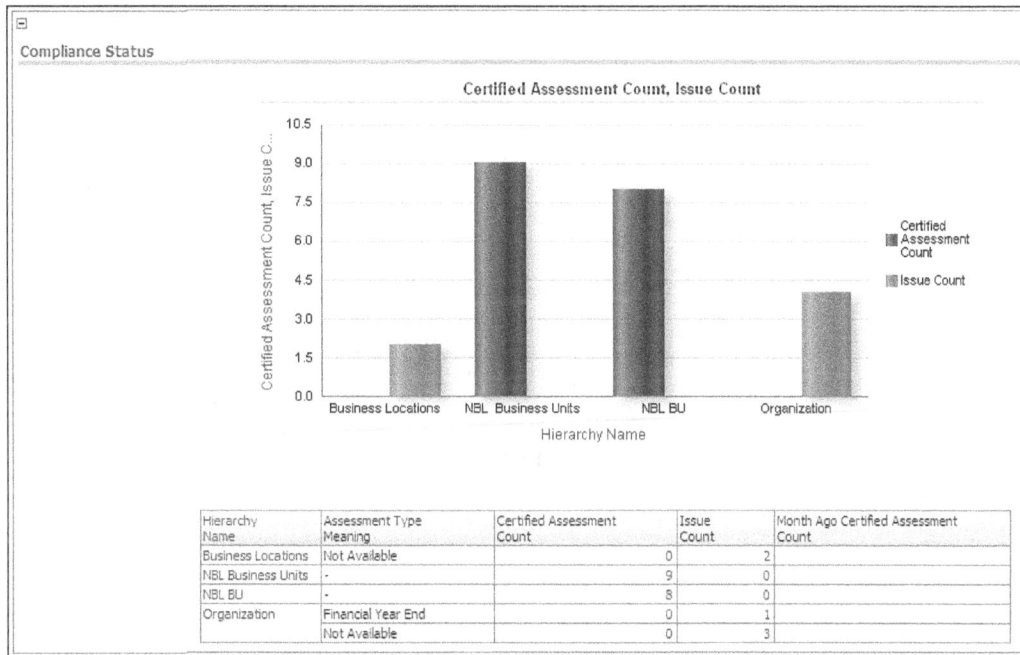

In this report, *certified* means simply that an assessment has been completed by a manager responsible for compliance over a process, risk, or control within an InFission business unit. It also indicates if the manager certifies with issues. The graph presents pairs of bars, each of which applies to assessments of process, risks, or controls associated with a specified regional compliance framework. In each pair, the height of one bar shows the number of complete assessments, and the other shows the number with issues.

You can review the control assessment results that show the number of controls that have passed or failed assessment, as shown in the following screenshot:

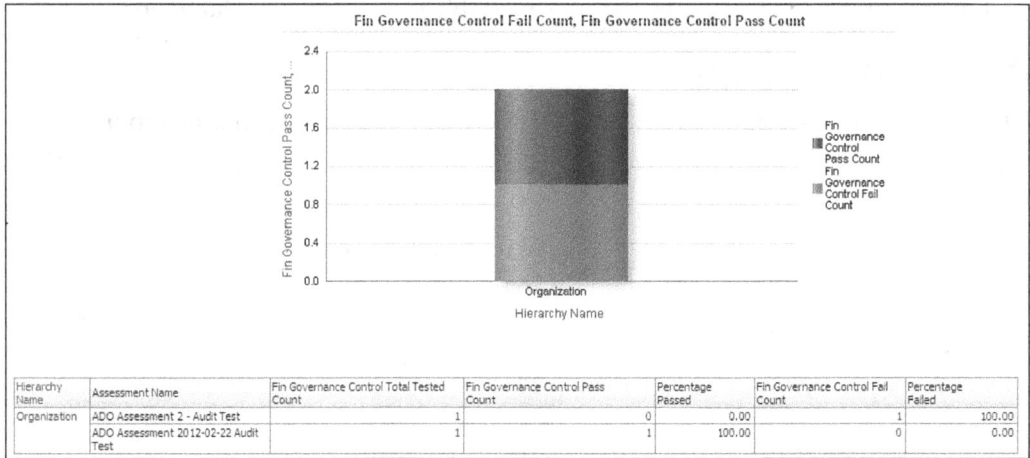

In the Control Assessment report, each bar in the graph represents controls associated with a specified perspective hierarchy; each includes a segment for passed controls and another for failed controls. The table contains a row for each assessment in which controls have passed or failed (and a given control may be included in any number of assessments). It displays the total number of controls in each assessment, the number (and percentage) of passed and failed controls, and the compliance framework with which the assessment and its controls are associated.

Issue reports

Compliance Managers can view the open issues by severity within the compliance framework by clicking on the **Issues** tab to see the following report:

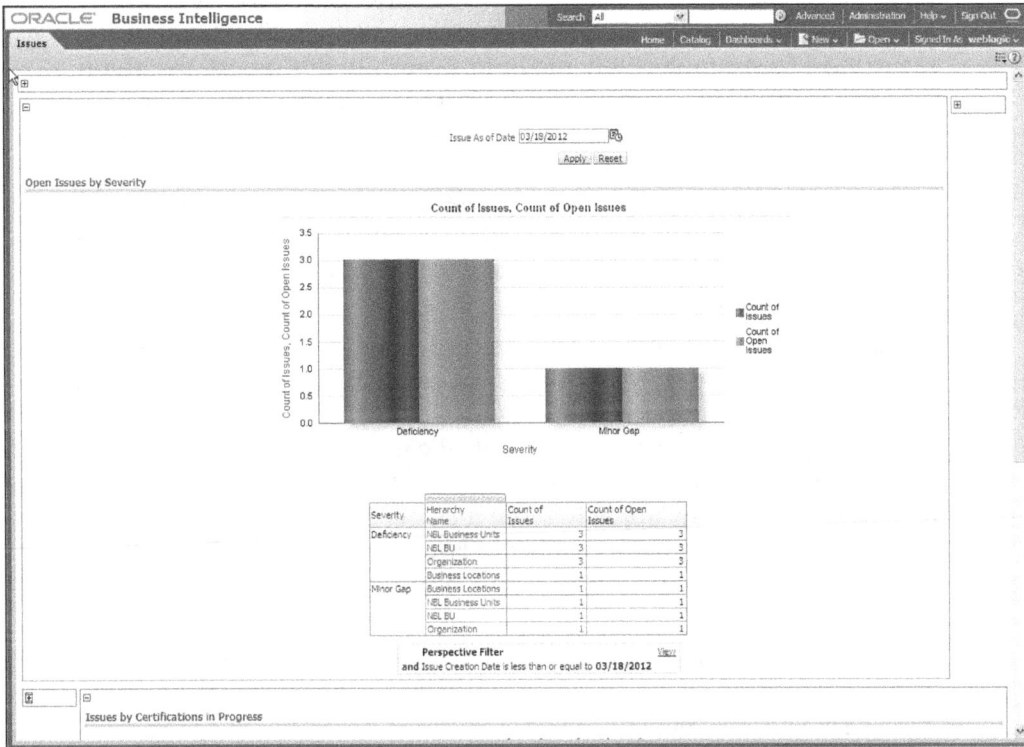

As issues are created by Regional Managers, they are assigned labels that rate their severity. In the previous report, the graph presents pairs of bars, each of which represents issues at a given severity, raised against objects associated with a specified compliance framework. In each pair, the height of one bar corresponds to the number of total issues, and the other to open issues. The graph may contain a pair with no severity label; if so, the pair represents issues that have not been assigned any severity.

The following issue reports are available in GRC Intelligence to help you track and analyze regional compliance issues:

- **Issues by Likelihood of Recurrence**: Compliance Managers also analyze issues using the Issues by Likelihood of Recurrence report. As issues are created, they may be assigned labels that rate their likelihood of recurring—for example, high, medium, or low. In this report, the graph presents pairs of bars, each of which represents issues with a given likelihood. In each pair, the height of one bar corresponds to the number of total issues, and the other to open issues. The graph may contain a pair with a no likelihood label; if so, it represents issues that have not been assigned any likelihood. The table not only shows issue counts, but also identifies perspective hierarchies, assessments, and risks with which the issues are associated.

- **Impact of Issues**: The impact of issues is defined as the cost of their remediation. In the graph for this report, each bar represents the number of issues within an **impact cost category**—a range of cost percentiles. The 0.75–1 category, for instance, represents the number of issues above the seventy-fifth percentile. In the table, each row shows an issue and the process it affects (an issue may apply to more than one process, so the table may contain more rows than the number of issues in the graph). Each row also shows the perspective hierarchy with which an issue is associated in addition to its impact cost category, its impact cost percentile, and impact cost.

- **Issues by Certifications in Progress**: This report compares the number of issues to the number of open issues raised in assessments of the Certification type. Each pair of bars in the graph represents issues raised against objects associated with a given perspective hierarchy. In each pair, the height of one bar corresponds to the number of total issues, and the other to open issues. The table shows the number of Certification assessments for objects associated with each perspective, as well as the total and open issue counts for those assessments.

Analysis reports

Click on the **Analytics** tab to view the following reports:

- **Control Count Trend**: This report shows the change in the number of controls implemented as time passes. The graph is a linear track of control counts from one quarter to the next. The table shows the controls created within each perspective hierarchy from one quarter to another.

The following screenshot shows control count for InFission Compliance framework:

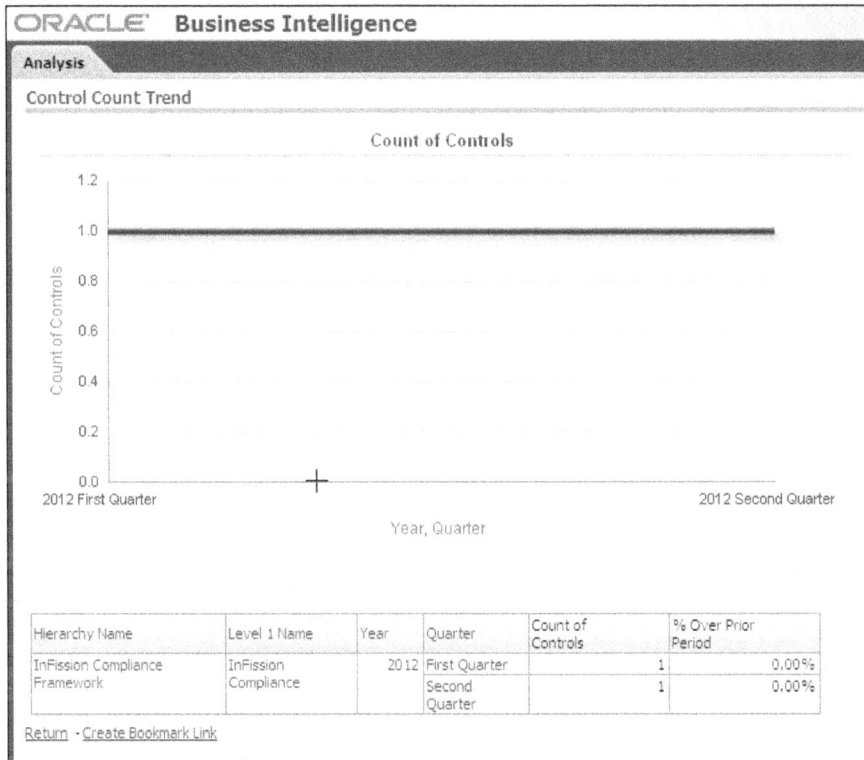

- **Control by Risk Type**: Each risk is assigned a type value. Each control is created to address one or more risks. This report shows the number of controls created for each risk type. The graph includes a bar for each risk type, the height of which corresponds to the number of controls. The table includes a row for each risk type within each perspective hierarchy, showing the number of controls and the percentage that value is over the number for the previous period.

Standard reports

InFission Compliance PMO also utilizes the *out of the box* reports available in the GRC Manager's **Reports** menu, as shown in the following screenshot:

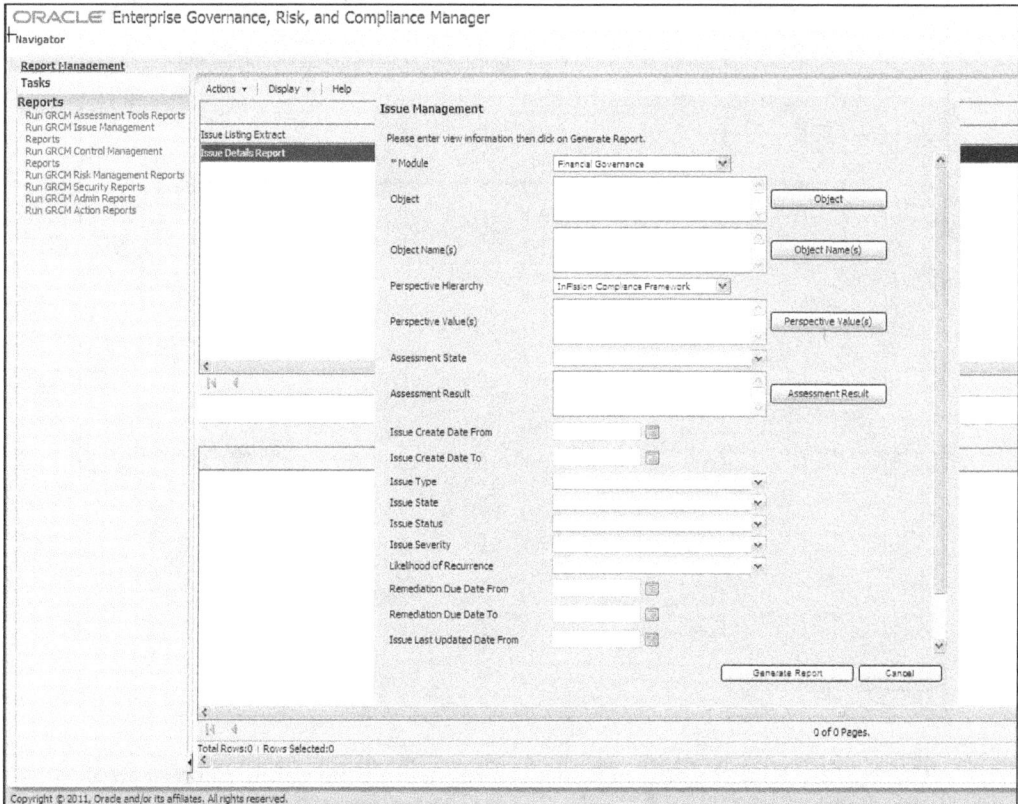

Oracle GRC Manager has the following reports available:

- **Assessment Activity Detail**: Displays all details related to a set of activities included in an assessment
- **Assessment Detail**: Displays all the details related to a set of assessments
- **Certification Detail Report**: Displays all the details related to a set of Certification activity assessments
- **Control Detail**: Displays all the details configured for a set of controls
- **Issue Detail**: Displays all the details related to a set of issues
- **Issue Detail – As of Date**: Displays all the details related to a set of issues as of a specified date

- **Issue Remediation Cycle Time**: Displays the cycle time for remediating open issues
- **Risks by Open Issues**: Displays the risks associated with each open issue
- **Risk Detail**: Displays all the details related to a set of risks
- **Risk Level Reduction**: Displays the reduction in risk level by control type
- **Treatment Cost Benefit**: Displays the cost and benefit of each risk treatment

Summary

Organizations can gain efficiency and reduce compliance costs by taking a more holistic approach to implement an integrated framework for coordinating and monitoring compliance activities.

A holistic compliance approach requires a central compliance management office to identify common regulatory requirements across the regions. The COSO framework can serve as a template for building an integrated framework to comply with regional regulations across major economic zones including the United States' Sarbanes-Oxley, Canada's Bill 198, the United Kingdom's Corporate Governance Code, the European Union's 8th Directive, Japan's Financial Instruments and Exchange Law, and Australia's Corporate Law Economic Reform Program (CLERP).

Oracle GRC Manager can be easily configured for managing different regional compliance activities. This application provides options to create *perspectives*, select compliance *objects* such as process, risks, and controls, add user defined attributes, document types, and create security roles to ensure that all regional compliance activities can be managed within the same platform. Compliance Managers can also use this platform to manage compliance activities with overlapping control objectives to comply with regional regulations. The compliance self-assessment can be performed for each regulatory region using this platform to identify issues and assign remediation tasks.

Purpose-built business intelligence tools, such as GRC Intelligence, can provide a holistic view of compliance across the integrated framework to streamlined regional compliance activities and full visibility of the management into the risks across its local entities and global processes. Regional Compliance Managers and corporate compliance PMO can see a common view through dashboards. The out of the box dashboard and reports can be used to monitor certification process, track issues and actions, as well as analyze regional compliance trends.

Index

model analysis process, AACG
  about 241
  deploy control 244
  remediation plan 243
  results, extracting to Excel 243
  view results online 242
  visualization 242
models 240
Model walk-through, AACG 241
Monitor and Evaluate (ME) 324
MSRP 60

N

National Labor Relations Act (NLRA) 50

O

Objectives 26
objectives, AACG
  identifying 238, 239
objects, Portfolio Planning System
  Planning Cycle 90
  Portfolio 90
  Portfolio Plan 90
  Project 90
  Project Scenario 90
  Project Scorecard 90
  Project Scorecard Objective 90
  Project Scorecard Objective Score 90
  Scenario 90
Occupational Health and Safety Act
    (OSH Act) 50
OEM Data Masking 333
Offering 36
Ontario Securities Act 407
operating environment security
  about 129
  IP filtering 130
  security incident response, through Oracle
    service 130, 131
operational risk 393
Oracle
  E-records Management System 384
Oracle Application Access Controls
    Governor 121
Oracle Applications Manager with Grid
    Control 99

Oracle Bills of Material 384
Oracle Business Intelligence
  about 65
  execution, monitoring with 65
Oracle database security
  about 126
  database links, reviewing 126
  XDB, disabling 126
Oracle Database Vault
  about 337, 338
  database objects, protecting 338
  pre-seeded realm authorizations 340
  preseeded realms, for E-Business Suite 338,
    339
Oracle E-Business Suite 135 320
Oracle Engineering 384
Oracle Enterprise Manager 11
Oracle Financial Analytics
  about 65, 67
  dashboards 66
Oracle Financial Services Data Warehouse
    architecture
  capital adequacy 395
  diagrammatic representation 394
  disclosure 398
  management review 396
Oracle Fusion GRC Intelligence (GRCI)
  regional compliance, monitoring 435
Oracle GRC applications
  IT processes, managing 315
Oracle GRC Controls Suite
  PCG 280
  TCG 257
Oracle GRC Intelligence
  about 144
  Risk of Material Misstatement (ROMM) 155
Oracle GRC Intelligence, risk assessment
    and control verification system
  assessment, evaluating 154
  assessment workflow 144
  quantitative risks, accessing 155
Oracle GRC Manager
  about 135, 143
  audit report, obtaining 229, 230
  InFission COBIT Framework setup 315
  management assessment survey 145

[PACKT] enterprise

PUBLISHING · professional expertise distilled

Thank you for buying
Governance, Risk, and Compliance Handbook for Oracle Applications

About Packt Publishing

Packt, pronounced 'packed', published its first book "Mastering phpMyAdmin for Effective MySQL Management" in April 2004 and subsequently continued to specialize in publishing highly focused books on specific technologies and solutions.

Our books and publications share the experiences of your fellow IT professionals in adapting and customizing today's systems, applications, and frameworks. Our solution based books give you the knowledge and power to customize the software and technologies you're using to get the job done. Packt books are more specific and less general than the IT books you have seen in the past. Our unique business model allows us to bring you more focused information, giving you more of what you need to know, and less of what you don't.

Packt is a modern, yet unique publishing company, which focuses on producing quality, cutting-edge books for communities of developers, administrators, and newbies alike. For more information, please visit our website: www.packtpub.com.

About Packt Enterprise

In 2010, Packt launched two new brands, Packt Enterprise and Packt Open Source, in order to continue its focus on specialization. This book is part of the Packt Enterprise brand, home to books published on enterprise software – software created by major vendors, including (but not limited to) IBM, Microsoft and Oracle, often for use in other corporations. Its titles will offer information relevant to a range of users of this software, including administrators, developers, architects, and end users.

Writing for Packt

We welcome all inquiries from people who are interested in authoring. Book proposals should be sent to author@packtpub.com. If your book idea is still at an early stage and you would like to discuss it first before writing a formal book proposal, contact us; one of our commissioning editors will get in touch with you.

We're not just looking for published authors; if you have strong technical skills but no writing experience, our experienced editors can help you develop a writing career, or simply get some additional reward for your expertise.

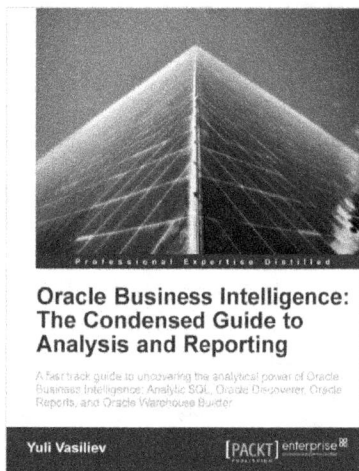

Oracle Business Intelligence : The Condensed Guide to Analysis and Reporting

ISBN: 978-1-84968-118-6   Paperback: 184 pages

A fast track guide to uncovering the analytical power of Oracle Business intelligence: Analytic SQL, Oracle Discoverer, Oracle Reports, and Oracle Warehouse Builder

1. Install, configure, and deploy the components included in Oracle Business Intelligence Suite (SE)

2. Gain a comprehensive overview of components and features of the Oracle Business Intelligence package

3. A fast paced, practical book that provides you with quick steps to answer common business questions and help you make informed business decisions

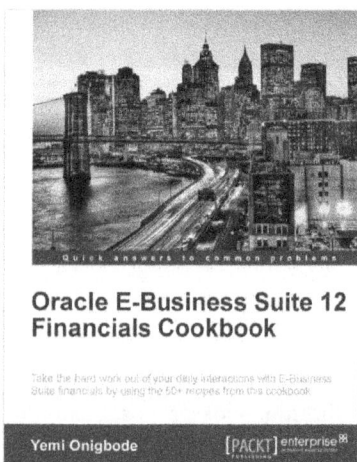

Oracle E-Business Suite 12 Financials Cookbook

ISBN: 978-1-84968-310-4   Paperback: 384 pages

Take the hard work out of your daily interactions with E-Business Suite financials by using the 50+ recipes from this cookbook

1. Delivers practical solutions that can be easily applied in functional EBS environments

2. A step-by-step tour through the EBS R12 Financials core modules in this book and eBook

3. Demonstrates the functional integration points between the EBS R12 Financial modules

Please check **www.PacktPub.com** for information on our titles

Oracle PeopleSoft Enterprise Financial Management 9.1 Implementation

ISBN: 978-1-84968-146-9   Paperback: 412 pages

An exhaustive resource for PeopleSoft Financials applicatio practitioners to understand core concepts, configurations, and business processes

1. A single concise book and eBook reference to guide you from PeopleSoft foundation concepts through to crucial configuration activities required for a successful implementation

2. Real-life implementation scenarios to demonstrate practical implementations of PeopleSoft features along with theoretical concepts

3. Expert tips for the reader based on wide implementation experience

Oracle SOA Suite 11g R1 Developer's Guide

ISBN: 978-1-84968-018-9   Paperback: 720 pages

Develop Service-Oriented Architecture Solutions with the Oracle SOA Suite

1. A hands-on, best-practice guide to using and applying the Oracle SOA Suite in the delivery of real-world SOA applications

2. Detailed coverage of the Oracle Service Bus, BPEL PM, Rules, Human Workflow, Event Delivery Network, and Business Activity Monitoring

3. Master the best way to use and combine each of these different components in the implementation of a SOA solution

Please check **www.PacktPub.com** for information on our titles

www.ingramcontent.com/pod-product-compliance
Lightning Source LLC
Chambersburg PA
CBHW080125220326
41598CB00032B/4953